T0184078

Lecture Notes in Artificial Intelligence 11556

Subseries of Lecture Notes in Computer Science

Series Editors

Randy Goebel
University of Alberta, Edmonton, Canada
Yuzuru Tanaka
Hokkaido University, Sapporo, Japan
Wolfgang Wahlster
DFKI and Saarland University, Saarbrücken, Germany

Founding Editor

Jörg Siekmann
DFKI and Saarland University, Saarbrücken, Germany

Uriel Martinez-Hernandez ·
Vasiliki Vouloutsi · Anna Mura ·
Michael Mangan · Minoru Asada ·
Tony J. Prescott · Paul F. M. J. Verschure (Eds.)

Biomimetic and Biohybrid Systems

8th International Conference, Living Machines 2019
Nara, Japan, July 9–12, 2019
Proceedings

Springer

Editors
Uriel Martinez-Hernandez ⓘ
University of Bath
Bath, UK

Anna Mura
SPECS, Institute for Bioengineering
of Catalonia
Barcelona, Spain

Minoru Asada
Osaka University
Suita, Japan

Paul F. M. J. Verschure ⓘ
SPECS, ICREA, BIST
Barcelona, Spain

Vasiliki Vouloutsi ⓘ
SPECS, Institute for Bioengineering
of Catalonia
Barcelona, Spain

Michael Mangan ⓘ
University of Sheffield
Sheffield, UK

Tony J. Prescott ⓘ
University of Sheffield
Sheffield, UK

ISSN 0302-9743   ISSN 1611-3349   (electronic)
Lecture Notes in Artificial Intelligence
ISBN 978-3-030-24740-9   ISBN 978-3-030-24741-6   (eBook)
https://doi.org/10.1007/978-3-030-24741-6

LNCS Sublibrary: SL7 – Artificial Intelligence

This Springer imprint is published by the registered company Springer Nature Switzerland AG
The registered company address is: Gewerbestrasse 11, 6330 Cham, Switzerland

Preface

These proceedings contain the papers presented at Living Machines 2019: the 8th International Conference on Biomimetic and Biohybrid Systems, held in the Kasugano International Forum, Nara, Japan, July 9–12, 2019. The international conferences in the Living Machines series are targeted at the intersection of research on novel life-like technologies inspired by the scientific investigation of biological systems, *biomimetics*, and research that seeks to interface biological and artificial systems to create biohybrid systems. The conference aim is to highlight the most exciting international research in both of these fields united by the theme of "Living Machines."

The Living Machines conference series was first organized by the Convergent Science Network (CSN) of biomimetic and biohybrid systems to provide a focal point for the gathering of world-leading researchers and the presentation and discussion of cutting-edge research in this rapidly emerging field. The modern definition of biomimetics is the development of novel technologies through the distillation of principles from the study of biological systems. The investigation of biomimetic systems can serve two complementary goals. First, a suitably designed and configured biomimetic artifact can be used to test theories about the natural system of interest. Second, biomimetic technologies can provide useful, elegant, and efficient solutions to unsolved challenges in science and engineering. Biohybrid systems are formed by combining at least one biological component—an existing living system—and at least one artificial, newly engineered component. By passing information in one or both directions, such a system forms a new hybrid bio-artificial entity.

The earth has continuously changed over billions of years, causing living beings to evolve their capabilities to adapt optimally to the changing environment. The result from this evolving process has marveled humans since many centuries ago, inspiring them to build machines and transform their world by mimicking the power accomplished by nature and animals. The approach of creating technology by imitating nature receives the term "biomimetics," coined by the American biophysicist and inventor Otto Schmitt in the 1950s, putting together the Greek words "bios" (life) and "mimesis" (imitate).

Although sometimes it is imperceptible, biomimetics has been with human beings along history and across the world, making life easier and comfortable. China is one of the first civilizations that took inspiration from nature by employing silk for the fabrication of fabrics, and making it one of the oldest examples of biomimetics. Lu Ban, a Chinese inventor, also made use of silk to create the first umbrella that mimicked the shape, flexibility, and effectiveness of the lotus leaf. The Renaissance period in Italy gave birth to Leonardo da Vinci, one of the most prolific figures, whose work was largely inspired by nature. In the 15th century, da Vinci developed numerous designs of machines, including a humanoid robot and flying machines, inspired by his observations of mechanisms and the anatomy of natural systems. It was in the 20th century when the first-ever flying machine was successfully developed in America by the Wright brothers, who observed the way birds use their wings to gain lift and control the direction of flight. Ground transportation has also been reached by biomimetics through the development of highly efficient vehicles. For example, at the beginning of the 21st century the world witnessed the appearance of the first bionic car in Germany, inspired by the skeleton structure and shape of the boxfish. This bionic car proved to be aerodynamic, highly stable, and fuel efficient compared with any existing car.

Traditionally, Japanese culture has exhibited a special bond with nature, which has been reflected in the technological developments in that country. In the 1990s, Japan unveiled the first bullet train implementing biomimicry inspired by the kingfisher's beak. The large head, long and sharp beak of this bird inspired the design for the shape of the front of the bullet train, resulting in a train slicing the wind rather than trapping it when entering a tunnel. This imitation of nature allowed the bullet train to minimize the air resistance and booming sound, while increasing acceleration and energy efficiently not seen before. The efficient evolution of the human body has inspired the creation of robots that look like people known as humanoids. In 2006 in Japan, Minoru Asada and his group developed the CB2 robot, a biomimetic humanoid that mimics the physical, mental, and social capabilities of a 2-year-old child. The CB2 robot is able to perform these capabilities by the use of biomimetic touch, vision, and auditory sensors inspired by the human body. In the past decade, exhaustive research by Hiroshi Ishiguro culminated in the first Geminoid robot, whose name is derived from the Latin word "geminus" (twin). Geminoids aim to be indistinguishable from real humans at first sight, by mimicking the human body anatomy, hair, skin, facial expressions, and interaction with others.

Biomimetics has brought together researchers from a wide variety of fields, to build machines and tools for the advancement of society, economy, and living style. However, biomimetics still has plenty of opportunities for research and applications. For that reason, the Living Machines conference provides the environment for the presentation, evaluation, and discussion of cutting-edge and next-generation technologies under investigation by researchers across the globe.

The main conference, during July 10–12, took the form of a three-day single-track oral and poster presentation program that included five plenary lectures from leading international researchers in biomimetic and biohybrid systems: Hiroshi Ishiguro (Osaka University) on studies on interactive robots; Michael Milford (Queensland University of Technology) on navigation, neuroscience, and neural networks – a quest to understand intelligence and build better technology for robots and autonomous vehicles; Andre van Schaik (Western Sydney University) on feature extraction using adaptive selection thresholds; Yukie Nagai (University of Tokyo) on cognitive development in robots – a unified theory based on predictive coding; and Koh Hosoda (Osaka University) on soft body as source of intelligence. There were also 26 regular talks and one poster session and poster spotlight (featuring approximately 16 posters).

Session themes included: advances in soft robotics; 3D-printed bio-machines; bio-hybrid actuators and muscles; bio-inspired locomotion; robots and society; biomimetic vision and control; deep learning for bio-robotics; collective and emergent behaviors in animals and robots; and bio-inspired flight.

The conference was complemented by two workshops on July 9, 2019, held at the Kasugano International Forum, Nara, Japan. More specifically, the "Closing Vico's Loop: Addressing Challenges in Science and Society with Living Machines" workshop was organized by Paul Verschure and Tony Prescott, and the "Bioprinting" workshop was organized by Cellink.

Consistent with the Living Machines' tradition of choosing historical venues at the crossroads between life and human sciences, the main conference was hosted at the Kasugano International Forum in the town of Nara, the old capital of Japan up until the 8th century. Nara is located less than one hour from Kyoto and Osaka. Thanks to its past as the first permanent capital, Nara is full of historic treasures, including some of Japan's oldest and largest temples. Deer roam free in Nara Park, by the Tōdai-ji temple where Daibutsu, the 15-m-high bronze Buddha, is displayed in a large wooden hall. On the park's east side is the Shinto shrine Kasuga Taisha, which dates to 768 A.D. and more than 3,000 lanterns. This year Living Machines was held in Nara after successful previous editions in Paris, France, in 2018; Stanford, USA, in 2017; Edinburgh, UK, in 2016; Barcelona, Spain, in 2015; Milan, Italy, in 2014; London, UK, in 2013, and Barcelona, Spain, in 2012.

We would like to thank our hosts for the conference, workshops, and poster sessions held at the Kasugano International Forum in Nara.

We also wish to thank the many people that were involved in making the eighth edition of Living Machines possible: Minoru Asada and Paul Verschure co-chaired the meeting; Uriel Martinez-Hernandez, Vasiliki Vouloutsi, and Michael Mangan chaired the Program Committee and edited the conference proceedings; Tony Prescott chaired the international Steering Committee; Anna Mura was the general organization chair and also coordinated the Web and communication; Minoru Asada, Koh Hosoda, and their group provided administrative and local organizational support in Nara. We are grateful to the SPECS lab and the Communication Unit at the Institute for Bioengineering of Catalonia (IBEC) in Barcelona for the assistance in the organization and for technical support. We would also like to thank the authors and speakers who contributed their work, and the members of the Program Committee for their detailed and considered reviews. We are grateful to the five keynote speakers who shared with us their vision of the future.

Finally, we wish to thank the organizers and sponsors of LM 2019: the Convergence Science Network for Biomimetic and Neurotechnology (CSNII; ICT-601167), the Institute for Bioengineering of Catalonia IBEC, and the Catalan Institution for Research and Advanced Studies (ICREA), and Cellink company.

Additional support was provided by Springer. Living Machines 2019 was also supported by: the IOP Physics journal *Bioinspiration & Biomimetics*, which will publish a special issue of articles based on the best conference papers: *Biomimetics – Open Access Journal* will publish a special issue of articles based on the best conference posters, and an award will be given for best paper with a social impact.

July 2019

Uriel Martinez-Hernandez
Vasiliki Vouloutsi
Anna Mura
Minoru Asada
Michael Mangan
Tony J. Prescott
Paul F. M. J. Verschure

Organization

Conference Chairs

Minoru Asada · Osaka University, Japan
Paul F. M. J. Verschure · Institute for Bioengineering of Catalonia (IBEC), Spain
Institute of Science and Technology (BIST), Spain
Institution for Research and Advanced Studies (ICREA), Spain

Program Chairs

Uriel Martinez-Hernandez · University of Bath, UK
Vasiliki Vouloutsi · Institute for Bioengineering of Catalonia (IBEC), Spain
Michael Mangan · University of Sheffield, UK

Local Organizers

Masahiro Shimizu · Osaka University, Japan
Koh Hosoda · Osaka University, Japan

Communications

Anna Mura · Institute for Bioengineering of Catalonia (IBEC), Spain

Workshop Organizers

Anna Mura · Institute for Bioengineering of Catalonia (IBEC), Spain
Tony Prescott · University of Sheffield, UK

International Steering Committee

Minoru Asada · Osaka University, Japan
Joseph Ayers · Northeastern University, USA
Mark Cutkosky · Stanford University, USA
Marc Desmulliez · Heriot-Watt University, UK
José Halloy · Université Paris Diderot, France
Nathan Lepora · University of Bristol, UK
Uriel Martinez-Hernandez · University of Bath, UK
Barbara Mazzolai · Istituto Italiano di Tecnologia, Italy
Anna Mura · Institute for Bioengineering of Catalonia (IBEC), Spain
Tony Prescott · University of Sheffield, UK
Roger Quinn Case · Western Reserve University, USA

Paul Verschure   Catalan Institution for Research and Advanced Studies
                                     (IBEC-BIST) and Catalan Institution for Research
                                     and
                                     Advanced Studies, Barcelona, Spain
Vasiliki Vouloutsi   Institute for Bioengineering of Catalonia (IBEC), Spain
Stuart Wilson   University of Sheffield, UK

Program Committee

Arockia Selvakumar A.   VIT Chennai, India
Hossam Abd El Munim   Ain Shams University, Egypt
Alireza Abouhossein   Shahid Beheshsti University of Medical Sciences, Iran
Andrew Adamatzky   University of the West of England, UK
Shady Ahmed   Ain Shams University, Egypt
Jonathan Aitken   University of Sheffield, UK
Matías Alvarado   Center for Research and Advanced Studies,
                                     CINVESTAV-IPN, Mexico
Sean Anderson   University of Sheffield, UK
Xerxes Arsiwalla   Pompeu Fabra University, Spain
Farshad Arvin   University of Manchester, UK
Tareq Assaf   University of Bath, UK
Mohammed Awad   Ain Shams University, Egypt
Joseph Ayers   Northeastern University, USA
Yoseph Bar-Cohen   Jet Propulsion Lab, USA
Mark Baxendale   University of the West of England, UK
Paul Baxter   University of Lincoln, UK
Lucia Beccai   Istituto Italiano di Tecnologia, Italy
Carlos Beltran-Perez   University of Sheffield, UK
Ben Bolen   Portland State University, USA
Frank Bonnet   École polytechnique fédérale de Lausanne, Switzerland
Luke Boorman   University of Sheffield, UK
Jordan Boyle   University of Leeds, UK
Nicolas Bredeche   Sorbonne Université, France
José Luis Briseño   CICESE, Mexico
Edgar Buchanan   University of York, UK
David Buxton   University of Sheffield, UK
Héctor Báez Medina   Instituto Politecnico Nacional, Mexico
David Cameron   University of Sheffield, UK
Daniel Camilleri   University of Sheffield, UK
José Juan Carbajal   National Polytechnic Institute, Mexico
   Hernández
Bernardo Castro   University of Bath, UK
   Dominguez
Leo Cazenille   Université Paris Diderot, France
Victor Cedeno   University of Sheffield, UK
Hillel Chiel   Case Western Reserve University, USA
Eris Chinellato   Middlesex University, UK

Matteo Cianchetti	Scuola Superiore Sant'Anna, Italy
Emily Collins	University of Liverpool, UK
Jorg Conradt	KTH, Sweden
Alex Cope	University of Sheffield, UK
Heriberto Cuayáhuitl	University of Lincoln, UK
Pete Culmer	University of Leeds, UK
Mark Cutkosky	Stanford University, USA
Vassilis Cutsuridis	University of Lincoln, UK
Kathryn Daltorio	Case Western Reserve University, USA
Abbas Dehghani-Sanij	University of Leeds, UK
Luis Gerardo de la Fraga	CINVESTAV-IPN, Mexico
Angel P. del Pobil	Jaume I University, Spain
Richard Suphapol Diteesawat	University of Bristol, UK
Tony Dodd	University of Sheffield, UK
Sanja Dogramadzi	University of the West of England, UK
Stéphane Doncieux	UPMC, France
Christian Dondrup	Heriot-Watt University, UK
Volker Dürr	Bielefeld University, Germany
Jonathan du Bois	University of Bath, UK
Gamal Ebrahim	Ain Shams University, Egypt
Tobias Fischer	Imperial College London, UK
Ioannis Georgilas	University of Bath, UK
Maria Elena Giannaccini	University of Bristol, UK
Benoît Girard	Sorbonne Université, CNRS, France
Jorge Gomes	University of Lisbon, Portugal
Alfonso Gómez-Espinosa	ITESM, Mexico
José Halloy	Université Paris Diderot, France
Tim Helps	University of Bristol, UK
Ivan Herreros	Universitat Pompeu Fabra, Spain
J. Michael Herrmann	University of Edinburgh, UK
Toby Howison	University of Cambridge, UK
David Hu	Georgia Tech, USA
Marcello Ienca	ETH Zürich, Switzerland
Ioannis Ieropoulos	University of the West of England, UK
Calum Imrie	University of Edinburgh, UK
Jesung Koh	Ajou University, South Korea
Agamemnon Krasoulis	Newcastle University, UK
Konstantinos Lagogiannis	King's College London, UK
Nathan Lepora	University of Bristol, UK
William Lewinger	University of Dundee, UK
Wei Li	University of York, UK
Omar Lopez-Botello	Tecnologico de Monterrey, Mexico
Shan Luo	University of Liverpool, UK
Alexis Lussier Desbiens	Université de Sherbrooke, Canada
Imran Mahmood	University of Leeds, UK

Michael Mangan	University of Sheffield, UK
Hector Marin-Reyes	University of Sheffield, UK
Jose Martinez-Carranza	Instituto Nacional de Astrofisica Optica y Electronica, Mexico
Uriel Martinez-Hernandez	University of Bath, UK
Israel Martinez	CICESE, Mexico
Barbara Mazzolai	Italian Institute of Technology, Italy
Adriana Menchaca Mendez	ENES Morelia, UNAM, Mexico
Amilcar Meneses Viveros	CINVESTAV-IPN, Mexico
Lin Meng	Tianjin University, China
Benjamin Metcalfe	University of Bath, UK
Stefano Mintchev	EPFL, Switzerland
Ben Mitchinson	University of Sheffield, UK
Jesus Yalja Montiel Perez	Centro de Investigacion en Computacion, Mexico
Vishwanathan Mohan	University of Essex, UK
Roger Moore	University of Sheffield, UK
Jose Emmanuel Morales Robles	University of Leeds, UK
Eduardo Morales Sanchez	Instituto Politecnico Nacional, Mexico
Kenneth Moses	Case Western Reserve University, USA
Anna Mura	University Pompeu Fabra, Spain
John Murray	University of Hull, UK
Vincent C. Müller	University of Leeds, UK
Gerhard Neumann	University of Lincoln, UK
Sancho Oliveira	ISCTE-Instituto Universitário de Lisboa, Portugal
Maria Panagiotidi	University of Salford, UK
Iordanka Panayotova	Christopher Newport University, USA
Diogo Pata	Universitat Pompeu Fabra, Spain
Martin Pearson	Bristol Robotics Laboratory, UK
Maxime Petit	Ecole Centrale de Lyon – LIRIS, France
Hemma Philamore	Bristol Robotics Laboratory, UK
Andrew Philippides	University of Sussex, UK
Tony Pipe	Bristol Robotics Laboratory, UK
Saskia Pollack	University of Sussex, UK
Tony Prescott	University of Sheffield, UK
Roger Quinn	Case Western Reserve University, USA
Andreagiovanni Reina	University of Sheffield, UK
Guillaume Rieucau	LUMCON, USA
Benjamin Risse	University of Münster, Germany
Alejandro Rodriguez Angeles	CINVESTAV-IPN, Mexico
Francisco Romero-Ferrero	Champalimaud Research, Spain
Elsa Rubio	CIC-IPN, Mexico
Adrian Rubio Solis	University of Sheffield, UK
Elmar Rueckert	University of Lübeck, Germany
Sylvain Saighi	University of Bordeaux, France

Contents

Full Papers

Feed-Forward Selection of Cerebellar Models for Calibration of Robot Sound Source Localization

M. D. Baxendale[1,3](✉) [iD], M. Nibouche[1] [iD], E. L. Secco[3] [iD], A. G. Pipe[2] [iD], and M. J. Pearson[2] [iD]

[1] University of the West of England, Bristol, UK
mark2.baxendale@live.uwe.ac.uk, mokhtar.nibouche@uwe.ac.uk
[2] Bristol Robotics Laboratory, Bristol, UK
{tony.pipe,martin.pearson}@brl.ac.uk
[3] Liverpool Hope University, Liverpool, UK
{mark.baxendale,seccoe}@hope.ac.uk

Abstract. We present a *responsibility predictor*, based on the adaptive filter model of the cerebellum, to provide feed-forward selection of cerebellar calibration models for robot Sound Source Localization (SSL), based on audio features extracted from the received audio stream. In previous work we described a system that selects the models based on sensory feedback, however, a drawback of that system is that it is only able to select a set of calibrators *a-posteriori*, after action (e.g. orienting a camera toward the sound source after a position estimate is made). The responsibility predictor improved the system performance compared to that without responsibility prediction. We show that a trained responsibility predictor is able to use contextual signals in the absence of ground truth to successfully select models with a performance approaching that of a system with full access to the ground truth through sensory feedback.

Keywords: Robot audition · Responsibility prediction · Multiple models · Cerebellum · Adaptive filter

1 Introduction

Vision is often used as the primary sensory modality in mobile robots, however, there are situations where vision can become impaired or completely unavailable such as in the aftermath of a disaster. A robot attempting to locate a person in distress, for example, may be unable to do so using vision alone due to airborne particles or collapsed infrastructure. In these situations, audio localization could be used as it does not rely on a direct field of view to the source. Robot audition is a relatively recent field [1] which includes the field of Sound Source Localization (SSL)- the identification of the location of sounds in a robot's environment (azimuth, elevation and distance to source). When operating in challenging acoustic environments such as disaster sites, errors will inevitably occur in the SSL estimation due to reflection, distortion and attenuation of the sound source.

© Springer Nature Switzerland AG 2019
U. Martinez-Hernandez et al. (Eds.): Living Machines 2019, LNAI 11556, pp. 3–14, 2019.
https://doi.org/10.1007/978-3-030-24741-6_1

Moreover, as the robot navigates through multiple environments the nature of these errors in the SSL estimate will vary according to the acoustic characteristics of those environments. In previous work, we proposed a multiple adaptive filter approach inspired by a cerebellar micro-circuit, to learn to calibrate the output of a SSL system operating in multiple acoustic environments [2]. Subsequently, the system was demonstrated selecting the best calibrator (or set of calibrators) for the robot's current environment, including novel environments through a process of responsibility estimation based on model prediction error. The prediction error is determined through comparison of a model's estimate of the sound source location with the ground truth sound source location. Although that work demonstrated an improvement in SSL, including in comparison to Generalized Cross-Correlation with Phase Transform (GCC-PHAT), a limitation is that it relied on establishing the ground truth location by orienting a camera toward the sound source in order to derive the model prediction errors. This can not always be assumed to be the case for a robot operating in an unstructured disaster site. To make the system more robust we introduce a means of pre-selecting the calibrators before the ground truth becomes available, using features extracted from the audio stream itself. We call this new component the *Responsibility Predictor* (RP) after the Modular Selection And Identification for Control (MOSAIC) framework, which uses the same cerebellar inspired adaptive filter model architecture to learn the contextual cues of the environment [5].

The paper is composed as follows: Sect. 2 provides background of the biological inspiration and computational implementation of the cerebellar inspired multiple model adaptive filter approach to calibrate a simple SSL algorithm. This is followed in Sect. 3 by a description of the proposed extension to this sensory learning architecture through inclusion of the RP. The experimental apparatus and data capture protocol designed to test the RP are described in the methods Sect. 4, followed by results and discussion of the influence on performance in Sect. 5.

2   Background

2.1   Cerebellar Role in Binaural Sound Source Localization

Until recently, the cerebellum was considered to mainly be involved in motor control, but there is increasing evidence that it plays a role in non-motor functions, and especially in perceptual processes [8]. The role of the cerebellum in auditory processing in particular was recognised several decades ago [9], but only recently has this aspect of cerebellar function received much attention. Work in this area has mainly focused on speech perception and production; until now there has been very little research on the role of the cerebellum in SSL. A review of binaural SSL in robotics is given in [10]. SSL systems are typically setup in a single, controlled acoustic environment [11,12], whereas challenging environments such as those described in Sect. 1 can introduce SSL errors, which may depend non-linearly on the azimuth position of the sound source due to complex and unpredictable environmental acoustics. The requirement for non-linear learning was the motivation for applying a computational model of the cerebellum to this problem.

2.2 Adaptive Filter Model of the Cerebellum

The adaptive filter model of the cerebellum was proposed by Fujita [13] and emphasizes the resemblance of the cerebellar microcircuit to an adaptive filter [14], Fig. 1. The model is characterised by a rich set of inputs/basis filters analogous to the large number of granule cells and Golgi cells in cerebellar cortex, contributing to the power of the adaptive filter function by providing a massive signal analysis capability. This allows a large number of inputs to the model, analogous to the mossy fibres in cerebellum, from very diverse areas of the brain and sensory systems. The parallel fibre signals are synthesised at the Purkinje cell according to the parallel fibre-Purkinje cell synaptic weights, analogous to the summing junction of the adaptive filter.

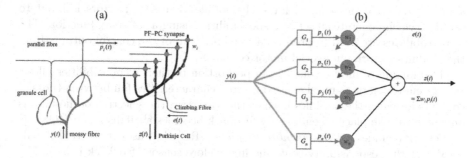

Fig. 1. Adaptive filter model of the cerebellum. (a) Cerebellar microcircuit. (b) Adaptive filter equivalent. Adapted with permission of Royal Society, from [3].

2.3 Multiple Internal Models and the Assignment of Responsibility

It has long been hypothesized that the brain possesses internal models to allow the prediction of how the world will respond to actions made, and that the cerebellum is a strong candidate for the site of such models [4]. There are many examples where a single internal model would not be able to capture the range of contexts encountered in real world situations. There have been a number of computational frameworks proposed, including MOSAIC [5] and Hierarchical Attentive Multiple Models for Execution and Recognition of actions (HAMMER) [6], contending that the central nervous system makes use of multiple modules (containing models), each specialised for a specific context. Both frameworks competitively select action, with HAMMER focusing on robot imitation [7]. The MOSAIC framework was used as an inspiration in this study as it has a number of advantages, including proportional combination of module outputs along with both prior and posterior contribution to the production of module probabilities (known in MOSAIC as *responsibilities*), with HAMMER lacking MOSAIC's RP, which underpins the current work.

MOSAIC was developed in the context of motor control, and consists of an array of modules each of which could have influence or control in a particular context. For example the task of lifting an object where objects having differing weights would each represent a different context, requiring a unique force profile. A key problem is that it may not be clear which module would be appropriate until the lifting action has commenced. In MOSAIC, each module consists of a paired forward and inverse model along with a responsibility predictor. There is a single *Responsibility Estimator* (RE) that operates across all modules. Each module receives an efference copy of the motor command, and, within each context, each predicts the state of the system under control as a result of the motor command, assuming it is in the context in which it learnt. After action has commenced or taken place, the ground truth state of the system under control is determined through sensory feedback (such as vision or proprioception), and a prediction error determined for each module. The set of errors is input to the RE, which generates a set of responsibilities using a soft-max function. The responsibilities are used to produce a weighted sum of the control outputs from the modules to form an overall motor command.

This mixing of module outputs in proportion to their responsibilities allows the system to adapt to novel contexts whose characteristics fall between those of contexts in which the modules have learnt. However, the selection of modules is only able to take place when sensory feedback becomes available. The MOSAIC framework includes a *Responsibility Predictor* (RP) that uses contextual signals to predict the responsibility of its module, before sensory feedback is available. By combining the outputs of the RPs with the outputs of the RE, an interplay takes place between the RP and RE. The RP can make an early prediction of the responsibility, potentially reducing performance error when the context changes but the RE outputs have not yet updated in response to sensory feedback. The example used in [15] is that lifting a transparent bottle allows the brain to make a prediction through vision and select appropriate modules for light or heavy objects.

It might seem that an RP that learns to predict its module's responsibility from contextual signals renders the RE redundant. However, the example also points out that an opaque carton would make this impossible, and the brain would need to select models based on prediction error after action has taken place, for which the RE would still be required. Also, the RP could mis-classify the context and select a set of modules that is inappropriate. In [16], Haruno et al. simulated an RP error and showed that in the next time step of the simulation, the RE corrected for the error introduced by the RP once the ground truth had become available through sensory feedback.

2.4 Cerebellar Calibration of SSL Using Multiple Models

The overall system, including the RP developed in this study, is shown in Fig. 2. It consists of multiple adaptive filter models of the cerebellum each of which learn the SSL error at different azimuths in a given acoustic environment, or context, and adds a compensatory shift to the SSL output. In this study only

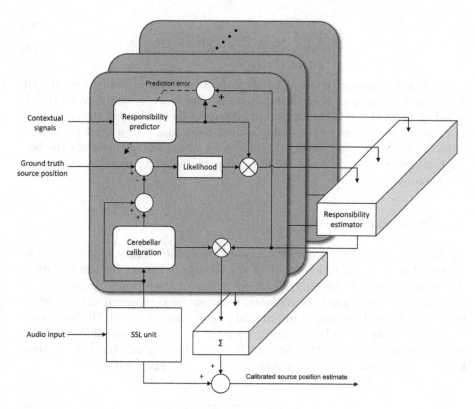

Fig. 2. Responsibility predictor as part of the overall multiple models calibration system.

azimuth is considered. The cerebellar calibration model was adapted from previous work that calibrated the whisker map of a robot [17]. The amount of calibration required will depend on the azimuth estimate, as different locations within an environment may experience different degrees of error, and is coded in the parallel fibre-Purkinje cell weights through training. A means is required to select the appropriate model for the robot's current environment, and a candidate framework is the MOSAIC described in Sect. 2.3. On receiving audio input the SSL unit makes an estimate of the azimuth position of the sound source. Each model produces a calibration signal, based on the SSL estimate, assuming that the robot is in the environment in which that model trained. In the field, the robot orients its camera toward the sound source using the calibrated estimate, to obtain the ground truth sound source position, from which an error is computed for each model. The likelihood that each model is the best suited to calibrate in the current environment is then computed, and from this a softmax function is used by the *Responsibility Estimator* (RE) to compute a responsibility λ_i for each model

$$\lambda_i = \frac{e^{-|\theta_t-\theta_i|^2/\sigma^2}}{\sum_{j=1}^n e^{-|\theta_t-\theta_j|^2/\sigma^2}} \tag{1}$$

where θ_t is the ground truth azimuth, θ_i is the estimate produced by the ith model, n is the number of estimates (models) and σ is a scaling factor which is tuned by hand as in [5]. The calibrated outputs of the models are then combined in proportion to their responsibility values to produce an overall calibration signal. In this way, the system can select a set of models (rather than the best single model) to best calibrate the SSL estimate, including allowing adaption to novel contexts.

3   Proposed System

As mentioned in Sect. 2.4, computation of the responsibility signals, required to apportion the calibration effort of the models, relies on the availability of the ground truth. As already discussed in Sect. 1, the ground truth may be unavailable. Even where it is available, it cannot be determined until after the robot has oriented its camera toward the sound source. MOSAIC includes feed-forward selection of models through prediction of the responsibilities based on contextual signals, rather than sensory feedback. Contextual signals are derived from the environment to form a prior prediction of responsibility:

$$\lambda_i = \frac{\lambda_{pi}e^{-|\theta_t-\theta_i|^2/\sigma^2}}{\sum_{j=1}^n \lambda_{pj}e^{-|\theta_t-\theta_j|^2/\sigma^2}} \tag{2}$$

where λ_{pi} is the predicted (prior) responsibility of the ith model. Contextual signals could be of any form, auditory, visual, tactile and so on, and in this study are derived from the audio stream itself, using just one feature, the mean zero crossing rate of the audio signal. This feature was chosen for computational simplicity and alone proved sufficient in the experiments conducted here. However, a range of features could have been used, and more challenging real-world environments may require a different set of features. Zero crossing rate is the ratio of the signal zero crossings to the number of audio samples over the analysis frame, and provides a rough indication of the frequency content of the signal (so will tend to be higher where higher frequencies dominate, especially "noisy" signals). Features were extracted using an adapted version of the *Audio Analysis Library* [18]. The RP is shown in the context of the multiple-models calibration system in Fig. 2. There is one RP associated with each model in the system, and it learns to predict the responsibility of the model based on contextual signals from the environment. The RP based on the adaptive filter model is shown in Fig. 3. Features are analysed into parallel fibre signals, based on the value of the feature, such that a low value of the feature would activate a parallel fibre toward one end of the array (with the value of the feature), while a high value would activate a fibre toward the other end of the array. This was chosen as an approach to be close to the use of the cerebellar model that calibrates the

SSL estimate as described in [2], in which the parallel fibres transmit activity on the robot's audio map. The output of the adaptive filter is a prediction of the associated model's responsibility $\hat{\lambda}$ and is the sum of the parallel fibre signals (the feature value) multiplied by the parallel fibre-purkinje cell weights

$$\hat{\lambda}_i = \sum_{i=0}^{n} w_i p_i \qquad (3)$$

where p_i is the ith parallel fibre signal and w_i is the corresponding weight. The parallel fibre-purkinje cell weights are updated according to the covariance learning rule [19] as shown in Fig. 3, with the teaching signal based on the overall responsibility signal, as shown in Fig. 2.

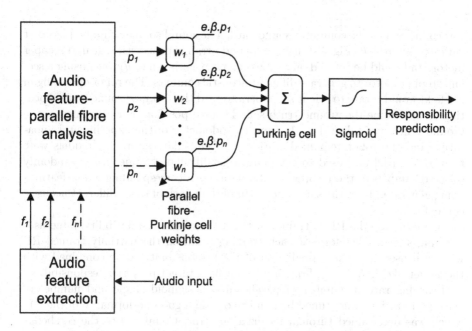

Fig. 3. Cerebellar implementation of the responsibility predictor.

4   Method

Matlab was used to control experiments and for implementation of algorithms. Two microphones (Audio-Technica ATR-3350 omnidirectional condenser lavalier) with an inter-microphone distance of 0.25 m were mounted in free field at either end of a horizontal bar, itself mounted on a Pan and Tilt Unit (PTU). The microphones were connected to a computer using a M-Audio MobilePre USB audio capture unit with a sampling rate of 44100 Hz. A sound source (Logitech Z150 Speaker) was positioned at a distance of 0.4 m from the robot (Fig. 4) and

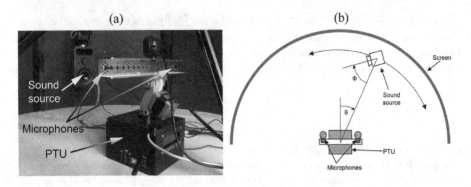

Fig. 4. (a) The experimental arena. (b) Plan view.

was connected to the computer sound card. The sound source could be placed at various azimuths θ (Fig. 4b), using a tripod arrangement with a geared stepper motor, and could be rotated on its axis (angle ϕ as shown in Fig. 4b) using a second stepper motor to generate different acoustic contexts. The robot operating in the field would rotate to orient its camera toward the assumed sound source location to determine the ground truth sound source position. For convenience, the ground truth was taken directly from the odometry of the experimental apparatus, and the robot remained stationary. Cerebellar calibration models were trained as in [2] and used to generate target likelihood values using randomly selected samples of the recorded audio data, with corresponding audio features being generated from the same audio samples, in each of three different acoustic contexts.

In MOSAIC, the RP is trained with the posterior responsibility value as a teaching signal. Therefore, at each training iteration the partially trained RP was itself used to make a prediction of the responsibility to be combined with the target likelihood using Eq. 2 in generating a target posterior responsibility.

Learning rate β, number of parallel fibres, sigmoid shape and number of learning iterations were tuned by hand to obtain a good performance of the RP, which was determined through localization error. Compared to the cerebellar calibration models described in [2], larger values of β and number of training iterations were required to achieve satisfactory performance of the RP. The robot head was presented with a sequence of acoustic contexts each consisting of 5 trials with randomly selected azimuths. In each trial, a 1 s duration Gaussian noise stimulus was used and the SSL unit generated an estimate of azimuth. Each model's calibration output was compared to the ground truth position of the sound source to generate a prediction error for that model. This was carried out in the next trial, because in the field, ground truth would be determined only after the robot had oriented its camera toward the sound source. 10 runs of each experiment were conducted to obtain performance statistics (mean squared error and accuracy rate as percentage of trials in which the absolute error was less than 5°).

5   Results

Figure 5a shows the responsibility signals of the system as it progressed through trials in contexts in which the calibration models had been pre-trained. By definition, the RPs had to be trained to predict the responsibilities of the calibration models in the same contexts. The blue curves show the normalized likelihood values, that is, the posterior responsibilities, generated after the ground truth becomes available, *without* being combined with RP output, to highlight the behaviour of the RE alone. These posterior responsibilities show the models dominating the responsibility in the context in which they learned (for example, model 1 learned in context 1). It can be observed that there is a delay of one trial before the RE responds to a change in context, as the responsibility values cannot be updated until after the ground truth becomes available in the next trial. Solid orange curves show the outputs of the RPs. The RP output is similar in shape to that of the RE alone, but because the RP is driven by contextual signals derived from the audio stream, it can update its prediction in response to a change in context before the ground truth becomes available. The broken red curve shows the overall responsibility computed using Eq. 2, so that it is the result of combination of RP output and likelihoods before input to the RE. The RP output closely follows the combined responsibility. Rows 1 and 2 of Table 1

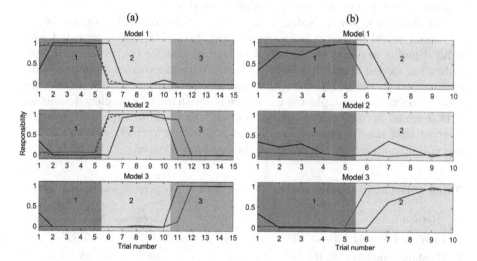

Fig. 5. Responsibility signals as the system progressed through trials. Each trial represents a randomly selected azimuth in one of a number of different contexts, indicated by the coloured boxes. (a) Learned contexts: Context 1 (blue) is $\phi = 90°$ left; context 2 (red) is $\phi = 0°$; context 3 (green) is $\phi = 90°$ right. The blue curve shows the output of the RE alone, the orange curve shows the output of the RP, and the red broken curve shows the overall responsibility calculated according to Eq. 2. (b) Novel contexts: Context 1 (blue) is $\phi = 72°$ left; context 2 (red) is $\phi = 72°$ right. (Color figure online)

show that the performance of the system with the presence of the RP (row 2) is improved over that without (row 1).

The system was tested in contexts that had not been previously experienced. The contexts were chosen to have characteristics that fell intermediate to those in which the calibration models had been trained, as the MOSAIC framework is unable to generalize to contexts that fall outside the learned state space [5]. Figure 5b shows that the system without the RP is able to generalize to the novel contexts, and the RPs appear able to predict this generalization reasonably well. Rows 3 and 4 of Table 1 show that the RP improves the performance in novel contexts.

As mentioned in Sect. 1, computation of the responsibility signals depends on the availability of the ground truth, which may not always be available. The ground truth was made to be unavailable in trial 6 (roughly half-way through the experiment), and remained unavailable throughout the remainder of the experiment. Rows 5 and 6 of Table 1 show that the performance with the RP present is improved over that relying on the RE alone. Further, row 7 shows that where the RP alone was used to provide the overall responsibility when the ground truth was unavailable, the performance was comparable with that of the system where the ground truth is available in all trials. However, it should be borne in mind that relying on the RP alone depends on a fully trained RE against which the RP was able to learn before the ground truth became unavailable. Figure 6a shows the profile of responsibilities in this scenario.

The experiment was repeated with a mis-classification of the context by the RPs as discussed in Sect. 2.3. During context 2, the RPs were presented with audio stimulus recorded for context 3 instead of that for context 2, whilst the calibration models themselves were presented with the correct audio recording from context 2. Figure 6b shows that the RPs (orange curve) mis-classify the context, so that, for example, the RP associated with model 3 predicts dominance by that model in context 2 as well as context 3, as would be expected. It can be observed that the RE (blue curve) causes a posterior correction of the overall responsibility, shown by the profile of the red broken curve.

Table 1. Localization performance. N = 150. Accuracy is percent less than 5° error

	Method	Accuracy	MSE (degrees^2)
1.	Combined models without RP	93%	5.5
2.	Combined models with RP	100%	1.12
3.	Combined models without RP in novel contexts	90%	9.3
4.	Combined models with RP in novel contexts	95%	5.7
5.	Ground truth missing from trial 6	71%	19.9
6.	Ground truth missing with RP	83%	14.5
7.	RP alone providing responsibility signals from trial 6	99%	1.7

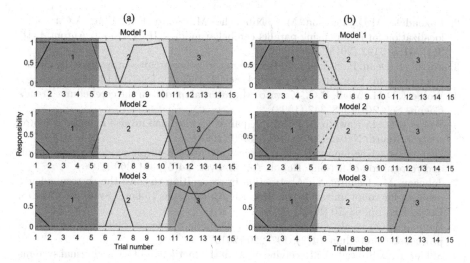

Fig. 6. Responsibility signals as the system progressed through trials. Each trial represents a randomly selected azimuth in one of three different contexts, indicated by the coloured boxes. Context 1 (blue box) is $\phi = 90°$ left; context 2 (red box) is $\phi = 0°$; context 3 (green box) is $\phi = 90°$ right. The blue curve shows the output of the RE alone, the orange curve shows the output of the RP, and the red broken curve shows the overall responsibility calculated according to Eq. 2. (a) Missing ground truth (b) RP mis-classification. (Color figure online)

6   Conclusion and Discussion

The RP based on the adaptive filter model of the cerebellum was able to successfully predict the responsibility values of the cerebellar models in the acoustic contexts presented, improving the performance compared to that without the RP. It did this through analysis of a single feature extracted from the audio stream allowing the system to predict the responsibilities of the models before the ground truth becomes available. The RP also improves the performance of the system with prolonged absence of the ground truth, allowing the robot to continue to calibrate its SSL even where it moves to a new acoustic environment, which is not addressed in the MOSAIC literature. The system was also able to predict, to a limited extent, the generalization of the models to novel contexts. Finally, it was shown that the RE is able to make a posterior correction to the responsibility values in the event that the RP mis-classifies the context.

References

1. Okuno, H.G., Nakadai, K.: Robot audition: Its rise and perspectives. In: 2015 IEEE International Conference on Acoustics, Speech and Signal Processing (ICASSP 2015), pp. 5610–5614 (2015)

2. Baxendale, M.D., Pearson, M.J., Nibouche, M., Secco, E.L., Pipe, A.G.: Audio localization for robots using parallel cerebellar models. IEEE Robot. Autom. Lett. **3**(4), 3185–3192 (2018)
3. Porrill, J., Dean, P., Stone, J.V.: Recurrent cerebellar architecture solves the motor-error problem. Proc. Roy. Soc. B Biol. Sci. **271**(1541), 789–796 (2004)
4. Wolpert, D.M., Miall, R.C., Kawato, M.: Internal models in the cerebellum. Trends Cognit. Sci. **2**(9), 338–347 (1998)
5. Wolpert, D.M., Kawato, M.: Multiple paired forward and inverse models for motor control. Neural Netw. **11**(78), 1317–1329 (1998)
6. Demiris, Y., Khadhouri, B.: Hierarchical attentive multiple models for execution and recognition of actions. Robot. Auton. Syst. **54**(5), 361–369 (2006)
7. Johnson, M., Demiris, Y.: Abstraction in recognition to solve the correspondence problem for robot imitation. In: Towards Autonomous Robotic Systems, TAROS, Essex, UK, pp. 63–70 (2004)
8. Baumann, O., et al.: Consensus paper: The role of the cerebellum in perceptual processes. Cerebellum **14**(2), 197–220 (2015)
9. Snider, R.S., Stowell, A.: Receiving areas of the tactile, auditory and visual systems in the cerebellum. J. Neurophysiol. **7**, 331–357 (1944)
10. Argentieri, S., Danès, P., Souères, P.: A survey on sound source localization in robotics: From binaural to array processing methods. Comput. Speech & Lang. **34**(1), 87–112 (2015)
11. Davila-Chacon, J., Magg, S., Jindong, L., Wermter, S.: Neural and statistical processing of spatial cues for sound source localisation. In: The 2013 International Joint Conference on Neural Networks (IJCNN), pp. 1–8 (2013)
12. Youssef, K., Argentieri, S., Zarader, J.L.: A binaural sound source localization method using auditive cues and vision. In: 2012 IEEE International Conference on Neural Networks (IJCNN), Acoustics, Speech and Signal Processing (ICASSP), pp. 217–220 (2012)
13. Fujita, M.: Adaptive filter model of the cerebellum. Biol Cybern. **45**(3), 195–206 (1982)
14. Dean, P., Porrill, J., Ekerot, C.F., Jorntell, H.: The cerebellar microcircuit as an adaptive filter: Experimental and computational evidence (report). Nat. Rev. Neurosci. **11**(1), 30 (2010)
15. Imamizu, H., Kawato, M.: Brain mechanisms for predictive control by switching internal models: Implications for higher-order cognitive functions. Psycholog. Res. **73**(4), 527–544 (2009)
16. Haruno, M., Wolpert, D.M., Kawato, M.: MOSAIC model for sensorimotor learning and control. Neural Comput. **13**(10), 2201–2220 (2001)
17. Assaf, T., Wilson, E.D., Anderson, S., Dean, P., Porrill, J., Pearson, M.J.: Visual-tactile sensory map calibration of a biomimetic whiskered robot. In: Proceedings of the 2016 IEEE International Conference on Robotics and Automation (ICRA), pp. 967–972. IEEE (2016)
18. Giannakopoulos, T., Pikrakis, A.: Introduction to Audio Analysis: a MATLAB Approach, 1st edn. Academic Press, Amsterdam (2014)
19. Sejnowski, T.J.: Storing covariance with nonlinearly interacting neurons. J. Math. Biol. **4**(4), 303–21 (1977)

Determination of Artificial Muscle Placement for Biomimetic Humanoid Robot Legs

Ben P. Bolen$^{(\boxtimes)}$ (ID) and Alexander J. Hunt (ID)

Portland State University, Portland, OR 97207, USA
bbolen83@gmail.com

Abstract. Bipedal robotic leg kinematics and dynamics are a key component in designing biomimetic humanoid robots. This work describes the process of designing artificial muscle attachment locations of the legs of a bipedal robot utilizing pneumatic artificial muscles (PAMs). PAMs offer similar force and activation times to real muscles, while being lightweight and low power. However, not all properties are identical, and substituting artificial muscles in with the same attachment locations results in different torque profiles about each joint. This work analyzes muscle length, moment arm, and isometric force of muscles over a range of different joint configurations, based on muscle attachment and wrapping points of the Gait2392 model in OpenSim. These parameters are then used to find joint torques produced by each muscle. This process is repeated for a model of the robot actuated by PAMs. Joint torques for individual muscles and groups of muscles are then compared between the models. Results indicate that several muscles torque profiles in the robot model closely match that of the human model, however, many muscles fall far short of the human capabilities. Where appropriate, additional results demonstrate how muscle attachment locations on the robot have been modified to better match the torque capabilities demonstrated by the OpenSim model. Matlab tools created for this project will facilitate further design refinement before implementation on the robot.

Keywords: Biomechanics · PAMs · Moment arm · Joint torque ·
Humanoid robot · Biarticular muscles · Over-actuated system · OpenSim

1 Introduction

Biomimetic robots attempt to replicate the anatomical motions and biological systems of living organisms. Of particular interest to humans are biomimetic bipedal humanoid robots. Two different processes are often utilized in developing biomimetic robots. One approach is to engineer the robotic systems to match observed biological principles, while the other works to match the biology and then observe how the system behaves in order to gain insight into the inner workings of biological systems. The work presented here details part of the design process for developing human-mimetic robot legs that falls into the second category [1].

Several human-mimetic robots have been built that fall into this type. These include Lucy [2], Pneumat-BS [3], and the robot built by Zang et al. [4]. These robots utilize McKibben style Pneumatic Artificial Muscles (PAMs) to actuate the joints.

© Springer Nature Switzerland AG 2019
U. Martinez-Hernandez et al. (Eds.): Living Machines 2019, LNAI 11556, pp. 15–26, 2019.
https://doi.org/10.1007/978-3-030-24741-6_2

These artificial muscles have many gross properties that mimic those of human muscles [5]. These muscles can only be used to pull, not push. Force-length properties of PAMs have been shown in experiments to be similar to muscles [6] and they can be used in accordance with the Hill muscle model [7]. PAMs are also useful to use as they have a power-to-volume and power-to-weight ratios equal to or greater than other actuators used in robotics [7].

When these robots were developed, many simplifications were used to position artificial muscle attachment locations at the locations of the analogous muscle on the human body. These simplifications reduce the versatility of the robots and their bio-mimetic similarity to humans. The properties of the PAMs do not match as closely with human muscles as would be most beneficial. Specifically, these artificial muscles cannot contract as much as human muscles: up to 18% in the PAMs vs 38% in biological muscles [8]. As such, if the artificial muscles are positioned at the same locations as the human muscles, joint range of motion, and joint torques are severely limited as compared to humans. Therefore, it is more pertinent to have attachment locations that allow the muscles to match the resultant torque and range of motion profiles that each muscle is able to contribute to movement.

This work compares the torque profiles of multiple muscles for a bipedal robot designed with the same attachment locations as a human. This is done by creating tools in Matlab that accurately reproduce results from the OpenSim [9] benchmark human model Gait2392 [10]. A copy of this model is then made, and muscle properties are changed from human properties to those of the PAMs chosen to be used for the robot. After initial analysis between the robot and OpenSim model, several artificial muscles were removed from the robot model and the attachment points on others have been modified to enable larger joint ranges of motion. Individual muscles are compared, as are groups of muscles based on their anatomical function [11]. Next steps in the bipedal humanoid development process are described.

2   Materials and Methods

For this project, the model Gait 2392 was used from OpenSim. Gait 2392 has 23 degrees of freedom (DoFs), 92 musculotendon actuators to represent 76 real muscles of torso and lower limbs, and 12 rigid-body segments. This model is based on a human subject that is about 1.8 m tall [9]. We first reproduced the segment lengths, muscle attachment locations, and muscle model in Matlab to verify the design process for the robot model and enable more effective comparison of data between the robot and human model.

2.1 Bone Segments

Joint centers in the Matlab model are placed in the same locations with the same orientations as is found in the OpenSim model (see Fig. 1). Using the same bone segment geometry in both the robot model and OpenSim model eliminates the need to perform scaling. Included in the model are details such as the moving knee origin with respect the femur origin. In both models the patella is removed, and the quadriceps insertion location on the patella is modeled in the tibia frame as a function of knee angle.

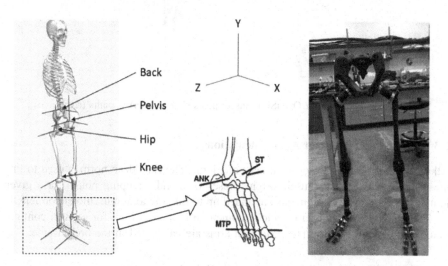

Fig. 1. Joint names and locations. Axis legend shows X axis (red), Y axis (green), and Z axis (blue). Close-up of ankle from Delp et al. [12]. ANK, ST, and MTP are the ankle, subtalar, and metatarsophalangeal joints, respectively. 3D printed robot skeleton shown on the right. (Color figure online)

2.2 Muscle Paths

Muscle attachment locations are also guided by GaitBody2392. Muscle origin and insertion points are kept the same, and the OpenSim moving wrapping points (to guide muscle paths) are replaced by fixed points in the Matlab human model. Several PAM attachment points in the robot model are modified to accommodate the contraction limits of Festo PAMs, and to try to accommodate 3D geometry realities that are not a component of the OpenSim model (i.e. avoiding interference with other actuators). Muscle path routings for GaitBody2392 are shown on the left hand side of Fig. 2, below. PAM routing paths for the robot design were exported to OpenSim and are shown on the right hand side for comparison.

Fig. 2. Skeleton w/ OpenSim muscle paths (left) and PAM paths (right).

2.3   Length and Moment Arm Calculations

All of the skeletal muscles cross at least one joint. The Euclidean norm is used to find the distance between all muscle origins, insertions, and wrapping points for a given joint angle. These norm segments are added up to find the total musculotendon length.

The method to acquire a muscle's moment arm about a joint for a given configuration is described by Hoy [13]. Moment arms are calculated in the body frame.

2.4   PAM Diameter and Resting Length Calculations

The Festo PAMs used for the robot come in three different diameters, 10 mm, 20 mm, and 40 mm [14]. The maximum theoretical force achieved by each actuator scales with diameter size. PAM diameter size for each muscle was chosen to match or exceed the muscle's maximum isometric force specified in the human model. The resting length is found so that it does not exceed maximum length of the muscle over the entire range of motion.

2.5   Force and Torque Calculations

Force used in the torque calculations is the isometric force for a muscle at a certain musculotendon length. This force scales with muscle length according to the force-length curves determined for each muscle. Force calculations for human muscles in the Matlab model were determined from the work of Millard [15], Thelen [16], and Hoy [13]. Details of the model can be found in Thelen [16].

For the Festo PAMs, force vs contraction percentage can be found in the work of Hunt et al. [17]. For the Festo PAMs, the maximum contraction is a function of the resting muscle length and varies from 14.91% to 17.50% [17].

Torque is calculated once muscle force and moment arm are known (Eq. 1).

$$Torque = force * moment\,arm \tag{1}$$

The calculations performed in the Matlab human model were checked against OpenSim results generated directly in the program. These are then also compared with the robot model.

3 Results

3.1 Validation of Matlab Human Model

Figure 3 compares the torque values of the sartorius muscle between OpenSim and the Matlab human model about the hip Z-axis for hip and knee flexion. The maximum difference between the Matlab model and OpenSim was 2%.

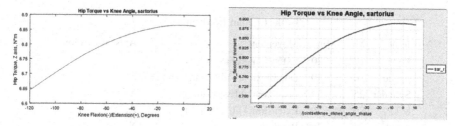

Fig. 3. Comparison of torque values between Matlab human model (left) and OpenSim (right) for hip Z-axis.

3.2 Robot Model

Joint angle limits for human model were determined from range of motion values listed by Platzer [19] and Kapandji [20]. The human model has a maximum hip flexion(+)/ extension(−) of +140°/−20°. Hip adduction (+) and abduction (−) is a function of hip flexion, ultimate maximum and minimums are +30°/−80°. Maximum internal hip rotation is 40°. Maximum external hip rotation is −30° with full hip extension and −50° with full hip extension. An initial pass at comparison of joint torques over these ranges of motion determined that even with the ability to change attachment locations, total range of motion would not be achieved due to the limited range of artificial muscle contraction. Therefore, desired joint limits in the robot were reduced. Limits were chosen to include the range of motion required for most human tasks including walking, sitting, and squatting. The robot model is limited to +110°/−15° for flexion (+)/extension(−), and +20°/−60° for ultimate adduction(+)/abduction(−) (Fig. 4). RoM limits for the other joints are listed in Table 1.

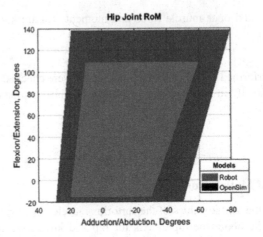

Fig. 4. RoM limits for hip flexion/extension and adduction/abduction for OpenSim (left) and robot (right) models.

Table 1. Joint RoM limits.

Joint	Max	Min	Movement	Axis of rotation
Knee	10°	−120°	Extension(+)/Flexion(−)	Z
Ankle	20°	−50°	Dorsiflexion(+)/Plantarflexion(−)	Z
Subtalar	25°	−35°	Inversion(+)/Eversion(−)	X
MTP	80°	−30°	Extension(+)/Flexion(−)	Z
Lumbar	20°	−20°	Bending	X
Lumbar	5°	−5°	Rotation	Y
Lumbar	20°	−60°	Extension(+)/Flexion(−)	Z

Table 2 shows the Festo diameter and resting PAM lengths calculated for the robot model's 27 actuators. These values were calculated for the DoF movements listed under the Motion column. Many muscles in the robotic model showed close matching to that of the human model, while several muscles require modifications to muscle attachment points. It is impossible to show the torque results for all muscles in the page limits of this manuscript, therefore only a few select muscles are shown.

Table 2. Resting muscle length and diameter for robot model.

	Resting muscle length, cm			DoF ranges investigated
Festo diameter, mm	**10**	**20**	**40**	
Glut Max			64	Hip adduction/abduction and flexion/extension
Semimembranosus			103	Hip and knee flexion/extension
Bicep Femoris, LH		85		Hip and knee flexion/extension

(*continued*)

Table 2. (*continued*)

	Resting muscle length, cm			DoF ranges investigated
Bicep Femoris, SH		34		Knee flexion/extension
Sartorius	150			Hip and knee flexion/extension
Adductor Magnus			61	Hip adduction/abduction and flexion/extension
TFL	84			Hip and knee flexion/extension
Gracilis	77			Hip and knee flexion/extension
Iliacus		52		Hip adduction/abduction and flexion/extension
Psoas		53		Hip adduction/abduction and flexion/extension
Rectus Femoris		70		Hip and knee flexion/extension
Vastus Int			41	Knee flexion/extension
Medial Gastro			46	Knee and ankle flexion/extension
Lateral Gastro		48		Knee and ankle flexion/extension
Soleus			36	Knee and ankle flexion/extension
Tibialis Posterior			38	Ankle flexion/extension and foot inversion/eversion
Flex. Digit. Longus	29			Ankle and MTP flexion/extension
Flex. Hallucis Long.	37			Ankle and MTP flexion/extension
Tibialis Anterior		42		Ankle flexion/extension and subtalar inversion/eversion
Peroneus Brevis	38			Ankle flexion/extension and subtalar inversion/eversion
Peroneus Longus		39		Ankle flexion/extension and subtalar inversion/eversion
Peroneus Tertius	40			Ankle flexion/extension and subtalar inversion/eversion
Ext. Digit. Long.	52			Ankle and MTP flexion/extension
Ext. Hallucis Long.	53			Ankle and MTP flexion/extension
Erector Spinae			27	Back flexion and bending
Internal Oblique		35		Back rotation and bending
External Oblique		27		Back rotation and bending

The gastrocnemius is a two-headed biarticular calf muscle modeled as two separate linear actuators in both the human and robot model (Fig. 5). Little modifications have been made to this muscle in the robot as the torque profiles closely match that of the human model. The origin points were moved slightly up the knee to increase the overall length of the muscles. A comparison of the torque over the knee Z-axis for these actuators for different knee and ankle orientations can be seen in Fig. 5.

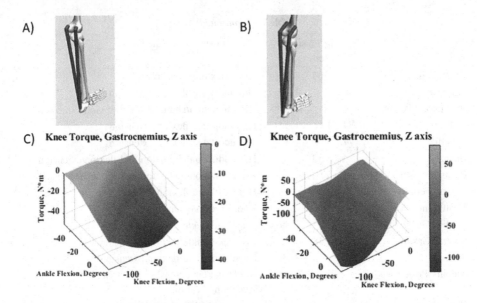

Fig. 5. Gastrocnemius muscle paths (A, B) and knee torque values (C, D) for human (A, C) and robot (B, D) models.

The biceps femoris muscle did not fare nearly as well in comparison. The action of this biarticular muscle is, in part, to perform hip extension and knee flexion. Even after significant lengthening of the muscle (lowering the insertion point on the tibia as shown in Fig. 6), there are still some areas in desired range of motion (maximal knee flexion and hip extension) in which the muscle is not able to produce any force.

Figure 7 groups and compares the uniarticular muscles of the hip joint (including the psoas). Since many of the gluteus, adductor, and external hip rotators in the model have similar joint torque functions, the number of muscles in the robot model was reduced. Simplification of muscle groups did not result in significant degradation in potential muscle groups. It is important to examine the group as a whole and see if the proposed changes in routings, and muscle consolidation, can provide similar torque. Hip rotation will not affect length as much as the other two hip DoFs and therefore was not investigated. The results demonstrate that the robot should be able to achieve the desired torques in all three degrees of freedom.

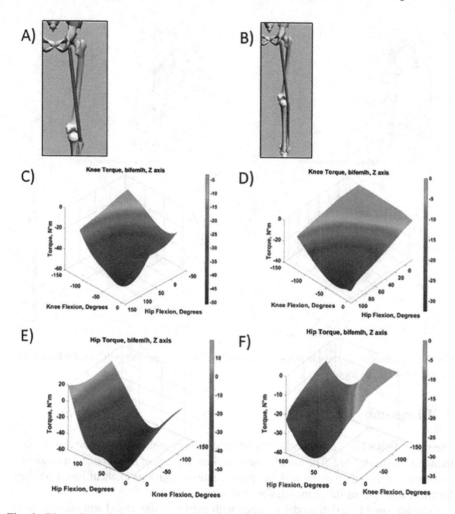

Fig. 6. Biceps Femoris Long Head muscle path (A, B) and torque values (C - F) for human (A, C, E) and robot (B, D, F) models, for knee (C, D) and hip Z-axis (E, F).

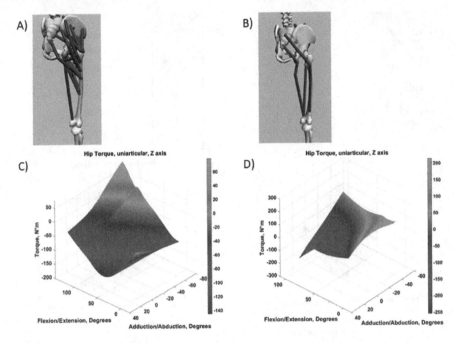

Fig. 7. Uniarticular hip muscle paths (A, B) and hip Z-axis torque values (C, D) for human (A, C) and robot (B, D) models.

4 Discussion

The robot design has 27 pneumatic actuators per side to replace the 46 muscles per side found in GaitBody2392. The muscles need various degrees of refinement. To make this refinement, it is important to look at specific muscles, groups of them based on their function, and groups of all muscles around a particular joint.

The humanoid Matlab model matches with the OpenSim model and enables us to create surface plots of calculated values over 2 degrees of freedom, enabling a more comprehensive view of muscle action than is available in the OpenSim program. This could be expanded to analyzing more than 2 degrees of freedom at once. For example, it could be used to analyze hamstring muscles during hip flexion, abduction, and knee extension movements, though visualizing the data might get difficult.

It is a challenge to achieve maximal joint RoMs and stay within the Festo maximum contraction capabilities. When the artificial muscle is fully contracted, and more range of motion is required, the artificial muscle would need to buckle.

Another limitation of this work is that there is currently little data on Festo hose diameters of 20 mm and 40 mm. These should be tested to see if they do indeed have the same maximum contraction capabilities as the 10 mm Festo muscle. The assumption that their force output will scale based on maximum theoretical force should also be tested. These tests will increase the accuracy of the robot model.

Many individual PAMs and muscle-actuator groups have torque values that have surface plots with significantly different shapes and torque ranges than the OpenSim model. An improvement in the biceps femoris maximum strain was achieved by changing the muscle origin, insertion, and wrapping points, but there are still joint angles in which the muscle is unable to provide any force (Fig. 6). Since this means that the maximum contraction is greater than 17.5%, it might be possible that moving the origin point up the sacrum and better modeling of the 3D geometry might further improve the muscle match. Other muscles that also need to be adjusted in a similar manner include the rectus femoris, psoas, erector spinae, abdominal muscles, calf muscles, and foot muscles.

The gastrocnemius in the robot model can resist much more torque than the one in the human model (Fig. 5), however one problem is that the gastrocnemius in the robot model also has positive torque value for certain ankle and knee position. This is not likely to occur in practice however, and can be eliminated by moving the attachment points out and away from the back of the knee. Solid modelling the skeleton geometry and how the PAMs will wrap around them will aid in this effort.

Looking at the groups of uniarticular hip muscles (Fig. 7), it can be seen that there is not yet a close fidelity between the human model and the robot model. It is also important to note that the Gait2392 model is not free of errors. For instance, at high degrees of hip flexion or extension some muscle routings pass through other muscles, or pass through bone [10]. Improvements might be made by solid-modeling PAM routings to get more accurate muscle paths or adding back in additional adductor/abductor hip muscles.

Range of motion limitations placed on the robot model helped specify acceptable resting lengths for the PAMs. Hip joint angles for flexion/extension and adduction/abduction were originally set to match the OpenSim model but after experimentation the limits were reduced. Further reducing of joint angle RoM was not as effective in achieving desired lengths when compared to moving the origin, insertion, and wrapping points for muscle actuators.

In all, these tools have been used to calculate and visualize values for length, moment arm, force, and torque for the robot design using PAMs, and they have been highly valuable in determining attachment locations for artificial muscles on a humanoid robot. Values produced in this model can be compared to existing human models. These tools will be effective for further refinement of the robot design. Additionally, more accurate modeling and refinement can be performed through the solid modeled and the final results will be tested with a 3D-printed skeletal structure, enabling us to investigate human control of muscles and movement in a more detailed manner than has yet been possible [1].

References

1. Steele, A.G., Hunt, A., Etoundi, A.C.: Biomimetic knee design to improve joint torque and life for bipedal robotics. In: Giuliani, M., Assaf, T., Giannaccini, M.E. (eds.) TAROS 2018. LNCS (LNAI), vol. 10965, pp. 91–102. Springer, Cham (2018). https://doi.org/10.1007/978-3-319-96728-8_8

2. Vanderborght, B., Van Ham, R., Verrelst, B., Van Damme, M., Lefeber, D.: Overview of the lucy project: dynamic stabilization of a biped powered by pneumatic artificial muscles. Adv. Robot. **22**(10), 1027–1051 (2008)
3. Ogawa, K., Narioka, K., Hosoda, K.: Development of whole-body humanoid "Pneumat-BS" with pneumatic musculoskeletal system. In: Amato, N.M. (ed.) IROS 2011, IEEE/RSJ, pp. 4838–4843. IEEE, San Francisco, September 2011
4. Zang, X., Liu, Y., Liu, X., Zhao, J.: Design and control of a pneumatic musculoskeletal biped robot. Technol. Health Care **24**(s2), S443–S454 (2016)
5. Chou, C.P., Hannaford, B.: Measurement and modeling of McKibben pneumatic artificial muscles. IEEE Trans. Robot. Autom. **12**(1), 90–102 (1996)
6. Klute, G.K., Czerniecki, J.M., Hannaford, B.: McKibben artificial muscles: pneumatic actuators with biomechanical intelligence. In: 1999 IEEE/ASME International Conference on Advanced Intelligent Mechatronics, Atlanta, pp. 221–226. IEEE (1999)
7. Tondu, B., Zagal, S.D.: McKibben artificial muscle can be in accordance with the Hill skeletal muscle model. In: 1st IEEE/RAS-EMBS International Conference on Biomedical Robotics and Biomechatronics, Pisa, pp. 714–720. IEEE (2006)
8. Gordon, A.M., Huxley, A.F., Julian, F.J.: The variation in isometric tension with sarcomere length in vertebrate muscle fibres. J. Physiol. **184**(1), 170–192 (1966)
9. Seth, A., Sherman, M., Reinbolt, J.A., Delp, S.L.: OpenSim: a musculoskeletal modeling and simulation framework for in silico investigations and exchange. Procedia Iutam **2**, 212–232 (2011)
10. Gait 2392 and 2354 Models. Stanford University. https://simtk-confluence.stanford.edu/display/OpenSim/Gait+2392+and+2354+Models. Accessed 22 Mar 2019
11. Gilroy, A., MacPherson, B., Ross, L., Schünke, M., Schulte, E., Schumacher, U.: Atlas of Anatomy, 2nd edn. Thieme, New York (2012)
12. Delp, S.L., Loan, J.P., Hoy, M.G., Zajac, F.E., Topp, E.L., Rosen, J.M.: An interactive graphics-based model of the lower extremity to study orthopaedic surgical procedures. IEEE Trans. Biomed. Eng. **37**(8), 757–767 (1990)
13. Hoy, M.G., Zajac, F.E., Gordon, M.E.: A musculoskeletal model of the human lower extremity: the effect of muscle, tendon, and moment arm on the moment-angle relationship of musculotendon actuators at the hip, knee, and ankle. J. Biomech. **23**(2), 157–169 (1990)
14. Festo Fluidic Muscle DMSP. https://www.festo.com/cat/en-us_us/data/doc_enus/PDF/US/DMSP_ENUS.PDF. Accessed 22 Mar 2019
15. Millard, M., Uchida, T., Seth, A., Delp, S.L.: Flexing computational muscle: modeling and simulation of musculotendon dynamics. J. Biomech. Eng. **135**(2), 021005 (2013)
16. Thelen, D.G.: Adjustment of muscle mechanics model parameters to simulate dynamic contractions in older adults. J. Biomech. Eng. **125**(1), 70–77 (2003)
17. Hunt, A.J., Graber-Tilton, A., Quinn, R.D.: Modeling length effects of braided pneumatic actuators. In: ASME 2017 International Design Engineering Technical Conferences and Computers and Information in Engineering Conference, ASME paper no. V05AT08A008. ASME, Cleveland (2017)
18. Platzer, W.: Color Atlas of Human Anatomy. Locomotor System, vol. 1, 5th edn., pp. 244–246. Thieme, New York (2004)
19. Kapandji, I.A.: Physiology of the Joints. Lower limb, vol. 2, 6th edn. Churchill Livingstone, London (1986)

Speedy Whegs Climbs Obstacles Slowly and Runs at 44 km/hour

William Breckwoldt, Richard Bachmann, Ronald Leibach[(✉)],
and Roger Quinn

Department of Mechanical and Aerospace Engineering,
Case Western Reserve University, Cleveland, OH 44106-7222, USA
rjl32@case.edu

Abstract. This work presents Speedy Whegs, a new Whegs vehicle that can climb over obstacles slowly and also run at a top speed of 44 km/hr (27 mph). It is powered by two parallel motor/transmission pairs modified from off-the-shelf components. Its three-speed transmissions can be shifted by remote control while the robot is in motion. Speedy Whegs accelerates to outrun all but the fastest humans in 40 yard and 100 yard distances. It is the fastest "multi-legged" robot in terms of gross speed and also the fastest of similar size or larger robots in terms of bodylengths per second. In fact, in terms of bodylengths per second it is faster than cheetahs. Despite having no suspension system or compliant legs, it is stable while running at top speed over grassy fields with minor irregularities.

Keywords: Wheel legs · Fast locomotion · Climbing · Mobile robot

1 Introduction

Mobile robot designers often struggle to balance speed, simplicity (reduced actuation), and rough-terrain navigation [1–3]. Wheeled robots can be fast and typically require simpler drive-train mechanisms than legged robots; however, compared to wheels, legs can allow movement over terrain with larger irregularities, but legged robots tend to be relatively slow. Two four-legged exceptions are Boston Dynamics' WildCat that runs at 32 km/hr (19.9 mph) [4] and MIT's electric Cheetah that runs at 23 km/hr (14.3 mph) and jumps fences [5]. However, these robots are complex machines.

RHex was invented to merge speed, simplicity and rough terrain navigation [4]. It has six motors, one for each of its legs, each of which rotates 360° about its axis. RHex was developed to model cockroach locomotion and, like insects, it can employ a range of gaits. Over rough terrain RHex can use a stance-to-swing speed ratio much less than one, producing an insect wave gait, with one leg in swing at a time. With a stance-to-swing speed ratio of one, the robot reaches its top speed while demonstrating the insect tripod gait, with the front and rear legs on one side of its body in phase with the middle leg on the opposite side. Its compliant legs provide a "suspension system" to absorb impacts and stabilize the robot and to store and release energy as in running animals [4]. To our knowledge, the fastest RHex robot has run at 10 km/hr (6.2 mph) [5].

U. Martinez-Hernandez et al. (Eds.): Living Machines 2019, LNAI 11556, pp. 27–37, 2019.
https://doi.org/10.1007/978-3-030-24741-6_3

Whegs was invented immediately after RHex and, in fact, RHex was one of its major influences [6]. Whegs was intended to be even simpler and less expensive than RHex while maintaining (and hopefully surpassing) its locomotion capabilities. For example, Whegs has only one propulsion motor that drives its six legs via sprockets and chains. Its wheel-legs have multiple spokes (see Fig. 1) so that its stance/swing leg function is produced with constant motor speed. Six-legged Whegs mimic a number of cockroach locomotion principles including the tripod gait described above. Most Whegs robots have a torsionally compliant mechanism in each of their hubs that allow them to adapt their gaits passively to the terrain. Some have a body joint powered by a series-elastic actuator. Some, such as in Fig. 1, have four wheel-legs. Two Whegs robots, DAGSI Whegs and Seadog, have climbed tall obstacles [1] and these robots have run at up to 8 km/hr (5 mph).

Fig. 1. Speedy Whegs on a football field. It is shown with the "Heel" design of rigid wheel-legs attached.

Reduced actuation robots have run fast in special cases and when miniaturized in terms of bodylengths per second. Miniature robots such as Mini-Whegs (8 cm long) ran at 10 bodylengths per second [7] and iSprawl (15 cm long) ran at 15 bodylengths per second [8]. Also, the wheel-like vehicle HexRunner runs at 51.8 km/hr (32.2 mph) but needs to be launched and falls over when it stops [9]. Therefore, we do not consider it comparable to a vehicle that can be autonomous.

To our knowledge, no full-size (50–100 cm) reduced actuation robot has successfully accomplished the combined capabilities of climbing and fast running at speeds comparable to BDI's WildCat.

The robot described in this paper was designed to answer the following questions: Can a Whegs robot run faster than BDI's WildCat with inexpensive, commercial off the shelf (COTS) drive train components and still climb irregular terrain at slow speeds? Also, will such a robot be stable while running at such a high speed?

In answering these questions, we will better understand and demonstrate the capability of wheel-legs in high-speed locomotion. This work presents Speedy Whegs, a Whegs vehicle designed to showcase the use of wheel-legs at high speed.

Fig. 2. Heel-Toe engagement. After the toe (front tip) of a wheel leg touches down on a step, the heel on the other front leg makes contact shortly after. Because these two contact points are not far out of phase, the robot is stable about its roll axis and does not need torsion devices to prevent rolling during climbing.

2   Robot Design

To address the questions posed in this study, it was decided that four wheel-legs would suffice. Also, based on our previous studies [7], four-spoke wheel-legs were chosen. In keeping with Whegs' design principles, a single propulsion system drives all of the wheel-legs via chains and sprockets.

The primary reason that previous Whegs robots were limited in speed was a lack of a multi-speed transmission. With a single speed transmission, for climbing obstacles with the necessary torque, controllability and limited current draw, the transmission needs to be geared for relatively slow movement, which limits the robot's top speed. Thus, a low gear is needed for climbing obstacles and at least one higher gear is needed for fast running.

To meet the design requirement of inexpensive COTS components, drill motors/ transmissions were identified as candidates for the propulsion system. Based on our previous experience with Whegs robots, we found that one such motor would not provide the necessary power. Therefore, Speedy Whegs is driven by two 18 V DeWalt Drill Motors (The Robot MarketPlace) each with an integral three-speed DeWalt Drill Motor Gearbox. The transmissions are shifted by rotating an external ring.

With the two motors operating in series, any difference in efficiency between the motors causes them to run at different speeds, which causes loading between the motors. Because of this, it is important for the motors to be back-drivable. The standard DeWalt gearbox is not suitable for this purpose, so two modifications had to be made. First, the back-drive disabling pins were removed from each gearbox. Second, the clutch of each gearbox was locked in place with a pin. This prevents the gearbox from slipping at high loads (Fig. 3).

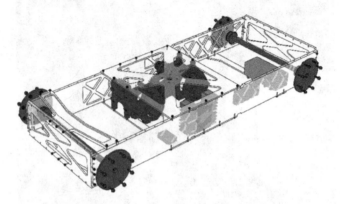

Fig. 3. CAD drawing of the Speedy Whegs assembly without wheel legs.

The Motor Mount (Fig. 4) serves two purposes. The first is to attach the motors rigidly to the chassis. The second is to facilitate shifting the transmissions of both motors simultaneously with a servo actuating the central Shifting Gear to rotate both C-Gears (C shaped sector gears) at once. Because of these parts' complex geometry, they were 3D printed out of PLA (polylactic acid). While a simpler, stronger structure could have been made of lightweight metal or durable plastic, 3D printing allows us to print material precisely where we need to in order to inexpensively create a lightweight, strong part.

The motor base is part of the motor mount and provides the primary support for the motor. The geometry is designed to snugly fit around the contours of the motor. The motor itself has two sections, the driver and the shifter. Each of these sections is held by a different clamp, and sits on a different part of the base, which is why the inner radius of the base changes. The Motor Shaft Subassembly mates with the front of the base with a press-fit bearing. The mounting of the base to the Chassis requires four supports jutting out of the bottom of the base.

The C Gears fit on the shifter of each motor and are actuated by the single central Shifting Gear (Fig. 4). A cutout on the inner diameter of the gear keys into the motor shifter. The pitch diameter and tooth shape are the same as that of the Shifting Gear. The shifting gear transmits torque from the shifting servo to the C Gear to shift the motors simultaneously.

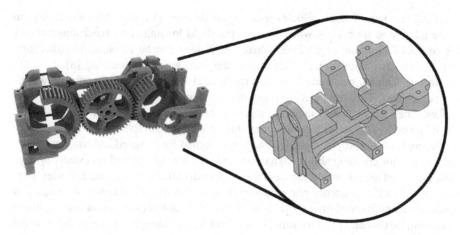

Fig. 4. Motor mount assembly. Shown here with all 3D printed components, as well as fasteners and servo. Motor Mount Base is emphasized. The motor and gearbox fit snugly in the 3D printed geometry of the Base.

To attach this gear to the servo's horn there are four clearance holes with hexagonal cutouts. The hexagonal cutouts allow the part to capture nuts. Because of this, assembly does not require holding the nut as the screws are tightened. A larger hole in the middle allows access to the screw that connects the horn to the servo itself. If the servo needs to be replaced, this can be used to transfer the horn to a new servo without having to unscrew the shifting gear from the horn. The pitch diameter and tooth shape are the same as that of the C Gear.

Speedy Whegs' wheel-legs all have a 45.7 cm (18 in.) diameter and are cut from 1.27 cm (0.5 in.) plywood on a CNC router. This allows for the rapid, low-cost production of various wheel leg designs. The wheel-legs also act as a roll cage during a crash. The wheel legs extend beyond the vehicle's chassis in every direction, ensuring they protect the vehicle in the event of a crash or roll. This may damage the vehicle's wheel-legs, but their replacement is easier and less expensive than replacing the vehicle's chassis or electronics.

Our hexapod wheel-legged robots typically use three spokes per wheel leg to maximize their ability to traverse rough terrain [1, 12]. On the other hand, our quadruped Whegs robots most often use four spokes per leg to smooth their body motions and this has shown to not decrease their climbing ability because the primary failure mode for quadruped climbing is pitching over backwards on higher obstacles. With more spokes, the frequency of vibrations experienced by Speedy Whegs increases while their amplitudes decrease. Increasing the number of spokes provides a smoother ride at high speeds. With these considerations, Speedy Whegs was designed with four-spoked wheel-legs.

Most previous Whegs vehicles use torsion devices to allow their wheel legs to rotate relative to their axles when above a threshold loading. This mechanism allows for enhanced climbing capabilities where wheel legs can be in phase for traversing steps, while also maintaining an alternating diagonal gait while running [8].

Spring-damping mechanisms in each leg have also proven to be effective on wheel-legged vehicles. These devices are pre-compressed and are in-line with the wheel legs' spokes. They act to absorb stepping impact to help smooth high-speed locomotion.

While both of these mechanisms are useful for Whegs vehicles, they are not necessary for the goals of this project. Speedy Whegs is designed for its speed and basic climbing, not for superior climbing ability, so torsion devices were not deemed necessary. Spring-damping mechanisms would increase the complexity of the robot, and are often only tuned to a specific frequency per ground condition. While some amount of damping is necessary for high speed running to be successful, natural turf provides damping without increasing the complexity of the robot. The wheel-legs are designed to be modular so that testing with spring and damping devices can be performed in the future.

This iteration of Speedy Whegs does not include the ability for steering. For the scope of this paper, it was important to confirm that stable locomotion could be achieved across the robot's entire range of speed. Turning mechanisms were not included because they could be used for active stabilization and we were interested to know if the robot would be passively stable at high speed (Table 1).

Table 1. Key dimensions of Speedy Whegs.

Dimension	Length (cm)	Length (in)
Body length	61	24
Body width	25.4	10
Chassis height	7.6	3.0
Wheelbase	53.3	21
Wheel leg diameter	45.7	18

3　Electronics and Control

Speedy Whegs is controlled with a handheld 2.4 GHz radio controller. The onboard circuit is comprised of a 2.4 GHz receiver, 50 A motor controller, two DeWalt Drill Motors, shifting servo, servo battery pack, and a 6-cell LiPo primary battery.

The radio receiver is a Futaba R2004GF 4-Channel FHSS Receiver. It is powered by the secondary battery and is connected to the motor controller and shifting servo. The motor controller is assigned to channel two and its 5 V line is not connected. The shifting servo is assigned to channel three.

The motor controller is the SyRen 50 A regenerative motor driver. It is controlled by the radio receiver but is not connected through its 5 V line. The controller is powered by the primary battery and powers both motors in parallel. The motor controller's current limiter is set to the maximum of 100 Amps. The six pin positions of the controller are 010100. This configuration uses the motor controller in standard R/C Input mode with auto-calibration to zero the incoming signal. This also enables the R/C Failsafe Timeout and automatic shutoff when the lithium battery is reduced to 3.0 V per cell.

The motors are two DeWalt 18 V New-Style Drill Motors. They are driven in parallel from the motor controller and attached to DeWalt gearboxes. These motors have a torque constant of 8.47 N-mm/amp and a voltage constant of 1125 RPM/volt. Their stall amperage is 155 Amps. The shifting servo is a HS-5085MG Premium Metal Gear Micro Servo. The servo is assigned to channel 3 of the radio receiver and turns the shifting gear in the motor mount subassembly.

The primary battery is the ZIPPY Flightmax 2200 mAh 6S1P 40C. This 22.2 V battery is connected only to the motor controller. The battery does not have enough energy for long-term use, but is enough to power the vehicle for several high speed test runs over the length of a football field. The battery voltage is slightly higher than the rated voltage of the motors, which causes the motors to output a higher than rated torque. The secondary battery is a Turnigy Receiver Pack 2/3A 1500 mAh 6.0V NiMH High Power Series. This battery connects to the radio receiver, and provides power to the receiver and servo. During testing, this battery pack failed and was replaced by a pack of four AAA batteries.

4   Testing

4.1   Speed

In testing for the vehicle's top speed, Speedy Whegs ran past a stationary camera at top speed. The video can be analyzed in at least two ways. The first option is to use markings on the ground and time the vehicle frame-by-frame as it passes them – this method can be performed on an American football field, or other field with constant-width markings. The second option is to use the vehicle as a gauge for length (see Fig. 6). Each frame, the distance between the front and rear axle is calculated in pixels. Because this has a constant length of 53.34 cm (21 in.), this gives a conversion factor from pixels to inches for each frame. The motion between frames can be taken in pixels and converted to inches using the average of both frames' conversion factors. Depending on the resolution of the video and how close the vehicle comes to the camera, this method may or may not have more error than the first method. For most of the speed tests recorded for this work, the first option was chosen (Fig. 5).

Fig. 5. Two overlapped video frames from a high-speed test. The blue and orange lines show the length between the front and back axles in their respective frames. These lengths are used to determine the actual distance moved by the vehicle between frames. (Color figure online)

4.2   Climbing

We showed that Speedy Whegs' climbing and rough terrain navigation were not sacrificed for speed. Several tests determined if it could climb obstacles as expected for a Whegs™ vehicle of its size. Speedy Whegs was tested over a range of step heights and videos were examined to determine its failure modes. Additionally, the transmission has been tested and has proven to allow torque selections during motion. This enables the robot RC operator to choose its torque in-situ.

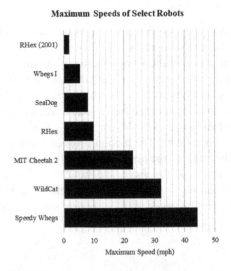

Fig. 6. Maximum speeds of selected robots. This chart represents a cross section of notable legged robots. Some were the fastest when they were created.

5   Results

5.1   Speed

Given enough room to accelerate (about 30–40 m), Speedy Whegs can reliably reach its top speed. Using the average of its three fastest runs, we find Speedy Whegs' top speed to be 44 km/hr (27 mph). This is equivalent to 20 bodylengths per second.

Speed tests were also run with a payload of 2.27 kg (5 lb). This payload is equivalent to a third of Speedy Whegs total mass. With this addition, the average of Speedy Whegs' three fastest runs was 38 km/hr (23.5 mph).

Figure 7 compares the speed of a number of legged robots developed over the past 18 years. It is not meant to be complete.

5.2   Stability

We found that Speedy Whegs can run with stability at high speed over asphalt/concrete and curbs and over grassy fields with minor irregularities. Introducing a 2.27 kg (5 lb) payload increases this stability but lowers the robot's maximum speed. However, we found that some irregularities caused the robot to leave the ground and somersault often resulting in broken wheel-legs. In these cases, an irregularity in the ground surface would cause the robot to leave the ground and suddenly yaw. When the robot landed, with a heading not in the direction of travel, its forward momentum would cause it to tumble. We believe that a turning mechanism may be useful to stabilize the robot in these situations and we leave this to future work.

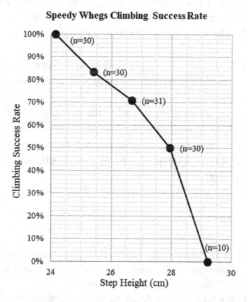

Fig. 7. Climbing success rate over a range of step heights.

5.3 Climbing

By shifting into its lowest gear, Speedy Whegs was able to make slow, controlled climbs. At a step height of 24 cm (9.5 in.), the vehicle had a 100% success rate of climbing (n = 30). At a step height of 29 cm (11.5 in.), the success rate was 0% (n = 10). For step heights between these two, results are shown in Fig. 7.

The vehicle exhibited two modes of failure while climbing, falling backwards or rolling to the side. If the attempt was made too quickly, as the rear wheel legs engaged the step, the front of the vehicle would rise up and Speedy Whegs would pitch backwards on its back. This could be improved by shifting the center of mass forward.

The second mode of failure occurred when the heel mechanism (Fig. 2) was not engaged while climbing. If the heel does not contact the step as the toe of the other front foot lifts the robot, the vehicle rolls while trying to push up. This comes from the vehicle's high center of gravity relative to its wheel base.

Precursors to these failures can be seen before the robot falls, making them avoidable for drivers with sight of the vehicle.

6 Conclusions

The purpose of Speedy Whegs is to go faster than the fastest legged vehicles while also retaining the climbing abilities of traditional wheel-legs and to do so with inexpensive COTS components and simplified actuation. It has fulfilled these goals including reaching a top speed of 44 km/hr (27 mph), or 20 bodylengths per second. This places Speedy Whegs faster than the fastest legged robot, WildCat. In terms of bodylengths per second, this places the vehicle faster than a cheetah (16 bodylengths per second).

Speedy Whegs achieves this speed while still being able to climb better than similar-sized wheeled vehicles, and maintaining simplicity in control and mechanism design.

Furthermore, despite not have a suspension or compliant wheel-legs, it remained stable while running at speed on asphalt/concrete surfaces, over curbs and on grassy fields with minor irregularities.

Can Speedy Whegs be volitionally turned while running at high speed and at what radius for a given speed? In future work, turning mechanisms will be added to address these questions. A future version will include steering either by splitting the motors to achieve "tank" steering or, as with previous Whegs robots, an independent steering rack for the front wheel-legs.

References

1. Boxerbaum, A.S., Oro, J., Peterson, G., Quinn, R.D.: The latest generation Whegs™ robot features a passive-compliant body joint. In: IEEE/RSJ International Conference on Intelligent Robots and Systems, pp. 1636–1641 (2008)
2. Eiji, N., Sei, N.: Leg-wheel robot: a futuristic mobile platform for forestry industry. In: IEEE/Tsukuba International Workshop on Advanced Robotics, Tsukuba, Japan (1993)

3. Kim, Y.-S., Jung, G.-P., Kim, H., Cho, K.-J., Chu, C.-N.: Wheel transformer: a wheel-leg hybrid robot with passive transformable wheels. IEEE Trans. Robot. **30**(6), 1487–1498 (2014)
4. WildCat, Boston Dynamics. https://www.bostondynamics.com/wildcat
5. Seok, S., Wang, A., Otten, D., Kim, S.: Actuator design for high force proprioceptive control in fast legged locomotion. In: IEEE/RSJ International Conference on Intelligent Robots and Systems (IROS), pp. 1970–1975 (2012)
6. Saranli, U., Buehler, M., Koditschek, D.E.: RHex: a simple and highly mobile hexapod robot. Int. J. Robot. Res. **20**(7), 616–631 (2001)
7. RHEX, Boston Dynamics. https://www.bostondynamics.com/rhex
8. Quinn, R., Offi, J., Kingsley, D., Ritzmann, R.: Improved mobility through abstracted biological principles. In: IEEE/RSJ International Conference on Intelligent Robots and Systems, vol. 3, pp. 2652–2657 (2002)
9. FastRunner – IHMC Robotics Lab. http://robots.ihmc.us/fastrunner
10. Morrey, J., Lambrecht, B., Horchler, A., Ritzmann, R., Quinn, R.: Highly mobile and robust small quadruped robots. In: IEEE/RSJ International Conference on Intelligent Robots and Systems, pp. 82–87 (2003)
11. Kim, S., Clark, J.E., Cutkosky, M.R.: iSprawl: design and tuning for high-speed autonomous open-loop running. Int. J. Robot. Res. **25**, 903–912 (2006)
12. Dunker, P.A.: A Biologically Inspired Robot for Lunar Exploration and Regolith Excavation. Case Western Reserve University, Cleveland (2009)

Automatic Calibration of Artificial Neural Networks for Zebrafish Collective Behaviours Using a Quality Diversity Algorithm

Leo Cazenille[1]([✉]), Nicolas Bredeche[2], and José Halloy[3]

[1] Department of Information Sciences, Ochanomizu University, Tokyo, Japan
leo.cazenille@gmail.com
[2] Sorbonne Université, CNRS, ISIR, 75005 Paris, France
[3] Univ Paris Diderot, Sorbonne Paris Cité, LIED, UMR 8236, 75013 Paris, France

Abstract. During the last two decades, various models have been proposed for fish collective motion. These models are mainly developed to decipher the biological mechanisms of social interaction between animals. They consider very simple homogeneous unbounded environments and it is not clear that they can simulate accurately the collective trajectories. Moreover when the models are more accurate, the question of their scalability to either larger groups or more elaborate environments remains open. This study deals with learning how to simulate realistic collective motion of collective of zebrafish, using real-world tracking data. The objective is to devise an agent-based model that can be implemented on an artificial robotic fish that can blend into a collective of real fish. We present a novel approach that uses Quality Diversity algorithms, a class of algorithms that emphasise exploration over pure optimisation. In particular, we use CVT-MAP-Elites [32], a variant of the state-of-the-art MAP-Elites algorithm [25] for high dimensional search space. Results show that Quality Diversity algorithms not only outperform classic evolutionary reinforcement learning methods at the macroscopic level (i.e. group behaviour), but are also able to generate more realistic biomimetic behaviours at the microscopic level (i.e. individual behaviour).

Keywords: Collective behaviour · Neural networks · QD-algorithms · CVT-MAP-Elites · Bio-hybrid systems · Biomimetic · Robot · Zebrafish · Fish

1 Introduction

Many models have been proposed for fish collective behaviours and motion [13,24,30]. At an early stage, they were developed to model realistic collective motion in computer simulation [28]. Nowadays, most of the models are developed to decipher the interaction rules of the animals and not to replicate their behaviour in autonomous agents be them robots or simulations. It is not clear that they can

© Springer Nature Switzerland AG 2019
U. Martinez-Hernandez et al. (Eds.): Living Machines 2019, LNAI 11556, pp. 38–50, 2019.
https://doi.org/10.1007/978-3-030-24741-6_4

be used to produce a realistic description of fish collective interactions with collective trajectories [19] similar to the observations. Moreover, most of the models consider an unbounded homogeneous space that could be the case in pelagic conditions but not in bounded and in-homogeneous environments. Only a few models consider the walls of the tanks that have a important effect on the fish [3,9,21]. In the robotic context, developing bio-mimetic and realistic fish behavioural models that can be implemented in robots are difficult to develop [5,6]. These issues are related: (i) how can we develop models producing good descriptions of fish collective behaviours and (2) that, when used as controllers, allow fully autonomous agents (robots, simulations) to cope with bounded inhomogeneous environments and social interactions?

For this type of question, currently two kind of modelling methods are pursued to simply take into account the tank walls and the social context. The first one is equation-based. Equations for the motion of the individuals are developed and calibrated on experimental data [3,21]. It has been shown that they give excellent results for groups of two fish (*Hemmigramus blerei*) in a circular bounded environment [3]. It remains to demonstrate that such method is scalable for groups made of more than two individuals and more elaborate set-ups. The second kind of modelling technique is agent based. For example, we have developed agent based models that take into account bounded in-homogeneous environment and the social context of the fish [6,9]. However, agent based models become rapidly complicated as the number of variables and parameters increases. The scalability of this modelling technique remains also an issue.

Here we explore how to develop scalable effective models to generate robot controllers producing realistic collective behaviours. We do not look for understanding specific collective behaviour mechanisms. In recent works, we explored the use of artificial neural network models (multilayer perceptrons) to generate realistic collective motion and trajectories of a group of five zebrafish in a bounded environment [7,8]. We compared supervised learning and reinforcement learning techniques to optimise the behaviour of artificial Zebrafish, so that they would match the trajectories obtained from real-world experimental data. In this setup, learning a behavioural model is challenging because of the continuous state and action spaces as well as the lack of a world model. We showed that evolutionary reinforcement learning, *i.e.* a direct policy search method [31,34], can be used to obtain relevant fish trajectories with respect to individual and collective dynamics, and outperforms results obtained by supervised learning. We also showed that while multi-objective evolutionary optimisation using NSGA-III [35] could provide different results over single objective optimisation using CMA-ES [1], the overall quality of trajectories generated is limited by the multiple aspects of behavioural dynamics to be captured simultaneously: wall-following, aggregation, individual trajectories and group dynamics. As a result, we showed that while the *global* biomimetic score (*i.e.* the aggregation of all criteria) is improved with these methods, there is no guarantee that *all* behavioural features will be optimised. In other words, generated trajectories may display unrealistic behaviours, such as low alignment between individuals or erratic wall-following behaviours, while matching real world data in term of inter-individual distances.

In order to improve the quality of biomimetic behavioural strategies, we propose to favour exploration over pure optimisation by using Quality-Diversity (QD) algorithms [12,27]. These algorithms are particularly successful in evolutionary robotics problems [11,15,25], either by improving diversity to overcome deceptive search spaces [23], or by generating a large repertoire of solutions instead of just one single solution [25]. In the current setup (Fig. 1), we enforce diversity to guide the search by exploring trade-offs between overall quality, which results from aggregating different criteria, and unique realistic behavioural traits, which focus on specific behavioural features, in this case: (1) inter-individual distances between agents, (2) polarisation of the agents in the group, (3) distribution of agent linear speed and (4) probability of presence in the arena. We use CVT-MAP-Elites [32], a variant of the MAP-Elites algorithm [25] using centroidal Voronoi tessellations to tackle high-dimensional feature spaces. CVT-MAP-Elites makes it possible to explore a range of both diverse and high-performing solutions by partitioning the search space into geometric regions according to features predefined by the user. It is then possible to find solutions that can be very different from one another.

We show that CVT-MAP-Elites outperforms state-of-the-art evolutionary optimisation methods (CMA-ES and NSGA-III) for revealing biomimetic behavioural strategies in a fish collective. Even more interestingly, we show that trajectories generated by individuals obtained with CVT-MAP-Elites are also more realistic (when compared to actual data from the fish) at the *microscopic* scale, with realistic behaviours at the level of the individuals. Quality Diversity algorithms offer a promising alternative to classical evolutionary optimisation and reinforcement learning algorithms with respect to learning biomimetic controller for artificial fish.

2   Methods

Experimental set-up. We apply the same experimental method, fish handling and set-up as in [6–8,29]. During experiments, fish are placed in an immersed square white plexiglass arena of $1000 \times 1000 \times 100$ mm. An overhead camera records a video of the experiment at 15 FPS with a 500×500 px resolution. It is them analysed to track the fish positions. Experiments were carried out with 10 groups of 5 adult (6–12 months old) wild-type AB zebrafish (*Danio rerio*) in ten 30-min trials as in [6,29]. Experiments conduced in this study were performed under the authorisation of the Buffon Ethical Committee (registered to the French National Ethical Committee for Animal Experiments #40) after submission to the French state ethical board for animal experiments.

Artificial neural network model. Artificial neural networks (ANN) are universal function approximators able to model phenomena with *a priori* information. They were used in previous studies [7,8,20] to model fish collective behaviour and generate biomimetic trajectories of fish in groups. However this

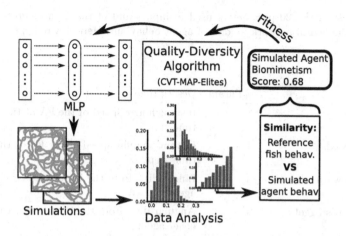

Fig. 1. Description of the presented methodology to calibrate artificial neural networks to generate fish trajectories. We apply CVT-MAP-Elites [32], a quality-diversity algorithm [27], to optimise the weights of a Multilayer Perceptron (MLP, 1 hidden layer, 10 neurons) that drive 5 fish-like agents in simulations. Simulated agents trajectories are compared to experimental fish trajectories. The fitness function corresponds to the biomimetism score of simulated agent groups. CVT-MAP-Elites is compared to CMA-ES [1] as in [7,8].

problem is challenging, and it is still possible to improve upon the biomimetism of resulting trajectories. Our methodology builds on Cazenille *et al.* [8] and calibrates Multilayer Perceptron (MLP) [2] artificial neural networks to drive simulated fish-like agents in groups of 5 individuals. All simulations involve 5 simulated agents driven by the optimised MLP (see workflow on Fig. 1).

MLP are a class of feedforward artificial neural networks. They can be employed in a wide variety of modelling and control tasks [26]. As in [7,8], our approach uses MLP with one hidden layer of 10 neurons with a hyperbolic tangent activation function. We use this simple and limited ANN as a baseline for bench-marking the various optimisation algorithms.

Table 1 lists the parameters used as inputs and outputs of the MLP controllers for each simulated focal agent. The 20 inputs parameters are often used in multi-agent models of animal collective behaviour [13,30], and can arguably be considered to be sufficient to model fish groups trajectories. As we consider fish trajectories observed in a bounded environment, we also take into account the presence of walls, which is often ignored in models of fish behaviour, and only found in a small number of recent studies [3,6–9].

Data analysis. As in [7,8], we analyse the tracked positions of agents in each trial e (experiments or simulations) and compute several behavioural metrics: (i) the distribution of *inter-individual distances* between agents (D_e); (ii) the distributions of *instant linear speeds* (L_e); (iii) the distribution of *polarisation* of the agents in the group (P_e); (iv) the *probability of presence of agents in the*

Table 1. List of the 20 parameters used in inputs and of the 2 parameters used as outputs of the neural network models of agent behaviour. Here, FA refers to the focal agent.

Inputs

Name	#Param.	Description
Linear speed	1	Instant linear speed of the FA at the prev. time-step
Angular speed	1	Instant angular speed of the FA at the prev. time-step
Distance towards agents	4	Linear dist. from the FA towards each other agent
Angle towards agents	4	Angular dist. from the FA towards each other agent
Alignment (angle)	4	Angular dist. between the FA heading and other agent heading
Alignment (linear speed)	4	Difference of linear speed between the FA and other agent linear speed
Distance to nearest wall	1	Linear dist. from the FA towards the nearest wall
Angle towards nearest wall	1	Angular dist. from the FA towards the nearest wall

Outputs

Name	#Param.	Description
Delta linear speed	1	Change of inst. linear speed of the FA from the prev. time-step
Delta angular speed	1	Change of inst. angular speed of the FA from the prev. time-step

arena (E_e). The polarisation of an agent group assesses the extent to which fish are aligned. It corresponds to the absolute value of the mean agent heading: $P = \frac{1}{N} \left| \sum_{i=1}^{N} u_i \right|$ where u_i is the unit direction of agent i and $N = 5$ is the number of agents [33]. Recent studies introduced more complex metrics to assess fish behaviour, like 2D features maps of neighbours compared to a focal fish used in [18,22]. Our approach here aims to provide a simple methodological baseline, so we only take into account simple and established behavioural metrics like polarisation and inter-individual distances. While more complex metrics based on 2D features maps could describe more accurately fish collective dynamics, they may also require quantities with higher dimensionality than simple metrics, which may make their synthesis into behavioural scores more difficult.

We quantify the realism of the simulated fish-like agents groups by computing a **biomimetism score** of their behaviour, as in [6–8]. It measures the similarity between behaviours exhibited by the simulated fish group and those exhibited by the experimental fish averaged across all 10 experimental trials (**Control** case e_c).

This score ranges from 0.0 to 1.0 and is defined as the geometric mean of the other behavioural scores:

$$S(e, e_c) = \sqrt[4]{I(L_e, L_{e_c})I(D_e, D_{e_c})I(P_e, P_{e_c})I(E_e, E_{e_c})} \qquad (1)$$

The function $I(X, Y)$ is defined as such: $I(X, Y) = 1 - H(X, Y)$. The $H(X, Y)$ function is the Hellinger distance between two histograms [14]. It is defined as: $H(X, Y) = \frac{1}{\sqrt{2}}\sqrt{\sum_{i=1}^{d}(\sqrt{X_i} - \sqrt{Y_i})^2}$ where X_i and Y_i are the bin frequencies. As opposed to [8], we do not take into account the distribution of angular speeds in the computation of the fitness. Indeed, the distributions of angular speeds of evolved individuals was always similar to the ones from random individuals. Thus, we removed this behavioural metrics from the features taken into account to reduce the dimensionality of the feature space.

Optimisation and illumination. We calibrate the weights of the MLP models driving agent behaviour to approximate as close as possible the trajectories and behaviours of groups of 5 fish-like agents, as in [5,7,8]. Simulations have a duration of 30 min (15 time-steps per seconds, *i.e.* 27000 steps per simulation).

In previous studies [7,8], we optimised these MLP controllers using evolutionary algorithms: CMA-ES [1] and NSGA-III [35].

Here, we use the CVT-MAP-Elites [32] QD algorithm, a variant of the popular MAP-Elites [25] algorithm, to search for interesting MLP controllers matching experimental fish trajectories across a user-provided space of features. The family of Map-Elites algorithms is based on the idea of exploring a clustered search space, retaining the best candidate solutions for each cluster. Clusters correspond to specific range of values for pre-defined features and each candidate solution is stored in a cell of a so-called map, which corresponds to its cluster. The seminal MAP-Elites algorithm uses a pre-defined clustering of the feature space, with the number of clusters (or "bins") quickly exploding as the number of feature dimensions considered grows. In order to tackle high-dimensional feature space, the CVT-MAP-Elite algorithm defines clusters as centroids of Voronoi tesselation, where centroids can be automatically positioned during exploration.

In our case, these features correspond to the four behavioural metrics L_e, D_e, P_e, E_e presented earlier. CVT-MAP-Elites is capable of handling high dimensional feature spaces (like our case) by using centroidal Voronoi tessellations to reduce the dimensionality of the feature space. Here, the CVT-MAP-Elites case only consider 32 bins of elites, which is far lower as what would be used with MAP-Elites in a reasonable configuration (*e.g.* with 32 bins per features, it would correspond to a grid with $32 \times 32 \times 32 \times 32 = 33554432$ bins of elites). We selected empirically 32 bins of elites in the CVT-MAP-Elites methods because it produced the best-performing results among tested numbers of bins.

We compare the generated trajectories using CVT-MAP-Elites with previous results from [7,8] where MLP controllers were optimised by the CMA-ES [1]. CMA-ES is a popular mono-objective global optimiser capable of handling problems with noisy, ill-defined fitness function.

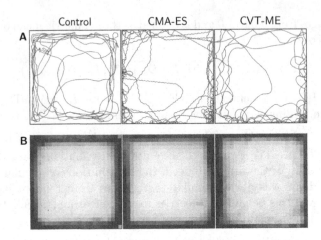

Fig. 2. Agent trajectories in the square (1 m) experimental arena after 30-min trials, for all considered cases: **Control** reference experimental fish data obtained as in [9, 29], **CVT-MAP-Elites** and **CMA-ES** corresponding to simulated MLP-driven agents. **A** Examples of an individual trajectory of one agent among the 5 making the group (fish or simulated agent) during 1 min out of a 30-min trial. **B** Presence probability density of agents in the arena.

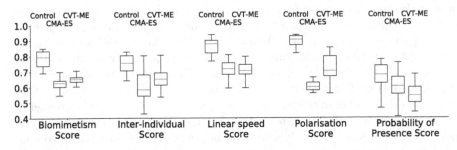

Fig. 3. Similarity scores between the trajectories of the experimental fish groups (Control) and those of the best-performing simulated individuals optimised by CVT-MAP-Elites or CMA-ES. All cases are tested across 10 different trials (experiments or simulations). Four behavioural features are considered to quantify the realism of exhibited behaviours. **Inter-individual distances** measures the similarity in distribution of inter-individual distances between all agents and corresponds to the capabilities of the agents to aggregate. **Linear speed distribution** measures to the distributions of linear speeds of the agents. **Polarisation** measures how aligned the agents are in the group. **Probability of presence** corresponds to the density of agent presence in each part of the arena (cf Fig. 2B). The **Biomimetic score** is computed as the geometric mean of the other scores.

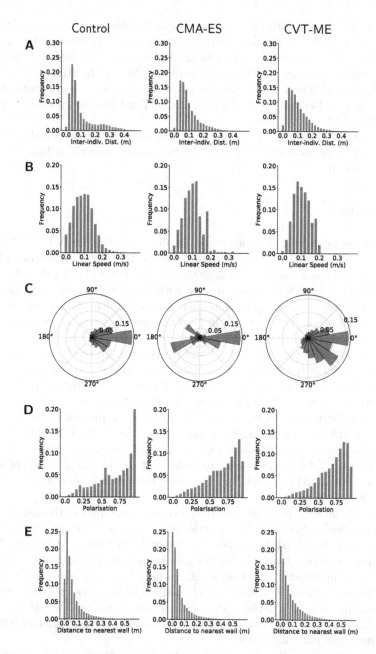

Fig. 4. Behavioural comparison between ten 30-min trials of experimental fish in groups of 5 and the 5-sized simulated fish groups for both tested cases. The following behavioural features are examined: inter-individual distances (**A**), linear (**B**) and angular (**C**) speeds distributions, polarisation (**D**), and distances to nearest wall (**E**). Note that distributions of angular speeds and distances to nearest wall are informative and not used in the calibration process.

In all cases, the algorithms aim to maximise the biomimetism score (S_{e_o,e_c}) of MLP-driven agents in simulations (e_o) compared to experimental fish groups (e_c). Both cases are tested in 10 different trials with the same budget of objective function evaluation (one simulation corresponds to one function evaluation): 60000 evaluations. The CVT-MAP-Elites case involves 6000 evaluations in the initial batch, and 450 batches of 120 individuals. The CMA-ES case involves 500 generations of 120 individuals.

We use a CVT-MAP-Elites implementation from the QDpy (Quality Diversity in Python) framework [4]. The CMA-ES implementation is based on the DEAP library [16].

3 Results

We analyse the behaviour of the simulated agent groups for the CVT-MAP-Elites and CMA-ES cases and compare them with the behaviour of experimental fish groups (Control case). In both cases, the agents are driven by MLP controllers, calibrated either by CVT-MAP-Elites or with CMA-ES to match as close as possible the behaviour of experimental fish across the behavioural metrics presented above. Each case is repeated in 10 trials and the following statistics only consider the best-evolved MLP controllers.

Figure 2A provides examples of agents trajectories. In the control case, fish tend to follow walls but retain a capability to go to the center of arena. This is also observed in trajectories from both MLP-driven cases. However, they also incorporate patterns not found in actual fish trajectories. Small circular loops can appear in both cases. A small periodic "shaking" is present in the trajectories of the CMA-ES case. Conversely, the trajectories of the CVT-MAP-Elites appear smoother and match more closely those of the experimental fish. This suggests that CVT-MAP-Elites is more realistic at the microscopic level of agent trajectories. Figure 2B presents the mean probability of presence of all agents in the arena for all cases.

We assess the realism of the two tested cases by computing the behavioural metrics presented in Sect. 2. These metrics serve as a base to compute similarity scores between the tested cases and experimental fish behaviour (Fig. 3). Both simulated cases display lower similarity scores than the experimental fish groups. Based on a comparison of the best solutions found by both algorithms, CVT-MAP-Elites outperforms CMA-ES with statistical significance (p-value $= 0.0227$ using the Mann-Whitney U-test). The best solution found by CVT-MAP-Elites also dominates all solutions found with CMAE-ES (best fitness: 0.724 with CVT-MAP-Elites *vs.* 0.704 with CMA-ES).

However, the controllers optimised by the two methods prioritise different features. The CVT-MAP-Elites case shows higher scores on inter-individual distances and polarisation than the CMA-ES case. In turn, CMA-ES exhibits higher probability of presence scores than the CVT-MAP-Elites case. Scores of linear speeds are roughly similar between the two cases. Overall, it means that the controllers optimised by the two methods exhibit different kind of behaviours and way of coping with the trade-offs between fish aggregative and wall-following behaviours. In term of group dynamics, the solutions of the CVT-MAP-Elites case are more cohesive than what is seen in the CMA-ES case, which evolves controllers that are more biased towards wall-following than group aggregation.

Histograms of all behavioural metrics are shown for all cases in Fig. 4, with two complementary metrics: the distribution of angular speeds (Fig. 4, related to polarisation) and distance to nearest wall (Fig. 4, related to probability of presence). They confirm the results from Fig. 3. The distributions of angular speed (Fig. 4C) of both cases are sub-optimal in term of realism. Figure 4E displays that simulated agents of both cases tend to exhibit correctly a wall-following behaviour.

The experimental fish groups of the **Control** case display a large behavioural variability across all investigated metrics (Figs. 3 and 4). Indeed, experiments were conduced with 10 groups of 5 fish (totalling 50 different fish) displaying disparate behaviours and individual preferences. This matches results from previous zebrafish collective behaviours studies [10,29]. Social (group composition) and environmental contexts impact fish behaviour: fish tend to aggregate in small short-lived sub-groups that follow walls from a distance that vary according to group composition. They also tend to exhibit an uniform degree of alignment within sub-groups.

4   Discussion and Conclusion

Calibrating artificial neural networks to model the collective behaviour of fish group and generate realistic fish trajectories is a challenging problem because fish behaviours involve several complementary dynamics with trade-offs between group-level dynamics (aggregative tendencies, group alignment), individual-level behaviours (agent linear speed) and response to environmental cues (wall-following behaviour, probability of presence in the arena). It is difficult to balance these conflicting behaviours during the calibration process.

Here, we show that the CVT-MAP-Elites [32], a quality diversity method that emphasises exploration over pure optimisation, calibrates controllers that are more realistic in term of agent groups polarisation and inter-individual distances when compared to previous results using stochastic optimisation methods such as the CMA-ES evolutionary method [7,8]. Moreover, QD algorithms also have the advantage of exploring a range of diverse solutions instead of searching for a single local optimum, and could be used to decipher the interrelation between features and behavioural biomimetism in order to draw biological conclusions.

Our approach could still be improved further, either by taking into account more behavioural metrics (tangential and normal accelerations, curvature or tortuosity) or by using more complex artificial neural networks than MLP, such as recurrent neural networks or deep neural networks.

Additionally, our methodology could be adapted to make possible to derive biological conclusions from the calibrated ANN models. ANN can be used as benchmarks to find the necessary information in experimental data to replicate experimental fish behaviour. Recently, Heras *et al.* [17] hinted at the possibility of this approach to decipher the interaction mechanism in large zebrafish groups. It remains to be shown that such ANN models can also produce collective trajectories similar to those observed experimentally. If it is shown to be the case, best-performing agents optimised through such methodology could be used as controllers to drive the behaviour of robots interacting experimentally with fish to study their collective dynamics.

Acknowledgement. This work was funded by EU-ICT project 'ASSISIbf', no. 601074.

References

1. Auger, A., Hansen, N.: A restart CMA evolution strategy with increasing population size. In: The 2005 IEEE Congress on Evolutionary Computation, vol. 2, pp. 1769–1776. IEEE (2005)
2. Bishop, C.: Pattern Recognition and Machine Learning. Information Science and Statistics. Springer, Heidelberg (2006)
3. Calovi, D.S., et al.: Disentangling and modeling interactions in fish with burst-and-coast swimming reveal distinct alignment and attraction behaviors. PLoS Computat. Biol. **14**(1), e1005933
4. Cazenille, L.: Qdpy: A python framework for quality-diversity (2018). https://gitlab.com/leo.cazenille/qdpy
5. Cazenille, L., et al.: Automated calibration of a biomimetic space-dependent model for zebrafish and robot collective behaviour in a structured environment. In: Mangan, M., Cutkosky, M., Mura, A., Verschure, P.F.M.J., Prescott, T., Lepora, N. (eds.) Living Machines 2017. LNCS (LNAI), vol. 10384, pp. 107–118. Springer, Cham (2017). https://doi.org/10.1007/978-3-319-63537-8_10
6. Cazenille, L., et al.: How mimetic should a robotic fish be to socially integrate into zebrafish groups? Bioinspiration & Biomimetics **13**(2), 025001 (2018). IOP Publishing
7. Cazenille, L., Bredeche, N., Halloy, J.: Evolutionary optimisation of neural network models for fish collective behaviours in mixed groups of robots and zebrafish. In: Vouloutsi, V., et al. (eds.) Living Machines 2018. LNCS (LNAI), vol. 10928, pp. 85–96. Springer, Cham (2018). https://doi.org/10.1007/978-3-319-95972-6_10
8. Cazenille, L., Bredeche, N., Halloy, J.: Modelling zebrafish collective behaviours with multilayer perceptrons optimised by evolutionary algorithms. arXiv preprint arXiv:1811.11040 (2018)
9. Collignon, B., Séguret, A., Halloy, J.: A stochastic vision-based model inspired by zebrafish collective behaviour in heterogeneous environments. Roy. Soc. Open Sci. **3**(1), 150473 (2016)
10. Collignon, B., Séguret, A., Chemtob, Y., Cazenille, L., Halloy, J.: Collective departures and leadership in zebrafish. PloS One **14**(5), e0216798 (2019). Public Library of Science
11. Cully, A., Clune, J., Tarapore, D., Mouret, J.B.: Robots that can adapt like animals. Nature **521**(7553), 503 (2015)
12. Cully, A., Demiris, Y.: Quality and diversity optimization: A unifying modular framework. IEEE Trans. Evol. Comput. **22**(2), 245–259 (2018)

13. Deutsch, A., Theraulaz, G., Vicsek, T.: Collective motion in biological systems. Interface Focus **2**(6), 689 (2012)
14. Deza, M., Deza, E.: Dictionary of distances. Elsevier (2006)
15. Duarte, M., Gomes, J., Oliveira, S.M., Christensen, A.L.: Evolution of repertoire-based control for robots with complex locomotor systems. IEEE Trans. Evol. Comput. **22**(2), 314–328 (2018)
16. Fortin, F.A., De Rainville, F.M., Gardner, M.A., Parizeau, M., Gagné, C.: Deap: Evolutionary algorithms made easy. J. Mach. Learn. Res. 13(July), 2171–2175 (2012)
17. Heras, F.J., Romero-Ferrero, F., Hinz, R.C., de Polavieja, G.G.: Aggregation rule in animal collectives dynamically changes between majority and minority influence. bioRxiv, p. 400747 (2018)
18. Heras, F.J., Romero-Ferrero, F., Hinz, R.C., de Polavieja, G.G.: Deep attention networks reveal the rules of collective motion in zebrafish. bioRxiv, p. 400747 (2018)
19. Herbert-Read, J.E., Romenskyy, M., Sumpter, D.J.: A turing test for collective motion. Biol. Lett. **11**(12), 20150674 (2015)
20. Iizuka, H., Nakamoto, Y., Yamamoto, M.: Learning of individual sensorimotor mapping to form swarm behavior from real fish data. In: Artificial Life Conference Proceedings, pp. 179–185. MIT Press (2018)
21. Jeanson, R., Blanco, S., Fournier, R., Deneubourg, J., Fourcassié, V., Theraulaz, G.: A model of animal movements in a bounded space. J. Theor. Biol. **225**(4), 443–451 (2003)
22. Jiang, L., et al.: Identifying influential neighbors in animal flocking. PLoS Computat. Biol. **13**(11), e1005822
23. Lehman, J., Stanley, K.O., Miikkulainen, R.: Effective diversity maintenance in deceptive domains. In: Proceedings of the 15th Annual Conference on Genetic and Evolutionary Computation, pp. 215–222. ACM (2013)
24. Lopez, U., Gautrais, J., Couzin, I.D., Theraulaz, G.: From behavioural analyses to models of collective motion in fish schools. Interface focus **2**(6), 693–707 (2012)
25. Mouret, J.B., Clune, J.: Illuminating search spaces by mapping elites. arXiv preprint arXiv:1504.04909 (2015)
26. Norgaard, M., Ravn, O., Poulsen, N., Hansen, L.: Neural Networks for Modelling and Control of Dynamic Systems: A Practitioner's Handbook. Advanced Textbooks in Control and Signal Processing. Springer, Berlin (2000)
27. Pugh, J.K., Soros, L.B., Stanley, K.O.: Quality diversity: A new frontier for evolutionary computation. Front. Robot. AI **3**, 40 (2016)
28. Reynolds, C.: Flocks, herds, and schools: A distributed behavioral model. Comput. Graph. **21**, 25–34 (1987)
29. Séguret, A., Collignon, B., Cazenille, L., Chemtob, Y., Halloy, J.: Loose social organisation of ab strain zebrafish groups in a two-patch environment. arXiv preprint arXiv:1701.02572 (2017)
30. Sumpter, D.J., Mann, R.P., Perna, A.: The modelling cycle for collective animal behaviour. Interface Focus **2**(6), 764–773 (2012)
31. Sutton, R.S., Barto, A.G.: Reinforcement Learning: An Introduction. The MIT Press, Cambridge, USA (2018)
32. Vassiliades, V., Chatzilygeroudis, K., Mouret, J.B.: Using centroidal voronoi tessellations to scale up the multidimensional archive of phenotypic elites algorithm. IEEE Trans. Evol. Comput. **22**(4), 623–630 (2018)
33. Vicsek, T., Czirók, A., Ben-Jacob, E., Cohen, I., Shochet, O.: Novel type of phase transition in a system of self-driven particles. Phys. Rev. Lett. **75**(6), 1226 (1995)

34. Whiteson, S.: Evolutionary computation for reinforcement learning. In: Wiering M., van Otterlo M. (eds.) Reinforcement Learning, vol 12, pp. 325–355. Springer, Heidelberg (2012). https://doi.org/10.1007/978-3-642-27645-3_10
35. Yuan, Y., Xu, H., Wang, B.: An improved NSGA-III procedure for evolutionary many-objective optimization. In: Proceedings of the 2014 Annual Conference on Genetic and Evolutionary Computation, pp. 661–668. ACM (2014)

Affective Visuomotor Interaction: A Functional Model for Socially Competent Robot Grasping

Eris Chinellato[1]([⊠]), Gabriele Ferretti[2], and Lucy Irving[1]

[1] Faculty of Science and Technology, Middlesex University,
The Burroughs, London NW4 4BT, UK
e.chinellato@mdx.ac.uk
[2] Dipartimento di Lettere e Filosofia, Università di Firenze,
Via Bolognese 52, 50139 Florence, Italy

Abstract. In the context of human-robot social interactions, the ability of interpreting the emotional value of objects and actions is critical for robots to achieve truly meaningful interchanges with human partners. We review here the most significant findings related to reward management and value assignment in the primate brain, with particular regard to the prefrontal cortex. Based on such findings, we propose a novel model of vision-based grasping in which the context-dependent emotional value of available options (e.g. damageable or dangerous items) is taken into account when interacting with objects in the real world. The model is both biologically plausible and suitable for being applied to a robotic setup. We provide a testing framework along with implementation guidelines.

Keywords: Human-Robot Interaction · Prefrontal cortex · Action selection · Visual streams · Emotional processing · Visuomotor processing

1 Introduction

Due to the ever-increasing diffusion of robots in our lives, Human-Robot Interaction (HRI) is a quickly developing field. It is nowadays considered essential that robots supposed to interact with human partners are not only dexterous, but also offer the appropriate social skills (Pessoa 2017). Regarding sensorimotor interactions in natural and artificial systems, we currently have a good understanding of the neural mechanisms underlying the visuomotor transformation of object attributes into motor commands, such as identifying graspable portions on the object surface. Such mechanisms have been successfully modeled to produce advanced sensorimotor skills in bio-inspired robotics (Chinellato and del Pobil 2016). However, in humans and non-human primates (as well as in most mammals), motor behavior in general, and visuomotor representations for grasping in particular, are influenced by the affective perception of the salient properties - encoded from an emotional point of view - of the objects we interact with. In other words, the representation of object emotionally-relevant properties, or emotional representations, - e.g. perceiving something as dangerous, fragile, etc., can influence, through inhibition (or elicitation), the way in which we represent "affordances", i.e. the action properties/possibilities (being graspable, climbable, etc.), offered by an object.

© Springer Nature Switzerland AG 2019
U. Martinez-Hernandez et al. (Eds.): Living Machines 2019, LNAI 11556, pp. 51–62, 2019.
https://doi.org/10.1007/978-3-030-24741-6_5

In this paper, we review and integrate evidence about affective response to visual stimuli, and the mechanisms subtending reward management, particularly in humans. We aim to extend current models of vision-based grasping in order to include a fundamental additional component, namely, the emotional value that might be associated to performing a certain action or interacting with a particular object. In doing so, we pursue the dual goal of improving robot sensorimotor and social skills, while contributing to the interpretation of fundamental neural mechanisms in the human brain. Endowing a robot with the capability of evaluating environmental stimuli from an emotional point of view, similarly to how a human subject would do, can substantially improve its skills in interacting within the surrounding environment and with human partners in a more effective and competent way. Consider the case of a robot able to ensure human safety by always offering any tool to be grasped by their handles by human partners.

In the next section, we review the current state of the art regarding relevant visuomotor neurosciences and corresponding modeling effort for robotics implementations. Then, we outline our proposal for including the processing of affective information into the typical affordance selection process as performed by bio-inspired robots. We finally outline a possible set of experiments aimed at validating the model presented here and discuss how they could further clarify the nature of the mechanisms at the basis of reward processing during action selection.

2 Background

This section reviews the state of the art in the neuroscience of vision-based grasping, the current state of biomimetic modelling in the field, and the evidence of the role of the prefrontal cortex in informing sensorimotor interactions.

2.1 Visual Neuroscience of Grasping

Modern accounts of visuomotor processing typically build on the two visual streams hypothesis, which suggests the presence, in humans and other mammals, of a separation of the visual pathways, grounded on distinct anatomo-functional structures (Milner and Goodale 2006): one for visual recognition, the ventral stream, and one for visually guided action, the dorsal stream (Fig. 1). Despite their different roles, the interaction between the streams is crucial in order to shape reliable grasping actions (Chinellato and del Pobil 2016; Ferretti 2016, 2018; de Haan et al. 2018).

The dorsal visual stream is divided into (at least) two sub-streams: the medial, or dorso-dorsal stream (D-D) and the lateral, or ventro-dorsal stream (V-D) (Gallese 2007). Visuomotor transformation of object attributes in motor commands is primarily performed by a defined parietal-premotor network lying in between the parietal cortex and the premotor cortex, that is, a precise portion of the V-D. The main areas involved in this neural loop are the anterior intraparietal area AIP area and the ventral premotor cortex PMv (roughly corresponding to F5 in monkey studies) (Castiello 2005; Turella and Lignau 2014; Borghi and Riggio 2015; Ferretti 2016, 2018). AIP extracts visual object information concerning action possibilities for grasping purposes (Theys et al. 2015; Culham et al. 2006; Ferretti 2016, 2018); the loop with PMv, possibly based on a competitive framework, selects one action to perform, the signal for which is sent to activate the primary motor cortex.

The ventro-dorsal stream areas in the inferior parietal lobe constitute an ideal convergence focus for the integration of semantic ventral information with online sensory data, related to visuomotor processing, from upstream dorsal areas (Chinellato and del Pobil 2016; Gallese 2007; Ferretti 2016).

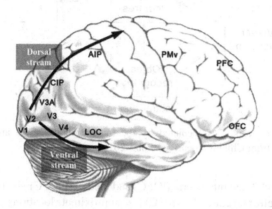

Fig. 1. Dorsal and ventral visual streams, highlighting areas most relevant for processing vision based grasping actions. See Chinellato and del Pobil (2016) for more details.

Despite its consolidated importance, robotic models of dorsal-ventral interactions are still rare. The conceptual schema in Fig. 2 illustrates how dorsal and ventral streams join their efforts to implement appropriate vision-based grasping actions (Chinellato and del Pobil 2016). No models so far have dealt with the additional role of affective encoding, managed by the prefrontal cortex. In fact, motor behavior in general, and visuomotor representations for grasping in particular, are influenced by the affective representation of the salient properties of the objects we want to interact with, encoded from an emotional point of view. This paper aims to fill such a gap.

2.2 Neural and Psychophysiological Evidence: Visuomotor Interactions and Affective Neuroscience

Evidence from the field of affective neuroscience suggests that the neural correlates of grasping are hugely interconnected with the neural correlates of object affective representations (Anelli et al. 2012). It is worth clarifying the terminology we will be using at this stage. We will be using *affective* and *emotional* as synonyms, referring at the same time to those concepts sometimes described in the neuroscientific literature as *drives* or *motives*. All of these are strongly interconnected with the concepts of value and reward, as we will see below. The prefrontal cortex (PFC) is considered to be in charge of the organization and orchestration of thoughts and actions in accordance with internal goals and attentional mechanisms (Lebedev and Wise 2002). In the specific case of grasping, the PFC is believed to mediate action selection with information on the specific task to perform (Johnson-Frey et al. 2005), integrating information about visual cues, actions, and potential rewards. Such an integration seems to be the main role of the orbitofrontal cortex (OFC), i.e. the orbital sector of PFC.

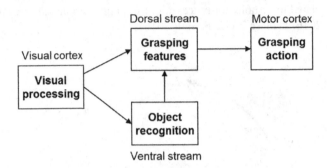

Fig. 2. Vision-based grasping is mediated by the integration of dorsal and ventral stream processing (adapted from Chinellato and del Pobil 2016).

The OFC is subdivided into lateral (lOFC) and medial (mOFC), the latter also known as ventromedial prefrontal cortex (VMPFC) (see approximate locations in Fig. 3). Whilst mOFC appears to be more directly connected to limbic areas, and has a faster response through its magnocellular projections, lOFC has stronger connections to sensory areas, and seems to receive more accurate, but slower, sensory information (Barrett and Bar 2009). Functionally, lOFC has been observed to process credit assignment, i.e. attributing a perceived reward to the correct stimulus, while mOFC appears to be involved in value-guided decision-making (Noonan et al. 2017). The strong connections of mOFC to other frontal and limbic areas suggest that relative values of options are computed in mOFC taking into account high-level, context-dependent goals. The OFC also has an anterior/posterior subdivision. Its frontal section is more responsive to secondary, deliberative reward tasks (e.g. monetary rewards), while the caudal one is more related to rewards of a primary, instinctive nature (e.g. sexual or food rewards, Sescousse et al. 2010; Klein-Flügge et al. 2013; Keller et al. 2018).

Recent evidence is shedding new light on the nature of the information exchanged by the OFC with many other brain areas (Rolls 2017). Some studies have highlighted substantial differences regarding the responsiveness of lOFC and mOFC regarding their role in decision-making and reward management. For example, it has been suggested that mOFC processes decision making using reward values provided by lOFC (Rushworth et al. 2012; Noonan et al. 2017). Another possible distinction is the prevalent relation of mOPC with internal motivations (Rolls and Grabenhorst 2008), compared with external information for lOFC. On the other hand, there seems to be a largely shared role of the various sections of OFC both for predicting reward probability and for potential decision risk (Li et al. 2016). Interspecies differences are pronounced, as can be expected when dealing with an evolutionary recent cortical area, and data from monkeys or other mammals are only of partial use to derive a model of neural mechanisms in humans (Donahue et al. 2018).

As summarized by Rudebeck and Murray (2014), there is substantial consensus on a medial-lateral gradient for relative reward values and a frontal-rostral gradient for reward type:

- **Medial/lateral gradient.** Whereas lOFC assesses options individually according to their implicit affective value, independently from alternative options, mOFC mediates choices by assessing the same options comparatively.
- **Anterior/posterior gradient.** The posterior portion of OFC is specific to primary instinctive rewards, whilst its anterior portion deals with secondary, more deliberative rewards.

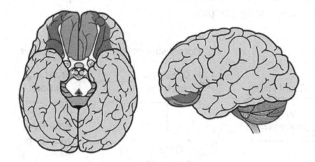

Fig. 3. Lateral OFC (purple); Medial OFC (light blue). (Color figure online)

2.3   Affective Processing in Applied Models of Visuomotor Interactions

The analysis of affective and emotional aspects in robotics have been a constant interest for researchers, especially regarding HRI applications (Ziemke and Lowe 2009). Recent efforts (Jung 2017; Barros et al. 2018) have been especially devoted to the development of robots more sensitive to human emotions. Specific efforts have been made to model emotions in artificial agents and humanoid robots. These have focused on several important aspects, among which reward management is certainly a very relevant one (Moerland et al. 2018). Other approaches have focused on the importance of episodic memories for complementing sensorimotor interactions through personal experience (Prescott et al. 2019). It is in any case increasingly accepted that intelligent robot design should include an emotional component in order to achieve proper autonomous behaviours in human environments (Pessoa 2017).

Of particular relevance is the work of Rolls and Grabenhorst (2008), which offers an insight into how neurons in OFC might be able to exhibit certain observed properties. Whilst this is a fundamental reference to take into account, we are more concerned here with higher level functionality and connectivity of OFC, in the context of complex sensorimotor, especially visuomotor interactions.

3   Coupling Visuo-Affective and Visuo-Motor Representations for Bio-Inspired Robotics Implementation

Pre-activation of premotor and parietal areas upon observation of graspable objects is well established in the neuroscientific literature: the mere observation of objects elicits facilitation effects of motor responses about action preparation (Fadiga et al. 2000). In addition, there is evidence that emotionally relevant properties of objects elicit a correspondent response compatible with their affective valence. For example, dangerous objects that pose a potential risk evoke aversive motor responses, generating an interference-effect (Anelli et al. 2012). In the context of shaping the appropriate response to potential affective rewards during actions selection, the OFC appears to be a critical actor. The conceptual schema in Fig. 4 extends the one shown in Fig. 2, by taking into account all the above considerations on affective processing, and how it is expected to intervene during grasping.

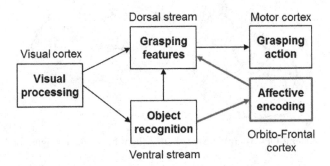

Fig. 4.   The interaction between the streams and the OFC. The affective encoding of the OFC is useful in managing the information encoded by both streams for grasping purposes with respect to affective properties linked to the visual cues offered by the object.

There is currently enough evidence to design a precise framework about how such intervention may occur. We aim to include rather specific functional roles for brain areas and the information flow among them, in order to be able to inform a computational model that can be applied to artificial agents. In Fig. 5 we thus propose a functional model implementing the conceptual schema of Fig. 4.

We propose here a two-stage account for the role of the OFC in shaping emotionally appropriate motor responses to sensory information about a specific object in a given context (see Fig. 5). We call the two stages of OFC intervention *instinctive* and *deliberative*. The first reaction is mediated by medial and posterior lateral OFC, upon reception of primary stimuli requiring a fast, instinctive response. Such response has been observed for positive rewards (Sescousse et al. 2010), but negative ones should follow the same trend, even more so considering the inconvenience of receiving a potentially painful reward. Known connections linking OFC to premotor cortex through dorsolateral PFC are consistent with such a framework. The second reaction would be through a *deliberative* pathway, from OFC directly to the striatum in the basal ganglia, a major input to the Inferior Parietal Lobe (IPL) and in particular to the primate grasping area, AIP. The OFC (and particularly the lateral and frontal sections) would thus act as a relay area along a possible ventral-dorsal stream connection, informing the pragmatic processing in the dorsal stream about the affective value of recognized visual stimuli, to be used in action selection and planning. The *instinctive* pathway would follow instead a more direct route to the premotor cortex, exploiting the connections running from mOFC to the premotor cortex, through superior areas of the PFC. The nature of this signal would be the one more traditionally associated with the OFC, i.e. the inhibition of motor plans.

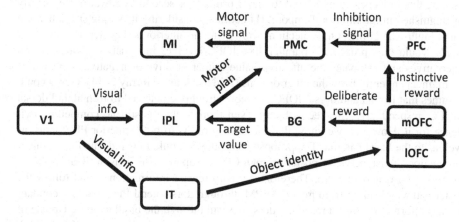

Fig. 5. Visuomotor affective model, from visual perception (Primary Visual Cortex, V1) to action release (Primary Motor Cortex, MI). Dorsal/ventral interactions is complemented by the visuo-affective representations provided by lateral and medial OFC.

Summarizing, whilst the faster channel running from posterior OFC would be crucial in quickly inhibiting unsuitable motor responses, the slower link to ventral and dorsal areas, through anterior OFC, may be devoted to guiding potential object-related responses that are most salient, or emotionally appropriate, in a given context.

The Basal Ganglia (BG), and particularly the *striatum*, are likely to assume a fundamental role in the above framework. They are involved in mediating between rival perceptions and/or competing motor actions (Clower et al. 2004). They are also strongly connected with the prefrontal cortex. Furthermore, different areas of the basal ganglia project to the dorsal and ventral streams. It seems, thus, that the basal ganglia help establish "go/no-go" responses and reward values concerning motor performance (Munakata et al. 2011), sending the information about such values to the IPL (Nakata et al. 2008; Budisavljevic et al. 2016), either directly or through ventral stream processing.

As explained above, lOFC is likely to assign an absolute reward value to object/action alternatives, whilst mOFC is in charge of comparing those alternatives to perform an informed choice, in accordance to the nature of a given, high-level context. How can this insight fit with the above two stages account? It may be that a single computational process allows to subtend both the *instinctive* and *deliberative* pathways.

In such a case, different activation intensities could evoke information flow in either or both of them. As an alternative, there could be two different processes running concurrently in different sections of the OFC: one for quickly detecting primary reward situation and acting promptly in consequence, and another for processing, more slowly, the convenience of alternative action options associated to secondary rewards. While both alternatives are plausible, the anterior/posterior activation gradients observed for secondary/primary rewards and the nature of the projections to other areas make the second possibility more likely (Sescousse et al. 2010; Klein-Flügge et al. 2013).

Here is a plausible explanation concerning the computational flow at the basis of such a process. Starting from object recognition in the ventral stream, it is plausible to assume that objects/actions related to either primary or secondary rewards are already distinguished in the Inferior Temporal (IT) cortex, considering its strong specialization for stimulus categorization. Projections from IT to the anterior and posterior sections of lOFC would thus proceed in parallel. The lOFC receives information about existing alternatives and estimates the affective value (either positive or negative) for each of them, independently from the other options (Rudebeck and Murray 2014). Our account assumes that frontal and dorsal lOFC are more strongly connected to frontal and dorsal mOFC, respectively. This seems likely, even though there is still no compelling evidence for it. However, we know that the OFC projects to both superior PFC areas, as well as to the basal ganglia. The proposed hypothesis would thus indicate that stronger connections exist between posterior mOFC and superior PFC, as well as between anterior mOFC and striatum. Therefore, primary reward information would follow the faster pathway leading from mOFC to PM, through dorsolateral PFC, while secondary reward information would reach the dorsal stream through the basal ganglia. Update of reward value according to a given action outcome would be done in lOFC in both cases, but it may well be that learning in anterior and posterior areas may follow slightly different computational solutions.

There is indeed some evidence that the basal ganglia-IPL circuit is based on slower learning processes, akin to standard reinforcement learning. These would be hardly suitable for critical action inhibition, in which even one mistake can be costly, as in the case of dangerous objects. Learning processes subserved by the anterior OFC can indeed progress on a rather typical reinforcement learning framework, in which different objects and action possibilities – as encoded by the ventral stream – are associated to a certain affective value and an appropriate reward signal, somehow proportional to the positive emotional value of each object. Values would be then sent to the IPL through the striatum in the basal ganglia. New experiences can be used to update affective values and rewards. It is also worth highlighting that, especially in humans, such experience does not need to derive from direct experience, but can also depend upon cultural transmission.

The type of signal sent more directly by OFC to the Premotor Cortex (PMC), through lateral PFC, should be of a different nature, more like a strong inhibitory projection, rather than a simple reward value. Equally, learning about strong experiences should be very fast, akin to a single-shot process, rather than a gradual reinforcement learning one. Cultural effects are also likely to assume a significant importance, since we usually prefer to know that something is dangerous before we have any interactions with it.

4 Experimental Validation Plan

As explained above, visuomotor representations in humans are influenced by emotional aspects, namely, by the representation of emotionally relevant/salient properties: we represent a graspable object as dangerous because we can represent an object as graspable, according to its affordances, and also as dangerous (e.g. because it is sharp, or hot), according to its identity associated with previous experiences or cultural knowledge. The same holds for fragile objects. We might represent an object as fragile, or deformable, and thus graspable under specific conditions: we should ensure a grip that is powerful enough to hold the object but not too powerful to break or crush the object.

The integration of the new frontal functions into neural models for bio-inspired robotic grasping, reported above (see Fig. 5) allows us to design new experiments aimed at verifying the influence of the visuo-affective level over standard visuomotor behavior of the robot. We are considering here two different families of objects: dangerous (as in the case of a red-hot object) and damageable (e.g. fragile or deformable). A possible experimental framework for testing our proposal would entail the presence of at least two alternative objects to handle, with choices depending on their aspect and on the action context. Let us imagine a possible set of experiments in which a robot needs to hand the right tool to a human partner.

In a first experiment, the robot would have to choose between two tools (e.g. a wrench and a hammer) according to the task at hand, or directly from human instructions. The robot would observe the two alternative objects, recognize them and judge their suitability for the task. In normal conditions, the match of object identity with an action goal of higher-level would provide the expected reward value for a certain alternative tool. Handing the right (or wrong) tool to a human partner in a certain context would reinforce, or reduce, the connectivity strength of that tool for the task at hand. Making an error would imply a negative reward, and improve the probability of making the right choice in the future.

Let us now consider a second setup, in which one of the two tools (e.g. the one constituting the most appropriate choice in the previous experiment) is recognizably presenting some alarming features. For example, it could be a red-hot metal tool, clearly indicating that handling it would be dangerous (for the robot, the human partner, or both). The importance of the ventral input to action selection in this second setup is clear. Affordance selection, as performed by the dorsal stream, is substantially bypassed by a strong affective bias provided by the ventral input mediated by the frontal cortex. The most typical motor response of the parietal-premotor visuomotor system is inhibited. The most important difference with the previous example is the necessary strength of the ventral influence over action selection. If the wrong action (i.e. grasping the hot object) were ever performed, there would be an extremely strong negative reward, aimed at ensuring that such a choice would never repeat again.

The ventral/prefrontal contribution to action selection could also be observed over alternative actions toward the same object. Let us now consider the third scenario, in which the robot has to handle a fragile object, which, due to its properties, needs to be grasped with particular care. This could be a precious item, but also a ripe fruit (crushing a ripe fruit in an automated food management line could have strong negative consequences on the whole handling process). Such an object would be graspable only under specific conditions, and the robot should try to avoid a possible damage of the object by using the correct grasping posture and the right amount of force, enough to ensure a solid grip, but not too powerful to damage the object. This case somehow seems to lie in between the two previous experiments: a wrong choice has a strong negative outcome, but not as strong as in the second scenario of a dangerous object. It would be the most interesting case from a computational point of view, as well as for testing the implementation of the proposed approach. The response might be mediated either by the *instinctive* or by the *deliberative* pathway from OFC to motor areas. This would arguably depend on the context, and on the negative or positive affective value associated to a certain outcome. Inhibition coming from frontal mOFC would possibly prevent the object from being grasped at all, while the bias coming from posterior mOFC bias would promote the choice of more careful grasping actions. Further experiments with human subjects would help in verifying the accuracy of such hypotheses.

5 Conclusion

Robotic grasping models aimed at emulating, in robots, the processing of affordance competition we find in humans, are not able to make an emotional evaluation of the environment. This lack of emotional encoding prevents robots from avoiding grasping dangerous objects, or selecting and performing suitable safe grasps on fragile objects.

Visuo-motor-affective evaluation of an object, as proposed in this work, relates to the affective value given to the object in a very specific visuo-motor context and with respect to the goal of the action. According to our proposal, such an evaluation is grounded on anatomo-functional orbitofrontal connections, related to the dorsal and ventral streams, and is able to drive the visuomotor interaction according to emotional considerations about action alternatives. Here we have proposed a two-stage approach capable of explaining common behavior in the presence of emotionally salient objects, while taking into account the state of the art regarding the functionality and connectivity of the orbitofrontal cortex in humans and other primates.

We have offered an overall framework for the model, some guidelines for computational implementation, and an overview of the type of experiments required to validate the model as well as to shed further light on the nature of reward management and action selection as mediated by the OFC.

From a robotics perspective, our model aims to constitute an important step towards including emotional encoding in order to make robots more capable of adapting to the ecological situations they deal with, not only from a visuomotor point of view, but also by relying on visuo-affective computations at the basis of motor responses.

References

Anelli, F., Borghi, A.M., Nicoletti, R.: Grasping the pain: motor resonance with dangerous affordances. Conscious. Cogn. **21**, 1627–1639 (2012)

Barrett, L.F., Bar, M.: See it with feeling: affective predictions during object perception. Philos. Trans. R. Soc. Lond. B Biol. Sci. **364**(1521), 1325–1334 (2009). https://doi.org/10.1098/rstb.2008.0312

Barros, P.V.A., Barakova, E.I., Wermter, S.: A Deep Neural Model Of Emotion Appraisal. CoRR abs/1808.00252 (2018)

Borghi, A.M., Riggio, L.: Stable and variable affordances are both automatic and flexible. Front. Hum. Neurosci. **9**, 351 (2015). https://doi.org/10.3389/fnhum.2015.00351

Budisavljevic, S., et al.: Asymmetry and structure of the fronto-parietal networks underlie visuomotor processing in humans. Cereb. Cortex (2016). https://doi.org/10.1093/cercor/bhv348

Castiello, U.: The neuroscience of grasping. Nat. Rev. **6**(9), 726–736 (2005). https://doi.org/10.1038/nrn1744

Chinellato, E., del Pobil, A.P.: The Visual Neuroscience of Robotic Grasping: Achieving Sensorimotor Skills through Dorsal-Ventral Stream Integration. CSM, vol. 28. Springer, Cham (2016). https://doi.org/10.1007/978-3-319-20303-4

Clower, D.M., Dum, R.P., Strick, P.L.: Basal ganglia and cerebellar inputs to 'AIP'. Cereb. Cortex **15**(7), 913–920 (2004)

Culham, J.C., Cavina-Pratesi, C., Singhal, A.: The role of parietal cortex in visuomotor control: what have we learned from neuroimaging? Neuropsychologia **44**(13), 2668–2684 (2006). https://doi.org/10.1016/j.neuropsychologia

de Haan, E.H.F., Jackson, S.T., Schenk, T.: Where are we now with 'What' and 'How'? Cortex **98**(1), 7 (2018). https://doi.org/10.1016/j.rehab.2017.02.002

Donahue, C.J., Glasser, M.F., Preuss, T.M., Rilling, J.K., Van Essen, D.C.: Quantitative assessment of prefrontal cortex in humans relative to nonhuman primates. Proc. Natl. Acad. Sci. **115**(22), E5183–E5192 (2018)

Fadiga, L., Fogassi, L., Gallese, V., Rizzolatti, G.: Visuomotor neurons: ambiguity of the discharge or 'motor' perception? Int. J. Psychophysiol. **35**, 165–177 (2000)

Ferretti, G.: Through the forest of motor representations. Conscious. Cogn. **43**, 177–196 (2016). https://doi.org/10.1016/j.concog.2016.05.013

Ferretti, G.: The neural dynamics of seeing-in. Erkenntnis (2018). https://doi.org/10.1007/s10670-018-0060-2

Gallese, V.: The "Conscious" dorsal stream: embodied simulation and its role in space and action conscious awareness. Psyche **13**(1), 1–20 (2007)

Johnson-Frey, S.H., Newman-Norlund, R., Grafton, S.T.: A distributed left hemisphere network active during planning of everyday tool use skills. Cereb. Cortex **15**(6), 681–695 (2005)

Keller, K.L., et al.: Brain response to food cues varying in portion size is associated with individual differences in the portion size effect in children. Appetite **125**, 139–151 (2018)

Klein-Flügge, M.C., Barron, H.C., Brodersen, K.H., Dolan, R.J., Behrens, T.E.J.: Segregated encoding of reward–identity and stimulus–reward associations in human orbitofrontal cortex. J. Neurosci. **33**(7), 3202–3211 (2013)

Lebedev, M.A., Wise, S.P.: Insights into seeing and grasping: distinguishing the neural correlates of perception and action. Behav. Cogn. Neurosci. Rev. **1**(2), 108–129 (2002). https://doi.org/10.1177/1534582302001002002

Li, Y., Vanni-Mercier, G., Isnard, J., Mauguière, F., Dreher, J.C.: The neural dynamics of reward value and risk coding in the human orbitofrontal cortex. Brain **139**(4), 1295–1309 (2016)

Jung, M.F.: Affective grounding in human-robot interaction. In: Proceedings of the 2017 ACM/IEEE International Conference on Human-Robot Interaction (HRI 2017), pp. 263–273. ACM, New York (2017). https://doi.org/10.1145/2909824.3020224

Milner, A., Goodale, M.: The Visual Brain in Action, 2nd edn. Oxford University Press, Oxford (1995/2006)

Moerland, T.M., Broekens, J., Jonker, C.M.: Mach. Learn. **107**, 443 (2018). https://doi.org/10. 1007/s10994-017-5666-0

Munakata, Y., Herd, S.A., Chatham, C.H., Depue, B.E., Banich, M.T., O'Reilly, R.C.: A unified framework for inhibitory control. Trends Cogn. Sci. **15**(10), 453–459 (2011)

Nakata, H., et al.: Somato-motor inhibitory processing in humans: an event-related functional MRI study. Neuroimage **39**(4), 1858–1866 (2008)

Noonan, M.P., Chau, B.K., Rushworth, M.F., Fellows, L.K.: Contrasting effects of medial and lateral orbitofrontal cortex lesions on credit assignment and decision-making in humans. J. Neurosci. **37**(29), 7023–7035 (2017)

Pessoa, L.: Do intelligent robots need emotion? Trends Cogn. Sci. **21**(11), 817–819 (2017)

Prescott, T.J., Camilleri, D., Martinez-Hernandez, U., Damianou, A., Lawrence, N.D.: Memory and mental time travel in humans and social robots. Philos. Trans. R. Soc. B Biol. Sci. (2019). https://doi.org/10.1098/rstb.2018.0025

Rolls, E.T.: The orbitofrontal cortex and emotion in health and disease, including depression. Neuropsychologia (2017). https://doi.org/10.1016/j.neuropsychologia.2017.09.021

Rolls, E.T., Grabenhorst, F.: The orbitofrontal cortex and beyond: from affect to decision-making. Prog. Neurobiol. **86**(3), 216–244 (2008)

Rudebeck, P.H., Murray, E.A.: The orbitofrontal oracle: cortical mechanisms for the prediction and evaluation of specific behavioral outcomes. Neuron **84**(6), 1143–1156 (2014)

Rushworth, M.F., Kolling, N., Sallet, J., Mars, R.B.: Valuation and decision-making in frontal cortex: one or many serial or parallel systems? Curr. Opin. Neurobiol. **22**(6), 946–955 (2012)

Saxena, A., Driemeyer, J., Ng, A.Y.: Robotic grasping of novel objects using vision. Int. J. Robot. Res. **27**(2), 157–173 (2008). https://doi.org/10.1177/0278364907087172

Sescousse, G., Redouté, J., Dreher, J.C.: The architecture of reward value coding in the human orbitofrontal cortex. J. Neurosci. **30**(39), 13095–13104 (2010)

Theys, T., Romero, M.C., van Loon, J., Janssen, P.: Shape representations in the primate dorsal visual stream. Front. Comput. Neurosci. **9**(43) (2015). https://doi.org/10.3389/fncom.2015. 00043

Turella, L., Lignau, A.: Neural correlates of grasping. Front. Hum. Neurosci. **8**(686) (2014). https://doi.org/10.3389/fnhum.2014.00686

Ziemke, T., Lowe, R.: Cogn. Comput. **1**, 104 (2009). https://doi.org/10.1007/s12559-009-9012-0

Measuring the Effectiveness of Biomimetic Robots as Therapeutic Tools: Translating the Felt Security Scale from English to Japanese

Emily C. Collins[1]([✉]), Tony J. Prescott[2], Yoichiro Yoshikawa[3], and Hiroshi Ishiguro[3]

[1] Department of Computer Science, University of Liverpool, Liverpool, UK
e.c.collins@liverpool.ac.uk
[2] Sheffield Robotics, University of Sheffield, Sheffield, UK
t.j.prescott@sheffield.ac.uk
[3] Intelligent Robotics Laboratory, Department of Systems Innovation, Graduate School of Engineering Science, Osaka University, Suita, Japan
{ishiguro,yoshikawa}@irl.sys.es.osaka-u.ac.jp

Abstract. Biomimetic robots that resemble companion animals, and that replicate aspects of animal social behavior, could play a useful therapeutic role in the treatment of disorders such as anxiety and depression, and could act as an alternative or complement to animal-assisted therapy (AAT). Previous work in AAT has noted the importance of feelings of care, love, self-esteem to the success of a therapeutic animal intervention. These feelings, alongside safety, have been measured in human-human interaction studies using a questionnaire-based measure called the Felt Security Scale (FSS). This paper presents the translation of the FSS into Japanese in order to produce a cross-cultural instrument for evaluating the effectiveness of robot-assisted therapy (RAT). We describe the development of the new Japanese Felt Security Scale (JFSS), its validation with native Japanese speakers, and a comparison of outcomes as measured against the Japanese Experiences in Close Relationships Scale (Japanese ECR). We propose that the FSS provides a useful tool for investigating the effectiveness of biomimetic robots as therapeutic tools in English- and Japanese-speaking cultural settings.

Keywords: HRI · Japanese · Felt security scale · Cross-cultural

1 Introduction

[P]eople's views of the world, of themselves, of their own capabilities, and of the tasks that they are asked to perform, or topics they are asked to learn, depend heavily on the conceptualisations that they bring to the task.

Donald A. Norman [14]

© Springer Nature Switzerland AG 2019
U. Martinez-Hernandez et al. (Eds.): Living Machines 2019, LNAI 11556, pp. 63–75, 2019.
https://doi.org/10.1007/978-3-030-24741-6_6

The objective of Robot-Assisted Therapy (RAT) is to create robots with the capacity to act as animal surrogates for individuals who do not have access to animals [30], for example with the PARO therapeutic robot, developed by AIST in Japan [29], and with the biomimetic robot MIRO [11]. The idea is not to replace animals, but to create opportunities for individuals to benefit from the positive effects of Animal-Assisted Therapy (AAT) in situations where AAT is not otherwise possible. For example, in many care facilities AAT is an infrequent scheduled event, taking place once or twice a week for a few hours or less [30]. Whilst some care homes entirely restrict animal visitations due to concerns about disease, allergies, aggressive outbursts from patients or animals that could result in injury, and other discretional reasons (e.g. see [25]). Controlled studies comparing animals and robots reveal that robots can be effective at reducing loneliness and anxiety [2], and can help counter cognitive decline via social facilitation. The comparison between experimental conditions in these studies is predominantly achieved using change scores, obtained via psychological or physiological metrics taken before and after the intervention.

Previous work in AAT has noted the importance of feelings of care, love and self-esteem to the success of a therapeutic animal intervention. Feelings of care, love and self-esteem, as well as safety, are components of felt security (FS) [6,24]. This can be measured by the Felt Security Scale (FSS; [19]), which captures the full dimensionality of FS. The FSS was developed as an attachment relationship priming manipulation check for use in human-human interaction (HHI) studies. According to the comparative framework proposed by Collins et al. [10], measures employed to explore other agents with which a human can interact, be they human, animal or object, can be drawn upon to explore and test the effectiveness of robots with which humans interact that have a similar morphology and use-case. Based on this framework, the FSS has also been successfully used in HRI studies with biomimetic robots (e.g. [9]).

However, an individual's mental model of a robot, which drives the extent to which they wish to engage with it, as well as the level of expectation, acceptance and believability they will have of the machine, is also in part constructed via the social culture in which an individual has been brought up and lives in. In this way it is apparent that when considering acceptance, use, and the development of robots intended for RAT, culture should be considered. It should not be assumed that the use of metrics to explore mechanisms of effect in RAT will work with equivalent success in all countries (as, for example, single methods of treating mental health are not always equally effective across different countries, see [32]). Indeed, when pairing a client with an AAT co-therapist the individual differences and cultural experiences of a client are taken into consideration (e.g. as explained in [21]). Comparatively, therefore, the individual differences and cultural experiences of users should also be considered important when considering the willingness of a user to engage with a biomimetic robot.

Differences between individuals' interactions with the world are related to differences between individuals' mental models of the world and its components [12]. This includes differences in interpersonal experiences across the lifespan which are internalised as cognitive models that guide behaviour and affect. An individual's mental model of a robot drives the extent to which they wish to engage with it, as well as the level of expectation, acceptance and believability they will have of the machine. A mental model provides an individual with the means of predicting and explaining their environment and its artefacts. They allow an individual to understand interactions via naturally evolving models which are not necessarily accurate, despite providing functionality. Mental models are constrained by such as an individual's background, their previous experiences, and the limitations of the processing power of the mind itself [14]. Aside from individual cognition and direct experience however, cultural models and social norms also have a powerful influence over structuring individuals' mental models of their environment [23]. Whilst it must be stressed that individuals are not cultural clones [5], social context is nonetheless integral to the construction of the context within which an individuals' working understandings of their world – their mental models – are formed.

Given this, consider robots: it could be argued that currently within the UK accurate depictions of state-of-the-art (SoA) robotics, as well as robot platforms themselves, are not ubiquitous. In the 2012 EU-wide 'Public Attitudes Towards Robots' report, 60% of responders wanted robots banned from the care of children, the disabled or the elderly [31]. Whilst according to the 2016 Robotics Business Review, the UK is currently home to only three of the top 50 robotics companies in the world [8].

Conversely, Japan is a world leader in robotics, with robots contributing to many areas of society, including entertainment and healthcare [20]. Globally, Japan has the one of the largest ratios of robots to manufacturing industry workers, with 323 robots per 10,000 workers in its factories [27]. Japan also dominates the manufacturing of robots, with 60% of the global market [27]. On May 16th, 2015, Japanese Prime Minister Abe opened the 'Robot Revolution Initiative Council' with a call to the nation's corporate sector to, "spread the use of robotics from large-scale factories to every corner of our economy and society" [13]. Historically Japan has been a world leader in social robotics too, with development on the PARO robot starting as early as 1993 [1]. Whilst the media continues to hail Japan as a country with a 'craze' for robots [20].

Level of exposure to robots occurs not only through direct experience of them but via the media too. In Japan robots are frequently portrayed in fiction, and in games and on TV, but unlike in western cultural portrayals of robots the typical 'robots will take over the world' scenario is not common [4]. Alternatively robots in Japanese media, such as manga, are not exclusively 'evil' but represent a variety of roles unrestrained by their technical nature [4]. [18] argues that this phenomenon is due to the traditional differences between western and eastern culture's analogies of machines. Western depictions are focussed on machines that challenge humanity's 'narcissistic shields' by their very existence [4], whilst eastern depictions, in particular those in Japan, are framed by a culture which does not distinguish artificial entities from natural ones, but rather views machines as opportunities to understand the natural laws of humanity instead [18]. With such complex nuances exposing populations to different degrees of tangible robotic technology and different social norms outlining the concept of what a robot *is*, it may well be concluded that culture does influence individuals' mental models of robots, and in turn how individuals take to robots on a personal level.

However, exactly how different cultural backgrounds might be impacting how individuals respond to robots is not as straightforward as simply stating that the Japanese love robots [4], whilst individuals from nominally western countries such as the UK or Australia are more wary (for example see [15]). In a cross-cultural study of negative attitudes towards robots [3] reported that in a sample of Dutch ($n = 24$), Chinese ($n = 19$) and Japanese ($n = 53$) participants the Japanese participants rated robots less positively than received opinion, that Japan is robot 'crazy', might have indicated. Instead the Japanese participants in the study expressed concern over the impact that robots might have on society. The study authors argued that high exposure to robot technology, aside from media portrayals, could be responsible for such an opinion. Exposure to real robots in recent years may have left the Japanese more aware of the actual abilities and constraints of SoA robotics. This begs the question of whether such a difference between individuals from countries that promote different levels of social exposure to SoA robots, would display different sympathies towards a robot that was behaving in a non-optimal manner.

Given the differences between the UK and Japan's socio-cultural exposure to SoA robotics then, perhaps individuals living in the UK would have different mental models of robots than those living in Japan. This example highlights that impact that culture can have on individual perspectives of robots. Thus, if culture is to be considered as having an impact upon the outcomes of HRI studies, cross-cultural explorations of HRI studies should be invested in. One way to do this is by translating more metrics between languages. This paper presents the process taken to translate the English Felt Security Scale into Japanese. Direct translation is rarely possible when dealing with psychological metrics. However, although difficult, this paper advocates for more attempts at metrics' translations to understand robotics, HRI, and RAT on a global scale.

2   Translating the Felt Security Scale (FSS)

2.1   Semantic Equivalence

It is well established that a single forward and back translation procedure is an insufficient method of making and checking the quality of a translation [33]. The process of translation must take into consideration semantic equivalence. Here, *equivalence* is when a pair of items, one from the original scale and one from the translated scale, are deemed to be measuring the same construct in equal proportions such that there is an equal probability of getting the same response from both items despite them being in different languages [17]. In order to achieve this a hierarchical procedure of translation, back-translation, and then verification is required to establish construct (semantic) equivalence [7].

Although attachment and related constructs, such as felt security, have been criticised for being ethnocentric [28], the Experiences in Close Relationships Scale (ECR) has been successfully translated into multiple languages including

Chinese [22] and Japanese [26]. This is because ideal translations take into consideration the fundamental need for semantic equivalence. A hierarchical translation process should incorporate not only an understanding of bilingualism from the translators, but also biculturalism such that the translators possess not only a knowledge of the instrument being translated, but are also very familiar with the target culture [22]. This is the most important process required when producing an adequate instrument translation in order to ensure semantic equivalence is truly established. As such translated instruments may ignore the idiosyncrasies of the original format, in order to incorporate necessary culturally specific adaptations. This is particularly the case when a culture is viewed as having a potentially significant impact on how concepts are expressed in various languages [16]. In the case of the presently translated FSS this meant taking into account the need for a translation that allowed for full sentences in order that the instrument's items were clearly contextualised. For example, eastern cultures have been reported to interpret 'self-esteem' (which the construct of felt security is in part comprised of) somewhat differently to western cultures [34], and understanding cultural nuances such as this was important when translating the FSS items in a way that made it clear to the Japanese individuals completing the instrument that the items it discussed where referring to them, as individuals, and not to others as might otherwise be unclear without the use of very specific sentences to convey each item. Thus, although limited by both time and resources in order to conduct as thorough a translation as would be desired (by, for example, validating the Japanese FSS with a participant sample numbering into the hundreds or thousands) the translation of the FSS conducted in Japan, and here reported, did take into consideration both the linguistic as well as the cultural differences required to convey the same concepts.

In translating the FSS into Japanese, having a Japanese version of the Adult Attachment Style Scale Experiences in Close Relationships Scale (Japanese ECR; [26]) proved extremely useful as a way of beginning to understand how felt security might be translated, without losing semantic equivalence. Having the Japanese ECR facilitated the translation of the FSS by providing an idea of the terms that could be used to express similar concepts seen in both the English FSS and ECR. For example, how to describe being cared for by another human as an adult (as opposed to an infant), and how to describe love (a term used with much nuance in Japanese). Finally, it should be noted that the description of the translation process given here is done so in as much detail as possible without going into linguistic specifics. Although examples will be given to highlight the process, note that for the ease of the reader these will be written in *romaji*, the romanised Japanese alphabet, and not in Japanese *kanji* or *hiragana* scripts.

2.2   Producing the Japanese Felt Security Scale (JFSS)

The English FSS [19] is a psychological instrument for measuring felt security. This is a concept which comprises feelings of care, love and self-esteem, as well as safety [6,24]. The original instrument was reliably validated by [19]: Cronbach's $\alpha = .97$; $M = 4.25$, $SD = 1.39$.

In the first step of translating the FSS into Japanese a native Japanese speaker and a native English speaker reviewed all the terms of the English FSS: *comforted, supported, looked after, cared for, secure, safe, protected, unthreatened, better about myself, valued, more positive about myself, I really like myself, loved, cherished, treasured, and adored.* The concepts were then discussed as they are understood within Japanese, both linguistically and conceptually. Both translators were English-Japanese bilinguals, and also bicultural individuals who had extensive experience of the target culture (one being a native Japanese (co-author of this paper Y. Yoshikawa), the other having lived in the country for five years and self-reported as very familiar with the Japanese culture (co-author of this paper E. C. Collins)); as well as having spent substantial time living outside their native countries (in America and Japan respectively). The native British translator also had a thorough knowledge of the English FSS, which allowed the translators to work beyond merely having knowledge of the two languages, by also having an in-depth knowledge of the subject matter of the instrument.

Direct translation of each item was not possible due to several reasons. For example, it is difficult to translate the item *protected* whilst retaining semantic equivalence with the English. Directly translated into Japanese, *protected* is *hogo*, a word used when referring to children or an individual in need of social support (such as someone who is very ill). It would be unusual for an adult, speaking about themselves, to rate themselves as requiring protection at all, given the Japanese cultural ideal that adults should not need to be protected. Further, words which conceptually group together in one language do not necessarily share the same conceptual family in the other. For example, in the English FSS, *cherished, treasured* and *adored* are all separate items, although they respectively cover the same conceptual idea: to protect or care or value someone lovingly. However, in Japanese these terms are difficult to translate as individual items. For example, the single idea of 'value' covers both being *cherished* and *treasured*, whilst *adored* is considered close to simply being loved by another human.

Given this issue the original 16 items were initially translated into an alternative English sentence that more clearly described the conceptual meaning that the item was conveying. In doing this some of the 16 items were grouped together, or placed in more than one group. Thus, for example, the original FSS items *treasured* and *cherished* were grouped together and translated as *I feel like an invaluable person,* whilst *cared for, valued* and *cherished* were also grouped together and translated as *I feel I am an important/valued person* (see Table 1). Note in this last translation that 'important' and 'valued' are given equal weighting in the translated sentence, this is because the Japanese equivalent of the concept, *taisetsu,* means both 'important' and 'valued'. Understanding the Japanese version of each of the secondarily translated English concepts was an important part in the translation process, and required bicultural understanding in order to be fully realised. One item, *better about myself* was not included in this stage as it is difficult to convey this concept in Japanese without a temporal explanation. However, there does exist a short version of the English FSS [19], comprising 10 items: *comforted, secure, supported, safe, loved, protected, better about themselves, encouraged, sheltered, and unthreatened*. Internal consistency was measured by [19], who reported high reliability: Cronbach's α = .97; M = 4.17, SD = 1.53. From this shorter 10-item FSS *encouraged* and *sheltered* were taken and included in this stage of the translation process. See Table 1, for the 15 alternative English sentences that were produced at this stage.

Table 1. The original 16-items of the FSS (excluding *better about myself*), plus two extra items from the 10-item FSS (*encouraged, sheltered*) were conceptually grouped (with some item overlap) and modified to create 15 new English sentences which more clearly described the concept each item conveyed. This was an important step to take prior to translating the items into Japanese in order to maintain semantic equivalency.

Item from English FSS (Single or Grouped)	Secondary English Translation
Comforted	I feel comforted
Supported	I feel supported
Looked after	I feel looked after
Cared for/Valued/Cherished	I feel I am an important/valued person
Secure (reassured)	I feel I am reassured
Safe	I feel safe
Protected/Sheltered	I feel I am protected/sheltered
Loved	I feel loved
Treasured/Cherished	I feel like an invaluable person
Loved/Adored/Cherished/Esteemed	I feel like I am dear to someone
That I like myself	I like myself
Sheltered/Positive about myself	I feel comfortable depending on others
Encouraged	I feel I can ask for help without resistance
Unthreatened	I do not think my environment is threatening

The secondary English translations, listed in Table 1, were then further reduced via another grouping method, in which sentences that when translated into Japanese were almost identical, were reduced to a single item. For example *I feel I am reassured* and *I feel safe* are conceptually similar, therefore only a single version of the Japanese translation of each was a chosen as the new item. In this case that was *anshin* (safety), which was used to create a new single item.

Finally the remaining sentences were translated into full Japanese sentences for the JFSS. Unlike in the English FSS, where single words are used to describe the terms, in the JFSS it was necessary to use full sentences to convey the concepts within a context. This was to ensure that the final JFSS would be readily understandable by all users. It can be difficult when using adjectives in Japanese to understand their meaning outside of a specific context. Therefore the use of full sentences in the JFSS allowed the instrument to be read as clearly indicating that each item was referring to how the reader felt at the time of completing the instrument. It should be noted that the final item-sentences were constructed in such as way as to ensure that no double-barrelled items were included, such that no single item contained two or more components that could warrant separate responses.

This resulted in 11 sentences which together conveyed the concept of felt security. In the English FSS each item was listed with its corresponding negative version, thus for the JFSS each item-sentence has a negative equivalent. See Table 2, for the English translations of the Japanese sentences.

Table 2. The final 11-items of the Japanese Felt Security Scale (JFSS), full positive and negative sentences are given. Concept being conveyed by each item in italics. Notes in brackets indicate information explicitly conveyed by the Japanese translation of the sentence.

Positive JFSS Item-Sentence	Negative JFSS item-Sentence
I feel that I am being *supported*	I do not feel that I am being *supported*
I feel I am *cared for/looked after*	I do not feel I am *cared for/looked after*
I feel *secure* (subjective sense)	I do not feel *secure* (subjective sense)
I do not feel that I am *threatened*	I feel that I am *threatened*
I feel that I am *loved*	I do not feel that I am *loved*
I feel I am an *important* person	I do not feel I am an *important* person
I *like myself*	I do not *like myself*
I am *not hesitant to ask other people for help* (reassured)	I am *hesitant to ask other people for help* (not reassured)
I feel I am *valued/treasured/cherished*	I do not feel I am *valued/treasured/cherished*
I think I am *respected/adored/esteemed*	I do not think I am *respected/adored/esteemed*
I think I am *encouraged/supported* (to do things)	I do not think I am *encouraged/supported* (to do things)

The 11 items of JFSS sentences (22, including the negatives) were then passed to three Japanese bilinguals, who though native to the target culture had spent substantial time in English speaking countries. They were naïve to both the FSS and its intended use. These individuals back-translated the Japanese sentences into English sentences they felt best expressed the concepts being described in Japanese. There was almost no variation between the three back-translations received from the secondary translators. Through this process it was established that the Japanese translations were good matches for the original English.

Finally, in order to fully establish face validity, one more individual, who was not associated with the location where the scale translation was taking place, and who was neither an English speaker, nor someone who had spent any substantial amount of time outside of Japan, was given the JFSS and asked if they could completely understand the form, including the Japanese translation of the instruction[1]. This volunteer had no problem at all understanding the JFSS, and was able to complete it in a manner they felt truly reflected how they felt at the time. At this stage as face validity had been fully established it was concluded that the translation was effective, and was ready to be used in a cross-cultural experiment.

2.3 Aims of the Current Paper

In the current study results from the administered JFSS were used to assess the instrument's internal consistency, as well as its performance adequacy via a test of convergent validity against results from the Japanese Adult Attachment Style Scale Experiences in Close Relationships Scale (Japanese ECR; [26]). Results from the Japanese ECR produce two scores, one of attachment anxiety and one of attachment avoidance. As both of these dimensions are tapping into two forms of insecurity these sets of scores can be used to assess the performance adequacy of the JFSS via convergent validity, as both scales should negatively correlate with each other.

2.4 Methods

41 participants (20 female; M age = 19.9, SD = 1.7) recruited from Osaka University via the Intelligent Robotics Laboratory volunteer email list completed the JFSS and the Japanese ECR. All participants were healthy, with no known physical, auditory or visual impairment. Prior to study participation written informed consent was obtained from each participant.

2.5 Results

Total scores for the pre-interaction JFSS items were computed, and internal consistency was confirmed, with high reliability, Cronbach's α = .871. This score indicates that items within the questionnaire are measuring the same construct. Participants also completed the 26-item Japanese ECR [26]. After computing a Pearson product-moment correlation coefficient to assess the relationship between JFSS scores and the attachment anxiety and attachment avoidance Japanese ECR scores, negative correlations between both sets of variables was found, Pearson's $r(41) = -.36$, $p = .010$ (anxiety), and $r(41) = -.32$, $p = .021$ (avoidance). Scatterplots were produced to summarise the results (Figs. 1 (anxiety) and 2 (avoidance)). Overall, there was a strong negative correlation between JFSS pre-interaction scores and Japanese ECR scores, such that the larger a participant's pre-interaction JFSS score, the smaller the participant's Japanese ECR scores.

---

[1] In English the Japanese instruction translates as: *Place a vertical mark on each line in a place that best indicates how you feel right now.*

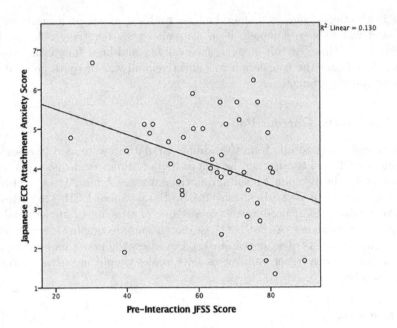

Fig. 1. Scatterplot showing negative correlation between completed JFSS scores and attachment anxiety Japanese ECR scores.

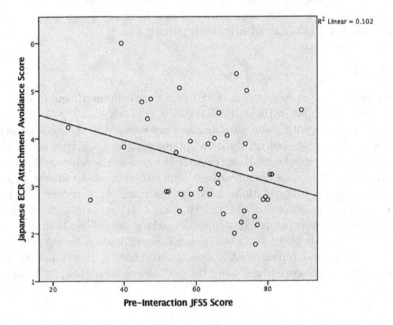

Fig. 2. Scatterplot showing negative correlation between completed JFSS scores and attachment avoidance Japanese ECR scores.

3 Conclusion

The study presented here shows the successful translation of the FSS into Japanese, with the new instrument validated both semantically and through comparison with similar measures already validated for Japanese populations (i.e. the Japanese ECR). Although the participant sample used to assess the JFSS were not representative of a clinical sample, such as that which would receive RAT, the translated instrument performed well. This production of this new instrument has provided a new instrument for measuring the performance of robots intended for RAT, and demonstrates a positive step towards the production of more comparative methodologies that can be utilised for cross-cultural HRI research.

Acknowledgements. This work was funded by the Engineering and Physical Sciences Research Council (EPSRC), and The Japan Society for the Promotion of Science (JSPS). The production of this paper was also partially supported by the RAIN (Robotics and Artificial Intelligence for Nuclear) Hub, which is funded by the Industrial Strategy Challenge Fund, part of the government's modern Industrial Strategy. The fund is delivered by UK Research and Innovation and managed by EPSRC [EP/R026084/1]. This paper also acknowledges support from The Human Brain Project.

References

1. AIST: Mental commit robot for psychological enrichment (2006). http://www.paro.jp/english/therapy.html. Accessed 30 August 2016
2. Banks, M.R., Willoughby, L.M., Banks, W.A.: Animal-assisted therapy and loneliness in nursing homes: Use of robotic versus living dogs. J. Am. Med. Directors Assoc. **9**(3), 173–177 (2008)
3. Bartneck, C., Nomura, T., Kanda, T., Suzuki, T., Kennsuke, K.: A cross-cultural study on attitudes towards robots. In: HCI International (2005)
4. Bartneck, C., Suzuki, T., Kanda, T., Nomura, T.: The influence of people's culture and prior experiences with aibo on their attitude towards robots. AI & Soc. **21**(1–2), 217–230 (2007)
5. Beach, L.R.: Image theory: Decision making in personal and organizational contexts. Wiley Chichester (1990)
6. Bowlby, J.: Attachment and Loss, Volume I: Attachment. Hogarth Press (1969)
7. Brislin, R.W.: Back-translation for cross-cultural research. J. Cross-Cultural Psychol. **1**(3), 185–216 (1970)
8. Carroll, J.: Top robotics companies for 2016 named by Robotics Business Review (2016). http://www.vision-systems.com/articles/2016/03/top-robotics-companies-for-2016-named-by-robotics-business-review.html. Accessed 30 August 2016
9. Collins, E.C.: Drawing parallels in human-other interactions: A trans-disciplinary approach to developing human-robot interaction methodologies. Philos. Trans. Roy. Soc. B **374**(1771), 20180433 (2019)
10. Collins, E.C., Millings, A., Prescott, T.J.: Attachment to assistive technology: A new conceptualisation. In: Proceedings of the 12th European AAATE Conference (Association for the Advancement of Assistive Technology in Europe) (2013)

11. Collins, E.C., Prescott, T.J., Mitchinson, B., Conran, S.: Miro: A versatile biomimetic edutainment robot. In: Advances in Computer Entertainment. Springer (2015)
12. Denzau, A.T., North, D.C.: Shared mental models: Ideologies and institutions. Kyklos **47**(1), 3–31 (1994)
13. Fensom, A.: Japan's robot revolution (2015). http://thediplomat.com/2015/07/japans-robot-revolution/. Accessed 30 Aug 2016
14. Gentner, D., Stevens, A.L.: Mental Models. Psychology Press (2014)
15. Haring, K.S., Silvera-Tawil, D., Matsumoto, Y., Velonaki, M., Watanabe, K.: Perception of an android robot in Japan and Australia: A cross-cultural comparison. In: Beetz, M., Johnston, B., Williams, M.-A. (eds.) ICSR 2014. LNCS (LNAI), vol. 8755, pp. 166–175. Springer, Cham (2014). https://doi.org/10.1007/978-3-319-11973-1_17
16. Herdman, M., Fox-Rushby, J., Badia, X.: 'Equivalence' and the translation and adaptation of health-related quality of life questionnaires. Qual. Life Res. **6**(3) (1997)
17. Hulin, C.L.: A psychometric theory of evaluations of item and scale translations fidelity across languages. J. Cross-Cult. Psychol. **18**(2), 115–142 (1987)
18. Kaplan, F.: Who is afraid of the humanoid? Investigating cultural differences in the acceptance of robots. Int. J. Humanoid Rob. **1**(03), 465–480 (2004)
19. Luke, M.A., Sedikides, C., Carnelley, K.: Your love lifts me higher! The energizing quality of secure relationships. Pers. Soc. Psychol. Bull. **38**(6), 721–733 (2012)
20. MacDorman, K.F., Vasudevan, S.K., Ho, C.C.: Does Japan really have robot mania? Comparing attitudes by implicit and explicit measures. AI & Soc. **23**(4), 485–510 (2009)
21. MacNamara, M., Moga, J., Pachel, C.: What's love got to do with it? Selecting animals for animal-assisted mental health interventions. Handbook on Animal-Assisted Therapy (2015)
22. Mallinckrodt, B., Wang, C.C.: Quantitative methods for verifying semantic equivalence of translated research instruments: A Chinese version of the Experiences in Close Relationships Scale. J. Couns. Psychol. **51**(3), 368 (2004)
23. Mantovani, G.: Social context in HCI: A new framework for mental models, cooperation, and communication. Cognit. Sci. **20**(2), 237–269 (1996)
24. Murray, S.L., Holmes, J.G., Griffin, D.W.: Self-esteem and the quest for felt security: How perceived regard regulates attachment processes. J. Pers. Soc. Psychol. **78**(3), 478 (2000)
25. Murthy, R., et al.: Animals in healthcare facilities: Recommendations to minimize potential risks. Infect. Cont. & Hosp. Epidemiol. **36**(05), 495–516 (2015)
26. Nakao, T., Kato, K.: Developing the Japanese version of the adult attachment style scale (ECR). Shinrigaku Kenkyu: Japanese J. Psychol. **75**(2), 154–159 (2004)
27. Prodhan, G.: China to have most robots in world by 2017 (2015). http://www.reuters.com/article/robots-china-idusl6n0vf52o20150205. Accessed 1 Feb 2015
28. Rothbaum, F., Weisz, J., Pott, M., Miyake, K., Morelli, G.: Attachment and culture: Security in the United States and Japan. Am. Psychol. **55**(10), 1093 (2000)
29. Shibata, T.: PARO (2016). http://www.parorobots.com/. Accessed 2 Feb 2016
30. Stiehl, W.D., Lieberman, J., Breazeal, C., Basel, L., Lalla, L., Wolf, M.: Design of a therapeutic robotic companion for relational, affective touch. In: IEEE International Workshop on Robot and Human Interactive Communication, ROMAN 2005, pp. 408–415. IEEE (2005)

31. The European Commission: Special Eurobarometer 382: Public attitudes towards robots (2012). http://ec.europa.eu/publicopinion/archives/ebs. Accessed 1 Aug 2016
32. US Surgeon General: Culture counts: The influence of culture and society on mental health. US and Center for Mental Health Services (2001)
33. Van Widenfelt, B.M., Treffers, P.D., De Beurs, E., Siebelink, B.M., Koudijs, E.: Translation and cross-cultural adaptation of assessment instruments used in psychological research with children and families. Clin. Child Family Psychol. Rev. 8(2), 135–147 (2005)
34. Wang, Y., Ollendick, T.H.: A cross-cultural and developmental analysis of self-esteem in Chinese and Western children. Clin. Child Family Psychol. Rev. 4(3), 253–271 (2001)

MiniBee: A Minature MAV for the Biomimetic Embodiment of Insect Brain Models

Alex J. Cope[✉], Ali Ahmed, Fadl Isa, and James A. R. Marshall

University of Sheffield, Western Bank, Sheffield S1 2TN, England
a.cope@sheffield.ac.uk

Abstract. Flying insects embody many properties that are desirable for Micro Aerial Vehicles (MAVs) including agile flight, low weight, small size, and low energy consumption. Research into embodiment of insect brain models therefore provides a clear avenue for improving the capabilities of MAVs. Here the MiniBee is presented - an open source quadrotor platform design to facilitate such research. The final design exceeds the design requirements, weighting 200 g with a hover flight time of 7 min. The platform provides panoramic vision with onboard remapping and stabilisation, which can reproduce the visual field of the honeybee or other insects. Visual information and control signals are robustly transmitted wirelessly to a ground station for integration with insect brain models.

Keywords: Biomimetics · Embodiment · Gaze stabilisation · Honeybee · Quadrotor

1 Introduction

Studying flying insects is of interest to the design of small Micro Aerial Vehicles (MAVs, [19]), as insects embody many properties that are desirable for MAVs including agile flight, low weight, small size, and low energy consumption. Insects such as the honeybee *Apis mellifera* are also capable of desirable behaviours including complex obstacle avoidance, vertical take-off and landing, and long range navigation [4,7,16]. These behaviours are performed using passive visual processing [15] with a brain consisting of only one million neurons [21]. Designing MAVs that can provide embodiment of models of insect brain function therefore provides a clear avenue for improving the capabilities of MAVs.

When considering how a brain functions it is vital that the sensory environment and motor plant are considered. The neural connections in the brain are influenced by the sensory information it receives, which in turn is largely determined by motor outputs. This is especially important when considering the visual pathways in insect brains. Insect vision consists mainly of two compound eyes with a wide field of view, but coarse resolution [14]. Despite limited resolution [6]

© Springer Nature Switzerland AG 2019
U. Martinez-Hernandez et al. (Eds.): Living Machines 2019, LNAI 11556, pp. 76–87, 2019.
https://doi.org/10.1007/978-3-030-24741-6_7

insects are able to perform discrimination tasks on detailed visual stimuli [22]. Analogous to primate vision, which uses the eye motor control to move the high resolution fovea onto visual points of interest, insects visual fidelity is increased by moving their entire bodies closer to the points of interest [3]. This means that insects' motor control of movement and sensory perception are inextricably linked, and it is vital when creating an agent to embody a model of insect brain function that it can reproduce both the sensory and motor systems of the insect body.

In this paper, a platform for the embodiment of insect brain models of vision-based flight control is introduced. This work updates a previous platform and methodology, the 'BeeBot' quadrotor [11,13]. Recent developments in MAV components designed for drone racing have led to a step change in the ability to approach the design goals. The goals for this platform are to optimise for minimum size, weight and cost, while still allowing accurate reproduction of several aspects of insect vision. By designing a cheap and small MAV using off-the-shelf parts this platform aims to make this research more accessible. Onboard computation of insect brain models is not a design goal for this quadrotor, as it has been established that remote computation is sufficient for initial research work [12] providing suitably low signal latency. In contrast to the BeeBot, here the focus is not only on replicating the sensory system and flight characteristics of insects but also an aspect of their behaviour which is closely linked to visual perception: head movement. Accounting for head movements requires different decisions in the MAV design. In addition, experience with electronic olfaction sensing has led to the conclusion that this is not currently useful for mounting on a MAV.

The fundamental requirements for a ultra-wide field of view and low cost means that existing solutions from the literature are unsuitable for providing this embodiment platform. The GRASP lab's VIO-swarm quadrotor is the closest match to the design goals, however it lacks a large enough field of view, and the use of development platform components for flight control increases the cost significantly [20].

2 Background

Much of the background for the design parameters of this quadrotor is well described in Sabo et al. [13], and the interested reader is referred there for details, however a summary will be presented here along with additional background on the differences in the current approach.

2.1 Vision

Insect vision has been widely studied, notably in the honeybee *Apis mellifera*. Honeybees have bilateral compound eyes composed of 5500 facets, or ommatidia, each arranged in a roughly parametrically varying array spanning over 270° azimuthally [14]. Several algorithmic models have been described, which derive from Andrew Giger's original model [5]. Each ommatidium has photoreceptors that are sensitive to three wavelengths of light: blue, green and ultra-violet [3]. These shorter wavelengths are important for flower recognition, as well as sky segmentation. Visual motion processing has been shown to primarily use the green photoreceptor output. Temporally, the honeybee eye has been measured as having a resolution between 165–300 Hz, implying that temporal resolution of 300 Hz may be needed for some behaviours [10,17]. The latency of the insect visual system from visual stimulus to motor action has been measured, with the dragonfly response to prey movements measured to have a latency of 30 ms [9].

2.2 Motor Control and Embodiment

MAVs are classified into three main types: fixed-wing, flapping-wing, and rotary-wing [19]. Of these fixed-wing does not match the agile flight of insects, and was therefore discounted. Flapping-wing and rotary-wing MAVs provide efficiency trade-offs that alter with the scaling of the MAV mass, thus payload requirements feature heavily in which is most suitable [8].

Honeybees also use motor control to affect the visual sensory information that they receive. As a bee controls its flight the attitude of the body and stroke plane of the wings vary considerably. If the eyes were fixed to this attitude then significant visual motion due to the bees attitude corrections would be observed. The bee's brain would have to process the motion signals to determine which were caused by the bee's motion, and which were caused by the environment. This processing would require a large investment of neurons. High speed footage of bees shows that instead of this investment honeybees stabilise their heads to movement of the body across the three rotational axes: termed 'gaze stabilisation'. To change heading the bee makes a rapid, saccadic head movement, with the body following with a delay [1]. Thus honeybees will only perceive translational motions on their visual field, simplifying the decomposition of visual motion into a measure of real world movement.

3 Design Requirements

Quadrotor MAVs have evolved considerably since the design of the BeeBot quadrotor platform [13], as has the understanding of what is required for the embodiment of insect brain models. There is therefore a need for an improved quadrotor platform with more capable sensory equipment in order to embody models of insect brain function. Notably the BeeBot quadrotor platform camera system is unable to mimic the head movements that honeybees use to stabilise their gaze.

3.1 Problem Description

As stated, there is a need for a platform to test the embodiment of flying insect brain models. Regulatory and practical concerns require that testing of such models should occur in a controlled laboratory environment. This serves a dual purpose. Firstly, the performance of the model can be evaluated in a controlled sensory environment where disturbances such as wind can be removed or added in a controlled manner. This is especially important for reactive models where behaviour is a product of the environment and the MAV's movement. Once validated in the lab, the MAV and brain model can then be tested in less constrained environments. Secondly, the laboratory can be instrumented with a motion tracking system. The tracking system allows both a ground truth measurement of the performance of the MAV, as well as a means of constraining certain degrees for freedom while others are controlled by the model. This aids analysis of performance and provides a virtual 'safety net', whereby a stable controller can assert itself over the brain model to prevent damage to the MAV if it moves outside of a predefined position and motion envelope.

For the testing presented here the Sheffield Aerial Robotics Lab (SARL) and a Vicon Motion Tracking System (MTS)[1] are used.

3.2 Design Requirements

The design requirements are listed below. For temporal resolution the value is scaled by a factor of 10 from that of the honeybee. This is due to the lower desired flight speed of the MAV from that of the honeybee, see Sabo et al. [13] for further discussion.

- Less than 250 g weight
- Less than 30 × 30 cm
- Inexpensive (off-the-shelf and 3D-printed components)
- Replicate insect field-of-view, spatial and temporal resolution
- Replicate insect visual field stabilisation
- Reliable communication of uncompressed video off-board and control signals on-board

The MAV design is then evaluated against these requirements using the lab environment described previously.

4   MiniBee Design

The rapid growth of first-person view (FPV) drone racing has lead to the development of a range of cheap consumer available parts for building quadrotor MAVs. Drone racing MAVs match many of the design requirements for our platform, being manoeuvrable, lightweight and relatively cheap compared to their larger commercial quadrotor counterparts. This is achieved in part by forgoing many of the features that can be found in larger quadrotors, notably GPS, barometric sensors and ultrasonic sensors. As insects do not have any of these sensors, with the possible exception of the barometric sensor, these omissions do not conflict with our design requirements.

---

[1] Vicon Motion Tracking System, https://www.vicon.com/.

4.1   Visual Sensing Design

To reproduce the visual sensing of the honeybee there are three main design requirements: reproduction of the field of view; reproduction of the gaze stabilisation; reliable transmission of uncompressed image data. Each of these will now be considered in turn.

Reproduction of the field-of-view requires the use of either multiple cameras or complex optics. The use of multiple cameras adds weight for each camera, as well as creating issues with synchronisation of the cameras frames. Correctly synchronising requires dedicated hardware where multiple cameras can be simultaneously activated over an I2C bus by a single controller. This conflicts with the requirement that off-the-shelf components should be used. Complex optics can consist of either lenses, mirrors, or a combination. Combined mirror lens systems such as a catadioptric system [18] have been previously used to reproduce insect vision, but again conflict with the requirement for off-the-shelf components. Given that only a single camera can be used, and off-the-shelf lenses do not offer greater then diagonal 220° field of view, a mirror system is left. The design incorporates a single hemispherical mirror from the Bubblescope panoramic camera system[2].

Stabilisation of the visual scene can be performed in one of two ways: a mechanical gimbal or in software. No gimbal system for stabilisation exists off-the-shelf that would meet the weight requirement of this design, and thus a software solution has been developed. Before describing this solution it is important to describe the possible solutions to reliably transmit uncompressed image data to a ground station.

Uncompressed image data, especially at the frame rates required by our design, consume considerable bandwidth. The BeeBot design used analog transmission to attempt to solve this issue, with remapping to the honeybee ommatidial layout performed post transmission [11]. Analog transmission at legally permitted transmission power introduces considerable noise, as well as picture tearing, both of which are undesirable as input into brain models. To avoid this issue the MiniBee camera system is digital, using a Raspberry Pi Zero W and camera. The Raspberry Pi camera is capable of 90 fps at 640×480 pixel resolution, and therefore well exceeds the speed requirements of the design. In order to focus the camera onto the mirror a macro lens is required between the camera and mirror.

The design as described requires both stabilisation and a means of transmitting the video data reliably. Both of these issues are solved using on-board processing on the Raspberry Pi Zero W, followed by WiFi transmission of the processed image data. The processing unwraps the distorted image of the mirror into either an ommatidial or cylindrical projection, which reduces the image size down to 152×72 pixels consisting either of the green colour channel, or all three colour channels, and thereby reduces the bandwidth cost of communication. In addition a Bosch BNO055 orientation sensor is connected to the Raspberry Pi

---

[2] https://www.tomlawton.com/bubblescope.

over a serial connection, and this is used to change the unwrapping to stabilise the field of view. Due to the processing limitations of the Raspberry Pi Zero the unwrapping and stabilisation is performed by an array of pre-calculated look up tables, indexed by the roll and pitch orientation of the quadrotor. It was calculated that a look-up with one degree resolution over $\pm35°$ in roll and pitch was possible to be stored in the Raspberry Pi RAM.

4.2 MiniBee Platform Design

Flapping-wing MAVs cannot currently carry the sensor payload described above, so a rotary-wing quadrotor MAV design was selected. The quadrotor design process for the MiniBee largely followed the iterative process outlined by Bouabdullah [2]. Following propulsion group choice (EMAX RS1106 II brushless motors) the eCalc online tool[3] was used to provide a guideline of the suitability of the components, and to iterate the design. Multiple considerations must be met to meet the strict weight limit, while allowing sufficient payload capacity for the visual sensor. Bouabdullah used gearing to pair smaller, high kV motors with larger propellers, however the size requirements of the design do not permit this choice for the MiniBee. Instead, high kV motors were paired with low pitch angle twin-blade 3 in. propellers (DYS 3020). This choice provides over 800 g of thrust for minimal weight, thus providing a high-manoeuvrability thrust-to-weight ratio close to 4.

The choice of motors and propellers along with the space required centrally to mount the components determines the minimum size of the frame: a 160 mm wheelbase. For the frame the Diatone Grasshopper 160 carbon fibre frame was chosen to minimise weight.

Weight was also a consideration in the choice of flight controller, and therefore a lightweight all-in-one board, the Airbot Asgard, comprising a STM32F4 processor to run the flight controller firmware, power distribution, and four 24A BL_Heli_32 electronic speed controllers (ESCs) at a total weight of 15 g was selected. The ESCs can provide more than the maximum current draw of the motors, and therefore not limit performance. The flight controller runs the open source BetaFlight firmware[4], which exposes a high degree of control over the attitude controller PID parameters. BetaFlight was chosen due to the open source community support it provides, as well as the lack of complex features such as GPS waypointing, which are not required by the design.

Bi-directional communication between the host and MiniBee flight controller is via an XBee3 serial wireless network. The MultiWii Serial Protocol is used, which is a simple and lightweight extensible message protocol used by the BetaFlight firmware for configuration and control.

A custom mount for the components was designed in Blender3D[5] and printed with a Stratasys Mojo Desktop 3D printer[6]. The mount secures the battery

---

[3] eCalc https://www.ecalc.ch/.
[4] BetaFlight https://github.com/betaflight/betaflight.
[5] Blender https://www.blender.org/.
[6] Mojo3D https://www.stratasys.com/.

between the soft mounted flight controller and the Raspberry Pi Zero W, as well as providing structure to support the camera, lens and mirror in place. The design mounts the battery high to move the centre of mass above the centre of thrust, thus improving the manoeuvrability of the quadrotor and requiring active attitude control. The design of the MiniBee is open source and can be found on GitHub (https://github.com/BrainsOnBoard/MiniBee).

4.3 MTS Flight Control and Safety

The integration of the ground station and MTS with the MiniBee is shown in Fig. 1.

The MiniBee has no position holding mechanism built into the flight controller and currently no insect brain model controlling its behaviour. In the absence of these, the MTS must be used to perform position holding and movement. To perform this function a velocity-based PID positional controller was implemented using the MTS data to provide an error signal. The assumption of small angles of roll and pitch, and therefore linear response, is made in the controller. A waypoint position vector $\mathbf{P}_w$ is set and the target velocity $\mathbf{V}_t$ is calculated as follows, where $\mathbf{P}_b$ is the MiniBee position.

$$\mathbf{P}_t = \mathbf{P}_w - \mathbf{P}_b$$
$$V_t = \begin{cases} 0.1v\mathbf{P}_t, & \text{if } |\mathbf{P}_t| < 10 \\ v\hat{\mathbf{P}}_t, & \text{otherwise} \end{cases} \tag{1}$$

The error is the difference between the MiniBee velocity and a constant target velocity in the direction of the target position. To avoid discontinuities in the control signal the target velocity is filtered using an infinite impulse response filter, where the new control velocity value $\mathbf{C}_i$ is related to the old control value $\mathbf{C}_{i-1}$ and the target control value $\mathbf{C}_t$ by the time constant τ using the following equations:

$$\mathbf{C}_i = \lambda \mathbf{C}_{i-1} + (\lambda - 1)\mathbf{C}_t$$
$$\lambda = e^{-1/\tau}$$

A τ value of 20 was used. In addition the target velocity scales as the target is approached, as described in Eq. 1.

If a waypoint is attempted to be set outside a safety box, then the waypoint is not accepted by the position controller. This allows initial testing of models to proceed though the safeguard of the MTS based positional controller, preventing damaging crashes.

5 Results

5.1 Visual Sensing Results

The visual sensor can transmit unwrapped and stabilised images at a range of rates depending on the method of transmission and the number of colour channels transmitted. WiFi transmission involves greater overhead, and decreases

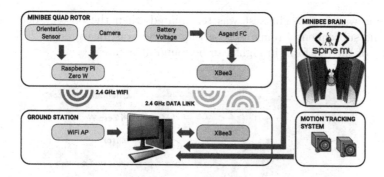

Fig. 1. MiniBee interfaces.

frame rate due to computational constraints. A list of frame rates along with the WiFi latency is shown in Table 1. All frame rates are well in excess of the design requirements. Latency was measured using a video of both a clock and the visual sensor's transmitted view of the clock, averaged over 16 frames. As the measured latency includes additional latency from displaying the camera data on the receiving device it is an upper bound on the true latency. The latency measured is within requirements, as it is considerably lower than the latency found in the insect visual system, factoring in the temporal resolution scaling factor of 10 ($30\,\text{ms} \times 10 = 300\,\text{ms}$ [9]).

Table 1. Transmission parameters for the MiniBee camera system.

Transmission method	Quantity	Value
WiFi	Mono (8bpp)	77 FPS
WiFi	Colour (24bpp)	60 FPS
USB Ethernet	Mono (8bpp)	90 FPS
USB Ethernet	Colour (24bpp)	70 FPS
WiFi	Latency	$142.5 \pm 14.4\,\text{ms}$

The MiniBee camera is capable of 360° azimuthal field of view, and 120° vertical field of view. The vertical field of view is less than that of the honeybee, but is at the limits of what can be achieved with a single camera mirror system.

Video of the camera output can be found online[7].

5.2 MiniBee Platform Results

The final MiniBee design is shown in Fig. 2, with the details shown in Table 2 and the weight and cost breakdown in Fig. 3. A hover test determined that the

---

[7] Camera footage https://youtu.be/SLpMH2qa98o.

hover time was 7 min. The test was terminated when the battery declined to 10.7V, and subsequently remaining battery charge was measured at 20%.

Video of the platform in flight can be found at online[8].

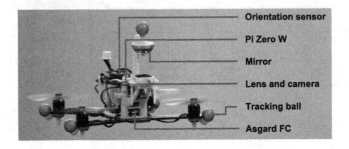

Fig. 2. Key components of the MiniBee.

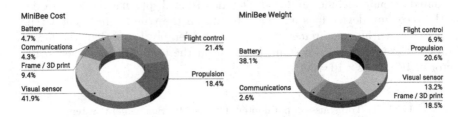

Fig. 3. Cost and weight breakdowns for the MiniBee.

A throughput test of the MultiWii Serial Protocol using the XBee was performed by sending control commands to the flight controller every loop, along with requests for battery status every 10 loops. Using this test protocol an average of 100 loops per second was achieved, which is in excess of that needed for flight control, and equal to the temporal resolution of the MTS. Thus the MiniBee meets the requirement of reliable wireless flight control.

5.3 MTS Control Results

To test the control of the MiniBee using the MTS a trajectory is constructed of several waypoints describing a closed loop. The controller traverses towards a waypoint until it is within a radius of 10 cm, and then switches to the next waypoint. Figure 4 shows the path of the MiniBee over several traversals. The trajectory shows high consistency and accuracy, with no overshoot of the waypoints. Thus the controller is suitable for the purpose of acting as a simple safety

---

[8] Minibee footage http://brainsonboard.co.uk/2018/10/26/introducing-the-minibee-v1/.

Table 2. MiniBee design results.

Quantity	Value
Total weight	200 g
Total size (inc. propellers)	21.1 × 18.3 × 14 cm
Total cost	$306
Voltage	11.1V (3S LiPo)
Average hover current draw	5.5 A
Average hover flight time	7 min
Estimated thrust-to-weight ratio (eCalc)	3.5

net, although it should be noted that due to the small angle approximation used for the linear control model large perturbations to attitude may be unrecoverable with this method.

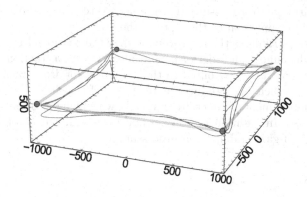

Fig. 4. Flight trajectory for MiniBee waypoint following.

6   Discussion and Conclusions

A complete system for the embodiment of flying insect brain models in a MAV is described here. The design requirements for this MAV were almost all met, and in some cases exceeded. The final design has lower weight (80% of the target)and smaller size (70% in the largest dimension) than the requirements. The final design also proved inexpensive by using only use off-the-shelf components, yet still has the ability to replicate the stabilisation and temporal resolution requirements on board. The field of view requirement is partially met, but this can be addressed by constructing a catadioptric camera. Communication both to the flight controller and of the image data is reliable, with latency and frame rate for image data suitable for the design requirements.

One drawback of the design is the choice of high kV motors and low pitch angle propellers, which leads to very high propeller tip speeds. This was found to create vibration problems if the propellers were unbalanced due to damage, and required careful vibration damping of the flight controller's integrated inertial measurement unit and the orientation sensor. This choice therefore decreases the robustness of the design to damage, and if robustness is a consideration other design choices should be considered.

No existing platform of this size is capable of reproducing the stabilised panoramic view of the MiniBee. The closest comparison is GRASP lab's state-of-the-art VIO-swarm quadrotor [20], fulfilling many of the design parameters. However the VIO-swarm quadrotor utilises a Qualcomm flight controller which is considerably more expensive ($800), and a custom carbon-fibre balsa wood composite frame. The VIO-swarm quadrotor can therefore be considered less easily constructed than the MiniBee, and potentially in conflict with the requirement for off-the-shelf components. The flight time of the VIO-swarm quadrotor is comparable (MiniBee: 7 min hover; VIO-swarm quadrotor up to 8 min) with the VIO-swarm quadrotor weighing 50 g more, and using larger propellers (MiniBee: 3-in.; VIO-swarm quadrotor: 4-in.). This demonstrates that the MiniBee design performs well in comparison to the state-of-the art.

What is most striking is the improvement over the previous BeeBot platform [13], with weight almost an order of magnitude lower for a fraction of the cost. This can in large part be attributed to the popularity of drone racing in recent years, a market which has produced a range of off-the-shelf components well suited to the embodiment of insect brain models, with high performance and light weight prioritised. In addition the design addresses a drawback of the BeeBot design: the lack of gaze stabilisation processing.

References

1. Boeddeker, N., Dittmar, L., Stürzl, W., Egelhaaf, M.: The fine structure of honeybee head and body yaw movements in a homing task. Proc. Roy. Soc. Biol. Sci. **277**(1689), 1899–1906 (2010). https://doi.org/10.1098/rspb.2009.2326
2. Bouabdallah, S.: Design and control of quadrotors with application to autonomous flying. https://doi.org/10.5075/EPFL-THESIS-3727
3. Dyer, A.G., Spaethe, J., Prack, S.: Comparative psychophysics of bumblebee and honeybee colour discrimination and object detection. J. Comp. Physiol. A **194**(7), 617–627 (2008). https://doi.org/10.1007/s00359-008-0335-1
4. Egelhaaf, M., Boeddeker, N., Kern, R., Kurtz, R., Lindemann, J.P.: Spatial vision in insects is facilitated by shaping the dynamics of visual input through behavioral action. Front. Neural Circ. **6**, 108 (2012). https://doi.org/10.3389/fncir.2012.00108
5. Giger, A.: Honeybee vision: analysis of pattern orientation. Ph.D. thesis, Australian National University (1996)
6. Hecht, S., Wolf, E.: The visual acuity of the honeybee. J. Gen. Physiol. **12**(6), 727–760 (1929)
7. Labhart, T., Meyer, E.P.: Neural mechanisms in insect navigation: polarization compass and odometer. Curr. Opin. Neurobiol. **12**(6), 707–714 (2002). https://doi.org/10.1016/S0959-4388(02)00384-7

8. Mulgaonkar, Y., Whitzer, M., Morgan, B., Kroninger, C.M., Harrington, A.M., Kumar, V.: Power and weight considerations in small, agile quadrotors. Int. Soc. Opt. Photonics, p. 90831Q. https://doi.org/10.1117/12.2051112

9. Olberg, R.M., Seaman, R.C., Coats, M.I., Henry, A.F.: Eye movements and target fixation during dragonfly prey-interception flights. J. Comp. Physiol. A Neuroethol. Sens. Neural Bhav. Physiol. **193**(7), 685–693 (2007). https://doi.org/10.1007/s00359-007-0223-0

10. Ruck, P.: A comparison of the electrical responses of compound eyes and dorsal ocelli in four insect species. J. Insect Physiol. **2**(4), 261–274 (1958). https://doi.org/10.1016/0022-1910(58)90012-X

11. Sabo, C., Chisholm, R., Petterson, A., Cope, A.: A lightweight, inexpensive robotic system for insect vision. Arthropod Struct. Dev. (2017). https://doi.org/10.1016/j.asd.2017.08.001

12. Sabo, C., Cope, A., Gurny, K., Vasilaki, E., Marshall, J.: Bio-inspired visual navigation for a quadcopter using optic flow. In: AIAA Infotech @ Aerospace Conference (2016)

13. Sabo, C., et al.: An inexpensive flying robot design for embodied robotics research. In: Proceedings of the International Joint Conference on Neural Networks, May 2017. https://doi.org/10.1109/IJCNN.2017.7966383

14. Seidl, R., Kaiser, W.: Visual field size, binocular domain and the ommatidial array of the compound eyes in worker honey bees. J. Comp. Physiol. A **143**(1), 17–26 (1981). https://doi.org/10.1007/BF00606065

15. Srinivasan, M., Zhang, S., Lehrer, M., Collett, T.: Honeybee navigation en route to the goal: visual flight control and odometry. J. Exp. Biol. **199**(Pt 1), 237–244 (1996)

16. Srinivasan, M.V.: Honeybees as a model for the study of visually guided flight, navigation, and biologically inspired robotics. Physiol. Rev. **91**(2), 413–460 (2011). https://doi.org/10.1152/physrev.00005.2010

17. Srinivasan, M.V., Lehrer, M.: Temporal acuity of honeybee vision: behavioural studies using moving stimuli. J. Comp. Physiol. A **155**(3), 297–312 (1984). https://doi.org/10.1007/BF00610583

18. Stürzl, W., Boeddeker, N., Dittmar, L., Egelhaaf, M.: Mimicking honeybee eyes with a 280 degrees field of view catadioptric imaging system. Bioinspiration Biomimetics **5**(3), 036002 (2010). https://doi.org/10.1088/1748-3182/5/3/036002

19. Ward, T.A., Fearday, C.J., Salami, E., Binti Soin, N.: A bibliometric review of progress in micro air vehicle research. Int. J. Micro Air Veh. **9**(2), 146–165 (2017). https://doi.org/10.1177/1756829316670671

20. Weinstein, A., Cho, A., Loianno, G., Kumar, V.: VIO-Swarm: a swarm of vision based quadrotors. IEEE Robot. Autom. Lett. (2018)

21. Witthöft, W.: Absolute anzahl und verteilung der zellen im him der honigbiene. Zeitschrift für Morphologie der Tiere **61**(1), 160–184 (1967). https://doi.org/10.1007/BF00298776

22. Wu, W., Moreno, A.M., Tangen, J.M., Reinhard, J.: Honeybees can discriminate between Monet and Picasso paintings. J. Comp. Physiol. A **199**(1), 45–55 (2013). https://doi.org/10.1007/s00359-012-0767-5

Bio-inspired Stochastic Growth and Initialization for Artificial Neural Networks

Kevin Dai⬭, Amir Barati Farimani⬭, and Victoria A. Webster-Wood$^{(\boxtimes)}$⬭

Carnegie Mellon University, 5000 Forbes Ave, Pittsburgh, PA 15213, USA
barati@cmu.edu, vwebster@andrew.cmu.edu
https://www.baratilab.com, http://engineering.cmu.edu/borg

Abstract. Current initialization methods for artificial neural networks (ANNs) assume full connectivity between network layers. We propose that a bio-inspired initialization method for establishing connections between neurons in an artificial neural network will produce more accurate results relative to a fully connected network. We demonstrate four implementations of a novel, stochastic method for generating sparse connections in spatial, growth-based connectivity (GBC) maps. Connections in GBC maps are used to generate initial weights for neural networks in a deep learning compatible framework. These networks, designated as Growth-Initialized Neural Networks (GrINNs), have sparse connections between the input layer and the hidden layer. GrINNs were tested with user-specified nominal connectivity percentages ranging from 5–45%, resulting in unique connectivity percentages ranging from 4–28%. For reference, fully connected networks are defined as having 100% unique connectivity within this context. GrINNs with nominal connectivity percentages $\geq$20% produced better accuracy than fully connected ANNs when trained and tested on the MNIST dataset.

Keywords: Sparse neural networks · Weight initialization · Bio-inspired · Growth-based connectivity · GrINN

1 Introduction

From the initial development of perceptron networks [28] to modern deep neural networks, neural network approaches have sought to capture or mimic the abilities of biological brains [2,4,8,9,11,23]. Despite recent advances in the development of neural network architectures, ranging from traditional artificial neural networks (ANNs) to convolution neural networks (CNNs) [13,24,27] and recurrent neural networks (RNNs) [16,20,33,34], these neural networks still fail to capture the learning rates and developmental capabilities observed in animals. Some biologically-inspired approaches to establish deep neural networks have used evolutionary algorithms based on genetic theory to heuristically determine network architectures [15,21,29]. Evolutionary algorithms can effectively search

© Springer Nature Switzerland AG 2019
U. Martinez-Hernandez et al. (Eds.): Living Machines 2019, LNAI 11556, pp. 88–100, 2019.
https://doi.org/10.1007/978-3-030-24741-6_8

for an optimal architecture over a wide space of parameters but do not inherently capture the spatiotemporal aspect of neuronal development in biological systems. To bridge the gap between biological neural networks and *in silico* network models, research efforts have investigated the creation of synthetic nervous systems [3,19,30,31] and evolving spiking neural networks [10,32]. However, the use of time-dependent spiking neuron models in both approaches prevents the application of such networks with modern deep learning techniques.

Whereas biological neural networks have dynamic spatial and connectivity architectures as well as synaptic plasticity, most ANN approaches that are compatible with modern deep learning techniques rely on fully connected networks. In fully connected networks, each artificial neuron in a given layer inherently has connections to every neuron in its neighboring layers. In reality, there are many complex factors that determine how biological neurons may grow to form network architectures and synaptic weights [7,12,25]. Biological neurons begin as independent cells with no connections between neurons, similar to the artificial neurons of an ANN with initial weights set to zero. During network development, the axons of the biological neurons are encouraged to grow by following chemical distributions in the surrounding tissue. These axons continue to grow until they reach and establish a connection with another biological neuron. This is akin to drawing a weighted link between two artificial neurons in an ANN. Biological neuronal growth is characterized by a chemical balance that can change whether axons extend their length by building a single chain of microtubules, or whether the axon splits into multiple dendrites that each grow independently.

To move towards a biological basis for artificial neural network connectivity and synaptic weight initialization within a deep learning compatible framework, a method for the creation of growth-based connectivity (GBC) maps and associated weight initialization is presented here. This growth-based initialization method aims to develop a first principles explanation for neural network initialization methods, based on approximating natural biological phenomenon. To reduce the complexity of the proposed neuronal growth model, the model ignores the chemical distribution typically found in biological systems and instead approximates axon growth based on stochastic growth parameters. This framework provides a foundation for future investigation on the role of continual network growth and adaptation on learning and perception.

2   Methods

2.1   Dataset Selection

Since the proposed growth-based weight initialization method is a novel concept that requires validation, the MNIST dataset was selected for its history as a common benchmark in training neural networks [17]. Each image in the dataset contains 784 pixels, with 10 possible class outputs (Fig. 1). In addition, even simple neural networks can achieve accuracy >95% on the MNIST dataset [17].

2.2   Network Connectivity and Weight Initialization

A basic, linear ANN consists of an input layer, a hidden layer, and an output layer. For the presented study, all networks are sized for the MNIST dataset, which requires 784 input neurons and 10 output neurons. The hidden layer is arbitrarily chosen to contain 100 hidden neurons with a ReLU activation function [6]. A softmax activation function is applied to the output layer for classification into one of ten possible classes (the digits 0 to 9).

Fully connected networks serve as the control when evaluating the performance of growth-initialized neural networks. Each layer in the fully connected network maintains full connections to adjacent layers.

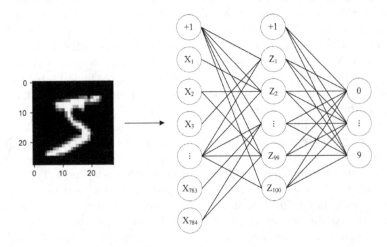

Fig. 1. Sample architecture of a GrINN for the MNIST dataset [18]. The input layer forms sparse connections with the hidden layer. In this study, the hidden layer is fully connected to the output layer for all GrINNs.

Stochastic Growth-Based Connectivity Map Creation: In contrast to fully connected neural networks, growth-initialized neural networks (GrINNs) do not assume full connectivity between the input and hidden layers (Fig. 1). The input layer for GrINNs is initially assumed to have zero connectivity with the hidden layer. Connections between these two layers are established by simulating the growth of connective "axons" from the input layer to the hidden layer.

The proposed, growth-based weight initialization method (Fig. 2) requires a spatial map of neuron positions to mimic the physical growth of axons and synapse formation during biological network development. The growth based connectivity (GBC) map is established in a unitless, 2D Cartesian coordinate system. 784 input layer neurons and 100 hidden layer neurons are each given a coordinate in the spatial map. Input layer neurons are represented by evenly

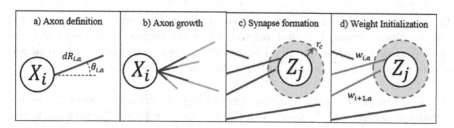

Fig. 2. Schema explaining stages in stochastic growth-based connectivity map creation and weight initialization. (a) Each neuron in the input layer is assigned a random number of axons. Each axon is defined by a growth rate, $dR_{i,a}$, and growth angle, $\theta_{i,a}$. (b) At each step, each axon is extended by its assigned growth rate. (c) Once an axon is within a specified capture radius of a hidden neuron, r_c, the origin neuron in the input layer and the relevant neuron in the hidden layer are considered connected and growth of the axon ceases. (d) Once the specified connectivity percentage is achieved, the weights of each unique axon are assigned. Any missing connections are assigned zero weight.

spaced points that form a vertical line at $x = 0$ from $y = 0$ to $y = -784$. The hidden layer neurons are represented by points on a vertical line at $x = 100$ from $y = 0$ to $y = -784$. The spacing between the two lines was set at 100 units.

Each input neuron is randomly assigned an integer number of axons using a uniform distribution $U(0, 100)$. This determines the maximum number of possible connections from a specific input neuron to the hidden layer. The resulting neural network will not be fully connected unless every input neuron is assigned at least 100 axons (the same number of axons as there are hidden layer neurons). As a consequence, it is likely that the input layer will be sparsely connected to the hidden layer as in Fig. 1. Note that for the GrINNs presented here, the growth-based initialization method is not applied between the hidden layer and the output layer, so the hidden layer is fully connected to the output layer.

Each axon, $A_{i,a}$, is initially positioned at its corresponding input neuron, X_i, and randomly assigned a growth angle, $\theta_{i,a}$, using a uniform distribution such that $\theta_{i,a} \sim U(-\pi, \pi)$ and a growth rate, $dR_{i,a}$ as described for each initialization method below (Fig. 2a). The model grows all axons step-by-step (Fig. 2b). During each step, the position of each axon's tip $(x_{i,a}, y_{i,a})$ is incremented by:

$$\Delta x_{i,a} = dR_{i,a} \cos(\theta_{i,a}) \qquad (1)$$

$$\Delta y_{i,a} = dR_{i,a} \sin(\theta_{i,a}) \qquad (2)$$

After each growth step, the model checks if any axon tips are close to a neuron in the hidden layer (Fig. 2c). If an axon tip is within a specified capture radius ($r_c = 4$ units) of a hidden neuron, then a connection is established between the axon's input neuron and the corresponding hidden neuron. The capture radius, r_c, spans over half the distance between adjacent neurons in the hidden layer.

To investigate the effect of stochastic GBC map growth parameters on image classification accuracy, four connection initialization methods were tested:

Initialization Method with Gaussian Growth Rate Distribution, Mean 0. This initialization method, hereafter referred to as "Gaussian 0", follows the step-by-step growth process described above. $dR_{i,a}$ growth rates for each axon are selected from a Gaussian distribution with $\mu = 0$ and $\sigma = 1$.

Initialization Method with Gaussian Growth Rate Distribution, Mean 1. In this initialization method ("Gaussian 1"), the growth rates for each axon are selected from a Gaussian distribution with $\mu = 1$ and $\sigma = 1$.

Initialization Method with Uniform Growth Rate Distribution. In this initialization method ("Uniform"), growth rates for each axon are selected from a uniform distribution such that $dR_{i,a} \sim U(0,1)$.

Reflective Initialization Method. This initialization method ("Reflective") uses the same step-by-step growth process and initialization distributions as described for Gaussian 0. However, axons are bounded to prevent growth beyond the y-bounds of the spatial map at $y = 0$ and $y = -784$. The $\theta_{i,a}$ of any axons that exceed these map boundaries is reflected across the x-axis by multiplying $\theta_{i,a}$ by -1. In subsequent growth steps, any reflected axons continue to grow as described previously, with their reflected $\theta_{i,a}$ values.

Connectivity Percentage: GBC maps were generated with each of the four initialization methods for user-specified nominal connectivity percentages ranging from 5% to 35% in increments of 5%. The Reflective method was also used to generate GBC maps with 40% and 45% nominal connectivity percentages (see Sect. 2.2). The nominal connectivity percentage is calculated as:

$$P_c = \frac{n_{axon,c}}{n_{input} \cdot n_{hidden}} \cdot 100\% \tag{3}$$

where P_c is the nominal connectivity percentage, $n_{axon,c}$ is the number of axons that have formed connections, n_{input} is the number of neurons in the input layer, and n_{hidden} is the number of neurons in the hidden layer. This is different than the percentage of unique connections, P_u, calculated as:

$$P_u = \frac{n_{conn}}{n_{input} \cdot n_{hidden}} \cdot 100\% \tag{4}$$

where n_{conn} is the number of connected input neuron-hidden neuron pairs. Because multiple axons from the same input layer neuron may form duplicate connections with a hidden layer neuron, the percentage of unique connections, P_u, will be lower than the nominal connectivity percentage, P_c.

Weight Initialization: Axon weights are initialized once an axon tip grows within the specified capture radius ($r_c = 4$) of a hidden layer neuron (Fig. 2d). Each weight is randomly selected from a uniform distribution such that $w_{i,a} \sim$

$U(0, 1)$. When the same input neuron-hidden neuron pair is connected by multiple axons, the total connection weight between the pair is determined by summing the weights of each connected axon between these two neurons. To facilitate translation of the GBC map to an ANN framework, the total connection weights are stored in a weight tensor of size $n_{hidden} \times n_{input}$. All other weights between unconnected neurons are set to zero. The weight tensor is assigned as the initial weights between the input and hidden layer of a GrINN in an ANN framework.

Training and Testing: Following creation of the weight tensor, each GrINN is trained on the MNIST dataset for 25 epochs using backpropogation. The accuracy of each GrINN is compared to that of a fully connected neural network. All neural networks are created using the PyTorch framework (Version 1.0.0) [26]. They utilize a cross-entropy loss function and an Adam optimizer [14] with learning rate set to 0.005. Batch size is set to 100 samples. For GrINNs, the input layer is constructed using a custom modified PyTorch linear module. The module uses a Boolean mask to ensure that unconnected weights, which should remain set to zero, will not change due to backpropagation during neural network training.

2.3 Statistical Analysis

For each combination of initialization method and connectivity percentage, designated hereafter as a group, fifty networks were generated. All statistical tests were performed in Minitab. Prior to statistical analysis, accuracy distributions for each group were assessed for normality using the Anderson-Darling test [1]. Due to several groups exhibiting non-normal distributions, Mann-Whitney analysis [22] was used for subsequent comparisons. All groups were independently compared to the control group (fully connected networks) with statistical significance determined by $p < 0.05$. Additionally, at each connectivity percentage, 2-sample Mann-Whitney comparisons were made between each of the initialization methods. This resulted in 6 comparisons at each connectivity percentage. A Bonferroni correction [5] was applied such that significance for comparisons between initialization methods was determined by $p < 0.0083$.

3 Results and Discussion

3.1 Connections

A characteristic example of the intermediate growth steps of the Gaussian 0 growth-based initialization method is shown in Fig. 3. Initially, the axon tip positions coincide with their input neurons. As growth progresses, the axon tip positions spread across the inter-layer space. For the characteristic example shown, many axons have reached the hidden layer by step 80, resulting in connections between their input neuron and the corresponding hidden neuron. This is evident by the clustering of points around the line at $x = 100$.

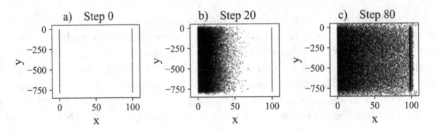

Fig. 3. A characteristic example of all axon tip locations in the spatial growth model for the Gaussian 0 initialization method (a) before growth, (b) after 20 steps of growth, (c) after 80 steps of growth. Input layer neurons are represented by the vertical line at $x = 0$. Hidden layer neurons are represented by the vertical line at $x = 100$.

Using the GBC map initialization methods presented in Sect. 2.2, growth is incremented until the connectivity percentage, P_c, reaches a user-specified threshold. However, for the Gaussian 0, Gaussian 1, and Uniform initialization methods, the maximum achievable connectivity percentage is limited by the growth angles, $\theta_{i,a}$, of the axons. As these initialization methods are spatially unbounded, axons may fail to be captured by the hidden layer neurons (Fig. 4a–c). Bounding the axons with the Reflective initialization method results in higher achievable connectivity percentages (Fig. 4d). For all initialization methods, the percentage of unique connections, P_u, was lower than the nominal connectivity percentage, P_c, by ~1–16% depending on P_c (Fig. 5).

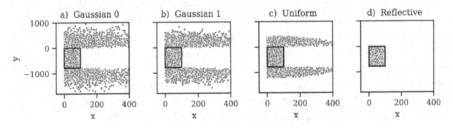

Fig. 4. Characteristic examples of axon tip positions (colored circles) at 25% connectivity using the (a) Gaussian 0, (b) Gaussian 1, (c) Uniform, and (d) Reflective initialization methods. The black rectangle indicates the boundaries of the spatial map formed by the input layer, the hidden layer, and horizontal lines at $y = 0$ and $y = -784$. In all but the Reflective initialization method, a substantial percentage of the axons fail to be captured by the hidden layer. (Color figure online)

3.2 Weights

For all tested GBC initialization methods, a significant portion of the tensor remains unconnected with weights set to zero. Most established connections coincide with the diagonal of the weight tensor running from $(0,0)$ to $(100, 784)$, which can be observed in visualizations of the trained weight tensor (Fig. 6c–j). The visible diagonal is due to the randomization of the axons' $dR_{i,a}$ and $\theta_{i,a}$ values. For example, input neurons positioned near $y = -200$ will tend to establish connections with hidden layer neurons also positioned near $y = -200$. Simultaneously, axons with a small $\theta_{i,a}$, close to zero, will likely reach the hidden layer in fewer steps and establish the majority of connections in GrINNs with lower connectivity percentages (Fig. 6c, e, g and i). As connectivity percentage increases, a greater number of axons with larger $\theta_{i,a}$ will establish connections (Fig. 6d, f, h and j).

In addition, the diagonal of non-zero weights in Fig. 6 is noticeably broader at 30% connectivity than the diagonal of non-zero weights at 10% connectivity for each of the initialization methods tested. This is likely because reaching 30% connectivity typically requires more steps than 10% connectivity, allowing more time for axons with larger $\theta_{i,a}$ to spread out and establish connections.

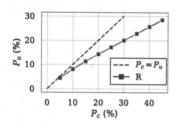

Fig. 5. P_c vs. P_u for the Reflective method. All methods followed a similar trend despite the spatial map boundaries for the reflective method.

Following training, the magnitudes of many connection weights are significantly increased. The weight visualization in Fig. 6(b–j) reveals that the trained weight tensors tend to form vertical bands. This banding effect is particularly visible at the low and high-numbered input neurons, indicating that these neurons do not transfer information to the hidden layer. It is possible that these non-contributing input neurons correspond to border pixels in MNIST images that are blank and do not contain information about the handwritten digit.

3.3 Accuracy

All neural networks produced accuracy >95% after 25 training epochs, as shown in Fig. 7. GrINNs with nominal connectivity >35% for the Gaussian 0, Gaussian 1, and Uniform methods, and connectivity >45% for the Reflective method were not tested due to diminishing returns in connectivity resulting from axon spread during initialization. GrINNs with higher percentages of connectivity tended to produce higher accuracy.

The test accuracy distributions for each GrINN group were compared to the test accuracy distributions for fully connected neural networks using the

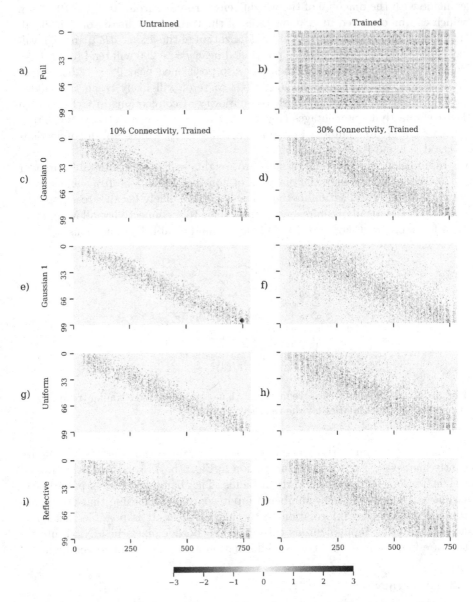

Fig. 6. Visualization of characteristic weight values for neural networks with varying connectivity (P_c): (a) untrained weights in a fully connected network, (b) trained weights in a fully connected network, and trained weights in the following GrINNs – (c) Gaussian 0 with 10% connectivity, (d) Gaussian 0 with 30% connectivity, (e) Gaussian 1 with 10% connectivity, (f) Gaussian 1 with 30% connectivity, (g) Uniform with 10% connectivity, (h) Uniform with 30% connectivity, (i) Reflective with 10% connectivity, and (j) Reflective with 30% connectivity.

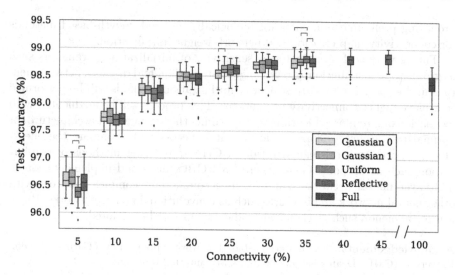

Fig. 7. Accuracy of neural networks at increasing nominal connectivity percentages (P_c). The fully connected neural network is indicated as 100% connectivity. Outliers are designated with *. Statistical significance bars show comparisons between initialization methods within each connectivity percentage, with a Bonferroni correction ($p < 0.0083$). All groups ($n = 50$) with 20–45% nominal connectivity exhibited a significantly higher accuracy than the fully connected control group ($p < 0.05$).

2-Sample Mann-Whitney test ($n = 50$). All groups exhibited a statistically significant difference from the fully connected control group ($p < 0.05$). For all initialization methods, the GrINNs with 20–45% nominal connectivity typically resulted in higher accuracy than fully connected neural networks. The higher accuracy of these GrINNs may result from the sparse connections in each network acting as an architectural regularization in a similar manner to dropout regularization. However, unlike dropout regularization, which temporarily removes connections in a neural network during training, the growth-based initialization methods additively and permanently form connections before training.

Additionally, at each connectivity percentage, 2-sample Mann-Whitney comparisons were made between each of the initialization methods with a Bonferroni correction ($p < 0.0083$). No initialization methods consistently demonstrated significant differences from the other methods across all connectivity percentages.

4   Conclusion

The growth-based initialization methods presented here produce neural networks with comparable, and possibly higher, accuracy relative to fully connected neural networks when trained on the MNIST dataset. Using the developed initialization methods, GrINNs with 20–45% nominal connectivity have significantly higher accuracy than the linear, fully connected ANNs used as a control. This is a promising preliminary outcome for biologically-inspired growth-based methods for connectivity map creation and network weight initialization.

Future work will investigate the sensitivity of initialization parameters such as growth rate distribution, growth angle distribution, and distance between neurons in the spatial map. Adjustment of initialization methods will be performed to achieve higher connectivity percentages. This process will be augmented with feedback using reinforced learning to determine the settings and architecture for optimal test accuracy [35]. In addition, it is necessary to compare the effects of sparse, architectural regularization of GrINNs to other methods of regularization such as dropout. Generation of 3D GBC maps and implementation in multilayer neural networks will seek to accommodate complex datasets with other neural network architectures such as convolutional neural networks. Physical phenomenon such as chemical gradients will also be explored.

Acknowledgements. This material is based on work supported by a Carnegie Mellon University (CMU) Dean's Fellowship and CMU internal funding.

References

1. Anderson, T.W., Darling, D.A., et al.: Asymptotic theory of certain "goodness of fit" criteria based on stochastic processes. Ann. Math. Stat. **23**(2), 193–212 (1952)
2. Chin, L., Mital, D.P.: Application of neural networks in robotic control. In: IEEE International Sympoisum on Circuits and Systems, vol. 5, pp. 2522–2525 (1991)
3. Deng, K., et al.: Neuromechanical model of rat hind limb walking with two layer CPGs and muscle synergies. In: Vouloutsi, V., et al. (eds.) Living Machines 2018. LNCS (LNAI), vol. 10928, pp. 134–144. Springer, Cham (2018). https://doi.org/10.1007/978-3-319-95972-6_15
4. Diamond, A., Schmuker, M., Berna, A.Z., Trowell, S., Nowotny, T.: Classifying continuous, real-time e-nose sensor data using a bio-inspired spiking network modelled on the insect olfactory system. Bioinspiration & Biomimetics **11**(2), 026002 (2016)
5. Dunn, O.J.: Multiple comparisons among means. J. Am. Stat. Assoc. **56**(293), 52–64 (1961)
6. Glorot, X., Bordes, A., Bengio, Y.: Deep sparse rectifier neural networks. In: Proceedings of the Fourteenth International Conference on Artificial Intelligence and Statistics, pp. 315–323 (2011)
7. Graham, B.P., van Ooyen, A.: Mathematical modelling and numerical simulation of the morphological development of neurons. BMC Neurosci. **7**(Suppl 1), S9 (2006)
8. Huang, S., Hu, C.: Neural network controller for robotic motion control. Int. J. Adv. Manuf. Technol **43**, 450–454 (1996)
9. Kar, A.K.: Bio inspired computing - a review of algorithms and scope of applications. Expert Syst. Appl. **59**, 20–32 (2016)
10. Kasabov, N., Dhoble, K., Nuntalid, N., Indiveri, G.: Dynamic evolving spiking neural networks for on-line spatio- and spectro-temporal pattern recognition. Neural Netw. **41**(1995), 188–201 (2013)
11. Kheradpisheh, S.R., Ganjtabesh, M., Masquelier, T.: Bio-inspired unsupervised learning of visual features leads to robust invariant object recognition. Neurocomputing **205**, 382–392 (2016)

12. Kiddie, G., McLean, D., Van Ooyen, A., Graham, B.: Biologically plausible models of neurite outgrowth. Prog. Brain Res. **147**, 67–80 (2005)
13. Kim, Y.: Convolutional neural networks for sentence classification. arXiv (2014)
14. Kingma, D.P., Ba, J.: Adam: a method for stochastic optimization. CoRR abs/1412.6980 (2014). http://arxiv.org/abs/1412.6980
15. Kitano, H.: Designing neural networks using genetic algorithms with graph generation system. Complex Syst. **4**(4), 461–476 (1990)
16. Lai, S., Xu, L., Liu, K., Zhao, J.: Recurrent convolutional neural networks for text classification. In: Proceedings of the 29th AAAI Conference on Artificial Intelligence (AAAI 2015), pp. 2267–2273 (2015)
17. LeCun, Y., Bottou, L., Bengio, Y., Haffner, P., et al.: Gradient-based learning applied to document recognition. Proc. IEEE **86**(11), 2278–2324 (1998)
18. LeCun, Y., Cortes, C., Burges, C.: Mnist handwritten digit database. AT&T Labs [Online], vol. 2, p. 18 (2010). http://yann.lecun.com/exdb/mnist
19. Li, W., Szczecinski, N.S., Hunt, A.J., Quinn, R.D.: A neural network with central pattern generators entrained by sensory feedback controls walking of a bipedal model. In: Lepora, N., Mura, A., Mangan, M., Verschure, P., Desmulliez, M., Prescott, T. (eds.) Living Machines 2016. LNCS (LNAI), vol. 9793, pp. 144–154. Springer, Cham (2016). https://doi.org/10.1007/978-3-319-42417-0_14
20. Liu, P., Qiu, X., Xuanjing, H.: Recurrent neural network for text classification with multi-task learning. In: IJCAI International Joint Conference on Artificial Intelligence, January 2016, pp. 2873–2879 (2016)
21. Maniezzo, V.: Genetic evolution of the topology and weight distribution of neural networks. IEEE Trans. Neural Netw. **5**(1), 39–53 (1994)
22. Mann, H.B., Whitney, D.R.: On a test of whether one of two random variables is stochastically larger than the other. Ann. Math. Stat. **18**(1), 50–60 (1947)
23. Martinetz, T., Schulten, K.: A neural network for robot control: cooperation between neural units as a requirement for learning. Comput. Electr. Eng. **19**(4), 315–332 (1993)
24. Mccann, M.T., Jin, K.H., Unser, M.: Deep learning for visual understanding convolutional neural networks for inverse problems in imaging. IEEE Signal Process. Mag. **34**(6), 85–95 (2017)
25. McLean, D.R., van Ooyen, A., Graham, B.P.: Continuum model for tubulin-driven neurite elongation. Neurocomputing **58–60**, 511–516 (2004)
26. Paszke, A., et al.: Automatic differentiation in PyTorch (2017)
27. Rawat, W., Wang, Z.: Deep convolutional neural networks for image classification: a comprehensive review. Neural Comput. **29**, 1–98 (2017)
28. Rosenblatt, F.: The Perceptron: a probabilistic model for information storage and organization in the brain. Psychol. Rev. **65**(6), 386–408 (1958)
29. Suganuma, M., Shirakawa, S., Nagao, T.: A genetic programming approach to designing convolutional neural network architectures. In: Proceedings of the Genetic and Evolutionary Computation Conference, pp. 497–504. ACM (2017)
30. Szczecinski, N.S., Hunt, A.J., Quinn, R.D.: A functional subnetwork approach to designing synthetic nervous systems that control legged robot locomotion. Front. Neurorobotics **11**, 37 (2017)
31. Szczecinski, N.S., Quinn, R.D.: Leg-local neural mechanisms for searching and learning enhance robotic locomotion. Biol. Cybern. **112**(1–2), 99–112 (2017)
32. Wysoski, S.G., Benuskova, L., Kasabov, N.: Evolving spiking neural networks for audiovisual information processing. Neural Netw. **23**(7), 819–835 (2010)
33. Zaremba, W., Sutskever, I., Vinyals, O.: Recurrent neural network regularization. arXiv (2015)

34. Zhang, H., Wang, Z., Liu, D.: A comprehensive review of stability analysis of continuous-time recurrent neural networks. IEEE Trans. Neural Netw. Learn. Syst. **25**(7), 1229–1262 (2014)
35. Zoph, B., Vasudevan, V., Shlens, J., Le, Q.V.: Learning transferable architectures for scalable image recognition. In: Proceedings of the IEEE Conference on Computer Vision and Pattern Recognition, pp. 8697–8710 (2018)

Characterization of Biomimetic Peristaltic Pumping System Based on Flexible Silicone Soft Robotic Actuators as an Alternative for Technical Pumps

Falk Esser[1,2,3]([✉]) [iD], Friederike Krüger[1], Tom Masselter[1,2] [iD], and Thomas Speck[1,2,3] [iD]

[1] Plant Biomechanics Group, Faculty of Biology,
Botanic Garden University Freiburg, Freiburg im Breisgau, Germany
Falk.esser@biologie.uni-freiburg.de
[2] FMF – Freiburg Materials Research Center, Freiburg im Breisgau, Germany
[3] Cluster of Excellence *liv*MatS @ FIT –Freiburg Center for Interactive
Materials and Bioinspired Technologies, University of Freiburg,
Freiburg im Breisgau, Germany

Abstract. In nature and technology fluids are often transported directionally via pumping systems. Technical pumps often show signs of wear caused by abrasion of moving parts, erosion and fluid impurities, which can result in damage and excessive noise in the system. Pumping systems for electric cars (in e.g. cooling systems) should emit little noise as combustion engine noise, which normally 'masks' the noise caused by pumping systems, is missing. The biological peristaltic pumping principle was identified as having the highest biomimetic potential in terms of space requirements and transport capabilities (flow rate, pressure and transported media) for a transfer into silent and safe pumping systems. The peristaltic pumping of the esophagus directionally transports various media in a simple, silent and secure way and was therefore used as a biological role model for abstraction and technical implementation. For the present study, a biomimetic tubular pump was developed allowing for a simple, quiet and safe transport of a wide variety of Newtonian and non-Newtonian fluids with variable viscosity. The system is actuated by eight silicone-based pneumatic ring actuators with an elliptical inner conduit longitudinal diameter of 2 cm. The influence of actuation frequency and varying peristaltic actuation patterns on the flow rate achieved were investigated. The results indicate that the developed flexible and elastic silicone-based self-priming peristaltic pump achieves sufficient flow rates over 250 l/h and can serve as an alternative to conventional technical pumps in the field of electro-mobility.

Keywords: Silicone-based ring actuators · Soft robotics ·
Peristaltic pumping system · Biomimetics

© Springer Nature Switzerland AG 2019
U. Martinez-Hernandez et al. (Eds.): Living Machines 2019, LNAI 11556, pp. 101–113, 2019.
https://doi.org/10.1007/978-3-030-24741-6_9

1 Introduction

Peristaltic pumping in nature and technology is used to safely transport a wide variety of media. In technics most peristaltic pumps are roller or finger driven [1]. These pumps are built with a rigid framing and their only flexible part is the tube or hose being compressed via rollers or fingers. Furthermore technical pumping systems like rotary and positive displacement pumps, e.g. centrifugal pumps, rotary vane pumps and gear pumps are the technological state-of-the-art with flow rates from 100 to 1000 l/h for automotive coolant pumps depending on engine conditions [2, 3].

In contrast to their technical counterparts, biological peristaltic pumps are usually highly integrated and specifically adapted systems, which can only be considered to a limited extent detached from the complex overall system [4, 5]. They consist of flexible self-healing composite materials and contraction is generated by means of flexible actuators (muscles) integrated into the pump. This arrangement does not require bearings or moving parts that rotate or translate and thereby offers advantages over technical systems in terms of wear [4]. In addition, biological peristaltic pumps can realize a continuous flow of viscous liquids containing solids [4, 6]. The example of the (ciberial) "mouth" pump of the mosquito shows that different Newtonian and non-Newtonian fluids can be transported with one single pump [4, 7]. In addition, biological pumps in general have a long service life and are flexible, quiet and adaptive systems [4, 5, 8–10].

In nature, peristaltic pumps are formed mostly by soft hollow organs (e.g. mammalian esophagus and intestines, dorsal vessels of arthropods) [4, 6, 8], in which a contraction wave runs along the conduit fully closing the conduit diameter [4, 6, 11]. The biological peristaltic pumping principle was identified as having the highest biomimetic potential for a transfer into a technical application [9, 11, 12]. The peristaltic pumping of the esophagus directionally transports various media in a simple and secure way, via propagative anterograde peristalsis (forwards) or via propagative retrograde peristalsis (backwards) [6, 13]. Therefore the esophagus was used as biological role model for abstraction and technical implementation in our biomimetic soft-robotic demonstrators [11, 12] (Fig. 1).

In principle, peristaltic pumping allows for not only reducing wear but also offers solutions for other technical problems often seen in conventional technical pumping systems like cavitation and excessive noise. These problems may become critical in various technological fields, as e.g. cooling systems in electro-mobility or in medical applications, where a safe and reliable (cavitation-free) pumping of liquids is essential. The advantages of natural peristaltic pumping are being transferred to technology in various soft-robotic pumping systems utilizing different types of actuators, ranging from actuators with pneumatic chambers, dielectric elastomer actuators to shape memory alloys and magnetic actuators [11, 14–20]. In 2017, Dirven et al. presented a biomimetic swallowing robot as a medical, rheological instrument for characterization of different bolus viscosities [21]. The system consists of silicone FEA (fluidic elastomer) ring actuators that can contract via air-filled chambers. This system, however, as others, requires a stiff frame [20, 22]. For example the pressure actuated peristaltic pump system patented by Feygin (1993) requires rigid jackets as an expansion

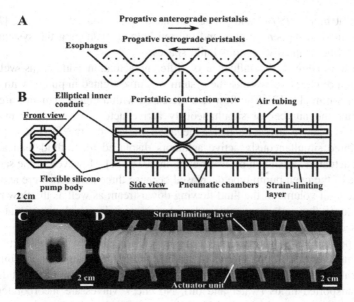

Fig. 1. Schematic drawing of peristaltic principle and silicone-based biomimetic peristaltic pump (SBPP). **A:** Two modes of peristalsis pumping – propagative anterograde (forwards) peristalsis and propagative retrograde (backwards) peristalsis – are shown in a conduit. The dotted lines represent the conduit walls at rest. The peristaltic contraction wave propagates along the conduit length facilitating transport in one direction. **B:** Simplified blueprint of the soft robotic silicone-based biomimetic peristalsis pump (SBPP). The basic biological principle of peristaltic contraction wave is abstracted into consecutively pressurized pneumatic chambers occluding the conduit. **C** and **D:** Fully flexible soft robotic silicone-based biomimetic peristalsis pump (SBPP) with a strain-limiting layer, which is flexible inextensible in the radial direction but allows for flexibility in longitudinal direction. **C:** Frontal view of the SBPP. **D:** Side view of the SBPP (reproduced with permission. [11] Copyright 2018, Springer Nature).

limitation for the tubular bladders used as actuators [20]. A rigid framing is not needed in the natural system for pumping.

In contrast to these systems, we achieved a fully flexible design with a silicone-based biomimetic peristaltic pump (SBPP) (Fig. 1 B–D) [11]. Eight soft-robotic silicone pneumatic actuators bonded together form the flexible tube pump, which is outfitted with a strain-limiting layer on the outside, which consists of polypropylene tape (curling ribbon). By wrapping the tape around the silicone actuators the peristaltic pump remains flexible in longitudinal direction but becomes inextensible in the radial direction, achieving an entirely flexible system capable of transport without rigid framing. In pressurization of the pneumatic chambers, the strain-limiting layer on the outside directs all expansion inward and the inner conduit is occluded. The system is able to produce sufficient flow rates by consecutive activation of the actuators with a peristaltic activation pattern. Flexible silicone rubber material EcoflexTM 00-50 (EF50; KauPo Plankenhorn, e.K.) was used as base material for actuator production. EF50 is a two component platinum-catalyzed addition cure silicone that is easy to mix and exhibits a short curing time ($\approx$3 h) at room temperature. EF50 was selected due to its high strain at break (980%) and for its sufficient water and oil resistance [23]. The whole systems can be bent, pulled and twisted without damaging the system, so the system could be adapted to various build spaces.

In previous studies, the influence of different actuation patterns as well as the incorporation of check valves into the system was investigated in pumps with a tubing diameter of 8 mm [11, 12]. The flow rate increased with a higher actuation frequency, but not with the number of simultaneously active actuators. A higher number of simultaneously active actuators had a negative impact on the flow rate [11]. For example, three simultaneously active actuators displaced more fluid than a smaller number of actuators, as shown by Esser et al. in 2018 [11]. However, at the same time, the volume of the open pump tube decreased because three actuators were active. This reduced the total volume of the fluid flowing downstream as well as the flow rate. The highest volume flow rate was achieved with a pattern in which the actuators were activated sequentially one at a time [11].

In the present study we characterize the developed SBPP with higher tubing longitudinal diameter of 20 mm in terms of produced flow rate and power consumption at two different sequential activation durations, activation patterns and transport directions for two transported fluids (water and oil). No check valves are incorporated in the system. The main goal of this study is the biomimetic implementation of peristalsis into a flexible, silent, robust, energy efficient, space-saving and low cost technical application for the usage in combustion engines, electric engines and cooling systems.

2   Materials and Methods

2.1   Characterization of Volume Flow Rate of the SBPP

In this study the SBPP is further characterized in view of the influencing factors on the volume flow rate. First measurements of influences on the volume flow rate produced by the SBPP with a greater longitudinal tubing diameter of 2 cm were performed with water as transport fluid. Oil was used in a second set of measurements in order to clarify if the SBPP is able to transport more viscous fluids with a sufficient volume flow. In Table 1 the properties of the two fluids are highlighted:

Table 1. Properties of the test fluids at 20 °C

Fluid	Kinematic viscosity υ [m²/s]	Density ρ [kg/m³]	Dynamic viscosity μ [N*s/m²]	Ref.
Water	$1.00*10^{-6}$	998.2	$1.00*10^{-3}$	[24]
Oil	$4.72*10^{-5}$	830.6	$3.75*10^{-2}$	[25]

Additionally in order to investigate differences between the pumps within the production process, four equally produced SBPPs were characterized with respect to their produced flow rate while transporting water when reversing the flow direction and adding a pause within the actuation cycle (Table 2) at three different actuation durations (AD) (75 ms, 100 ms and 125 ms) of the individual actuators. The AD describes how long each actuator was pressurized during an actuation cycle. The reverse patterns were only used for the characterization with water as transport fluid.

Table 2. Peristaltic actuation patterns of the silicone-based biomimetic peristaltic pump (SBPP), one actuation cycle per pattern is shown. O: open state, X: occluded state.

Pattern 1	Pattern 1 reverse	Pattern 2 incl. pause	Pattern 2 incl. pause reverse
XOOOOOOO	OOOOOOOX	XOOOOOOO	OOOOOOOX
OXOOOOOO	OOOOOOXO	OXOOOOOO	OOOOOOXO
OOXOOOOO	OOOOOXOO	OOXOOOOO	OOOOOXOO
OOOXOOOO	OOOOXOOO	OOOXOOOO	OOOOXOOO
OOOOXOOO	OOOXOOOO	OOOOXOOO	OOOXOOOO
OOOOOXOO	OOXOOOOO	OOOOOXOO	OOXOOOOO
OOOOOOXO	OXOOOOOO	OOOOOOXO	OXOOOOOO
OOOOOOOX	XOOOOOOO	OOOOOOOX	XOOOOOOO
		OOOOOOOO	OOOOOOOO

For comparability of data by Esser et al. (2018) [11] with test series of the present study, the frequencies are here related to the actual actuation durations of the solenoid valves (Fig. 2 (7)) as in Esser et al. (2018). The frequency of 5 Hz equaled 200 ms AD, 3 Hz equaled 334 ms AD and 1 Hz equaled 1000 ms AD.

Fig. 2. Test bench with biomimetic peristaltic pump. (1) Camera setup with transmitted light table to characterize the expansion of the individual actuators. (2) Gas volume flow sensor (mounted on the rear). (3) System air pressure sensor. (4) Pressure gauge for setting the system pressure. (5) Data acquisition devices. (6) SBPP: silicone-based biomimetic peristaltic pump. (7) Solenoid valves. (8) Actuator air pressure sensors. (9) Microcontroller. Scale bar: 5 cm.

A custom-built test bench was used for characterizing the contraction rate of the actuators, the fluid flow rate produced by the pump as well as pressure and pump power consumption (Fig. 2) [11].

In the characterization the actuators were pressurized with 0.4 bar to guarantee full closure of the inner conduit, as shown by Esser et al. 2018 [11]. The actuators were pressurized via solenoid valves activated in the peristaltic actuation patterns via the Arduino based microcontroller. To determine the volume flow rate, the transported fluid volume was measured via weighing after 50 actuation cycles and each pump was tested 10 times. In order to determine the power consumption of the pumps, a gas volume flow sensor was added to the pump test bench and recorded the volume flow of the system air during the measurements. In addition, the hose diameter at the inlet and outlet was adapted to the target parameters of 2 cm. This system allows for a feasibility study as a principle demonstrator for a novel biomimetic peristaltic pumping system as an alternative for technical pumping systems. In order to identify the suction pressure the geodetic rise height was estimated to 0.1 bar [26–28].

By means of a gas volume flow sensor it was possible to measure the air volume required for the actuation. From this value the power consumption can be calculated, and, paired with the fluid volume flow and the fluid pressure, this allows for calculating the pump efficiency. The sensor data was recorded using the DAQ and a self-programmed LabVIEW program. For the determination of the pumping capacity, the pressure difference along the tube has to be assessed. The pressure difference Δp can be determined by subtracting the suction pressure from the air pressure. The hydraulic power P_H of a pumping system is determined by the following formula (in the case of laminar flow) (Eq. 1):

$$P_H = Q\Delta p = \frac{\pi r^4 \Delta p^2}{8l\mu} \ [W] \tag{1}$$

With volume flow Q, radius of the tube r, pressure difference along the tube Δp, length of the considered section of tube l, and dynamic viscosity of the fluid μ. The hydraulic power is obtained by multiplying the volume flow Q by the generated pressure difference Δp [26, 29, 30]. This formula can also be used to calculate the power consumption P_M [31]. Here Q corresponds to the measured gas volume and thus to the consumed compressed air.

The efficiency of pumps η_P can be calculated from the power consumption and the hydraulic power [27, 29, 32].

$$\eta_P = \frac{P_H}{P_M} = \frac{Q * \Delta p}{P_M} \tag{2}$$

With hydraulic power P_H, power consumption P_M, volume flow rate Q and the pressure difference Δp.

2.2   Statistics

The software GNU R 3.4.3 was used for statistical analyses (R Core Team, 2017) [33]. We performed a two-way ANOVA on ranked transformed data, having checked for normal distribution (Shapiro–Wilk test) and homoscedasticity of variances in advance (Levene test). This allowed for determining the significance of correlation between varying actuation frequencies and actuation pressures on actuator occlusion rate, as also different actuation frequencies and the presence of check valves in the setup, on the transported fluid volume of the SBPP pumping with different peristaltic patterns. Post-hoc tests were performed via multiple comparisons using Tukey's test.

3   Results

3.1   Characterization of the SBPP with Water as Transported Fluid

In the characterization of SBPP with water as transported fluid four different activation patterns and three different activation durations were used. The results of the volume flow rate measurements for four SBPP are presented in Fig. 3(A). The four pumps were tested 10 times with 50 actuation cycles during each individual test. In a direct comparison of the volume flows the pumps achieved the highest flow rates with pattern 2 (which includes a pause). An influence of the AD was observed as the pumps achieved higher peak values at 75 ms AD than at 100 ms AD, but the median of the volume flows was higher at 100 ms AD (276 l/h) than at 75 ms AD (270 l/h) and 125 ms AD (230 l/h) (Fig. 3A). The flow rate decreased with longer AD or lower actuation frequency, on average the pumps transported up to 40 l/h less with 125 ms AD than with shorter AD. The range of the difference of the volume flows between the pumps was smaller at 125 ms AD (11 l/h at pattern 1) and 100 ms AD (14 l/h at pattern 1) than at 75 ms AD (38 l/h at pattern 1), this was also observed within the other actuation patterns. The reversal of flow direction had only marginal influence on the flow rate and the results indicate no significant difference in volume flow rate between the different directions of flow.

The average power consumption of the pumps at 100 ms AD and 125 AD were below those at 75 ms (Fig. 3B). A difference in power consumption could be observed also between the different actuation patterns. Pattern 2 incl. pause, in which a pause occurs after an actuation cycle, shows lower power consumption as no air is consumed during the pause. No significant difference could be observed upon reversal of the actuation (Fig. 3B). For the analysis of the performance and efficiency of the pump, pressure sensors at the pump inlet and outlet were used to determine the pressure difference across the pump. Using the hydrostatic equation and manual measurement of the suction height of the pump, an initial estimate of the pump performance could be made. The SBPPs had a suction height of 1.2 m. This corresponds to a pressure difference of approximately 0.1 bar (calculated by hydrostatic equation). With a flow rate of over 276 l/h (median achieved with pattern 2 incl. pause at 100 ms AD) a pump power of 0.77 W can be calculated. These data were used for a quantitative estimation of the efficiency as a measure of the pump efficiency, which results for the SBPP in an efficiency of 6.6% when transporting water.

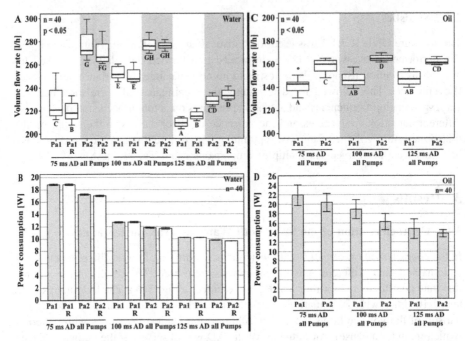

Fig. 3. Volume flow rates of water (**A, B**) and oil (**C, D**) of four silicone-based biomimetic peristaltic pumps with different actuation patterns and three actuation durations (AD), and the respective power consumption. (**A**): Volume flows of water produced by the pumps with three different AD. The highest volume flow rates are achieved with pattern 2 (at 75 ms AD of 298 l/h, at 100 ms AD of 286 l/h, at 125 ms AD of 241 l/h). The capital letters represent significance levels; different letters correspond to a significant difference in the achieved volume flow with p-values below 0.05. The sample size for the box plots is n = 40 each test consisting of 50 actuation cycles. (**B**): Power consumption of the pumps for different actuation durations and patterns. Pa1: Pattern 1; Pa1R: Pattern 1 Reverse; Pa2: Pattern 2 incl. Pause; Pa2R: Pattern 2 incl. Pause Reverse. Light grey bars indicate results in normal flow direction and white bars indicate results in reverse flow direction. The power consumption was averaged over the four pumps, error bars show the standard deviation, n = 40 each test consisting of 50 actuation cycles. (**C**): Volume flows of oil produced by the pumps with three different AD. The highest volume flow rates are achieved with pattern 2 (at 75 AD of 164 l/h, at 100 ms AD of 169 l/h, at 125 ms AD of 166 l/h). The capital letters are significance levels; different letters correspond to a significant difference in the achieved volume flow with p-values below 0.05. The sample size for the box plots is n = 40 each test consisting of 50 actuation cycles. (**D**): Power consumption of the pumps for different actuation durations and patterns. Pa1: Pattern 1; Pa1R: Pattern 1 Reverse; Pa2: Pattern 2 incl. Pause; Pa2R: Pattern 2 incl. Pause Reverse. Light grey bars indicate results in normal flow direction and white bars indicate results in reverse flow direction. The power consumption was averaged over the four pumps, error bars show the standard deviation, n = 40 each test consisting of 50 actuation cycles.

3.2   Characterization of the SBPP with Oil as Transported Fluid

The volume flow rate measurements with water indicated no significant difference in flow rate and power consumption between reversed and normal pumping direction. The pump was constructed with no preferred geometric direction influencing internal flow. As a consequence, only the forward transporting patterns were investigated in the characterization of flow rate with oil as transported medium.

The characterization of the flow rate of the pumps with oil indicated an influence of the actuation pattern on the flow rate as the highest flow rates were achieved with pattern 2. In a direct comparison of the volume flows, the pumps achieved higher peak values at 100 ms AD than at 75 and 125 ms AD, the median of the volume flows was higher at 100 ms AD (164 l/h) than at 75 ms AD (160 l/h) and 125 ms AD (161 l/h) (Fig. 3C). The flow rate decreased with shorter AD, on average the pumps transported up to 4 l/h less with 75 ms AD than with longer AD.

The average power consumption of the pumps decreased with longer AD, consumption at 100 ms AD and 125 AD were below those at 75 ms (Fig. 3D). A difference in power consumption could be observed also between the different actuation patterns. Pattern 2, in which a pause occurs after an actuation cycle, shows lower consumption because no air is consumed during the pause (Fig. 3D).

For the analysis of the performance and efficiency of the pump, pressure sensors at the pump inlet and outlet were used to determine the pressure difference along the pump. Using the hydrostatic equation and manual measurement of the suction height of the pump, an initial estimate of the pump performance could be made. The SBPPs had a suction height of 1.2 m. This corresponds to a pressure difference of approximately 0.1 bar (calculated by hydrostatic equation). With a flow rate of over 164.7 l/h (median achieved with pattern 2 at 100 ms AD) a pump power of 0.45 W can be calculated. These data were used for a quantitative estimation of the efficiency as a measure of the pump efficiency; which results for the SBPP in an efficiency of 2.8% when transporting oil.

4   Discussion

The silicone-based biomimetic peristaltic pumps with larger hose diameters (2.0 cm compared to 0.8 cm) at the inlet and outlet tested in the present study showed higher volume flows of more than 200 l/h (Fig. 3) compared to results from previous studies with maximum volume flows of 60 l/h [5]. In the previous test series the volume flow was restricted by the small diameter of the inlet and outlet (0.8 cm), whereas in the present test series the flow rate occurs to be limited by the performance of the pumps. The latter can be inferred from the finding that with an increase of the inlet diameter from 0.8 cm (in previous tests) to 2.0 cm in the present test series the volume flow increases by a factor of approx. 3-5 "only" (with 2.0 cm inlet) whilst the increase in radius of the inlet by 2.5 theoretically would allow for an increase of volume flow by a factor of >39, as the radius influences volume flow with r4 (Eq. 1). Our data indicate that by utilizing actuation patterns with a pause the pumps produced significantly higher volume flows (up to 298 l/h at 75 ms AD for water (Fig. 3 A), up to 169 l/h at

100 ms for oil (Fig. 3C)). Reversal of the pumping direction had marginal effect on the volume flow rate, the values achieved were within the same range as for normal flow. This was consistent with the null hypothesis that the deformation of the actuators was not affected by the direction of actuation.

Furthermore our data show that mass inertia of the less viscous fluid affect the volume flow in a similar way as with increasing actuation duration (AD): the fluctuation within the measurements of the individual pumps decreased. The impact of mass inertia on the volume flow was probably further augmented by actuation patterns with pause. In this type of actuation pattern, after an actuation cycle, the inner conduit of the pump remained completely open for a short time, allowing the water already in motion to flow unhindered through the pump. According to Newton's law of inertia, a body retains its motion quantity if it is not prevented from doing so by external forces [29, 34]. Therefore, the fluid is considered to retain a large part of its momentum or kinematic energy after the pumping cycle, even when losses by closing actuators or wall friction are taken into account [34]. Before the mass momentum of inertia of the fluid is reduced, the next actuation cycle already started, whereby the pauses in the pump cycle showed a positive effect on the flow rate.

In direct comparison in between the four (equally produced SBPP) pumps a (small) difference in produced flow rate could be determined. This difference can be attributed to the manual manufacturing process. Also the pressure for actuator pressurization had to be adjusted manually to 0.4 bar after each pump change. This can lead to variations, which can result in the observed (small) differences between the pumps.

The highest volume flow rates could be achieved with water as transported fluid, over 100 l/h more than in the measurements with oil as transported fluid. For the oil measurements the same actuation pressure and actuation duration was used to enable a direct comparison. The reason for the lower volume flow rates is the higher viscosity of the oil (up to approx. 40 times higher than water see Table 1). In viscous liquids the particles are more strongly bound to each other and less mobile (internal friction) [24, 35]. The effect of internal friction can be simplified by the movement of two superimposed, interlocked molecule layers [24, 35]. When flowing, the molecules glide past each other, and in order to overcome the interlocking, a certain force is required [24, 35]. In viscous fluids like the oil this force needs to be higher than in less viscous fluid water. The oil is therefore more resistant to displacement in the pump tube. Accordingly, more energy has to be used to attain the same pressure in the actuators, which explains the higher power requirement (Fig. 3D). Due to the higher viscosity of the oil more energy was necessary to produce a flow and a lower overall volume flow rate was achieved (Fig. 3D) [24, 35].

The investigation of the power consumption in the transport of water and oil showed a decrease of the power demand over time with increasing actuation time, since the actuators are activated less frequently in the same time. The efficiency of the pump (for transport of water and oil) is low compared to technical peristaltic pumps (60 to 90% [1]). The used pneumatic drive of the SBPP has a strong negative influence on the efficiency. For the drive of the pump, a larger air volume is required in comparison to the delivery volume. An increase in pump efficiency can be achieved by using alternative actuators as e.g. electric drives or actuators (possible actuators include flexible dielectric elastomers or magnetic elastomers as base material for the tube actuated by electromagnets). In general, the efficiency of hydraulic and pneumatic drives is lower than that of mechanical drives as a result of pressure losses due to fluid friction in pipes and elements and as a result of leakage and flow losses in gaps (at hose attachments or between actuator elements) [26]. Additionally, the size of pressure chambers of each actuator could be decreased, to the extent that full closure of the inner conduit is still guaranteed. This could reduce overall air consumption and increase the efficiency of the pump. To increase the efficiency furthermore a smooth transition between active actuators could be incorporated into the system via proportional valves, resulting in a more sinus wave like motion [21].

5 Conclusion

The biomimetic silicone-based biomimetic peristaltic pumps (SBPPs) with a tubing diameter within the range of the most relevant target applications in engineering achieved a sufficient fluid flow rate by various peristaltic activation patterns. A short interruption (pause) of actuation within the activation pattern increased fluid transport, and decreased power consumption for certain durations or frequencies of actuation. In addition, a significant influence of the actuation duration on the flow rate was shown. The volume flow rate measurements with oil further indicate that a sufficient transport of viscous fluids is possible. For future studies higher actuation pressures and actuation patterns with more actuators at the same time should be investigated to achieve higher volume flow rates. The influence factors for the transport of viscous fluids should be investigated in more detail.

In comparison with the demonstrators developed by Dirven et al. (2013) [14] and Suzuki and Nakamura [36], the SPBB distinguishes itself from other demonstrators by its simple and completely flexible design and the significantly higher volume flows produced (up to 4 l/min produced by the SBPP compared to 2 l/min flow rate of water produced be the demonstrator of Suzuki and Nakamura [36]).

The developed biomimetic SBPP is an efficient, self-priming, flexible alternative to conventional pumping systems, e.g. for electro-mobility in which pumping not only has to be efficient and durable, but also silent. In future studies alternative electrically based actuation principles will be developed and utilized to actuate an electrically based biomimetic soft-robotic tube pump.

Acknowledgements. We thank Marc Desmuliez (Hyatt Watt University Edinburgh) and various colleagues within the framework of the cluster of excellence 'Living Materials Systems (*liv*MatS)', funded by the Deutsche Forschungsgemeinschaft (DFG, German Research Foundation) under Germany's Excellence Strategy – EXC-2193/1–390951807, for inspiring scientific discussions.

References

1. Nesbitt, B.: When is a tube not a tube? When it's a pump! World Pumps **2004**, 20–23 (2004)
2. Krutzsch, W.C., Cooper, P.: Introduction: classification and selection of pumps. In: Karassik, I.J., Cooper, P., Messina, J.P., and Heald, C.C. (eds.) Pump Handbook. Mc Graw Hill (2008)
3. Pierburg Pump Technology GmbH: Water circulation pump–compact and versatile (2018). http://www.kspg.com
4. Vogel, S.: Living in a physical world X. Pumping fluids through conduits. J. Biosci. **32**, 207–222 (2007)
5. Bach, D., Schmich, F., Masselter, T., Speck, T.: A review of selected pumping systems in nature and engineering—potential biomimetic concepts for improving displacement pumps and pulsation damping. Bioinspir. Biomim. **10**, 051001 (2015)
6. Cannon, W.B.: The nature of gastric peristalsis. Am. J. Physiol.-Leg. Content. **29**, 250–266 (1911)
7. Kim, B.H., Kim, H.K., Lee, S.J.: Experimental analysis of the blood-sucking mechanism of female mosquitoes. J. Exp. Biol. **214**, 1163–1169 (2011)
8. Vogel, S.: Nature's pumps. Am. Sci. **82**, 464–471 (1994)
9. Esser, F., Bach, D., Masselter, T., Speck, T.: Nature as concept generator for novel biomimetic pumping systems. In: Kesel, A.B. and Zehren, D. (eds.) Bionik: Patente aus der Natur, Tagungsbeiträge zum 8. Bionik-Kongress in Bremen, pp. 116–122 (2017)
10. Fratzl, P.: Biomimetic materials research: what can we really learn from nature's structural materials? J. Roy. Soc. Interface **4**, 637–642 (2007)
11. Esser, F., Krüger, F., Masselter, T., Speck, T.: Development and characterization of a novel biomimetic peristaltic pumping system with flexible silicone-based soft robotic ring actuators. In: Vouloutsi, V., et al. (eds.) Living Machines 2018. LNCS (LNAI), vol. 10928, pp. 157–167. Springer, Cham (2018). https://doi.org/10.1007/978-3-319-95972-6_17
12. Esser, F., Steger, T., Bach, D., Masselter, T., Speck, T.: Development of novel foam-based soft robotic ring actuators for a biomimetic peristaltic pumping system. In: Mangan, M., Cutkosky, M., Mura, A., Verschure, P.F.M.J., Prescott, T., Lepora, N. (eds.) Living Machines 2017. LNCS (LNAI), vol. 10384, pp. 138–147. Springer, Cham (2017). https://doi.org/10.1007/978-3-319-63537-8_12
13. Sinnott, M.D., Cleary, P.W., Arkwright, J.W., Dinning, P.G.: Investigating the relationships between peristaltic contraction and fluid transport in the human colon using smoothed particle hydrodynamics. Comput. Biol. Med. **42**, 492–503 (2012)
14. Dirven, S., Xu, W., Cheng, L.K., Allen, J., Bronlund, J.: Biologically-inspired swallowing robot for investigation of texture modified foods. Int. J. Biomechatronics Biomed. Robot. **2**, 163–171 (2013)
15. Yoshihama, S., Takano, S., Yamada, Y., Nakamura, T., Kato, K.: Powder conveyance experiments with peristaltic conveyor using a pneumatic artificial muscle. In: 2016 IEEE International Conference on Advanced Intelligent Mechatronics (AIM), pp. 1539–1544 (2016)
16. McCoul, D., Pei, Q.: Tubular dielectric elastomer actuator for active fluidic control. Smart Mater. Struct. **24**, 105016 (2015)
17. Sun, X., Hao, Y., Guo, S., Ye, X., Yan, X.: The development of a new type of compound peristaltic micropump. In: 2008 IEEE International Conference on Robotics and Biomimetics, pp. 698–702 (2009)
18. Lotz, P., Matysek, M., Schlaak, H.F.: Peristaltic pump made of dielectric elastomer actuators. In: Electroactive Polymer Actuators and Devices (EAPAD) 2009. International Society for Optics and Photonics, p. 72872 (2009)

19. Fuhrer, R., Schumacher, C.M., Zeltner, M., Stark, W.J.: Soft iron/silicon composite tubes for magnetic peristaltic pumping: frequency-dependent pressure and volume flow. Adv. Funct. Mater. **23**, 3845–3849 (2013)

20. Feygin, I.: Pressure actuated peristaltic pump (1993). https://patents.google.com/patent/US5273406A/en

21. Dirven, S., Allen, J., Xu, W.P., Cheng, L.K.: Soft-robotic esophageal swallowing as a clinically-inspired bolus rheometry technique. Meas. Sci. Technol. **28**, 035701 (2017)

22. Ilievski, F., Mazzeo, A.D., Shepherd, R.F., Chen, X., Whitesides, G.M.: Soft robotics for chemists. Angew. Chem. Int. Ed. **50**, 1890–1895 (2011)

23. Smooth-on Inc. Safety data sheets (2018). https://www.smooth-on.com

24. Munson, B.R., Young, D.F., Okiishi, T.H.: Fundamentals of Fluid Mechanics, 6th edn. Wiley, New York (2010)

25. Fuchs Schmierstoffe GmbH. Datasheet TITAN G 52529. https://www.fuchs.com/de

26. Watter, H.: Hydraulik und Pneumatik. Springer, Wiesbaden (2017). https://doi.org/10.1007/978-3-658-18555-8

27. Karassik, I.J., Messina, J.P., Cooper, P., Heald, C.C.: Pump Handbook. Mcgraw-Hill Professional, New York (2008)

28. Stepanoff, A.J.: Definitionen und Terminologie. In: Stepanoff, A.J. (ed.) Radial- und Axialpumpen: Theorie, pp. 16–23. Springer, Heidelberg (1957). https://doi.org/10.1007/978-3-662-25101-0_2

29. Tschöke, H., Hölz†, H.: Verdrängerpumpen. In: Grote, K.-H., Feldhusen, J. (eds.) Dubbel, pp. P12–P25. Springer, Heidelberg (2011). https://doi.org/10.1007/978-3-642-17306-6_193

30. Vogel, S.: Comparative Biomechanics: Life's Physical World, 2nd edn. Princeton University Press, Princeton (2013)

31. Wang, T., Ren, H.: Reduction of power consumption for fluidic soft robots using energy recovery technique. In: 2016 IEEE International Conference on Information and Automation (ICIA), pp. 1403–1408 (2016)

32. Will, D., Gebhardt, N., Nollau, R., Herschel, D., Ströhl, H.: Pumpen und Motoren. In: Will, D., Gebhardt, N. (eds.) Hydraulik, pp. 121–176. Springer, Heidelberg (2011). https://doi.org/10.1007/978-3-540-79535-3_6

33. R Core Team: R: A language and environment for statistical computing (2017). https://www.R-project.org/

34. Gülich, J.F.: Kreiselpumpen. Handbuch für Entwicklung, Anlagenplanung und Betrieb. Springer, Heidelberg (2010). https://doi.org/10.1007/978-3-642-05479-2

35. Bauer, P.D.-I.G.: Physikalische Grundlagen. In: Ölhydraulik, pp. 17–53 (2011)

36. Suzuki, K., Nakamura, T.: Development of a peristaltic pump based on bowel peristalsis using for artificial rubber muscle. In: 2010 IEEE/RSJ International Conference on Intelligent Robots and Systems, pp. 3085–3090 (2010)

Adaptive Biomimetic Actuator Systems Reacting to Various Stimuli by and Combining Two Biological Snap-Trap Mechanics

Falk Esser[1,2,3(✉)] (ID), Frank D. Scherag[3,4] (ID), Simon Poppinga[1,2] (ID),
Anna Westermeier[1,5] (ID), Max D. Mylo[1,3] (ID), Tim Kampowski[1,2] (ID),
Georg Bold[1,2,5] (ID), Jürgen Rühe[3,4], and Thomas Speck[1,2,3] (ID)

[1] Plant Biomechanics Group, Faculty of Biology,
Botanic Garden University Freiburg, Freiburg im Breisgau, Germany
falk.esser@biologie.uni-freiburg.de
[2] FMF – Freiburg Materials Research Center, Freiburg im Breisgau, Germany
[3] Cluster of Excellence livMatS, @ FIT –Freiburg Center for Interactive
Materials and Bioinspired Technologies, University of Freiburg,
Freiburg im Breisgau, Germany
[4] Laboratory for Chemistry and Physics of Interfaces,
Department of Microsystems Engineering (IMTEK),
University of Freiburg, Freiburg im Breisgau, Germany
[5] Freiburg Center for Interactive Materials and Bioinspired Technologies (FIT),
Freiburg im Breisgau, Germany

Abstract. In our project we aim to develop living, adaptive and energy-autonomous material systems that show dynamic, life-like and non-equilibrium (energy) features. Our demonstrators represent a first step towards future implementation of novel technologies into industrial products and everyday life applications. In this study, we present bioinspired demonstrators which not only incorporate the actuation principles and motion behaviors of two carnivorous plant species (Venus flytrap and waterwheel plant), but also show adaptive responses to different environmental triggers. The presented actuator systems are the first to successfully implement several plant movement actuation and deformation systems into one versatile adaptive technical compliant mechanism.

Keywords: Bioinspired materials systems · Actuator systems ·
Hinge-less movements · Snap-trap · Snap-buckling · Kinematic amplification ·
Curved-line folding

1 Introduction

Living organisms like plants and animals have evolved a multitude of mechanisms for sensing and adapting to the environment, e.g. by harvesting and storing energy, which can then be used to power movement. Such adaptability is based on the respective structure's material building blocks, i.e. biological composites, which are to the very most part multifunctional [1]. Such systems are of very high interest as biological role models for the development of bioinspired technical living, adaptive and energy-autonomous

© Springer Nature Switzerland AG 2019
U. Martinez-Hernandez et al. (Eds.): Living Machines 2019, LNAI 11556, pp. 114–121, 2019.
https://doi.org/10.1007/978-3-030-24741-6_10

material systems. Our main goal is to use, combine and advance bioinspired paradigms and patterns for the development of novel dynamic, life-like, non-equilibrium materials systems. In this preliminary study, we concentrate on constructing and experimentally testing demonstrators, which can snap shut and re-open by different actuation and deformation principles in response to two different external stimuli and/or changing environmental conditions. The further demonstrator generations, despite being made from purely artificial materials, work by these bioinspired compliant mechanisms. They are currently being developed and will incorporate characteristics of the motion behavior and actuation principles with varying degree of resemblance to the natural Venus flytrap and waterwheel plant resulting in technical chimera demonstrators with compliant movement principles.

The biological role models, the Venus flytrap (*Dionaea muscipula*) and the waterwheel plant (*Aldrovanda vesiculosa*), are two closely related carnivorous plants, which are able to sense prey and perform very fast catching movements upon triggering of sensitive hairs on the trap lobes [2–4] (Fig. 1). In both species, the traps are modified leaves consisting of two lobes connected via a midrib (Fig. 1B, C) [2].

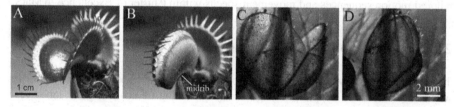

Fig. 1. Trap movement of *Dionaea muscipula* (A, B) and *Aldrovanda vesiculosa* (C, D). (A) The trap of *Dionaea muscipula* in open resting state, with the lobes showing an outwards curvature. (B) The trap after snapping. The curvature of the lobes is reversed and now inwardly directed. (C) The trap of *Aldrovanda vesiculosa* in open resting state with a straight midrib. (D) After triggering, the trap is closed and the curvature of the midrib changed but no change in curvature of the lobes has occurred. Images modified after [3].

The aerial traps of *Dionaea muscipula* are approximately 2 cm long and the lobes typically close within 100–300 ms [2, 5]. The underwater traps of *Aldrovanda vesiculosa* are significantly smaller (between 2–4 mm long) and close within approximately 20–100 ms [2, 3, 6]. The trap shutting of *Dionaea muscipula* is the result of a combination of a turgor change-based slower movement, and a second passive, fast movement by the release of stored elastic energy due to a sudden geometric change of its trap lobes (snap-buckling) [2–4]. The trap lobes of *Aldrovanda vesiculosa* close via a rapid turgor change of epidermal cells located near the midrib in combination with the release of prestress stored in the initially bent midrib. Due to kinematic coupling to the midrib, the lobes move towards each other [3]. The lobes of *Aldrovanda vesiculosa* do not change curvature during trap closure.

In literature, some artificial Venus flytraps have already been described using mostly stiff base materials for the lobes, like the system of Kim et al. [7]. This system has bi-stable artificial lobes made from asymmetrically laminated carbon fiber reinforced prepregs

(CFRP) using shape memory alloy (SMA) springs to actuate the lobes. Besides this example, there are various actuator systems described in literature to realize closing motions. For example, hydrogel bilayer systems with an enzyme triggered closure movement [8], pneumatic actuation opening of a flexible 3D-printed "Venus flytrap" with two layered lobes (closing by pressure release) [9], pneumatic closure of the *Aldrovanda vesiculosa* inspired Flectofold system for applications in architecture [10, 11], or a non-contact magnetic drive of the CFRP closure [12].

In this study, we will highlight novel actuator systems implementing both movement principles of the Venus flytrap and the waterwheel plant. We abstracted the basic snap-trap form of the plants into a foil model, which was able to perform a closure movement of its "lobes" via kinematic coupling by curved folds (inspired by *Aldrovanda*) and an inverse snap-buckling movement for opening (inspired by *Dionaea*). To drive these movements we used pneumatic actuators, thermally driven shape memory alloy springs and magnetic displacement of attached magnets. Additionally, we will show the possibility of energy storage and movement locking via hydrogel based actuators. The novel actuator systems presented in this study can serve as a basic outline for developments of smart bioinspired and autonomous demonstrators with tailored motion sequences and movement speeds within Cluster of Excellence *liv*MatS.

2   Compliant Foil Model Demonstrator

The basic morphology of the two carnivorous plants (two lobes connected by a midrib) was abstracted into a simple planar geometry consisting of two triangular lobes vertically connected by a rectangle that was joined by two circles as "ears" for actuation (Fig. 2A). The sketch was printed onto a foil and cut out (coated copying film 5001476 with 0.1 mm thickness from Streit GmbH & Co). The foil was buckled at the

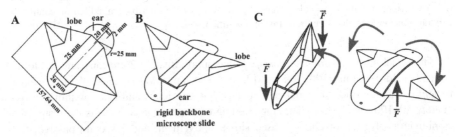

Fig. 2. Compliant foil model demonstrator. (A) Technical sketch of simplified bioinspired geometry (carnivorous plant trap morphology). (B) The foil was folded at the connection of the triangles (lobes) to the rectangle. An acrylic microscope slide was attached to the rectangle as (modifiable) backbone. (C) Left: Closure movement of the lobes in response to an applied downward force to the "ears". Right: Snap-buckling of the backbone in response to an applied bending force to the backbone, resulted in an opening of the lobes.

connection of the triangles to the rectangle. An acrylic plastic microscope slide was fixed under the rectangle (same size) as a rigid backbone, to enhance structural mechanical stability (Fig. 2B). When the "ears" were pressed down manually, the lobes underwent a closing movement due to the curvature of the "ears" and their attachment points to the lobes (kinematic coupling, as present in the *Aldrovanda* trap). Alternatively, when the "ears" were fixed and the rigid backbone was moved upwards, this will result in the same movement. Applying an additional force exerted from below towards the center of the backbone will result in a bending of the backbone and cause a snap buckling motion (as present in *Dionaea*), which re-opened the lobes (Fig. 2C).

2.1 Actuator Systems for Closure Movement

For the actuation of the closing movement three different actuator systems were used. The demonstrator was actuated via pneumatic cushions (pneumatic model) (Fig. 3A–D), a shape memory alloy (SMA) spring was attached to the "ears" (thermal model) (Fig. 3E–G), or magnets attached to one "ear" and actuated contactless by a magnetic stirrer (magnetic model) (Fig. 3H–I). The pneumatic model was based on three pneumatic cushions in a frame (Fig. 3A) to which the "ears" of the demonstrator are fixed at the edge (adhesive tape). The cushions were pressurized via air-filled syringes (Fig. 3B). The two outer pneumatic cushions lifted the entire backbone, while the "ears" are fixed at the edge (adhesive tape), which resulted in a rather slow closing movement (>1 s) of the trap (Fig. 3C). By pressurizing the central pneumatic cushion, the curvature of the backbone was altered and the lobes open again quite fast (ms range) (Fig. 3D). After the pressure was released, the system returned to the initial state (Fig. 3B). The pneumatic system represented a dual actuation system with two distinctive activation stimuli.

In the second model, thermal actuation was used. The foil demonstrator was attached to an aluminum plate and its "ears" were connected by an SMA spring (Fig. 3E–G). An aluminum tube, through which the spring passed contact-free, was heated by means of an electrical resistor, which in turn heated the spring until it reached its threshold temperature (65 °C). Then the spring contracted and closed the trap within 50 s (Fig. 3E–G).

The third model utilized magnets to actuate the trap movement Fig. 3(H–I). Therefore, a magnet was attached to one "ear" and actuated contactless via a magnet stirrer. The rotating magnetic field deflected the magnet and caused a flapping movement (Fig. 3I).

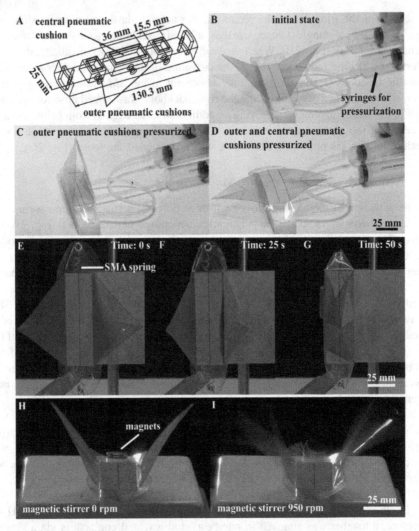

Fig. 3. Three different actuator systems of the demonstrator. The pneumatic actuator system (A)-(D): (A) A technical sketch of the pneumatic frame with two smaller outer pneumatic cushions for the closure movement and a central cushion for the opening movement. (B) The initial state. (C) The outer pneumatic cushions lifted the backbone, resulting in a slow closure of the model. (D) Additionally pressurizing the central cushion to bend the backbone and thereby opening the model by snapping open of the lobes. (E)-(G) The thermal actuation via contactless heating of a SMA spring that resulted in a contraction of the spring, which pulled the "ears" "back" and closed the model within 50 s (E)-(G)). (H)-(I) The magnetic actuation of the model. (H) Magnets were attached to one "ear" and actuated via the rotating magnetic field of a magnetic stirrer. (I) At 950 rpm the trap performed a flapping motion.

2.2   Locking of Demonstrator Movement via Hydrogel-Coating

The fourth model used a combination of two stimuli occurring together, which unlocked and initialized the model for possible movements. In this model a 3D printed backbone with a low glass transition temperature (T_G) was used, that became flexible when heated over 50 °C. A central groove of the backbone was filled with a cross-linked and surface-attached hydrogel. By drying the hydrogel ($T_G > 100$ °C) on a heating plate at 60 °C, it shrank, which lead to a curvature and prestressing of the backbone (which was heated over its T_G) and locked the demonstrator model in a snap-through state (Fig. 4A–B). Only the combination of the triggers heat (heated backbone over its T_G) and moisture (swelling and softening agent for the dry hydrogel layer, e.g. by steam) enabled the model to turn back to its initial state, in which a closing movement was possible (Fig. 4C). As a result, the hydrogel swelled and the prestressed backbone could return to its original straight state, thereby enabling the model to be actuated again (Fig. 4D–F). This system could also be used to harvest thermal energy, as shrinkage of the hydrogel causes the system to bend, thus storing elastic energy in the system.

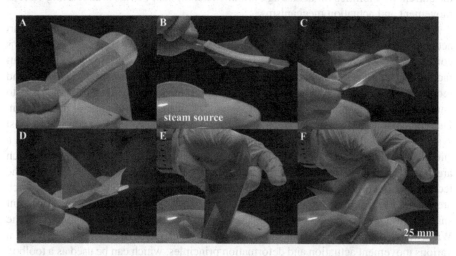

Fig. 4. Fourth demonstrator model with two stimuli serving as system initialization. (**A-B**) A curved 3D printed backbone with a low T_G (50 °C), covered with a hydrogel locked the model in the snap-trough state. (**C**) Hot steam rehydrated the hydrogel (which lead to a swelling) and heated the backbone (increasing its flexibility). The backbone straightened and the model returned to its initial state (**D**), thereby enabling it for closure via kinematic amplification (**E**) or opening via snap-buckling instability (**F**).

3 Conclusion and Outlook

In this preliminary study, new artificial, adaptive, and versatile bioinspired demonstrators with compliant motion were developed that combined two different hinge-less movement principles. The presented systems were inspired by the snap traps of carnivorous plants. Three model systems were presented that utilize different (state-of-the-art) actuation systems for the movement of the model lobes (based on pneumatic actuators, SMA spring contraction via thermal heating and magnetic actuators). The slow heat induced spring contractions and the fast magnetic actuation simply moved the lobes from an open to a closed state with different kinetics when they received a change of the "environmental condition", i.e. a heat or magnetic stimuli. In contrary, the pneumatic actuation combined a rather slow closing of the lobes with a fast opening that could be triggered by threshold driven pressures or two distinctive pressure stimuli. A fourth model highlighted the combination of two distinctive triggers (moisture and heat), which were both needed for the movement initialization of the prior locked system. The latter two systems were also a showcase for self-regenerative systems with slow recovery at dry heat on the one hand and instantaneous recovery at pressure release on the other. These different systems highlight the current possibilities for actuating biomimetic compliant demonstrators using various movement and actuation mechanisms.

The artificial fly trap models described in current literature highlight complex smart actuation of bistable systems for the function of snapping shut [7–10, 12]. These systems consist of highly complex material systems, which are costly and involve high manufacturing costs. The system from Fan et al. 2019 [13] is also able to perform shutting and reopening motions. In comparison to the other presented systems it is also able react to changing environmental conditions. All systems react in the time frame of up to 6 min. Our demonstrators can react within a much shorter time frame of 5 s. In contrast to most systems described in literature, the demonstrators presented in this study are based on a simple compliant mechanism, with low-cost actuator systems of low complexity, which are however able to perform highly complex motion sequences and reactions. The technical chimera demonstrators with compliant movement resulting from our research are uncoupled from our biological concept generators, as the combination of different snap-trap motion mechanics does not occur in nature, neither in the Venus flytrap nor the Waterwheel plant alone. In our approach we demonstrate that nature holds ready a various movement actuation and deformation principles, which can be used as a toolbox for developing bioinspired motile devices with tailored movement capabilities.

Our biomimetic approach is the first to successfully combine different principles in one biomimetic device, which highlights the multitude of possibilities resulting from this toolbox. However, such chimeras are, of course, even one step further away from the biological concept generator resulting from the biomimetic abstraction and transferring processes.

In following studies, the developed actuators will be further characterized with regard to their energy requirements, acting forces and the factors influencing the closing time. Furthermore the systems will be further analyzed utilizing simulations and mathematical modeling. The further development of our demonstrators, among others into an artificial Venus fly trap system, is subject of our ongoing project to increase adaptability, longevity, robustness and resilience of material systems and potentially lead to systems with self-improving properties.

Acknowledgement. Funded by the Deutsche Forschungsgemeinschaft (DFG, German Research Foundation) under Germany's Excellence Strategy – EXC-2193/1–390951807. AW, GB, SP & TS are grateful to the Deutsche Forschungsgemeinschaft for the funding our research on the biological role models within the framework of the CRC-Transregio 141 "Biological Design and Integrative Structures – Analysis, Simulation and Implementation in Architecture". SP acknowledges funding by the Joint Research Network on Advanced Materials and Systems (JONAS).

References

1. Eder, M., Amini, S., Fratzl, P.: Biological composites—complex structures for functional diversity. Science **362**, 543–547 (2018)
2. Westermeier, A.S., et al.: How the carnivorous waterwheel plant (*Aldrovanda vesiculosa*) snaps. Proc. Roy. Soc. B Biol. Sci. **285**, 20180012 (2018)
3. Poppinga, S., Joyeux, M.: Different mechanics of snap-trapping in the two closely related carnivorous plants *Dionaea muscipula* and *Aldrovanda vesiculosa*. Phys. Rev. E **84**, 041928–041935 (2011)
4. Poppinga, S., Masselter, T., Speck, T.: Faster than their prey: New insights into the rapid movements of active carnivorous plants traps. BioEssays **35**, 649–657 (2013)
5. Poppinga, S., Kampowski, T., Metzger, A., Speck, O., Speck, T.: Comparative kinematical analyses of Venus flytrap (*Dionaea muscipula*) snap traps. Beilstein J. Nanotechnol. **7**, 664–674 (2016)
6. Ashida, J.: Studies on the leaf movement of *Aldrovanda vesiculosa*. L. Mem. Coll. Sci. Univ. Kyoto Ser. B. **9**, 141–244 (1934)
7. Kim, S.-W., Koh, J.-S., Lee, J.-G., Ryu, J., Cho, M., Cho, K.-J.: Flytrap-inspired robot using structurally integrated actuation based on bistability and a developable surface. Bioinspir. Biomim. **9**, 036004 (2014)
8. Athas, J.C., Nguyen, C.P., Zarket, B.C., Gargava, A., Nie, Z., Raghavan, S.R.: Enzyme-triggered folding of hydrogels: toward a mimic of the venus flytrap. ACS Appl. Mater. Interfaces. **8**, 19066–19074 (2016)
9. Temirel, M., Yenilmez, B., Knowlton, S., Walker, J., Joshi, A., Tasoglu, S.: Three-dimensional-printed carnivorous plant with snap trap. 3D Print. Addit. Manuf. **3**, 244–251 (2016)
10. Körner, A., et al.: Flectofold—a biomimetic compliant shading device for complex free form facades. Smart Mater. Struct. **27**, 017001 (2017)
11. Poppinga, S., et al.: Compliant mechanisms in plants and architecture. In: Knippers, J., Nickel, Klaus G., Speck, T. (eds.) Biomimetic Research for Architecture and Building Construction. BS, vol. 8, pp. 169–193. Springer, Cham (2016). https://doi.org/10.1007/978-3-319-46374-2_9
12. Zhang, Z., Chen, D., Wu, H., Bao, Y., Chai, G.: Non-contact magnetic driving bioinspired Venus flytrap robot based on bistable anti-symmetric CFRP structure. Compos. Struct. **135**, 17–22 (2016)
13. Fan, W., et al.: Dual-gradient enabled ultrafast biomimetic snapping of hydrogel materials. Sci. Adv. **5**(eaav7174), 1–6 (2019)

Rose-Inspired Micro-device with Variable Stiffness for Remotely Controlled Release of Objects in Robotics

Isabella Fiorello[1,2(✉)], Fabian Meder[1], Omar Tricinci[1],
Carlo Filippeschi[1], and Barbara Mazzolai[1(✉)]

[1] Center for Micro-BioRobotics@SSSA, Istituto Italiano di Tecnologia,
Pontedera, Italy
{isabella.fiorello,barbara.mazzolai}@iit.it
[2] The BioRobotics Institute, Scuola Superiore Sant'Anna, Pontedera, Italy

Abstract. In this work, we present a biomimetic device, with micro-prickle-like hooks capable of variable stiffness remotely controlled by a laser. We designed artificial prickles taking inspiration from the geometry of the natural prickles of the climbers *Rosa arvensis* 'Splendens', which has a peculiar downward orientation of the tip. We fabricated artificial arrays with micro-prickles using a combination of different microfabrication techniques, including direct laser lithography (DLL), micro-moulding of PDMS and thermoplastic polycaprolactone polymer (PCL) with incorporated rod-shaped gold nanoparticles (PCL@Au NPs). Due to the plasmonic effect, Au NPs heat upon laser irradiation and thus induce a controlled softening of the PCL polymeric matrix. Thermal characterization of the device under different laser intensities was performed using a dedicated setup and it provided suitable output for remotely controlling the device. The developed micro-device can hook and release a weight of 2 g varying the prickle stiffness by using a laser power with on-off cycles. This biomimetic approach permits to gain new insights for developing innovative intelligent systems in robotics, such as controllable adhesion-based grippers for micromanipulation.

Keywords: Biomimetics · Soft robotics · Rose prickles · Variable stiffness · Direct laser lithography · Thermoplastic polymer

1 Introduction

The development of novel intelligent controllable devices has obtained an increasing interest in robotics [1]. One key approach to develop such devices is to take inspiration from biological systems: structures, mechanisms and underlying principles of living organisms can lead to new ideas for robotics applications, kicking off a new branch of science known as "Bioinspired Robotics". Several devices have been fabricated by mimicking the animal kingdom [2–4] or the plant kingdom [5], creating a growing

---

F. Meder and O. Tricinci contributed equally.

© Springer Nature Switzerland AG 2019
U. Martinez-Hernandez et al. (Eds.): Living Machines 2019, LNAI 11556, pp. 122–133, 2019.
https://doi.org/10.1007/978-3-030-24741-6_11

research field. In particular, the investigations of surface patterns and biomechanics of climbing animals and plants have allowed to the development of different attachment technologies in robotics [3, 4]. One of the main attachment strategy include the use of hook-like microstructures for generating high friction and adhesion [8]: for instance, arrays of spines and hooks are used for prototyping novel probabilistic fasteners [6–10], or for attaching rough surfaces using various climbing robots [11–13] or grippers [14, 15].

Among living organisms, climbing plants represent an outstanding biological model, due to their unique adaptive behavior which has allowed them to colonize most environments on planet Earth [16]. They have different climbing mechanisms, including twining, coiling, adhesive pads, adventitious roots and hooks [17–23]. The geometrical properties of needle or hook-like structures such as spines, thorns and in particular prickles (which are small and hard hooks at the epidermis), working as attachment system in the cultivar climbers *Rosa arvensis* 'Splendens', have shown high resistance to mechanical stress due to the peculiar downward orientation of the tip [23].

A biomimetic artificial translation of rose prickles can lead to innovative devices for climbing, grasping and realising objects for different applications, which strongly dependent on scale size and material choice.

Among fabrication techniques, the combination of direct laser lithography (DLL) and micro-moulding has the excellent potentiality for the production of bio-mimetic micro-patterns with three-dimensional features and resolution at the nanoscale, allowing a good flexibility in the scale and material selection for micro-robotics applications [24–27].

In this work, we present the first prototype of a novel micro-scale device with arrays of rose-inspired prickle-like hooks capable of reversible and variable stiffness. The system is made by means of DLL, micro-moulding and casting using thermoplastic polycaprolactone polymer with incorporated gold nanoparticles (PCL@Au NPs). The rod-shaped Au NPs induce a photon to heat conversion due to their surface plasmon effect under near-infrared light irradiation [28]. Heat transfer from the NP surfaces to the PCL will generate a stiffness variation (hard/soft) controlled by laser on/off switching. The thermal characterization over time of the micro-fabricated device at different laser intensities is performed making use of a dedicated experimental setup. At last, the potentiality of a proof-of-concept device is demonstrated for easily interlocking and releasing objects by NIR light-based remote control.

2 Materials and Methods

2.1 Morphological Characterizations

Samples of the cultivar climbers *Rosa arvensis* 'Splendens' were collected in February from a garden in Pisa (Italy) to analyze the geometrical properties of their prickles. The structure of rose prickle was observed by using a digital microscope Hirox KH-7700. Samples of artificially fabricated micro-devices with prickles arrays were mounted onto aluminium stubs using adhesive carbon discs and coated with a 15 nm gold layer using a sputter coater (Quorum Q150R ES). The surface topography characterizations of rose-inspired artificial micro-devices were made using a Scanning Electron Microscope (SEM) (Zeiss EVO LS10).

2.2   Synthesis of PCL @ Au NPs

We synthesized rod-shaped Au Nps with a plasmon resonance peak of ~ 810 nm using the procedure detailed in [29]. After synthesis, the suspensions (~ 10 mL) were centrifuged at 14000 x g for 20 min, the supernatants discarded and the Au NPs were redispersed in 10 mL of 0.69 M polyvinylpyrrolidone, with a molecular weight of 40 kDa. After 24 h, the Au NPs were centrifuged, supernatants discarded and redispersed in about 1 mL of methanol. Five grams of PCL were heated at about 70 °C and 300 µL Au NPs in methanol were added and immediately mechanically mixed with PCL to obtain PCL@Au NPs.

2.3   Micro-device Fabrication

A 3D biomimetic design of the rose prickle-like hook was made by extracting the morphological parameters from the natural sample, such as diameter, length, width and angle (Fig. 3a-c). Then, a 3D model was designed in SolidWorks® 2010 (Fig. 3d). In order to use our device for micro-scale robotics tasks (e.g. micromanipulation in remote environments [30]), we scaled down the size of natural rose prickles to 1:16 respect to the selected natural model. For clarity, an overview of the microfabrication procedure was reported in Fig. 1. First of all, an array of artificial rose prickles (8 × 8 prickles) (Fig. 1, labels I) were printed in IP-S photoresist (Nanoscribe GmbH) on a glass substrate, by means of Photonic Professional GT system (Nanoscribe GmbH). The IP-S photoresist was poured on the glass substrate (covered with a nanometric layer of ITO) and exposed to the laser beam with a centre wavelength of 780 nm (Toptica laser source), using a scan speed of 10 mm/s with a power of 50 mW (Fig. 1, labels II). The printed samples were developed in SU-8 Developer (20 min) (MicroChem Corp) and rinsed with isopropyl alcohol (5 min) and deionized water (5 min). For making the moulding, the printed micro-devices were treated with plasma (Colibrì Plasma RF 50 kHz – Gambetti Kenologia) and chemical vapour deposition of 0.3% perfluorodecyltrichlorosilane (PFOTS) in cyclohexane. Finally, the structures were covered with poly(dimethylsiloxane) (PDMS) and left under vacuum for 48 h at room temperature (28 ± 2 °C) for PDMS curing (Fig. 1, labels III). Then, the PDMS mould was gently removed and used for the casting of PCL@Au NPs material. For casting, the PCL@Au NPs material was heated for 3 min at 200 °C and transferred to PDMS mould (Fig. 1, label IV). Finally, the PDMS mould is gently removed (Fig. 1, label V) and the rose-inspired micro-device with prickle-like hooks arrays was obtained (Fig. 1, label VI).

2.4   Thermal Characterization

The thermal characterizations of micro-fabricated artificial devices with prickle-like hooks arrays were performed using a dedicated experimental setup, equipped with a thermal camera (FLIR A325sc, FLIR System AB, Sweden), a NIR laser source ($\lambda = 808$ nm, maximum output power 500 mW, Roithner Lasertechnik, Vienna,

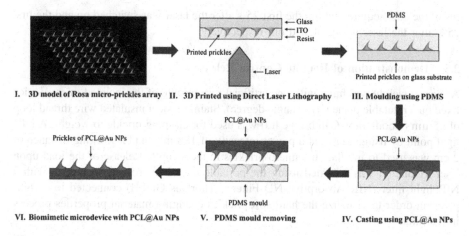

I. 3D model of Rosa micro-prickles array   II. 3D Printed using Direct Laser Lithography   III. Moulding using PDMS

VI. Biomimetic microdevice with PCL@Au NPs   V. PDMS mould removing   IV. Casting using PCL@Au NPs

Fig. 1. Schematic view of microfabrication process of rose-inspired micro-device with prickle-like hooks arrays.

Austria) and a portable digital microscope (Duratool, 25-400X Magnification, 0.3 Megapixel) (Fig. 2). The thermal camera was connected with a workstation PC with FLIR software (FLIR Research IR Max software) for extracting heating and cooling kinetics of the prickles; the portable digital microscope was connected with another PC in order to record videos during experiments in real time.

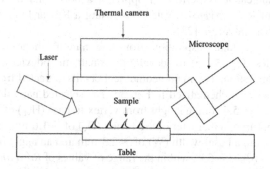

Fig. 2. Experimental set up for thermal characterization of the micro-fabricated devices.

A typical procedure consists of the following steps: (1) a sample was placed on an anti-vibration table, (2) the laser was placed at a working distance of 2 cm, and (3) the thermal characterization was performed under different laser power intensities (that are 0.5, 5, 94, 188, 277 and 361 mW) for a fixed time (3 min) at room temperature (28 ± 2 °C), while (4) the video recording by microscope was made at the same time. The temperature vs. time profile was normalized between three rose prickle-like hooks selected from each sample on the base of the highest temperature intensity of the laser spot. The heating and cooling rates of the artificial prickles were calculated from linear fits of the data acquired within the first 25 s after the laser was switched on and the first 25 s after the laser was switched off, respectively.

2.5 Demonstration of Remote Control Release

A 2-gram weight was hung with one artificial rose prickle of the inclined micro-device fixed on a rotatable plane ($\cong 75°$ angle degree). Stainless steel insulated wire thread loop of 25 μm (Goodfellow Cambridge ltd) was used for clasping prickle to weight. A NIR light point by using a laser at a power intensity of 188 mW and a working distance of 2 cm was used to irradiate the micro-prickles in the sample. Release of the load upon laser irradiation was recorded using the portable digital microscope equipped with a NIR light filter (NIR Absorptive ND Filter – Thorlabs GmbH) connected to a computer, in order to visualize the hard-soft prickles changing material properties process in real-time.

3 Results and Discussion

3.1 Biomimetic Design of Rose Prickle-Like Hooks

The spiky structures on roses, the prickles of the climber species *Rosa arvensis* differ considerably in morphological, geometrical, and biomechanical properties [23]. In particular, the prickle tip of the wild *Rosa arvensis* not has a particular orientation, in contrast to the cultivar *Rosa arvensis* 'Splendens' which gain a tip downward-orientation. Mechanical tests performed applying a horizontal traction force to the peculiar prickles of *Rosa arvensis* 'Splendens' using a Kevlar loop have shown high resistance to mechanical stress [23].

In this paper, we take inspiration from the natural shape of *Rosa arvensis* 'Splendens' prickles (Fig. 3a, b) for developing smart microdevices that can be controlled by light-stimulation. The main geometrical details extracted from *Rosa arvensis* 'Splendens' prickles are schematized in Fig. 3c. The selected natural prickles have an overall height (H) of ~ 5.4 mm, a height from vertex to base (H_{vb}) of ~ 2 mm, a basal diameter (D_b) of 6.4 mm, a diameter of the vertex (D_v) of ~ 1.6 mm, a diameter of the tip (D_t) of ~ 0.16 mm, a basal width (W) of ~ 2.3 mm and an angle between the basal axis and vertex axis (θ) *of* $\sim 53°$, within the range of values of *Rosa arvensis* Splendens prickles, type I [15]. On the base of natural geometrical details extracted from the natural samples, a biomimetic 3D model of rose prickle-like hooks was developed (Fig. 3d).

3.2 Results of Microfabrication of Biomimetic Devices

To apply our technology for micro-scale robotics tasks, such as micromanipulation of small objects for medicine and space exploration applications [31, 32], the model of rose prickle-like hooks was scaled down to 1:16 respect to the natural prickles. The artificial micro-prickles have been fabricated using a combination of DLL, micro-moulding and casting of PCL@Au NPs material, as explained in detail in Sect. 2.3.

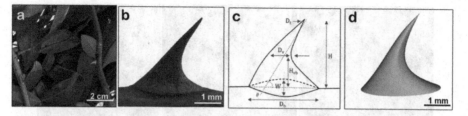

Fig. 3. (a) Climbing *Rosa arvensis* 'Splendens' species in natural environment. (b) Natural rose prickle hook. (c) Morphometric analysis of the rose prickle. D_b is the basal diameter, D_v is the diameter of the vertex, D_t is the diameter of the tip, W is the basal width, H is the height, H_{vb} is the height from vertex to base and θ is the angle between the basal axis and vertex axis. (d) 3D biomimetic CAD model obtained in SolidWorks® of the rose prickle.

The geometrical details and the microfabrication outcome observed with SEM are reported in Table 1 and Fig. 4, respectively.

Table 1. Geometrical details of rose-inspired artificial micro-prickles: N_{array} is the number of prickles (covering an area of 0.64 cm^2), H is the height, H_{vb} is the height from vertex to base, W is the basal width, D_b is the basal diameter, D_v is the diameter of the vertex, D_t is the diameter of the tip and d is the distance between prickles in the array.

Design	N_{array}	H (μm)	H_{vb} (μm)	W (μm)	D_b (μm)	D_v (μm)	D_t (μm)	d (μm)
Micro-prickles	64	344	125	144	400	100	10	800

The final microfabrication process has shown excellent results in terms of quality and resolution, particularly evident at the level of the tip (Fig. 4c, f). The device consists of an array of 8 × 8 structures at a distance of 800 μm one from the other, an overall height of 344 μm, a vertex to base height of 125 μm, a basal width of 144 μm, a basal diameter of 400 μm, a vertex diameter of 100 μm and a tip diameter of 10 μm (Fig. 4a–f).

3.3 Thermal Characterization

Thermal characterization of the artificial micro-devices using different laser intensities was performed to investigate how laser irradiation controls the temperature variation as a function of time of the thermoplastic PCL@Au NPs prickles (Fig. 5). PCL is a semi-crystalline, biodegradable polymer whose mechanical properties are affected by temperature so that it can be easily and fast switched from hard to soft [33, 34]. PCL has a relatively low melting point of 59–64 °C, and a glass transition temperature of about −60 °C [24]. A recent study has shown that the tensile modulus of PCL polymer can vary from about 107-90 to 80-68 MPa from 23 ± 2 °C to 37 ± 2 °C, respectively [33]. By doping of the polymer with Au NPs [26], it is possible to incorporate nanoscale heating elements that have a marginal influence on the polymer properties but enable varying the PCL stiffness upon laser irradiation in a fast and accurate way, by the efficiently varying temperature inside the material.

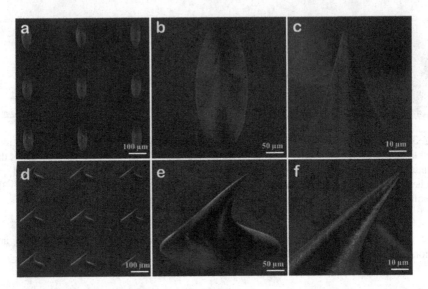

Fig. 4. SEM images of the results of the fabricated rose prickles at microscale. (a, d) (a) Frontal and (d) lateral view of the rose prickles array. (b, e) (b) Frontal and (e) lateral view of a single rose prickle and (c, f) detail of the tips.

During experiments, the response of the PCL@Au NPs prickle material strongly depends on the laser power (Fig. 5). In Fig. 5a, the temperature is plotted versus time. The plot shows two main phases, including a heating phase in which laser is switched on (first 180 s) with a certain power, and a cooling phase in which laser is switched off (last 100 s). At low power, as expected, the temperature variation is marginal (for 0.5 mW), and a variation of about 2 °C was found using a laser power of 5 mW (~ 2 °C) (Fig. 5a). However, further increasing the laser power, the temperature increases consequently, raising from room temperature (about 28 °C) to a maximum of 39 ± 0.44, 47 ± 0.56, 57 ± 0.93 and 64 ± 0.87 °C, using 94, 188, 278 and 361 mW, respectively (Fig. 5a). After switching the laser off, the temperature rapidly drops and approaches room temperature (Fig. 5a). In the first 25 s from switching the laser on, the temperature has the fastest increase after which it begins to stabilize; in the same way, in the first 25 s from switching laser off, the temperature has the fastest decrease, and then, slowly returns to room temperature (Fig. 5a). In particular, the heating rates are 0.24, 0.42, 0.76 and 0.85 °C/s at the laser power of 94, 188, 278 and 361 mW, respectively (Fig. 5b); while the cooling rates are 0.31, 0.43, 0.66 and 0.91 °C/s at the maximum temperatures of 39, 47, 57 and 64 °C, respectively (Fig. 5c).

The thermal camera view at the maximum temperature achieved during different laser power intensity experiments was reported in Fig. 5d, where prickle-like hooks are visible like "points" inside the spot. In addition, two examples of digital microscope views during the experiment at laser power intensity of 188 and 361 mW are reported in Figs. 5e and f, respectively, to visualize the structures during the thermal

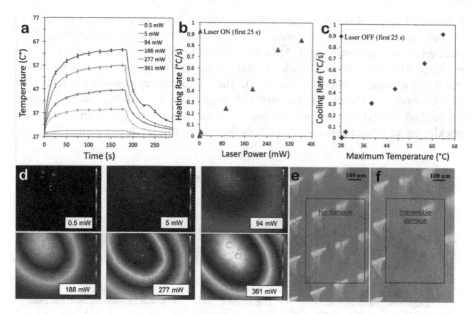

Fig. 5. (a) Temperature vs. time profile of the fabricated micro-device with rose-inspired micro-prickles under different laser intensities (from 0.5 mW to 361 mW). (b) Heating rate vs. laser power in the first 25 s of the experiments; (c) Cooling rate vs. maximum temperature in the first 25 s after that the laser is turned off. (d) Thermal view during experiment at different laser intensities. The boxes indicate three prickles inside the laser spot with maximum temperature. (f) Example of microscope view during the experiment at laser intensity of 188 mW (prickles remain intact after the experiment, red box) and (f) 361 mW (prickles are irreversible damaged, red box). (Color figure online)

characterization at real-time. The prickle structures remain intact after the test at 188 mW, in contrast to the test at 361 mW where prickles melt and are irreversibly damaged due to the too high temperature achieved. Considering that the PCL polymer becomes soft at about 37 °C [33] and melts at about 60 °C, we could hence define a feasible laser power for a controlled stiffness variation of the prickle-like hooks, which can be used for the controllable release of objects at a microscale.

3.4   Proof-of-Concept Prototype for Controllable Release of Objects

In order to perform a preliminary mechanical characterization and to demonstrate our technology, we developed and tested a proof-of-concept device with prickle-like hooks for controllable release of objects by means of stiffness variation (Fig. 6). The optical and schematic views of the tests, recorded in real time, are reported in Fig. 6a–c and d–f, respectively. A 2 g ($\sim$20 mN) weight was hung at a single artificial prickle at time 0 s, when the laser is off and the prickle is hard (Figure a, d). Then, a laser with 188 mW power was used to irradiate the device, which begins to heat. According to our thermal characterization results (Sect. 3.3), the device achieves a temperature of about 40 °C after 25 s, and then increases up to 43 °C after 50 s at 188 mW (Fig. 5a). This behaviour is correlated to polymer stiffness variation but does not induce irreversible melting [33]. As expected, after about 25 s the polymer becomes more flexible and the prickle tip starts to slowly bend. After 49 s, the tip bending is clearly visible (Fig. 6b, e). After 50 s, the soft prickle releases the weight and the prickle tip returns immediately in its initial position (Figs. 6c, f). These experiments confirm the reversible laser-controlled variation of the material properties at an initial stage. Further mechanical characterization will enable to adjust parameters like laser power and prickle size to certain applications such as the release of objects.

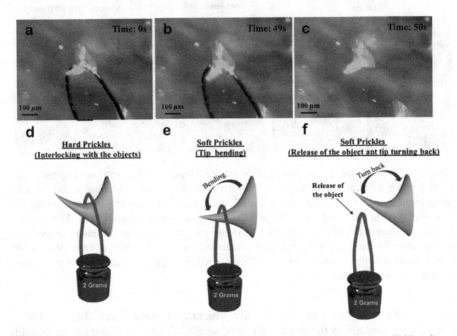

Fig. 6. (a–f) Proof-of-concept of the rose prickle-like device to demonstrate controllable release of objects. (a–c) Microscope view (extracted from a video) of a prickle, which interlocks a loop with a weight of 2 g at the (a) starting time (laser OFF, time: 0 s); after (b) 49 and (c) 50 s (laser ON, 188 mW). (d) Schematic draw of the controllable release process: (d) at the starting time the material of prickle is hard and it can hold a weight of 2 g; (e) when the laser is turned on, the prickle becomes soft and starts to bend, until (f) it releases the object and turns back.

4   Conclusions

In this work, we developed a rose-inspired device with micro-prickle-like hooks able to release objects by variable stiffness controlled using NIR light. Overall, the combination of DLL, micro-moulding and casting of PCL@Au NPs allowed to reproduce a rose micro-prickle-based design with outstanding fabrication results at the microscale. The thermal characterization of micro-prickles has permitted to investigate the most suitable laser power for achieving a temperature of about 40 °C in a controllable time interval (i.e. at 188 mW after 25 s), which is correlated to PCL polymer stiffness variation. At last, a demonstration of a single micro-prickle for hooking and releasing a weight of 2 g by remote laser controlled heating of PCL@Au NPs was tested and recorded, demonstrating the feasibility of our technology for developing the proposed innovative smart devices.

As future perspectives, devices will be fabricated at different dimensional scales (e.g. scaling down the size), mechanical characterizations on single rose micro-prickles and arrays will be performed in order to better characterize the performance of our technology for controllable micromanipulation tasks. For instance, the ability to manipulate small size objects in remote environments has become very attractive in a large variety of fields, including medicine (e.g. prickles placed in opposite direction can work like a microgripper for controlled release and microsurgery) and space exploration (e.g. these devices can be embedded in a multifunctional microrobot to perform manipulation of precious microsamples) applications.

Acknowledgments. This work was funded by RoboCom++, the European Commission under the FLAG-ERA Joint Transnational Call (JTC) 2016, and by GrowBot, the European Union's Horizon 2020 Research and Innovation Programme under Grant Agreement No. 824074.

References

1. Xia, Z.: Biomimetic Principles and Design of Advanced Engineering Materials. Wiley, Hoboken (2016)
2. Kim, S., Laschi, C., Trimmer, B.: Soft robotics: a bioinspired evolution in robotics. Trends Biotechnol. **31**(5), 287–294 (2013)
3. Mazzolai, B., Margheri, L., Laschi, C.: Quantitative measurements of *Octopus vulgaris* arms for bioinspired soft robotics. In: Bonsignorio, F., Messina, E., del Pobil, A.P., Hallam, J. (eds.) Metrics of Sensory Motor Coordination and Integration in Robots and Animals. CSM, vol. 36, pp. 3–14. Springer, Cham (2020). https://doi.org/10.1007/978-3-030-14126-4_1
4. Laschi, C., Mazzolai, B., Cianchetti, M.: Soft robotics: technologies and systems pushing the boundaries of robot abilities. Sci. Robot. **1**(1), eaah3690 (2016)
5. Mazzolai, B., Beccai, L., Mattoli, V.: Plants as model in biomimetics and biorobotics: new perspectives. Front. Bioeng. Biotechnol. **2**, 2 (2014)
6. Ji, Z., et al.: Biomimetic surface with tunable frictional anisotropy enabled by photothermogenesis-induced supporting layer rigidity variation. Adv. Mater. Interfaces, **6**(2), 1801460 (2018)
7. Afrisal, H., Sadati, S.H., Nanayakkara, T.: A bio-inspired electro-active Velcro mechanism using Shape Memory Alloy for wearable and stiffness controllable layers. In: 2016 IEEE International Conference on Information and Automation for Sustainability (ICIAfS), pp. 1–6. IEEE (2016)
8. Gorb, S.N.: Biological attachment devices: exploring nature's diversity for biomimetics. Philos. Trans. R. Soc. A Math. Phys. Eng. Sci. **366**(1870), 1557–1574 (2008)
9. Gorb, S.N., Popov, V.L.: Probabilistic fasteners with parabolic elements: biological system, artificial model and theoretical considerations. Philos. Trans. R. Soc. Lond. Ser. A Math. Phys. Eng. Sci. **360**(1791), 211–225 (2002)
10. Williams, J.A., Davies, S.G., Frazer, S.: The peeling of flexible probabilistic fasteners. Tribol. Lett. **26**(3), 213–222 (2007)

11. Provancher, W.R., Clark, J.E., Geisler, B., Cutkosky, M.R.: Towards penetration-based clawed climbing. In: Climbing and Walking Robots, CLAWAR 2004, pp. 961–970. Springer, Heidelberg (2005). https://doi.org/10.1007/3-540-29461-9_94

12. Birkmeyer, P., Gillies, A.G., Fearing, R.S.: CLASH: climbing vertical loose cloth. In: IEEE/RSJ International Conference on Intelligent Robots and Systems. IEEE (2011)

13. Kim, S., Asbeck, A.T., Cutkosky, M.R., Provancher, W.R.: SpinybotII: climbing hard walls with compliant microspines. In: Proceedings of the 2005 International Conference on Advanced Robotics, ICAR 2005 (2005)

14. Jiang, H., et al.: Stochastic models of compliant spine arrays for rough surface grasping. Int. J. Robot. Res. **37**(7), 669–687 (2018)

15. Parness, A.: Anchoring foot mechanisms for sampling and mobility in microgravity. In: IEEE International Conference on Robotics and Automation, pp. 6596–6599 (2011)

16. Niklas, K.J., Spatz, H.C.: Plant Physics. University of Chicago Press, Chicago (2012)

17. Isnard, S., Silk, W.K.: Moving with climbing plants from Charles Darwin's time into the 21st century. Am. J. Bot. **96**(7), 1205–1221 (2009)

18. Isnard, S., Cobb, A.R., Holbrook, N.M., Zwieniecki, M., Dumais, J.: Tensioning the helix: a mechanism for force generation in twining plants. Proc. R. Soc. Lond. B Biol. Sci. (2009). https://doi.org/10.1098/rspb.2009.0380

19. Melzer, B., Steinbrecher, T., Seidel, R., Kraft, O., Schwaiger, R., Speck, T.: The attachment strategy of English ivy: a complex mechanism acting on several hierarchical levels. J. R. Soc. Interface **7**(50), 1383–1389 (2010)

20. Rowe, N.P., Speck, T.: Stem biomechanics, strength of attachment, and developmental plasticity of vines and lianas. In: Ecology of Lianas, pp. 323–344 (2014)

21. Bauer, G., Klein, M.C., Gorb, S.N., Speck, T., Voigt, D., Gallenmüller, F.: Always on the bright side: the climbing mechanism of Galium aparine. Proc. Biol. Sci. **278**(1715), 2233–2239 (2011)

22. Steinbrecher, T., Beuchle, G., Melzer, B., Speck, T., Kraft, O., Schwaiger, R.: Structural development and morphology of the attachment system of Parthenocissus tricuspidata. Int. J. Plant Sci. **172**(9), 1120–1129 (2011)

23. Gallenmüller, F., Feus, A., Fiedler, K., Speck, T.: Rose prickles and asparagus spines-different hook structures as attachment devices in climbing plants. PLoS ONE **10**(12), e0143850 (2015)

24. Fiorello, I., Tricinci, O., Mishra, A.K., Tramacere, F., Filippeschi, C., Mazzolai, B.: Artificial system inspired by climbing mechanism of Galium aparine fabricated via 3D laser lithography. In: Vouloutsi, V., et al. (eds.) Living Machines 2018. LNCS (LNAI), vol. 10928, pp. 168–178. Springer, Cham (2018). https://doi.org/10.1007/978-3-319-95972-6_18

25. Tricinci, O., Terencio, T., Mazzolai, B., Pugno, N.M., Greco, F., Mattoli, V.: 3D micropatterned surface inspired by salvinia molesta via direct laser lithography. ACS Appl. Mater. Interfaces **7**(46), 25560–25567 (2015)

26. Tricinci, O., et al.: Dry adhesion of artificial gecko setae fabricated via direct laser lithography. In: Mangan, M., Cutkosky, M., Mura, A., Verschure, P.F.M.J., Prescott, T., Lepora, N. (eds.) Living Machines 2017. LNCS (LNAI), vol. 10384, pp. 631–636. Springer, Cham (2017). https://doi.org/10.1007/978-3-319-63537-8_60

27. Bernardeschi, I., Tricinci, O., Mattoli, V., Filippeschi, C., Mazzolai, B., Beccai, L.: Three-dimensional soft material micropatterning via direct laser lithography of flexible molds. ACS Appl. Mater. Interfaces **8**(38), 25019–25023 (2016)

28. Baffou, G., Quidant, R.: Thermo-plasmonics: using metallic nanostructures as nano-sources of heat. Laser Photonics Rev. **7**(2), 171–187 (2013)

29. Ali, M.R., Snyder, B., El-Sayed, M.A.: Synthesis and optical properties of small Au nanorods using a seedless growth technique. Langmuir **28**(25), 9807–9815 (2012)

30. Belfiore, N.: Micromanipulation: a challenge for actuation. Actuators **7**(4), 85 (2018)
31. Corradi, P., Menciassi, A., Dario, P.: Space applications of micro-robotics: a preliminary investigation of technological challenges and scenarios. In: Proceedings of the 5th Round Table on Micro/Nano Technologies for Space, Noordwijk, The Netherlands (2005)
32. Woodruff, M.A., Hutmacher, D.W.: The return of a forgotten polymer—polycaprolactone in the 21st century. Prog. Polym. Sci. **35**(10), 1217–1256 (2010)
33. Kurniawan, D., Nor, F., Lee, H., Lim, J.: Elastic properties of polycaprolactone at small strains are significantly affected by strain rate and temperature. Proc. Inst. Mech. Eng. [H] **225**(10), 1015–1020 (2011)
34. Corbierre, M.K., et al.: Polymer-stabilized gold nanoparticles and their incorporation into polymer matrices. J. Am. Chem. Soc. **123**(42), 10411–10412 (2001)

Robotic Simulator of Vocal Fold Paralysis

Maria Elena Giannaccini[(✉)], Andrew Hinitt, Edward Gough,
Andrew Stinchcombe, Keren Yue, Andrew Conn, and Jonathan Rossiter

University of Bristol, Bristol, UK
{maria.elena.giannaccini,andrew.hinitt,edward.gough,andrew.stinchcombe,
keren.yue,andrew.conn,jonathan.rossiter}@bristol.ac.uk
http://www.bristol.ac.uk/engineering/research/softlab/

Abstract. Vocal fold disorders impact significantly on quality of life. Specifically, vocal fold paralysis can affect the ability to speak and breathe. To date, there has been a shortage of studies providing a quantitative characterisation of the effect of paralysed vocal folds on the frequency and amplitude of sound in phonation. In this paper we propose a novel bioinspired robotic simulator that physically replicates both healthy vocal fold function and two main pathological conditions in vocal fold paralysis: bilateral and unilateral paralysis. By analysing the audio data produced by our robotic simulator a correlation can be drawn between each type of paralysis and the effects on amplitude and frequency. Results show that in a healthy configuration, frequency response and vocal fold stress are mostly proportional and that their relationship is highly impacted by paralysis. In addition, our experimental results provide a mapping between vocal fold position and tension in our simulator and the resulting sound. These insights will inform laryngeal surgical procedures and help improve the effectiveness of current implant systems.

Keywords: Bioinpired robotics · Vocalisation · Vocal fold paralysis

1 Introduction

Dysphonia (or hoarseness) is a symptom of pathologies that occur in the vocal folds (VF) of the larynx (Fig. 1). It is a disorder characterised by an alteration in voice, pitch or loudness [18]. It impacts communication and reduces voice-related quality of life (QOL) [13].

Hoarseness affects nearly 30% of the population at some point in their lives. The diagnoses can include acute/chronic laryngitis, functional dysphonia, benign tumors and neurological diseases such as vocal fold paralysis (VFP) [3]. The work presented in this paper focuses on the physical simulation and characterisation of VFP in comparison to healthy vocal folds.

VFP results in no movement (paralysis) or weak movement (partial paralysis) of the vocal folds. VFP can be unilateral or bilateral. The paralysed vocal fold may become immobilised in various positions: median (towards the centre),

© Springer Nature Switzerland AG 2019
U. Martinez-Hernandez et al. (Eds.): Living Machines 2019, LNAI 11556, pp. 134–145, 2019.
https://doi.org/10.1007/978-3-030-24741-6_12

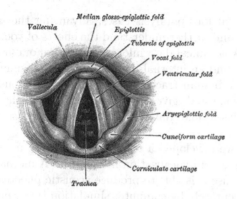

Fig. 1. The human vocal folds. Illustration by Henry Vandyke Carter, for the book 'Anatomy of the Human Body' by Henry Gray (1918). This work is in the public domain.

paramedian (1.5 mm from midline, the most frequent position) or, less often, intermediate (3.5 mm from midline) or lateral [17].

Current treatment options for VFP include voice therapy, which is effective in treating functional and organic dysphonia, and surgical intervention [12,16]. Types of surgery that are used to treat VFP include bulk injection, vocal fold repositioning and thyroplasty. Despite improvements in patients' QOL through developments of materials and technologies for laryngeal implants, in the state of the art there is no direct quantitative translation from VF tension, configuration and resulting vocalisation. In addition, most of the implants are permanent and can lead to suboptimal outcomes such as unsatisfactory vocalisation [20]. Hence the mapping between vocal fold position and tension and sound production we propose could provide a useful tool to improve on vocalisation results after surgery and laryngeal implant placement. The aim of this paper is to investigate the effect of different vocal fold positions on sound production by analysing the frequency and amplitude of the resulting sound.

The main function of the larynx during vocalisation is to control the position and tension of the vibrating vocal folds, hence modulating the vocalised sound. Many mathematical and computational models have been developed to simulate phonary VF functions and glottal flows, including continuum models for VF tissues and glottal aerodynamics [21], analysis on cartilage movements using finite element analysis tools [23] and surgery planning tools for VF paralysis [14].

Existing studies show mechanical vocalisation models, including von Kempelen's mechanical voice production machine [9], robots physically producing human speech [4,15], a vocal system with adaptive control for pitch learning [6] and the WASEDA anthropomorphic talking robot [5]. However, these models reproduce healthy vocalisation only. A mechanical model capable of varying vocal fold tension is described in [7], which is an initial exploration of potential pathological conditions, lacking the identification of a specific pathology. By contrast, our mechanical simulator focuses specifically on paralysis and mimics the full range of vocal fold paralysis cases, advancing the potential for using robots to reproduce and further understand the effects of vocal fold paralysis on sound production. Anatomical data informs the design of our robotic simulator: its length is 105 mm and an internal diameter of 19 mm, simulating the average dimensions of a male human trachea [8], air pressure is consistent with physiological values (0.1 bar) and, given the viscoelasticity of the human vocal fold tissues [2], a viscoelastic material (Theraband) has been selected as the vocal fold in our simulator.

In this research we developed a robotic simulator to investigate the contribution of VF to the human vocalisation mechanism. A mechanical and physical model is chosen because it is able to produce acoustic phenomena that are difficult to reproduce accurately by computer simulation [11]. Specifically, complexity is introduced by the non-linearity intrinsic to the human vocalisation system, caused by the interplay between the turbulent flow present in voice production, dynamic effects of the vocal folds, aeroelastic effects and viscoelasticity of the vocal folds tissue. Our robotic system focuses on exploring the effects on sound production of partially turbulent airflow on a viscoelastic latex membrane as it is symmetrically and asymmetrically tensioned and lateralised. By having a predominately rigid assembly, the non-linear effects of the membrane on phonation are isolated, in contrast to introducing further unknown interactions by having an entirely soft structure.

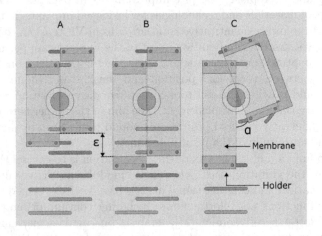

Fig. 2. Configuration of membranes, which represent VF in our simulator. A: unstrained (paralysed) configuration with symmetric and parallel membranes B: configuration with both membranes strained by 30% (ϵ) (healthy) C: configuration for unilateral paralysis in abducted position, which is in a different plate.

Our system can analyse sound quality by simulating vocal fold positions in healthy and paralysis cases. Specifically, we test bilateral paralysis and unilateral paralysis. The former is a rare but serious condition, where both VF are paralysed, that can cause vocal difficulties and significant problems with breathing and swallowing. In most cases of vocal fold paralysis, only one vocal fold is partially or completely paralysed (unilateral). We consider two types of unilateral paralysis: (i) the paralysed vocal fold is adducted (towards to the larynx midline) and partially obstructing the airway; and (ii) the paralysed vocal fold is abducted (away from the larynx midline) and preventing complete closure of the airway, as shown in Fig. 2.

2   Materials and Methods

The VF simulator mimics the opening of the vocal folds, which, in the human, is performed by the rotation of the arytenoid cartilages by the posterior cricoarytenoid muscles. The closing of the vocal fold is achieved by the lateral cricoarytenoid and oblique arytenoid muscles and is also reproducible in our simulator by moving the membranes along the slots shown in Fig. 2. The second degree of freedom of our simulator achieves the tensioning of the vocal folds, imitating the function of the cricothyroid muscle. A detailed explanation of the simulation methodology is described below.

- **Healthy Vocal Folds** - The membranes are parallel to each other and stretched by the same amount. The ability to simultaneously produce equal strain in both VF is found in healthy human VF. This results in three configurations with symmetric strain (30%, 60% and 90%).
- **Bilateral Paralysis** - Both membranes are kept in a flaccid state, at their unstretched, nominal length (0%).
- **Unilateral Paralysis** - Unilateral paralysis can be divided into the adducted case and the abducted case. In unilateral paralysis, the most common paralyzed position are paramedian, intermediary and lateral [19].
  - *Unilateral Paralysis in Adducted Position* - The paralysed membrane is kept at its unstretched, nominal length while the healthy membrane is progressively strained to 30%, 60% and 90%. For completeness a semi-paralysis of one vocal fold is also imitated and in this case the semi-paralysed fold is strained to 30% and 60%.
  - *Unilateral Paralysis in Abducted Position* - In patients with this condition, one vocal fold is paralysed in an abducted configuration. A custom test plate (Fig. 4) was fabricated to simulate this pathology. This test plate is modified to allow for the rotation of the paralysed membrane. This rotation pivots around the point where the paralysed membrane and the circumference of the acrylic trachea in the simulator intersect. To enable this rotation four arced slots are laser cut into the test plate. The healthy membrane is stretched to 30%, 60% and 90%, while the paralysed membrane is angled from 0° to 10° in increments of 2.5°. The angular variations are 0%, 2.5%, 5%, 7.5%, and 10%. This membrane is fixed on a C-shaped acrylic frame, which is dimensioned to keep the membrane at its unstretched, nominal length. The C-shaped frame ensures that, as the membrane is rotated from 0° to 10°, the length and tension remains constant.

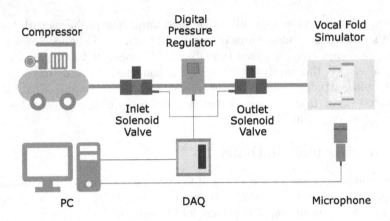

Fig. 3. Illustration of the experimental setup

The test bench utilised for the experiments is composed of an air pressure regulation system and a human vocal folds simulation system, shown in Fig. 3.

The VF simulator, shown in Fig. 2, comprises an acrylic tube, representing the trachea, bonded to an acrylic plate. The VF are represented by latex membranes (Theraband). The membranes to be used in a parallel configuration are bonded to an acrylic holder at each end using sil-poxy (Smooth-On), whereas the lateralized membrane is bonded to an acrylic bracket to ensure that transverse strains are not introduced as the membrane is rearranged. The membranes are bolted to the plate through laser-cut slots. PVF will be represented by unstrained membranes. There are four sets of slots to tension the membranes to linear strains of 0% (unstrained), 30%, 60% and 90% as shown in Fig. 2, where ϵ is the amount the membrane is strained from rest length. A 3D printed bracket is positioned above the membranes, as shown in Fig. 4, pressing onto them to ensure that all air is forced between the two membranes, rather than out the sides, and to simulate the connection between the VF and the upper larynx. Mounting the membranes using slots rather than holes enables fine adjustment to close the gap between the two membranes resulting from necking of the vocal fold material as it stretches. Curvature due to necking is predominantly towards the interface between holder and membrane; hence the membranes are sufficiently long (60 mm) so that the area above the airflow has a negligible curvature. A preliminary set of experiments, testing a variety of silicone and latex membranes, showed that Theraband had good sound production capability in the human vocalisation frequency range, whilst also having an elastic limit high enough to allow straining the membranes to the desired levels.

A Werther International compressor provides air to the proportional digital pressure regulator (Festo 8L-L-1-G14-0L2H-V1N-S1C1) through a solenoid (Festo VACS-H1P-A1-1) attached to a normally closed valve. A second valve controls airflow into the vocal fold simulator. The data acquisition system is controlled via a bespoke LabView logging system and interface.

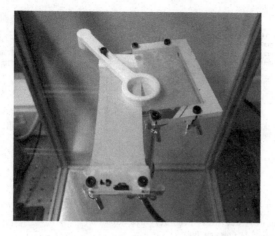

Fig. 4. Simulation of unilateral paralysis in adducted configuration. The healthy membrane is on the left of the rig and the paralysed and rotated membrane is on the right.

A USB microphone (Blue Yeti) is placed above the membranes to record the audio output. A sound level meter (Tenma ST-805) is used to record the sound amplitude in dB during tests.

Three experiments are conducted, each pertaining to the simulation of a specific vocal fold positioning: healthy vocal folds, bilateral paralysis and unilateral paralysis, which is further divided into the adducted position and the abducted position. Air flow from the pressure regulator is supplied to the trachea in the simulator and forced through the membranes. Each experiment is composed of 25 trials, adjusting the air pressure from 0.02 to 0.1 bar in intervals of 0.02 bar. The pressure range was chosen according to Titze's work on measuring relative lung pressures with an open-tube manometer [22]. The LabView control system allows the setting of the maximum and minimum pressures and the trial duration, which is set for all trials at 4 s.

3   Results

The experimental data is analysed in Matlab (Mathworks) to provide a comprehensive and detailed characterisation of each trial, including the input pressure, the input flow rate and the sound amplitude and frequency. The discrete fast Fourier transform of the audio data is utilised to obtain the dominant sound frequency in every experiment. The results for the three main cases are detailed in the following sections.

3.1   Healthy Vocal Folds and Bilateral Paralysis

The configuration of the membranes in these cases is shown in case (A) of Fig. 2. The bilateral paralysis configuration has the two VF parallel to each other and in

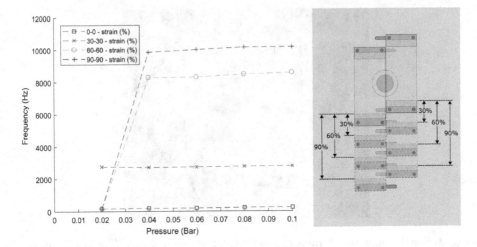

Fig. 5. Fundamental frequency response against pressure in the parallel and symmetric case. The case in which both membranes are flaccid (0% strain) mimics the bilateral paralysis case. Both membranes being stretched and by the same amount (30%, 60%, 90% in both right and left membrane) represents the healthy case.

their flaccid state (0% strain both in the right and left membrane). The healthy VF configuration has both membranes parallel and strained by the same amount (30%, 60%, 90% in both right and left membrane). For ease of convenience we tested the healthy and bilateral paralysis cases during the same experiment set, as the membrane configuration is similar, with only the membrane strain amount changing between the two cases. The results in Fig. 5 show that the increase in membrane extension (0%–90%) causes an increase in frequency. This result is in line with sound theory regarding the direct proportionality of sound frequency magnitude (F_0) and membrane elongation shown in Eq. 1, the well-known formula for vibrating strings [22].

$$F_0 = \frac{1}{2L}\sqrt{\frac{\sigma}{\rho}} \tag{1}$$

where L is the length of the vocal folds, σ is the longitudinal stress in vocal fold tissue and ρ is the tissue density. As notable in Fig. 5, non-linear hyperelastic stress-strain of the membrane causes the non-linear response at higher pre-stretches. The amplitude of the sound increases in an approximately proportional fashion to the increase of pressure (Fig. 6). Notably, the amplitude is lower in the 0% (or bilateral paralysis) case and 90% case than it is for the 30% and 60% strain cases. This shows the stronger resonance of the 30% and 60% cases. Background noise baseline is found to be 68 dB.

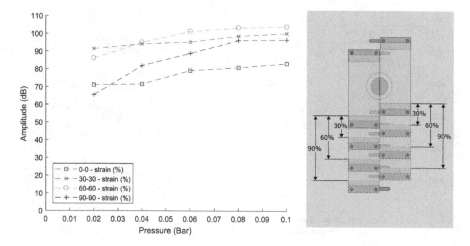

Fig. 6. Amplitude against pressure in the parallel and symmetric case, with 0–0% strain representing bilateral paralysis and 30–30%, 60–60%, 90–90% representing the healthy case.

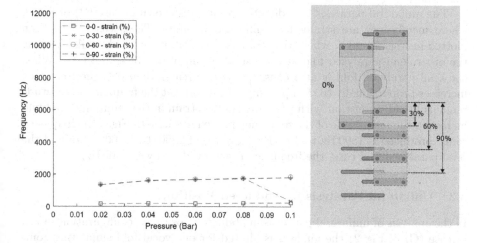

Fig. 7. Frequency against pressure in the parallel and unilateral paralysis case where the paralysed fold is untensioned and the other fold is tensioned to 30%, 60% and 90%.

3.2 Unilateral Paralysis in Adducted Position

Interestingly, the sound frequency in the unilateral paralysis in adducted position (Fig. 7) does not significantly increase between the cases in which the healthy membrane is strained by 30%, 60% and 90%. This indicates that proportionality between membrane elongation and sound frequency magnitude described in Eq. 1 does not hold true for considerable elongations if one of the vocal folds is paralysed.

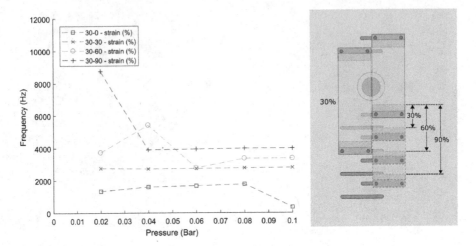

Fig. 8. Frequency against pressure in the parallel and unilateral paralysis case where the semi-paralysed fold is tensioned to 30%.

The unilateral paralysis for adducted position is shown in case (B) of Fig. 2, where membranes are strained by different amounts. These cases have been plotted in Figs. 7 and 8, where the strain was varied on one fold, whilst keeping the other semi-paralysed fold at a constant strain of 0%, 30% and 60%. When the semi-paralysed fold is at a constant strain greater than 0%, the frequency increases proportionally to the opposing fold strain, yet the frequency magnitude remains broadly constant with pressure. As the strain in the semi-paralysed fold increases, the magnitude of the frequency range increases. In Fig. 8 the frequency range produced is 1800 Hz to 4000 Hz - a range of 2200 Hz. In 60% strain of the semi-paralysed fold case, the frequency range produced was 6700 Hz.

3.3   Unilateral Paralysis in Abducted Position

In the analysis of unilateral paralysis in abducted positions (configuration shown in case (C) of Fig. 2) the angle α is altered for one vocal fold simulating complete paralysis (with 0% strain). The opposing vocal fold is medialised with different strains. In all cases only one frequency in the region of 1650 Hz is produced, otherwise no clear vocalisation is made. In each case where $\alpha = 7.5°$ and $\alpha = 10°$ no sound is produced and only background noise is recorded. This result suggests that in the unilateral paralysis in abducted position, VF can generate sound only if the abduction is small. Also, unilateral paralysis seems to notably restrict the frequency response. At 30% strain a sound is produced at an angle of $\alpha = 5°$, at an amplitude of 70–80 dB across the pressure range (which we identified as background noise). In all other cases vocalisation was produced with amplitudes in a comparable range across all strains where sound was produced - at 80 to 100 dB - as shown in Fig. 9.

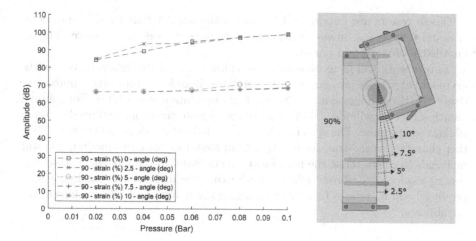

Fig. 9. Amplitude against pressure in the unilateral paralysis in abducted position case for abduction angles $\alpha \in 2.5, 5, 7.5, 10°$

In general, the results show a frequency response (1 kHz–10 kHz) which is compatible with biological data, as the frequency response of human voice is within 100 Hz and 10 kHz. Low male voices reach a fundamental frequency just below 100 Hz. Female voices start about an octave higher, around 200 Hz. Vowels primarily vocalise at lower mid frequencies (200 to 1 kHz) and the consonants at the upper mid frequencies: 2 kHz and upwards, with sibilant consonants reaching 8.4 kHz [1] with peaks at 10 kHz for the dental fricative for the female speaker [10]. However, it must be kept in mind that human speech frequencies are modulated by a full and dynamic vocal tract, the tongue and mouth, which are not present in our simulator. Hence, a one-to-one mapping between the sounds our simulator produces and consonant and vowel production should not be assumed.

4   Conclusion and Future Work

A novel robotic vocal fold simulator has been presented to replicate a variety of dysphonia configurations. The results of the tests conducted with this platform allow the comparison of sound frequency and amplitude between the simulation of healthy and paralysed membranes. The results show proportionality of sound frequency magnitude and membrane elongation in most cases with the important exception of the adducted unilateral paralysis with one relaxed membrane (0%). In this case the frequency magnitude does not increase with strain.

In the abducted unilateral paralysis case the ability to vocalise is directly limited by the abduction angle, which when increased beyond intermediate position (in this case $\alpha > 2.59°$) can produce no sound.

These results are important to quantify the impact that vocal fold orientation and tension has on vocalisation for pathological cases, hence increasing our knowledge of vocal fold paralysis.

Future work will focus on adding the third degree of freedom achieved by the arytenoid cartilages into our robotic simulator, in order to reproduce more effectively the three dimensional movement of the human vocal folds. Tongue and mouth structure will also be investigated to explore the cause and production of sibilant sound more. The system will be expanded to include an oral cavity to further characterise the transfer function from sound to voice production, and soft materials to characterise the non-linear effects found in the biological structure. Having explored the broad effects of adjusting the membranes, the frequencies produced will be refined further by changing the material and dimensions of the membranes.

References

1. Boothroyd, A., Medwetsky, L.: Spectral distribution of /s/ and the frequency response of hearing aids. Ear Hear. **13**(3), 150–157 (1992)
2. Chan, R.W., Titze, I.R.: Viscoelastic shear properties of human vocal fold mucosa: measurement methodology and empirical results. J. Acoust. Soc. Am. **106**(4), 2008–2021 (1999)
3. Cohen, S.M., Kim, J., Roy, N., Asche, C., Courey, M.: Prevalence and causes of dysphonia in a large treatment-seeking population. Laryngoscope **122**(2), 343–348 (2012)
4. Endo, N., Kojima, T., Ishihara, H., Horii, T., Asada, M.: Design and preliminary evaluation of the vocal cords and articulator of an infant-like vocal robot "lingua". In: 2014 IEEE-RAS International Conference on Humanoid Robots, pp. 1063–1068. IEEE (2014)
5. Fukui, K., Shintaku, E., Honda, M., Takanishi, A.: Mechanical vocal cord for anthropomorphic talking robot based on human biomechanical structure. Jpn. Soc. Mech. Eng. Int. **73**(734), 112–118 (2007)
6. Higashimoto, T., Sawada, H.: A mechanical voice system: construction of vocal cords and its pitch control. In: International Conference on Intelligent Technologies, vol. 7624768 (2003)
7. Honda, M., Fukui, K., Ogane, R., Takanishi, A.: Pathological voice production by mechanical vocal cord model. In: 9th International Seminar on Speech Production 2011, ISSP, Montreal, Canada, pp. 49–56 (2011)
8. Kamel, K.S., Lau, G., Stringer, M.D.: In vivo and in vitro morphometry of the human trachea. Clin. Anat. Off. J. Am. Assoc. Clin. Anat. Br. Assoc. Clin. Anat. **22**(5), 571–579 (2009)
9. von Kempelen, W.: Mechanismus der menschlichen Sprache nebst der Beschreibung seiner sprechenden Maschine. Uppsala Univ. (1982)
10. Lee, S.I.: Spectral analysis of mandarin Chinese sibilant fricatives. In: ICPhS, pp. 1178–1181 (2011)
11. Luo, X., Hinton, J., Liew, T., Tan, K.: Les modelling of flow in a simple airway model. Med. Eng. Phys. **26**(5), 403–413 (2004)
12. Maryn, Y., De Bodt, M., Roy, N.: The acoustic voice quality index: toward improved treatment outcomes assessment in voice disorders. J. Commun. Disord. **43**(3), 161–174 (2010)

13. Mirza, N., Ruiz, C., Baum, E.D., Staab, J.P.: The prevalence of major psychiatric pathologies in patients with voice disorders. Ear Nose Throat J. **82**(10), 808–812 (2003)
14. Mittal, R., Zheng, X., Bhardwaj, R., Seo, J.H., Xue, Q., Bielamowicz, S.: Toward a simulation-based tool for the treatment of vocal fold paralysis. Front. Physiol. **2**, 19 (2011)
15. Nishikawa, K., Asama, K., Hayashi, K., Takanobu, H., Takanishi, A.: Development of a talking robot. In: Proceedings of the 2000 IEEE/RSJ International Conference on Intelligent Robots and Systems (IROS 2000) (Cat. No. 00CH37113), vol. 3, pp. 1760–1765. IEEE (2000)
16. Reiter, R., Hoffmann, T.K., Pickhard, A., Brosch, S.: Hoarseness-causes and treatments. Deutsches Ärzteblatt Int. **112**(19), 329 (2015)
17. Rubin, A.D., Sataloff, R.T.: Vocal fold paresis and paralysis. Otolaryngol. Clin. North Am. **40**(5), 1109–1131 (2007)
18. Schwartz, S.R., et al.: Clinical practice guideline: hoarseness (dysphonia). Otolaryngol. Head Neck Surg. **141**(1–suppl), 1–31 (2009)
19. Schwarz, K., Cielo, C.A., Steffen, N., Jotz, G.P., Becker, J.: Voice and vocal fold position in men with unilateral vocal fold paralysis. Braz. J. Otorhinolaryngol. **77**(6), 761–767 (2011)
20. Sittel, C.: Larynx: implantate und stents. Laryngo-rhino-otologie **88**(S 01), S119–S124 (2009)
21. Titze, I.R., Alipour, F.: The myoelastic aerodynamic theory of phonation. National Center for Voice and Speech (2006)
22. Titze, I.R., Martin, D.W.: Principles of voice production (1998)
23. Yin, J., Zhang, Z.: Interaction between the thyroarytenoid and lateral cricoarytenoid muscles in the control of vocal fold adduction and eigenfrequencies. J. Biomech. Eng. **136**(11), 111006 (2014)

Drosophibot: A Fruit Fly Inspired Bio-Robot

Clarissa Goldsmith$^{(\boxtimes)}$, Nicholas Szczecinski, and Roger Quinn

Department of Mechanical and Aerospace Engineering,
Case Western Reserve University, Cleveland, OH 44106, USA
cag111@case.edu

Abstract. We introduce Drosophibot, a hexapod robot with legs designed based on the Common fruit fly, *Drosophila melanogaster*, built as a test platform for neural control development. The robot models anatomical aspects not present in other, similar bio-robots such as a retractable abdominal segment, insect-like dynamic scaling, and compliant feet segments in the hopes that more similar biomechanics will lead to more similar neural control and resulting behaviors. In increasing biomechanical modeling accuracy, we aim to gain further insight into the insect's nervous system to inform the current model and subsequent neural controllers for legged robots.

Keywords: Insect robot · Fruit fly · Dynamic scaling · Passive compliance

1 Introduction

Legged robots have been a key focus of robotic design for many years due to their promising capacity for mobility. While wheels or treads are easier to design and control, multi-legged robots in particular would be able to traverse far more complex terrains with greater robustness and maneuverability, making them valuable for a variety of exploratory and autonomous applications [8]. In regards to implementing legs, animals, and insects in particular, provide excellent models for legged locomotion over difficult terrains (for a review, see [3]). They are able to traverse punishing landscapes with speed and agility, and can quickly compensate to maintain efficient movement if legs become injured or lost by altering their stance and stepping pattern [1]. Fruit flies are particularly interesting for biologically inspired robotics due to the abundance of genetic tools available to manipulate their nervous systems. Examples include studying the neural control of locomotion in mutants that lack different neuromodulators and using light-activated ion channels to selectively deactivate proprioceptors in the legs during walking [11,22]. Experiments like these have huge potential to thoroughly explain the neural control of walking in insects in general and fruit flies

Supported by the National Science Foundation (Grant Number: 1704436).

U. Martinez-Hernandez et al. (Eds.): Living Machines 2019, LNAI 11556, pp. 146–157, 2019.
https://doi.org/10.1007/978-3-030-24741-6_13

Fig. 1. An assembled view of Drosophibot standing on six legs

in particular. Thus, to more directly apply these and other findings from fruit fly locomotion, we present Drosophibot, a hexapod robot with several key fruit fly-like characteristics (Fig. 1).

Our previous robot, MantisBot, provided significant insight and impetus for the design of Drosophibot. MantisBot is a 28 degree-of-freedom legged robot designed to mimic the dimensions and movement of a Chinese mantis, *Tenodera sinensis* [18]. The robot was used as a testing platform for a variety of biologically-inspired insect-like neural control networks [18–20]. While it was successful in some such testing, our design for Drosophibot seeks to improve four main characteristics of MantisBot:

1. Higher strength-to-weight ratio;
2. More animal-like distribution of weight;
3. More similar dynamic scale to that of an insect; and
4. Compliant tarsus-like feet that may be used to study substrate grasping reflexes

The decision to exclude some of these components in MantisBot is in-line with many other contemporary insect-like bio-robots, and all of these robots successfully fulfill their design goals. Ensuring a sufficient strength-to-weight ratio is

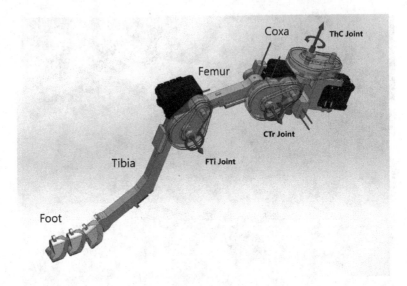

Fig. 2. A labeled schematic of Drosophibot's leg with axes of joint rotation and strain gauges in gold

a common design problem in legged robots and has been solved by including a spring in parallel with actuators [21], as we do in this study. Drosophibot's parallel springs enables it to support more weight, while simultaneously mimicking the passive forces of insect joint membranes [2,10] and helping to dynamically scale Drosophibot to be more similar to the insect. To our knowledge, no previous insect-like robot has explicitly addressed dynamic scaling of the robot relative to the animal. In addition, to our knowledge, no previous robots have addressed adhering to a more animal-like distribution of weight; robots such as OCTAVIO and HECTOR do not include the abdominal segments possessed by their insect inspirations in their designs, presumably to reduce the total body weight [9,14,21]. Last, legged robots do not typically include compliant feet in their designs, as they add complexity and are not totally necessary for stable locomotion. However, they add valuable compliance during walking, as well as a higher fidelity insect model [4,15,21].

In this manuscript, we describe the technical design of Drosophibot, including its electronics and mechanics. We include sections for each of the four aforementioned aspects that we sought to improve from MantisBot, describing the manners in which they are addressed in the design. Some preliminary electromechanical tests are presented to showcase the underlying capabilities of the robot, then we conclude by previewing the future uses of Drosophibot as a neural testing platform.

2   Overview of Design

Drosophibot's legs and body are designed based on the common fruit fly, *Drosophila melanogaster*. Each leg has three actuated joints (Fig. 2); the thorax-coxa (ThC) joint moves the leg forward and backward, the coxa-trochanter (CTr) joint elevates and depresses the leg, and the femur-tibia (FTi) joint extends and flexes the tibia segment. One additional servo attaches to the front of the thorax to actuate the head, totaling 19 degrees of freedom (DOF) throughout the robot. The included three DOF per limb comprise the minimum for movement in 3D space, and were selected due to their established role in insect locomotion and their usefulness in other insectoid robots [14,21]. We omitted any additional DOF in the insect to decrease complexity, as well as the lack of available data concerning their specific functions. Each leg also possesses three tarsal segments, which are passively actuated via an elastic tendon. All of the legs are homologous, each actuated by Dynamixel AX-12 smart servos (Robotis, Seoul, South Korea) with a stall torque of 1.5 Nm at 11.1V. The smart servos were selected over fluid actuated tendons or transmissions primarily for their simpler, strictly linear control scheme and the simplifications of the mechanical design they allowed.

Each leg has three strain gauges: two mounted on the trochanterofemur (anterior [Group 2] and dorsal [Groups 3 and 4] [24]), as well as one on the tibia (dorsal [Group 6A] [23]), to detect the strain of each leg during locomotion. Strain sensors in insects have long been known to work in conjunction with force sensors built into the muscle-apodeme complex, so strain gauge data combined with torque data from the servos will provide a useful analog for simulation [23].

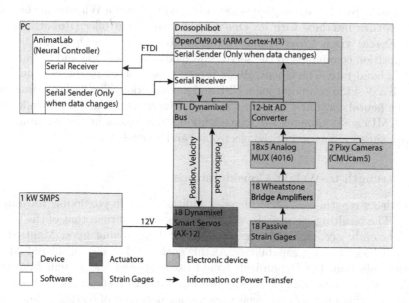

Fig. 3. A diagram of Drosophibot's electronics and control system

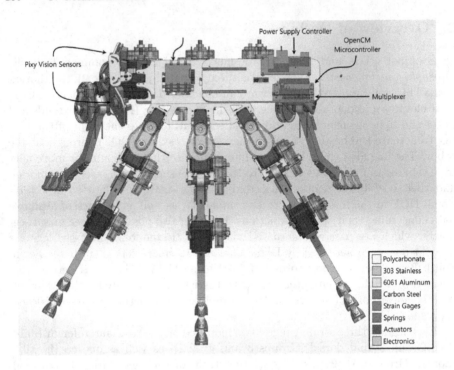

Fig. 4. A side view of Drosophibot with materials, springs, sensors, actuators, and electronic components color-coded.

Load signals from the strain gauges are amplified by custom Wheatstone bridges, which in turn interface with an OpenCM9.04 microcontroller (Robotis, Seoul, South Korea) via a 12-bit analog-to-digital converter. The OpenCM9.04 also sends position commands to the servos and reads their position and torque with a 1 MHz baud rate. The OpenCM9.04 functions as a serial tosser, communicating with a desktop computer via a USB serial connection. The desktop computer runs the neural controller in AnimatLab [6]. The robot's head also includes two Pixy (CMUcam5) cameras for recognizing specific colors in the environment. Figure 3 shows a diagram of the electronics and control system.

2.1   Strength-to-Weight Considerations

For needed strength, each servo includes additional gearing to double the output torque. The resulting strength-to-weight ratio is still less than that of the insect, but sufficiently accomplishes our stated goal of improving upon MantisBot's ratio to achieve walking capabilities. As this goal was the only considered during actuator selection, the Dynamixels would likely prevent the system from ever matching the ratio of *Drosophila*. The vast majority of the structural components are made of extruded polycarbonate, with some parts out of 6061-T6 aluminum. All gears are made out of 303 stainless steel and rotational shafts out of carbon steel. Figure 4 shows a color-coded view of the different materials and electronics that make up the robot.

2.2 Abdominal Segment for Weight Distribution

To more accurately mimic *Drosophila's* biomechanics, Drosophibot also includes an adjustable abdominal segment which houses all controllers and additional weight to achieve the insect's center of mass (COM). The COM of *Drosophila melanogaster* is approximately 1/10 of the length of the thorax behind the middle set of legs [16]. This bias is the result of the insect's abdominal segment making up the majority of its mass. By contrast, Drosophibot's actuators comprise the bulk of its mass, heavily biasing the COM to the middle of the thorax. The simplest way to shift this bias toward the rear is to add mass to the rear of the thorax; however, adding too much mass then risks making the entire robot too heavy for the Dynamixels. Therefore, the adjustable abdominal feature enables us to increase the impact of any added mass in redistributing the robot's COM, allowing us to more closely match the distribution of the animal with an acceptable amount of weight for the servos.

2.3 Dynamic Scaling

We placed torsion springs in parallel with all leg joints, such that the spring resists the servo's torque when raising the leg, and assists the servo in supporting the body weight throughout the stance phase. These springs additionally mimic the elastic forces in the legs of small animals in general, which shifts the animal's control strategy from one based on momentum, as in larger animals such as humans, to one more reliant on kinematics [10].

Matching the scaling in this way requires that the ratio between passive stiffness and inertia be the same for Drosophibot as in *Drosophila*. Figure 5A shows a simplified diagram for the CTr joint. This includes a torsional spring with stiffness k_T and the mass of the FTi actuator, m, located distance L from the joint. Figure 5B shows the associated free body diagram. Assuming that the joint angle θ is small, we can analyze the deflection of the mass in the x direction.

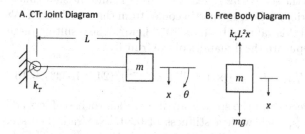

Fig. 5. A. Simplified functional diagram of the CTr joint with the parallel spring, the limb's mass, and the limb's length labelled. B. The associated free body diagram.

To do so, we calculate the equivalent linear spring stiffness $k_{eff} = k_T/L^2$. This enables us to write the equation of motion for this simple system,

$$m\ddot{x} = mg - \frac{k_T}{L^2}x. \tag{1}$$

Since the acceleration of gravity is scale-invariant, we can solve this equation for g, and use the resulting expression as a constraint on the inertia, length, and stiffness of the robot to ensure its dynamics are like those of the fly:

$$\ddot{x} + \frac{k_T}{mL^2}x = g. \tag{2}$$

This result is consistent with the finding in [10] that the ratio between a limb's stiffness k_T and its moment of inertia $I = mL^2$ defines the control regime that an animal must use (i.e. momentum- or kinematics-based). Thus, our constraint equation is

$$k_{\text{robot}}/I_{\text{robot}} = k_{\text{fly}}/I_{\text{fly}}. \tag{3}$$

Direct measurements of these quantities in the fruit fly are not available, but we can estimate them using measurements from other insects. In stick insects, the calculated joint stiffness is 10^{-6} Nm/rad [10]. Since muscle stiffness is proportional to the cross-sectional area squared, and a fruit fly is about 1/10 the scale of a stick insect, a fly's muscle's stiffness should be 1/100 that of a stick insect. In addition, the lever arm of the muscle is 1/10 as long, so this scales the muscle stiffness again by 1/100. The resulting joint stiffness of a fruit fly due to passive muscle forces should be about 1/10,000 that of a stick insect, $k_{\text{fly}} = 1 \times 10^{-10}$ Nm/rad. This does not include passive forces from the joint membranes of the exoskeleton, which are also known to contribute substantially to passive joint forces [2,10].

The fruit fly's leg is about 1 mm long, and has a mass of about $24\,\mu g$, which is 2% of its total mass of 1.2 mg [16,22]. Its moment of inertia should be on the order of $I_{\text{fly}} = 24 \times 10^{-15}$ kgm^2. We experimentally measured the moment of inertia of one of our Dynamixel AX-12 servos by using an unpowered unit as the hub of a large pendulum. We approximated the servo's moment of inertia and damping by measuring the pendulum's response, and then subtracting the inertia of the pendulum. Due to the servo's large gear ratio (508:1) and the small mass of the plastic legs, the majority of the leg's inertia comes from the servo's rotor. We experimentally measured this value to be 4.0×10^{-3} kgm^2. The resulting target stiffness for the servo to replicate the dynamics of the fruit fly is

$$k_{\text{robot}} = k_{\text{fly}}I_{\text{robot}}/I_{\text{fly}} = 1 \times 10^{-10}(4 \times 10^{-3})/(24 \times 10^{-15}) = 16 \text{ Nm/rad.} \tag{4}$$

Since the servo and the springs are in parallel, their stiffness adds. Each joint has two springs, each with a stiffness of 0.307 Nm/rad. The servo's stiffness, when set to its most compliant setting, is 9.17 Nm/rad. Therefore, the total joint stiffness is 9.78 Nm/rad, near to that of a fruit fly, and much greater than

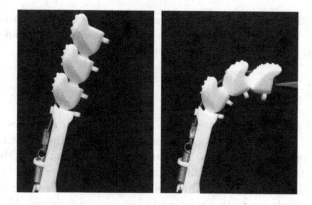

Fig. 6. Foot at its neutral position (left) and at maximum rotation (right)

that of a stick insect. We can further tune the stiffness of the joints by increasing the gain of the position feedback in the servo's controller. In this way, we can ensure that Drosophibot is dynamically scaled correctly and, therefore, is better suited as a test platform for testing for controllers based on nervous systems.

2.4   Compliant Feet

To further increase the fidelity of biomimicry of Drosophibot, we chose to add compliant foot segments. The design for MantisBot simply includes pointed tips at the bottom ends of the tibias to press into the ground, which makes walking on smooth, hard surfaces difficult. Other recent insectoid bio-robots circumvent this problem by including suction cups, rubber surfaces, and inline passive springs for better grip, but the robots are still functionally walking on the stubs of their tibia segments [9,14,21]. This lack of a dedicated foot segment or tarsus causes issues in replicating accurate biological motion, as most insects have fairly long tarsi, with *Drosophila's* foot segment measuring almost the same length as the tibia. Without feet, bio-inspired robots' torsos sit much closer to the ground, potentially causing collisions of the torso with the ground, and certainly leading to kinematics differing from the corresponding animal's. Additionally, a robot with compliant feet would have greater contact area with the ground and lower impact loading when a leg enters stance phase due to the elasticity of the feet, which should prolong the life of the actuators and the load-bearing components.

With these factors in mind, Drosophibot includes compliant feet that mimic those of *Drosophila* and other insects. Each foot is made up of a series of segments interconnected with a limited ball-and-socket joint and attached to an additional angled segment of the tibia. Thin wire cable routes through the underside of each segment and attaches to an extension spring mounted on the tibia to provide a restoring force throughout the ground contact deformation shown in Fig. 6. The morphology of the tarsal segments was loosely based on the tarsal shape present in *Drosophila*, while also maximizing ground contacting surface area.

Cleats were additionally added to these surfaces for better grip on the carpeted testing surface. Three tarsal segments have initially proven to provide the desired level of ground contact with minimal complexity.

3   Results

Several "proof of life" tests have been conducted on Drosophibot thus far to validate our calculations of its electro-mechanical capabilities. Most of the initial tests have involved validation of the strength-to-weight ratio of the robot, in particular the temperature behavior of the servomotors over time. This allowed us to confirm the expected capabilities of the robot and determine if there were any time constraints for testing relating to servomotor overheat. Figure 1 shows the robot standing on its six legs. Figure 7 shows the results of tests involving the robot standing on six and three legs, monitoring the average temperature at each load bearing servomotor over the span of 30 min, or until a servomotor surpassed the maximum operating temperature of 70 °C. For both tests, the center of mass of the robot was shifted to the biologically accurate position with the additional abdominal mass. Through these tests, we have also determined the read/write bandwidth to control all six legs as 44 ms.

We have also conducted center of mass tests with the robot suspended to confirm that an additional abdominal mass of 700 g sufficiently shifts the center of mass to within the desired location behind the middle set of legs. While no quantitative tests have yet been conducted specifically on the robot's tarsal segments and dynamic scaling, they show great improvements to the corresponding design of MantisBot.

4   Discussion

4.1   Interpretation of Temperature Data

In both sets of strength-to-weight validation testing, the temperature of the load bearing servomotors stabilized at a level at minimum 3° below the maximum operating temperature, in most cases well below this value, over the course of 30 min. The temperatures of the loaded legs also appear relatively unaffected by the number of legs involved in the stance, and in some cases stabilized at lower temperatures when in the three leg stance. This data proves promising in utilizing the robot for prolonged testing periods of 30–45 min, which MantisBot was previously not capable of. Additionally, these tests validated the usefulness of the equilibrium position in each joint between the springs and robot mass in servo cool-down, as the joints arbitrarily placed near their equilibrium exhibited temperatures close to ambient for the servo, and were able to stay relatively cool if perturbed while near equilibrium as in the case of the Right Front FTi joint in the three leg stance. This will prove useful in further extending the operating time of the platform by adding a cool-down procedure into the control when the system detects a joint getting too hot.

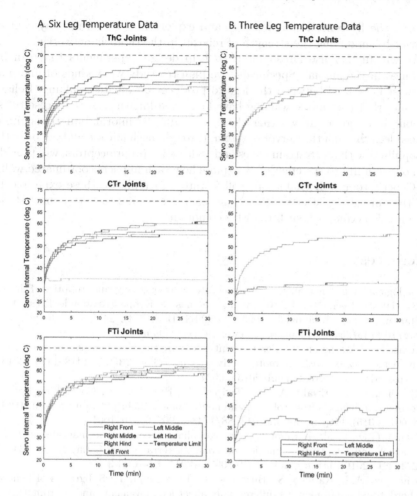

Fig. 7. Temperature data for each load bearing servo joint for a six leg stance (A) and three leg stance (B) over the course of 30 min or until a joint surpassed maximum operating temp of 70 °C.

4.2 Conclusions and Further Work

We have designed Drosophibot to mimic particular insect-like qualities and improve our previous robot, MantisBot. Drosophibot has a higher strength-to-weight ratio than MantisBot; it has the potential to distribute its weight more biologically accurately; its dynamic scale is more similar to that of its insect model; and it has compliant tarsi-like feet to better match the proportions of the animal, and reduce impact loading during walking. The next steps in Drosophibot's development will be to implement our dynamical neural control networks for walking [13,17]. We plan to specifically examine how strain-based reflexes may simplify the control of multiple legs simultaneously in stance phase, which forms a redundant manipulator. In addition, we will use Drosophibot to test our model of the fly central complex [12], and explore how the brain may control behavior by modifying the strength of reflexes in the thoracic networks.

We will further use Drosophibot to help design experiments that can be performed in the animal. Specifically, we plan to study what kinds of information must be shared between the legs to produce coordinated walking. Behavioral rules that coordinate walking have long been known (e.g. the Cruse rules, [7]), but it is not clear whether these arise due to information transmitted between legs through the nervous system, through mechanical coupling, or both. Drosophibot, with its 18 strain gages and 18 leg joint proprioceptors, will provide us an opportunity to systematically explore how each impacts coordinated walking. Genetic tools will enable our collaborators to replicate these experiments with the animal [5], after which we can compare results to better understand how animals accomplish such robust locomotion.

References

1. Biological neural networks in invertebrate neuroethology and robotics. Editors: Randall D. Beer, Roy E. Ritzmann, Thomas McKenna (Academic Press, Inc., Harcourt Brace Jovanovich, 1993). SIGART Bull. **7**(4), 24 (1996). https://doi.org/10.1145/264927.1066406, reviewer-Becker, Glenn

2. Ache, J.M., Matheson, T.: Passive joint forces are tuned to limb use in insects and drive movements without motor activity. Curr. Biol. **23**(15), 1418–1426 (2013). https://doi.org/10.1016/j.cub.2013.06.024

3. Buschmann, T., Ewald, A., von Twickel, A., Buschges, A.: Controlling legs for locomotion-insights from robotics and neurobiology. Bioinspiration Biomim. **10**(4), 41001 (2015). https://doi.org/10.1088/1748-3190/10/4/041001

4. Canio, G.D., et al.: A robot leg with compliant tarsus and its neural control for efficient and adaptive locomotion on complex terrains. Artif. Life Robot. **21**(3), 274–281 (2016). https://doi.org/10.1007/s10015-016-0296-3

5. Chockley, A.S., Ratican, S., Büschges, A., Bockemühl, T.: Subgroups of femoral chordotonal organ neurons differentially affect leg movements and coordination in *Drosophila melanogaster*. In: Proceedings of the 13th Goettingen Meeting of the German Neuroscience Society, Goettingen, Germany (2019)

6. Cofer, D.W., Cymbalyuk, G., Reid, J., Zhu, Y., Heitler, W.J., Edwards, D.H.: AnimatLab: a 3D graphics environment for neuromechanical simulations. J. Neurosci. Methods **187**(2), 280–288 (2010). https://doi.org/10.1016/j.jneumeth.2010.01.005

7. Cruse, H., Schwarze, W.: Mechanisms of coupling between the ipsilateral legs of a walking insect *Carausius morosus*. J. Exp. Biol. **138**(1), 455–469 (1988)

8. Delcomyn, F.: Foundations of Neurobiology. W.H. Freeman, New York (1998)

9. Goldschmidt, D., Wörgötter, F., Manoonpong, P.: Biologically-inspired adaptive obstacle negotiation behavior of hexapod robots. Front. Neurorobot. **8** (2014). https://doi.org/10.3389/fnbot.2014.00003

10. Hooper, S.L., et al.: Neural control of unloaded leg posture and of leg swing in stick insect, cockroach, and mouse differs from that in larger animals. J. Neurosci. **29**(13), 4109–4119 (2009)

11. Mendes, C.S., Bartos, I., Akay, T., Marka, S., Mann, R.S.: Quantification of gait parameters in freely walking wild type and sensory deprived *Drosophila melanogaster*. eLife **2**, e00231 (2013). https://doi.org/10.7554/eLife.00231

12. Pickard, S.C., Quinn, R.D., Szczecinski, N.S.: Simulation of the arthropod central complex: moving towards bioinspired robotic navigation control. In: Vouloutsi, V., et al. (eds.) Living Machines 2018. LNCS (LNAI), vol. 10928, pp. 370–381. Springer, Cham (2018). https://doi.org/10.1007/978-3-319-95972-6_40

13. Rubeo, S., Szczecinski, N., Quinn, R.: A synthetic nervous system controls a simulated cockroach. Appl. Sci. **8**(1), 6 (2017)

14. Schneider, A., Paskarbeit, J., Schilling, M., Schmitz, J.: HECTOR, a bio-inspired and compliant hexapod robot. In: Duff, A., Lepora, N.F., Mura, A., Prescott, T.J., Verschure, P.F.M.J. (eds.) Living Machines 2014. LNCS (LNAI), vol. 8608, pp. 427–429. Springer, Cham (2014). https://doi.org/10.1007/978-3-319-09435-9_51

15. Spenko, M.J., et al.: Biologically inspired climbing with a hexapedal robot. J. Field Robot. **25**(4–5), 223–242. https://doi.org/10.1002/rob.20238

16. Szczecinski, N.S., Bockemühl, T., Chockley, A.S., Büschges, A.: Static stability predicts the continuum of interleg coordination patterns in *Drosophila*. J. Exp. Biol. (2018). https://doi.org/10.1242/jeb.189142

17. Szczecinski, N.S., Brown, A.E., Bender, J.A., Quinn, R.D., Ritzmann, R.E.: A neuromechanical simulation of insect walking and transition to turning of the cockroach *Blaberus discoidalis*. Biol. Cybern. **108**(1), 1–21 (2014). https://doi.org/10.1007/s00422-013-0573-3

18. Szczecinski, N.S., et al.: Introducing MantisBot: hexapod robot controlled by a high-fidelity, real-time neural simulation. In: IEEE International Conference on Intelligent Robots and Systems, vol. 2015-Dec, pp. 3875–3881 (2015). https://doi.org/10.1109/IROS.2015.7353922

19. Szczecinski, N.S., Hunt, A.J., Quinn, R.D.: Design process and tools for dynamic neuromechanical models and robot controllers. Biol. Cybern. **111**(1), 105–127 (2017). https://doi.org/10.1007/s00422-017-0711-4

20. Szczecinski, N.S., Quinn, R.D.: Template for the neural control of directed stepping generalized to all legs of MantisBot. Bioinspiration Biomim. **12**(4), 45001 (2017). https://doi.org/10.1088/1748-3190/aa6dd9

21. von Twickel, A., Hild, M., Siedel, T., Patel, V., Pasemann, F.: Neural control of a modular multi-legged walking machine: simulation and hardware. Robot. Auton. Syst. **60**, 227–241 (2012)

22. Wosnitza, A., Bockemuhl, T., Dubbert, M., Scholz, H., Buschges, A.: Inter-leg coordination in the control of walking speed in *Drosophila*. J. Exp. Biol. **216**(Pt 3), 480–491 (2013). https://doi.org/10.1242/jeb.078139

23. Zill, S.N., Büschges, A., Schmitz, J.: Encoding of force increases and decreases by tibial campaniform sensilla in the stick insect, *Carausius morosus*. J. Comp. Physiol. A Neuroethol. Sens. Neural Behav. Physiol. **197**(8), 851–867 (2011). https://doi.org/10.1007/s00359-011-0647-4

24. Zill, S.N., Schmitz, J., Chaudhry, S., Büschges, A.: Force encoding in stick insect legs delineates a reference frame for motor control. J. Neurophysiol. **108**(5), 1453–1472 (2012). https://doi.org/10.1152/jn.00274.2012

Crab-Like Hexapod Feet for Amphibious Walking in Sand and Waves

Nicole M. Graf[✉], Alexander M. Behr, and Kathryn A. Daltorio

Case Western Reserve University, Cleveland, OH 44106, USA
nmg63@case.edu

Abstract. Sandy beaches can be smooth access points for future amphibious robots to enter and exit the water, but the terrain is challenging, especially for smaller scale robots. Strong hydrodynamic forces can interrupt navigation by displacing, reorienting, or even inverting the robot. Looking to animals that navigate these conditions, crabs have legs and gaits that are distinctive from land animals and robots. In order to better understand the potential advantages of crab-like legs for surf-zone terrain, our goal is to evaluate these legs on dry, wet, and submerged sandy terrain. With our modified 1.2 kg HEXY robot, we demonstrate two important advantages of crab-like legs. First, crab-like legs can allow the robot to resist vertical forces greater than the body weight (the maximum force required to lift the robot is 120% of the weight). This is important because, in contrast to robots that increase traction by adding weight, using the legs to effectively increase normal forces means that robots can be built lighter and smaller while still traversing the same environments. Secondly, we show distributed inward gripping with the crab-like legs reduce wave-induced displacement in lab tests (with default feet, waves displace the robot 1–4 cm, but with our crab-like feet, this displacement is eliminated). The modified foot designs of the robot are compatible with legged walking gaits (slow, medium, and fast). In the future, these leg designs and grasping strategies can be used to convert other land-based robots for amphibious locomotion.

Keywords: Bio-inspired robot · Amphibious robots · Legged locomotion

1 Introduction

Surf-zones (areas of the ocean with depth less than 10 m) are challenging but necessary environments for amphibious robots. Developing solutions for traversing sandy beaches may be a first step towards more capable robots for environmental monitoring, lifeguarding, or naval science.

Sand is a challenging substrate for robot locomotion because in some regimes it behaves like a solid and in others like a liquid [1]. Some researchers have adapted wheel designs [2, 3] to move around in sand. Wheel designs such as this are promising, yet legged locomotion has many benefits, such as the maneuverability [1], efficiency, speed, and versatility in rough terrains, natural environments, or unconstructed environments [4]. Full understanding of granular media is complex [5]. Many properties of the sand impact how the robot will move, including the packing [1], cohesion [6],

© Springer Nature Switzerland AG 2019
U. Martinez-Hernandez et al. (Eds.): Living Machines 2019, LNAI 11556, pp. 158–170, 2019.
https://doi.org/10.1007/978-3-030-24741-6_14

tensile strength [6], capillary forces [6], and moisture levels [6]. Different characteristics of the robot, such as the limb speed [6], mass [5], and driving patterns [5] will contribute to the movement in granular media as well. Because of this complexity empirical testing is essential and models such [7] show how results can be scaled from sandbox tests to different size vehicles.

More importantly, the presence of waves can limit locomotion. While a light robot might be displaced in the waves, a heavy robot's weight may be able to counteract the buoyancy and hydrodynamic forces. However, adding weight has disadvantages: a heavy robot may sink into the sand, have greater energy requirements, and incur higher material and delivery costs. In this paper we will show that grasping with legs can increase stability in waves without adding weight. This is critical for developing smaller, lighter robots for walking on shorelines.

At every length scale, animals transition between water and land, and amphibious robots are often inspired by biology. Nature hints at what is possible and design ideas that people may not have considered [8]. Inspired by cockroaches, Whegs IV is an all-terrain robot that can move efficiently both in and out of water [9, 10]. This robot incorporates the strengths of both wheels and legs for navigation; however, the gait cannot be varied. The MinTurtle-I aims to obtain efficient and easy amphibious locomotion based off of a turtle [11]. An otter robot, SeaOtter, is being developed to traverse and map surf zones [12]. The SeaOtter does move around in surf zones, but this crawler robot cannot adapt its gait either. Snake robots have been developed for both land and aquatic implementation that are very flexible and have advantages over legged robots [13, 14]; however, if a wave comes, they will go with the force of the current. Gecko robots can run across the surface of water [15] but will also succumb to waves. The same issue is true for duck robots, that have webbed feet capable of generating propulsion similar to real ducks, allowing it to swim and walk [16]. An insect robot was designed to swim and fly, transitioning between the air and water; however, this robot will also be ineffective in waves and the transition from water to air is unable to be controlled [17].

Crabs are arguably one of the most famous animals for adeptly walking in surf zones. Crabs use the sand's properties to help them dig hiding places [18] and oscillate their feet laterally to help dig into the sand [8]. Crabs can vary their gait between land and submerged environments. This has helped in the development of autonomous legged underwater vehicles [19]. These animals also have wide bodies with strong legs and tapered dactyls [20]. These dactyls help the crabs navigate in the sand. They walk forward in a gait cycle that alternates similar to insects [21]. Crabs are able to locomote without displacing from waves [22].

The advantages of crabs have inspired robot designs. The claw of the crab has also inspired the development of a compliant microgripper [23]. A lobster robot was developed to explore the advantages of lobster locomotion [24]. Horseshoe crab-inspired robots demonstrate the value of a tail for self-righting if flipped by waves [25]. A large crab robot, the Crabster CR200, is another amphibious robot being created to explore control techniques [26]. Autonomous legged underwater vehicles, Ursula and Ariel, were developed in the 1990s [27] to explore effects of walking with different stance widths [8]. In contrast, the gripping strategy proposed in this is to effectively change the stance width mid-stance (as discussed in Sect. 3.1).

The concept of deliberately gripping a substrate by pulling the legs inward is a strategy used in recent climbing robots [28, 29]. We, and others, have referred to it as "Distributed Inward Gripping" [30]. However, to our knowledge this has not been applied to amphibious robots. Here our goal is to determine whether and to what extent it is possible for a legged robot to "grip" fine sand.

This paper presents empirical evidence that grip force generated by a legged robot can withstand waves on granular media, supporting that DIG can be applied to legged robots locomoting in granular media. We modified off-the-shelf robot (HEXY, Arc-Botics, [31]) to mimic a crab-like grasp on dry, wet, or submerged granular media. The resulting robot (Fig. 1) can resist displacement from waves developed in a wave-tank significantly better than the original design (p = 5e^{-5}). The crab-like gripping actions and dactyl designs described in this work could enable legged robots to enter and exit water at shorelines-resulting in more capable amphibious robots.

Fig. 1. Our modified hexapod robot can walk submerged or partially submerged (as shown) in sand.

2   Experimental Methods

With many open source and commercially available robots, we realized that water-proofing and modifying an existing robot design would be more repeatable for others and expedient for baseline testing. Although several of the small servomotors have failed during the hundreds of trials, they are easy to replace.

We chose the HEXY robot kit from ArcBotics (Fig. 2A), a hexapod with three DOF per leg. This robot was chosen because it is convenient for indoor testing, it has an onboard Arduino-based board for control with Bluetooth or USB, and it is easy to modify the blue acrylic laser cut body parts. Another major advantage is that it comes in a metal geared servo version for higher actuator durability. HEXY comes with a rubber cap to act as the foot of the robot. This cap increases the surface area of the foot, allowing the unit to move better on normal land.

2.1   Robot Waterproofing

The HEXY kit was modified to waterproof the robot. The total body width of the robot is 200 mm. The coxa is 101.6 mm. The femur is 25.4 mm. The tibia and the dactyl are each 50.8 mm. The ultrasonic distance sensor was removed from the body. Next, all of the servos were disassembled, and the gears were coated with Lucas Hi-Performance Multi-Purpose Marine Grease. Then, the servos were reassembled, and thin coatings of silicone modified conformal coating (MG Chemicals), which glows under a blacklight, were added to the outside of the servos, by dipping each servo into a beaker with the solution. To make sure all of the needed seams were covered, each servo was examined under a blacklight to ensure full coverage. The marine grease and conformal coating ensured that the servos interior is protected from water. Once this coating dried, the HEXY robot was reassembled.

The controller was placed in a waterproof box (Adafruit Toyogiken Tibox Small Plastic Project Enclosure – Weatherproof with Clear Top) that was modified by removing most of the top of the box and adding a laser cut acrylic plate, which allowed for the wires to be connected to the board and for the wires to be waterproofed with the lid. The holes in this casing and the wires sticking out of it were then caulked shut to ensure a watertight seal. The batteries needed to be more accessible, so a Mpow 024 Waterproof Case, Universal IPX8 Waterproof Phone Pouch Underwater Protective Dry Bag was purchased. Gardner Bender LTB-400 Liquid Electrical Tape was painted along the edges of the battery cases and the waterproof box as an added precaution. The resulting robot is shown in Fig. 2B.

(a)   (b)

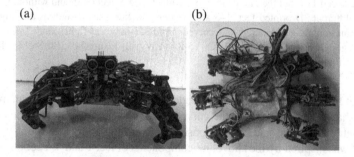

Fig. 2. (A) HEXY robot, before modification, on hard substrate (B) Top view after waterproofing.

2.2   Foot Designs

Each foot of the original HEXY robot is a flat piece of 6.35 mm thick acrylic that attaches to the servo and then narrows to a width of 7.9 mm for a length of 34.9 mm, including the rounded tip. The robot comes with a black rubber cap that fits snugly over the tip to increase foot compliance and friction.

In order to obtain the grip force needed to overcome the force of waves, different designs of the foot were tested to try to increase the amount of extraction resistance (measured vertically as described below) required to remove the robot from sand.

Nine different feet were prototyped, 3D printed on a Flashforge Creator Pro with white PLA material (30% rectilinear infill), and tested, along with the original foot with and without the rubber cap. These feet are shown in Fig. 3.

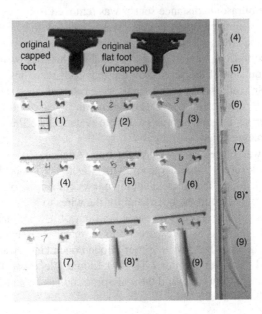

Fig. 3. We tested 11 robot feet: at the top, the original HEXY feet (with and without plastic cap) and then 9 different 3D printed feet. 1–3 are the same thickness and length as the original, 4–6 have the same length, but tapered and curved profiles (shown at right), and 7–9 are longer. https://drive.google.com/drive/folders/1FO0Y5-ZF_YWyvaIpXRnmQ4A3R6rSreMl for more detail on the foot design.

For feet four through six, a curve was added to mimic the dactyl of a crab more than a generic shape. The hope is that the curve from the foot will allow the component to easily penetrate the sand and hold its position better than a blockier foot.

Foot 7 was inspired by the shoveling components of feet 1 and 4. Feet 8 and 9 were designed to mimic the dactyl of an actual crab, but the length was not kept constant with the other designs. These feet were used to examine whether or not the profile of the natural crab would outperform the synthetic designs.

In preliminary characterization experiments, the curved feet were more successful at moving and gripping than the designs without the taper. For feet 7 and 9, the foot was too long to allow HEXY to walk, rendering them useless. Foot #8 had the advantages of the curved foot yet gripped better than all of the other modified designs. The inferences from these tests yielded that Foot #8 was the most promising design.

3 Crab-Like Robot Movement

3.1 Grip Definition

The coxa is 101.6 mm, the femur is 25.4 mm, and the tibia and the dactyl are each 50.8 mm. When the robot legs are completely horizontal in the X direction, the angles in the legs are all set to 0°. Each leg has a range of motion from –90° to +90°. The different grips being tested are generated by changing the angles between each of the joints.

Four grips were examined throughout this process: a home position, a small grip, a medium grip, and a large grip. As a result of the specified angles, leg tips are closer together when in a "Large Grip". The tip-to-tip distances and grip positions are shown in Fig. 4.

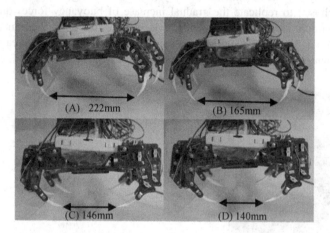

Fig. 4. Demonstration of grip positions in air with distance between front legs. (A) no grip, (B) small grip (C) medium grip (D) large grip

3.2 Walking Gaits

Three different walking speeds (slow, medium, and fast) were tested. Each step in the different tripod gaits moved approximately 19.1 mm. The only difference is the delay: 600 ms for slow (came preprogrammed in the HEXY software), 525 ms for medium (average of slow and fast delay), and 450 ms for fast (how fast the actuators can move).

4 Characterization of Resulting Robot

The resulting robot weighs 1.2 kg. The waterproofing and different feet designs can vary the weight by 40 g, and this variation is considered when normalizing subsequent data. The modified HEXY robot is smaller than existing crab-like robots [20, 21], and also has more degrees of freedom than other crab inspired robots [20, 21], which result in a more versatile range of applications.

4.1   Evaluation of Vertical Force (Ability to Grip the Ground)

Pavestone Natural Play Sand was purchased from Home Depot and poured into a dry tank and a wet tank. In the wet tank, a 10° incline was created. Water was added to create submerged areas below the waterline and wet but not submerged areas above the waterline. Between each test, a piece of metal was used to spread the sand back to a natural, flat surface. This resulted in each run of the test being conducted with the same initial conditions in the sand.

At the start of each test, the robot was placed in the appropriate sand and connected to the force gauge (Nextech DFS50 Digital Force Gauge, published resolution ±2.0 g force) by a wire connected to its body. The programmer would then have the robot reset on the sand and perform the appropriate grip. Some tests were ran without any grip to obtain a control set of data. After performing the grip, the gauge would be pulled vertically (by hand) until the robot yielded from the granular media. The slow speed was chosen to replicate the gradual increase of buoyancy forces due to rising water and to minimize the speed-dependent viscosity terms. Thus, these measurements are conservative. The force gauge would record the maximum load for each test. The setup is shown in Fig. 5, and an example single test result is shown in Fig. 6.

Fig. 5. Grip test example

Fig. 6. Example time-force profile for single Foot #8 in wet sand with a big grip.

The force gauge measures the total vertical forces, reflecting the sum total of all of the forces on the dactyls. Final grip testing was performed 30 times in each condition (dry, wet, and submerged sand) for each different grip (none, small, medium, large) for Foot #8 and the original foot with and without the cap. The results are in Fig. 7.

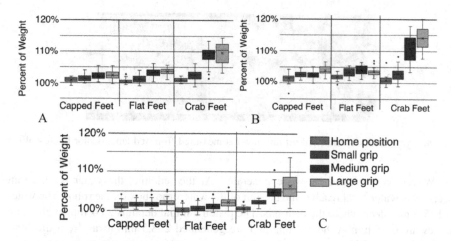

Fig. 7. (A) Summary of grip trials in dry sand (B) Summary of grip trials in wet sand (C) Summary of grip trials in submerged sand

The data in Fig. 7 shows that the dactyl and the grasp motion are both required to increase the removal force. With original feet (with or without cap), all of the performed consistently, with an average that is close to the robot's weight, no matter which sand was used.

Using the crab-like feet (Foot #8) resulted in higher removal forces than the weight when the grip positions were used. The force generally increases with grip size, so the largest forces correspond to the large grip. This grasping worked in all sand types, with removal force to weight of 110% in dry sand, 120% in wet sand, and 106% in submerged sand.

The outliers are present because the robot would occasionally not achieve a solid grip, and the crab feet increased the variance. All of the grips in this testing could have slight increases in weight caused from sand friction and small amounts of sand stuck on the feet.

A t-test was applied to no grip and large grip for each type of sand for Foot #8 and found that there was a significant increase in grip force. For the dry sand a p-value of 9.06×10^{-15} was achieved, for the wet sand a p-value of $p < 2.20 \times 10^{-16}$ was achieved, and for the submerged sand a p-value of 3.69×10^{-11} was achieved.

4.2   Characterization of Wave-Induced Displacement in Stance

The feet were also tested in a wave test using a wave generator. The modified HEXY robot was placed in the tank with its front legs at a point marked on the glass of the tank, shown in Fig. 8.

Fig. 8. Wave tank experimental set-up, travel is measured from red tape. (Color figure online)

Waves were created by wave generator. At the red line, the water is 76.2 mm deep. This water level reaches the bottom of the waterproof box on the robot. The water is 155.6 mm deep where the piston is. The piston's initial depth is 25.4 mm at 20°. The waves are 63.5 mm at the red line and are generated 298.5 mm away from the front feet of the robot. The board connected to the piston that is used to generate the waves is 228.6 mm x 301.6 mm. The stroke of the piston is 152.4 mm. The piston was powered with an air tank at 100 psi. The waves were then generated at 3.2 Hz for four waves. After that, the robot's total absolute displacement was recorded. The average over 10 trials is recorded in Table 1 along with std.

Table 1. Average displacement and standard deviation from the wave test in mm.

Grip	Original foot with cap				Original foot without cap				Foot #8			
	None	Small	Med.	Large	None	Small	Med.	Large	None	Small	Med.	Large
Wave-induced displacement (mm)	41	50	55	57	8	21	23	15	0	0	0	0
Std (mm)	10	12	3	4	6	5	3	6	0	0	0	0

When comparing the three feet, Foot #8 had no measurable displacement at all for every grip. These results show that the dactyl foot #8 is better at resisting displacement (without gripping the dactyl resists displacement significantly better than the original capped foot ($p = 5.2 \times 10^{-5}$, t-test in R)). Furthermore, without the dactyl foot, gripping did not help the robot attach to the ground.

4.3   Walking Speed Characterization

To show that the robot can navigate in granular media, the modified HEXY was timed as it traversed 457.2 mm (18in) of each type of sand. The robot was also timed for locomoting along a linoleum floor and in a container of rocks. The setup for this test on linoleum is shown in Fig. 9.

Fig. 9. Distance traveled in speed tests.

Each leg was able to successfully travel along the set distance on the dry, wet, and submerged sand, as well as in the rocks. On dry linoleum, with Foot #8, there was too much slip at the fastest speeds for the robot to move. In the submerged tests, the depth of the water is 25.4 mm above the sand, completely covering the feet. Three different walking speeds were performed fifteen times for consistent data. The average velocities are recorded in Table 2.

Table 2. Average velocities in mm/s.

Speed in sand (mm/s)	Original foot with cap			Original foot without cap			Foot #8		
	Slow	Med	Fast	Slow	Med	Fast	Slow	Med	Fast
Dry	55	63	73	61	68	77	34	39	42
Wet	48	55	57	43	55	65	33	37	36
Submerged	62	72	81	60	67	67	13	16	29
Linoleum	58	67	74	59	73	86	35	35	0
Rocks	54	60	67	50	57	54	28	28	37

While each of the feet were able to move, Foot #8 was slower than the original foot with and without the cap. At fastest, the robot was moving at ~ 2 body lengths per second with the original rounded feet. Switching to tapered feet reduces speed by approximately 58% on dry sand, 67% on wet sand, 28% on submerged sand, 37% on the linoleum floor, and 61% on the rocks.

5 Discussion and Conclusions

The contributions of this paper are two-fold. First, we show that a crab-like foot shape enables a grip motion in sand. Both the tapered foot shape and the inward grip motion after contact with the ground are needed to grip the granular media. These strategies can be applied to the design of smaller light weight robots to operate in areas where previously only robots that were large relative to the water depth have been used. The dactyl helps the foot penetrate the sand and increase the likelihood that the feet will successfully grasp the ground. The gripping acts as an anchor to keep the robot on the ground. The dactyl and the grip work together to keep the robot stationary in the sand until the robot is commanded to take a step.

Second, we show that the displacement due to waves is reduced when crab-like feet are added. Tapered dactyls increase the depth that the robot sinks into the sand, which better anchors the robot to the ground. Eliminating this displacement is important for walking in surf-zones.

The disadvantage of tapered feet is that for the same gait patterns, the overall walking speed roughly halved. Based on our observations, this is because our current gait pattern did not allow Foot #8 to fully exit the sand, reducing the velocities associated with that foot. In future work, new gaits can be explored that may increase the walking speed.

Taken together, these results provide an explanation for the distinctive pointed dactyls of biological crabs which are different from the flat feet of land animals and suggest potential designs for legged amphibious robots.

Acknowledgment. We would like to thank Ariel Foss for help with data entry, Noah Napiewocki and Justin Wong for constructing the wave tank, and Chenming Wei for helping make the drawings of the feet. This work was sponsored by the Office of Naval Research and CWRU Graduate Student Travel Award.

References

1. Li, C., Umbanhowar, P., Komsuoglu, H., Koditschek, D., Goldman, D.: Sensitive dependence of the motion of a legged robot on granular media. PNAS **106**, 3029–3034 (2009)
2. Sun, Y., Ma, S.: A versatile locomotion mechanism for amphibious robots: eccentric paddle mechanism. In: Advanced Robotics (2013)
3. J8 Atlas Xtreme Terrain Robot (XTR), Canada. http://www.army-technology.com/projects/j8-atlas-xtreme-terrain-robot-xtr/
4. Liang, C., Ceccarelli, M., Carbone, G.: Design and simulation of legged walking robots in MATLAB® environment. In: Perutka, K. (ed.) MATLAB for Engineers - Applications in Control, Electrical Engineering, IT and Robotics (2011). ISBN 978-953-307-914-1
5. Marvi, H., et al.: Sidewinding with minimal slip: snake and robot ascent of sandy slopes. Science **346**(6206), 224–229 (2014)
6. Kim, T.H., Nam, J.M., Yun, J.M., Lee, K.I., You, S.K.: Relationship between cohesion and tensile strength in wet sand and at low normal stresses. In: Proceedings of International Conference on Soil Mechanics and Geotechnical Engineering, pp. 364–367 (2009)
7. Askari, H., Kamrin, K.: Intrusion in heterogeneous materials: simple global rules from complex micro-mechanics. arXiv preprint arXiv:1510.02966 (2015)
8. Full, R.J.: Using biological inspiration to build artificial life that locomotes. In: Gomi, T. (ed.) EvoRobots 2001. LNCS, vol. 2217, pp. 110–120. Springer, Heidelberg (2001). https://doi.org/10.1007/3-540-45502-7_6
9. Boxerbaum, A.S., Werk, P., Quinn, R.D., Vaidyanathan, R.: Design of an autonomous amphibious robot for surf zone operation: Part I mechanical design for multi-mode mobility. In: Proceedings of 2005 IEEE/ASME International Conference on Advanced Intelligent Mechatronics, pp. 1459–1464. IEEE (2005)

10. Harkins, R., Ward, J., Vaidyanathan, R., Boxerbaum, A.X., Quinn, R.D.: Design of an autonomous amphibious robot for surf zone operations: Part II-hardware, control implementation and simulation. In: Proceedings of 2005 IEEE/ASME International Conference on Advanced Intelligent Mechatronics, pp. 1465–1470. IEEE (2005)
11. Han, B., et al.: Mechanism design and gait experiment of an amphibian robotic turtle. Adv. Robot. 25(16), 2083–2097 (2011)
12. SeaOtter. http://www.weeprojects.com/c-2-innovations-inc-c-2i.html
13. Kelasidi, E., et al.: Innovation in underwater robots: biologically inspired swimming snake robots. IEEE Robot. Autom. Mag. 23(1), 44–62 (2016)
14. Kelasidi, E., et al.: Locomotion efficiency optimization of biologically inspired snake robots. Appl. Sci. 8(1), 80 (2018)
15. Nirody, J.A., et al.: Geckos race across the water's surface using multiple mechanisms. Curr. Biol. 28(24), 4046–4051 (2018)
16. Kashem, S.B.A., Mujahid, T., Malcolm, C.: A novel design of an amphibious robot having webbed feet as duck. In: International Conference on Computer and Drone Applications (IConDA). IEEE (2017)
17. Chen, Y., et al.: A biologically inspired, flapping-wing, hybrid aerial-aquatic microrobot. Sci. Robot. 2(11), eaao5619 (2017)
18. Weis, J.S.: Walking Sideways: The Remarkable World of Crabs. Cornell University Press, Ithaca (2012). ISBN 978-0-8014-5050-1. OCLC 794640315
19. Martinez, M.M., Full, R.J., Koehl, M.A.: Underwater punting by an intertidal crab: a novel gait revealed by the kinematics of pedestrian locomotion in air versus water. J. Exp. Biol. 201(18), 2609–2623 (1998)
20. Cunningham, C.W., Blackstone, N.W., Buss, L.W.: Evolution of king crabs from hermit crab ancestors. Nature 355(6360), 539 (1992)
21. Herreid, C.F., Full, R.J.: Locomotion of hermit crabs (Coenobita compressus) on beach and treadmill. J. Exp. Biol. 120(1), 283–296 (1986)
22. Martinez, M.M.: Running in the surf: hydrodynamics of the shore crab Grapsus tenuicrustatus. J. Exp. Biol. 204(17), 3097–3112 (2001)
23. Nguyen, D.N., et al.: Multi-objective optimization design for a sand crab-inspired compliant microgripper. Microsyst. Technol. 1–19 (2019)
24. Ayers, J., Witting, J.: Biomimetic approaches to the control of underwater walking machines. Philos. Trans. R. Soc. Lond. A Math. Phys. Eng. Sci. 365(1850), 273–295 (2007)
25. Krummel, G., Kaipa, K.N., Gupta, S.K.: A horseshoe crab inspired surf zone robot with righting capabilities. In: ASME 2014 International Design Engineering Technical Conferences and Computers and Information in Engineering Conference, p. V05AT08A010. American Society of Mechanical Engineers, August 2014
26. Falconer, J.: Huge Six-Legged Robot Crabster Goes Swimming. IEEE Spectrum, 30 July 2013. https://spectrum.ieee.org/automaton/robotics/industrial-robots/six-legged-underwater-robot-crabster
27. Elsley, D.R., et al.: Autonomous legged underwater vehicles for near land warfare. In: Proceedings of the Autonomous Vehicles in Mine Countermeasures Symposium, Naval Postgraduate School, 4–7 April 1995
28. Wile, G.D., et al.: Screenbot: walking inverted using distributed inward gripping. In: IEEE/RSJ International Conference on Intelligent Robots and Systems, IROS 2008, pp. 1513–1518. IEEE, September 2008
29. Hawkes, E.W., et al.: Dynamic surface grasping with directional adhesion. In: IEEE/RSJ International Conference on Intelligent Robots and Systems, pp. 5487–5493. IEEE, November 2013

30. Palmer III, L.R., Diller, E., Quinn, R.D.: Toward gravity-independent climbing using a biologically inspired distributed inward gripping strategy. IEEE/ASME Trans. Mechatron. **20**(2), 631–640 (2015)
31. HEXY. http://arcbotics.com/products/hexy/

Highly-Integrated Muscle-Spindles for Pneumatic Artificial Muscles Made from Conductive Fabrics

Arne Hitzmann[✉], Shuhei Ikemoto, and Koh Hosoda

Osaka University, Toyonaka 1-3, Osaka 560-8531, Japan
arne.hitzmann@arl.sys.es.osaka-u.ac.jp

Abstract. Pneumatic artificial muscles (PAMs) actuating bio-inspired structures are widely used to mimic the human musculoskeletal system. The research in this field can improve the understanding of the human's physical abilities through a close recreation of its natural structure. This paper will introduce an enhancement to PAMs resembling the sensory-feedback of the muscles spindles' group Ia and II afferent neurons. The artificial muscle spindle presented in this paper is embedded into the muscle and wraps around like its biological counterpart. Previous publications of artificial muscle spindles mostly aimed to output a signal, which correlates to the length of the muscle. This approach, however, aimed to recreate the natural muscle spindle as close as possible in regards to its functional principal and positioning inside of the PAM. By using conductive fabrics, a deeply embedded sensor type was created, which feedback correlates to the expansion of the PAM's inner tube, as well as the pressure in-between of the inner tube and the outer braided sleeve. In this paper, a constructional approach on a biomimetic muscle spindle is introduced, including its Ia and II afferent neurons.

Keywords: Constructive approach · Soft-robotics · Sensory-feedback

1 Introduction

Research in bio-inspired humanoid robots and biomimetics is recently drawing an increasing amount of attention. One field beside the simple replication of the human morphology is its actuation using artificial muscles. The McKibben design of pneumatic artificial muscles (PAMs) is broadly used for this purpose. They show properties like fast response and are flexible by design. Using them to actuate a human-inspired robot can help to increase the capabilities of bio-inspired robots, as well as the understanding of the human body. One downside of this type of actuator is its low control precision. A typical approach, therefore, is to estimate the current length of the actuator and to control it through the applied pressure. Unfortunately is the relationship between pressure and length non-linear and highly dependent on factors like externally applied lateral forces, and internal properties like friction.

© Springer Nature Switzerland AG 2019
U. Martinez-Hernandez et al. (Eds.): Living Machines 2019, LNAI 11556, pp. 171–182, 2019.
https://doi.org/10.1007/978-3-030-24741-6_15

This problem was approached by introducing a new version of an artificial muscle spindle, which can be embedded into the PAM. This was achieved by using conductive fabrics, which were applied directly to the inner tube of the PAM. Therefore a change in dynamic properties like stiffness and flexibility could be avoided.

1.1   Related Work

This work relates to previous efforts of researchers to increase the precision, and therefore, the usability of PAMs. This paper is introducing a hardware extension to traditional PAMs, which closely oriented on its biological counterpart. The following paragraph lists research, which relates to the aim of adapting muscle spindles to PAMs.

Hardware. Jaax et al. [1] concentrated their efforts on creating a prototype of an artificial muscle spindle, without embedding it into a PAM. In their published design for an artificial muscle spindle, Erin et al. [2] proposed a PAM which is covered with a mesh of copper wire held in place by silicone. Their design allowed to estimate the muscle's displacement based on the inductance of the coil formed by the copper wire. A shape-memory alloy was used by Peng et al. [3] To measure the length of a PAM when it exerts a specific force. Hannaford et al. [4] published a platform to research human neural control. They described their setup to control PAMs by approaches inspired by motor units. However, it did not include the feedback of physically represented muscle spindles.

Contributions. The results and methodology of this work can aid the research of human muscle control and coordination on the lowest level. A broader understanding in this area in combination with seamlessly embedded sensory-feedback can drastically increase in the motoric abilities of PAM-actuated robots.

2   Neurophysiological Background of Muscle Spindles

In the following section, the sensory-feedback system will be introduced, which is described in the literature as muscle spindles. This introduction will explain why this type of receptor should be considered to be of high potential to advance the capabilities of PAMs in musculoskeletal robots. Further, will this form the foundation of the reasoning regarding the physical properties the artificial muscle spindle was designed for.

The biological muscle spindle consists of two different kinds of sensing neurons. Figure 1 visualizes the structure and the placement of the two neurons within the muscle.

The muscle spindle provides the input for the motor-units, which are essential for the muscles to maintain a specific length, as well as the cooperation of antagonistic muscles. To achieve this the two afferent neurons, which the muscle spindle consists of, modulate their firing rate based on two aspects of the muscle's state. The Ia afferent neuron is wrapped around the nuclear chain fiber and

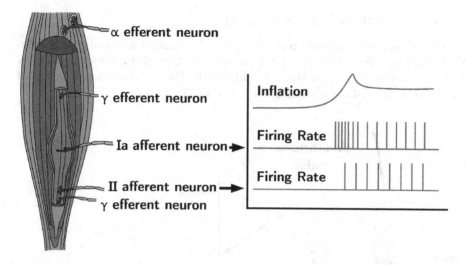

Fig. 1. This image shows the representation of the biological muscle spindle (Inspired by Purves [5]). On the right side the response to inflation of the Ia and II afferent neurons is also visualized. This is the feedback that allows the motor-units to effectively control the and maintain the length of muscles.

detects small changes of the muscle's inflation. Its firing rate hereby depends on the change rate of the muscle's inflation. The II afferent neuron, however, changes its firing rate regarding the sustained inflation of the muscle. Further, do the γ efferent neurons moderate the excitability of the Ia and the II afferent neurons.

3   Artificial Muscle Spindle

3.1   Concept

The vital information for the realization of a bio-inspired motor-unit is sensory-feedback of the muscles. In human anatomy, several receptors are responsible for this. Most notable are the muscle spindles and the Golgi tendon organs, whereby the latter is more involved in preventing over-stressing, and the first one supports the maintenance of the muscles' length. Therefore, the muscle spindles were chosen as the most desirable source of feedback to implement a more dexterous control scheme for PAMs. The biggest challenge was the choice of material for the artificial muscle spindle's Ia and II afferent neuron. The design described in this paper was defined after the following design requirements:

- can be embedded into the PAM
- fast response
- simplicity of measurements
- not causing the muscle to fail prematurely

– not changing the elasticity of the muscle

Other researchers already published several designs of artificial muscle spindles; however, they either could not be embedded, needed additional circuitry to be read or even reduced the durability of the PAMs. The design concept of this work's artificial muscle spindle is shown in Fig. 2.

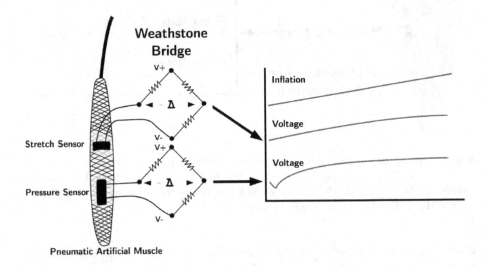

Fig. 2. This image shows the functional concept of the design for an artificial muscle spindle. Two sensors made from conductive fabrics are placed in similar locations on the PAM as their biological counterparts are on a muscle fiber.

The design integrates the Ia and II afferent neuron by placing two different kinds of conductive fabrics in-between the inner rubber tube and the outer braided sleeve of the PAM. The type which represents the Ia afferent neuron changes its resistance when it is stretched. It is positioned in the middle of the muscle and is partially wrapped around it. The second sensor which represents the II afferent neuron, is made from a piezoresistive fabric and changes its resistance under pressure.

The choice of two different fabrics was made so the stretch of an unpressured PAM can be detected as well. The stretch sensor alone is not capable of measuring this reliable, as the diameter of the PAM decreases and no stretching takes place. The pressure sensor, on the other hand, can easily detect the change of pressure in-between the rubber tube and the braided sleeve when an external force stretches an empty muscle.

The design recreates the structure of the biological muscle spindle in regards to the measured properties and the placement of the sensing elements within the muscle. However, the outputs of the afferent neurons in biological muscle spindles are signals in the form of spikes. The outputs of the artificial muscle spindle are continuous voltages. Further does the II afferent neuron represents the steadiness of the muscle's inflation. The artificial muscle spindle utilizes this element to measure the stretching of an unpressurized muscle.

With this setup, both outputs can be reproduced, which biological muscle spindles provide to the motor-units. Theoretically, only the version of the Ia afferent neuron would be sufficient. Because the sustained level of the stretch can be directly derived as the rate of change. The version of the II afferent neuron is therefore not needed for its biological purpose, but in an PAM it can provide data of an unpressurized muscle.

3.2 Components

To comply with the requirements which were defined in the concept section, the selection of materials were initially lead to a specific direction. External mechanisms were not feasible, due to their size and inevitable change of the muscles dimensions. Therefore a possibility was investigated to integrate the sensor in-between of the inner tube and the outer braided sleeve of the PAM. Using the work of Erin et al. [1] as a starting point, finding a way to preserve the original flexibility of PAM was focused on. It was found that the usage of conductive fabrics would allow this. The components, which were finally used for the artificial muscle spindle shown in Fig. 3.

Using two different types of conductive fabrics and directly attach them to the inner rubber tube of the PAMs, was found to be the most viable solution. The used fabrics change their resistance by stretch (EeonTex LTT-SLPA-20K) and pressure (EeonTex NW170-SLPA-2k). Small stripes of these materials are placed similar to their locations inside of real muscles. The stretch-sensitive fabric wraps around the middle part of the muscle and recreates the feedback of the Ia afferent neuron, while the pressure-sensitive material is placed longitudinally in the lower third of the muscle. Two magnet wires are glued to the fabric with conductive adhesive, which cures at room temperature (KAKEN TECH CN-7120). These wires are fed into a Wheatstone bridge to measure their resistance. The change in resistance causes a difference in measurements of up to 1.7 V using a 5 V reference voltage. Figure 4 illustrates the response time and the slew rate of the artificial muscle spindle.

It can be noticed that the response to a change in pressure reaches the threshold of 50 mV distributed over the complete pressure range of the muscle within 10 ms. The underlying electronics of the system samples the air pressure and voltages of the artificial muscle spindle at 100 Hz. The threshold of 50 mV was selected by evaluating the signals' noise. During this process, the noise was measured for 50 intermediate pressures between 0.0 MPa and 0.85 MPa. The pressure sensitive fabric showed no significant change in resistance when low pressures were applied. This can be explained by the fact that the outer sleeve is about 4 mm wider in diameter, and some inflation of the rubber tube has to take place before the material makes contact with the sleeve to register pressure. This property, however, was later found to be useful to detect external stretching of the relaxed muscle. In this case, the sleeve and the inner tube are pressed together by the external force and hereby can be measured.

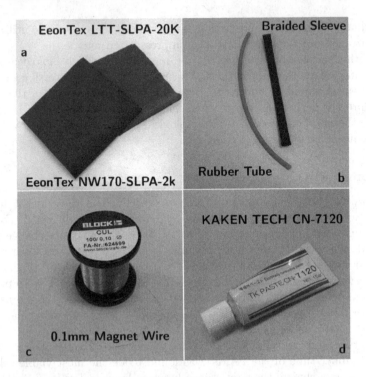

Fig. 3. The images above display the materials, which were finally used for the artificial muscle spindle. Image *a* shows the conductive fabrics, and *b* the inner tube made of rubber as well as the outer braided sleeve. In image *c* magnet wire is shown and *d* shows the conductive adhesive that was used.

3.3   Assembly

In this paragraph, the manufacturing process of the artificial muscle spindle will be described. Figure 5 shows the four most important steps of the process.

Preparing the Fabrics: The first step includes the connection of the two different fabrics *EeonTex LTT-SLPA-20K* and *EeonTex NW170-SLPA-2k* with the magnet wires. Creating a conductive and robust connection between these two different materials was one of the most significant issues. For this work, a conductive adhesive is used, that cures at room temperature *KAKEN TECH CN-7120* and therefore does not damage the fabrics through typical curing temperatures around 70 °C to 90 °C. Using this adhesive, the magnet wires are first sew-in into the fabrics and then secured into place using the conductive compound. A finished sensor of the stretch-type can be seen in Fig. 5 on the upper left image (*a*).

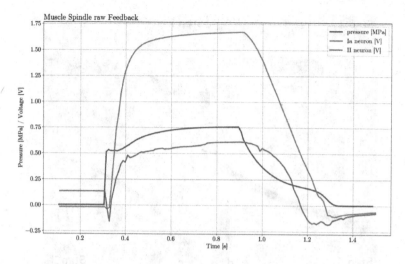

Fig. 4. The diagram above visualizes the feedback of the artificial muscle spindle. It further shows the response to a change in pressure. For this sample the valve was opened without ramping, which resulted in a response within 10 ms.

Attaching the Sensors: The second step is designated to fix the two individual sensors onto the rubber tube, so they stay in place during the assembly. After the assembly, the sensors stay in place due to the contact between the inner tube and the outer sleeve. However, having long wires attached to very light pieces of fabric exacerbate their handling. Therefore, the two sensors get fixed on one side before the insertion into the outer sleeve. For this step, *UHU Max Repair extreme* was used. Any adhesive, which does not degrade the rubber is usable for this purpose. The position of the sensors can be seen in Fig. 5 on the upper right image.

Preparing the Insertion: To be able to insert the inner tube into the sleeve the wires need to be organized in advance. This step can be seen in Fig. 5 on the lower right image. During this step, the plugs at both ends of the tube are inserted as well. This step is essential to decrease the twisting of the wires in the finished muscle. Therefore, the wires are threaded through the outer sleeve before the insertion.

Finalizing the Muscle: In the last step, the rubber tube is slide into the braided sleeve, while the wires need to be kept on minimal tension to avoid the creation of loops. The muscles are then finalized by sealing the ends using metal wires as it can be seen in the lower left image of Fig. 5.

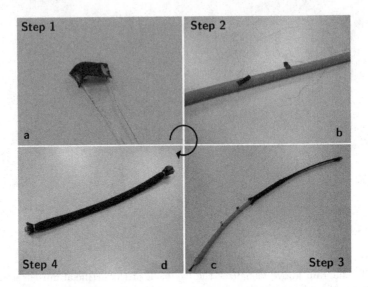

Fig. 5. Image *a* shows the magnet wire sewn-in and fixed with conductive adhesive. Image *b* shows the fabrics and wires being fixed as lightly as possible on one side to the rubber tube. Image *c* shows the tube plugged both sides and the wires already threaded through the sleeve at their final position. Image *d* shows the finished assembly of the muscle.

4   Evaluation

In this section, two essential aspects of the design's properties will be emphasized. The first important trait is the longevity of the assembly. Therefore several muscles $N = 10$ were tested and repeatedly pressurized to estimate the average lifetime under full load. The second characteristic is the stability of the muscle spindle's output.

4.1   Longevity

A primary design goal was the preservation of the PAM's durability; therefore, multiple endurance tests with these actuators were conducted. The PAMs were repeatedly contracted using a pressure of 0.85 MPa, during these tests. Of specific interest was the PAM's tendency to rupture, as well as the possible breakage of the magnet wires, which connect the fabrics to the Wheatstone bridge. It was found that out of the sample group $N = 10$, no actuator ruptured during 300 individual contractions. This fact validated the choice of adhesives as they did not weaken the inner rubber tube of the PAM. The magnet wires (0.15 mm diameter) however, showed increased sensitivity to fatigue breakage. This issue needs to be addressed in future revisions of the design.

4.2   Stability of Measurements

The visualizations in this section will illustrate the margin of variance of the spindles' output when actuated repeatedly. This data was generated by continuously actuating the PAMs with a constant airflow and recording their feedback. The actuation was repeated 30 times. It could be observed that once a set of repetitions were started, it took around 3 activations for the feedback to settle in a closer margin of variance. This warm-up period contributes significantly to the extent of the minimum and maximum values, which are shown in Figs. 6 and 7.

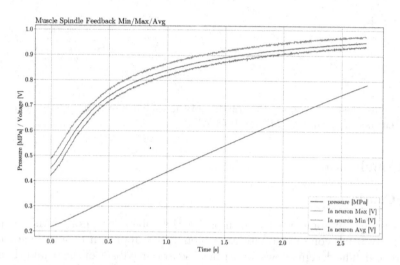

Fig. 6. This illustration shows the stability of the feedback over 30 repetitions for the Ia afferent neuron from 0.22 MPa to 0.78 MPa.

The evaluation of the Ia neuron shows a non-linear relationship between the pressure and its feedback. However, the stretchable fabric is sufficient to cover the whole actuation range of the PAM.

Like the Ia neuron did the II neuron show a non-linear relationship to the pressure of the PAM it was embedded into, as well as being able to cover the PAM's whole actuation range. For the piezoresistive fabric, the change in pressure shows an initial reduction of its output before it starts raising in a similar way to the Ia neuron. This can be explained by the free travel the inner tube of the PAM experiences due to the slight difference in diameter compared to the outer sleeve. Through this data, two analogies to biological muscles and their sensory feedback can be made. First, the design has a warm-up period once the muscles are activated from a cold state, till their feedback settles. Second, for the II afferent neuron to show predictable feedback, minimal pressure is needed to maintain firm contact in-between of the outer sleeve and the inner rubber tube of the PAM. This property can be interpreted as an analogy to the muscle tone of musculoskeletal systems.

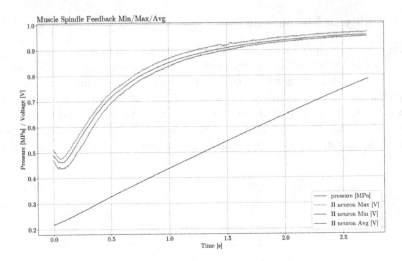

Fig. 7. This illustration shows the stability of the feedback over 30 repetitions for the II afferent neuron from 0.22 MPa to 0.78 MPa.

5   Conclusion

5.1   Conclusion

In this paper, an augmented version of the McKibben design of PAMs was presented. By using conductive fabrics, a biomimetic approach to muscle spindles was created. The design allows for artificial sensory feedback of the Ia and II afferent neurons. The usage of fabrics and their positioning in-between of the braided sleeve and the PAM's inner tube caused no noticeable changes in the muscle's characteristics. This work demonstrated that the significant difference in resistance, and therefore, the output voltage of the spindle, renders this design robust to inductive interference. The combination of these traits makes this design very favorable for musculoskeletal setups with a focus on the realism of muscular sensory feedback.

5.2   Discussion

The artificial muscle spindle followed a biomimetic approach for its design. However, the output is not electronically converted into neuron-like firing patterns. This transform of the output needs to be done in software. The selection of materials was a result of the goal to embed the muscle spindle seamlessly into the PAM. Conductive fabrics allow the placement of the sensors directly in-between of the inner tube and the outer braided sleeve of the PAM. This does not only replicate their respective location in biological muscle spindles, but it is also favorable for not changing the PAM's flexibility as well as its dimensions.

Another important aspect is the correlation between the non-linear signal of the artificial muscle spindles and the change in length and diameter of the PAM. In Fig. 8 the change in length and diameter is visualized for an unloaded PAM from its unpressurized state up to 0.41 MPa. This data was collected by 40 intermediate measurements and the pressure was raised till the PAM stopped expanding.

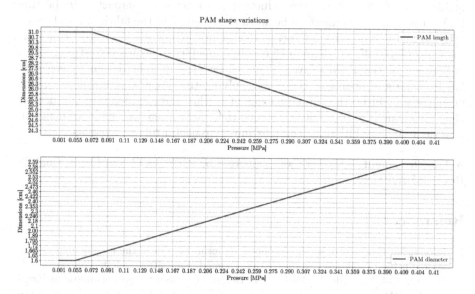

Fig. 8. This diagram shows the change of a PAM's shape during pressurization. The diameter starts to increase faster than the length because the inner rubber tube first needs to expand to make firm contact with the outer sleeve.

It can be noted that the change in length and diameter is linear as soon as the inner rubber tube makes contact with the outer sleeve. This need for the inner tube's initial expansion explains the PAM's delayed response to pressurization. Based on this data we can assume that the non-linearity of the artificial muscle spindle's output is caused by the fabrics. However, it needs to be considered that all measurements were made with unloaded muscles.

The decision to integrate both afferent neurons (Ia and II) was based on this design's biomimetic approach. It was found, that the second sensor (II) is not necessary to produce a similar feedback to the biological muscle spindle. However, in this case the position, which was adopted from the II afferent neuron, supported the measurement of an unpressurized PAM. This is possible due to the pressure between the inner tube and the outer braided sleeve when an external force stretches an unpressured PAM. This also justified the usage of a second type of conductive fabric. Positioning this sensor at the location of the II afferent neuron, further was tested to be highly effective.

5.3   Future Works

To allow a larger and more sophisticated robot, it would be advantageous to improve the embedding of the artificial muscle spindle further. The wiring of the current revision causes no problems in simple setups, but in a robot actuated with numerous PAMs, it will get convoluted quickly. Further development needs to be done to increase the longevity of the assembly. The current design focuses highly on its flexibility and the reduction of a mechanical impact to its hosting PAM. The adhesive connection between the wiring and the fabric was enhanced by choosing a conductive adhesive, which cures at low temperatures. However, the wires them-self, which are 0.15 mm in diameter, are exposed to strong forces in-between of the PAM's layers. This caused the current design to typically fail from fatigue breaks of the wires. Solving this issue, through adjustments in materials will be the primary focus of further improvements to the design. Once this issue is resolved, it is assumed that the sensory-wise enhancement can provide a viable solution for complex musculoskeletal robotic systems.

Acknowledgment. This work was supported by JSPS KAKENHI Grant Numbers 16KT0015 and 17H05908.

References

1. Jaax, K.N., Hannaford, B.: A biorobotic structural model of the mammalian muscle spindle primary afferent response. Ann. Biomed. Eng. **30**(1), 84–96 (2002)
2. Erin, O., Pol, N., Valle, L., Park, Y.L.: Design of a bio-inspired pneumatic artificial muscle with self-contained sensing. In: IEEE 38th Annual International Conference of the Engineering in Medicine and Biology Society (EMBC), pp. 2115–2119. IEEE, August 2016
3. Peng, C., Yin, Y.H., Hong, H.B., Zhang, J.J., Chen, X.: Bio-inspired design methodology of sensor-actuator-structure integrated system for artificial muscle using SMA. Procedia CIRP **65**, 299–303 (2017)
4. Hannaford, B., Winters, J.M., Chou, C.P., Marbot, P.H.: The anthroform biorobotic arm: a system for the study of spinal circuits. Ann. Biomed. Eng. **23**(4), 399–408 (1995)
5. Purves, D.: Neuroscience. Oxford University Press, Oxford (2012)

Insect Behavior as High-Sensitive Olfactory Sensor for Robotic Odor Tracking

Junji Horibe[1]($\boxtimes$), Noriyasu Ando[1,2] (iD), and Ryohei Kanzaki[1]

[1] The Research Center for Advanced Science and Technology,
The University of Tokyo, Tokyo, Japan
horibe@brain.imi.i.u-tokyo.ac.jp
[2] Department of Systems Life Engineering, Maebashi Institute of Technology,
Maebashi, Japan

Abstract. Highly sensitive odor sensors are required for odor tracking in mobile robots. The male silkmoth (*Bombyx mori*) is a candidate as a biosensor because of its high sensitivity to the sex pheromone with stereotypic searching behavior; further, genetic tools enable us to modify their odor preferences. Therefore, the development of techniques to detect odor response easily and sensitively from silkmoths has become important. Recently, machine learning has demonstrated the behavior discrimination of silkmoths to estimate the timing of odor reception. Therefore, it would be possible to leverage a silkmoth's behavioral response for odor tracking. In this research, we developed an odor-sensing device based on a silkmoth's walking pattern for mobile-robot odor tracking. To achieve this, we first collected behavioral data with and without odor stimuli, and subsequently predicted the presence of odor using a support vector machine (SVM). The F_1-score of our SVM classifier for the collected test data was 0.963. Finally, we implemented this sensing device to an odor-tracking robot.

Keywords: Olfactory sensor · Silkmoth · Odor tracking · Machine learning · Walking

1 Introduction

Odor tracking is an important task for the safety of our lives, such as finding explosives, drugs, hazardous material leaks, or victims in a disaster. We have been relying heavily on dogs for these types of tasks, while robotic odor searching is still ongoing and far from practical use. A reason for this is that artificial odor sensors are not sufficiently sensitive to detect odor from afar because odor flow is intermittent, unlike light or sound [1].

Meanwhile, it has been reported that flying moths can detect and tack the conspecific sex pheromone from at least 80 m [2, 3]. This high sensitivity was used for detecting specified chemicals by associative learning with a target odor and rewards. For example, an odor-sensing device that detects a specific behavior of parasitoid wasps in response to a learned odor [4], and a device that detects the odor of explosives by measuring the electromyograms of hawkmoths that learned the target odor [5].

© Springer Nature Switzerland AG 2019
U. Martinez-Hernandez et al. (Eds.): Living Machines 2019, LNAI 11556, pp. 183–192, 2019.
https://doi.org/10.1007/978-3-030-24741-6_16

These sensing devices demonstrated high sensitivity to target odors; however, they are not suitable as odor sensors for robotic odor tracking because the detection of the temporal dynamics of odor distribution, which is a requirement for robots, are not considered.

The silkmoth (*Bombyx mori*) (Fig. 1A) is now a biosensor candidate for robotic odor tracking. Male silkmoths exhibit a stereotypical odor searching behavior in response to the conspecific female sex pheromone. When they receive the pheromone, they walk forward during odor reception (surge), whereas they perform a zigzagging turn and finally circling after the loss of the pheromone (Fig. 1B) [6]. If they detect the odor again, they will restart the behavior from the surge. Owing to the simplicity of the behavior and intensive studies on its neural basis [7], various studies have been conducted on odor tracking using mobile robots: a robot bearing silkmoth's antennae and its neural circuit model [8], and mobile robots controlled by the walking or neural activity of silkmoths [9, 10]. As an olfactory sensor, recent advances in genetic tools have allowed us to express a specified olfactory receptor on the pheromone receptor neurons in silkmoths [11], and such transgenic silkmoths can respond to other odor without any training. Therefore, detecting the appropriate response to a specific odor is important for utilizing silkmoths as olfactory sensors.

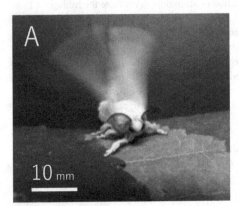 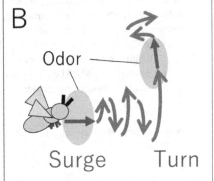

Fig. 1. Male silkmoth. (A) wing fanning elicited by the pheromone; (B) basic pattern of odor searching behavior

Detecting odor response as a behavior is sensitive and easy to perform. Recent studies on silkmoths demonstrated that machine learning can predict the timing of odor reception ($t_{reception}$) from the behavior, measured as the walking velocity or electromyograms of flight muscles [12, 13], which could be applied for sensors for robotic odor tracking. The goal of our study is to develop an odor-sensing system based on the behavior of silkmoths, and to implement it to an odor-tracking robot as a highly sensitive sensor (Fig. 2).

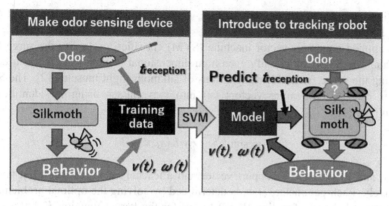

Fig. 2. Overview of this study

2 Odor Sensing Device

2.1 Experimental Setup for Behavioral Experiment

The thorax of a male silkmoth was tethered to the top of the device during the experiment. Once the moth received the conspecific sex pheromone, it walked on an air-supported polystyrene ball. The rotation of the ball was subsequently measured using an optical sensor (Fig. 3) that output the translational velocity (v) and angular velocity (ω) of the moth's walking behavior. An odor stimulus was applied using a piece of filter paper containing the major component of the female sex pheromone (bombykol, 1000 ng/paper) through a glass tube. Odor flow was created by a pump and the timing of the stimulus was controlled by an electromagnetic valve.

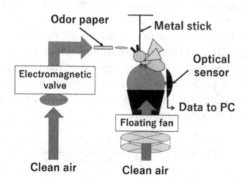

Fig. 3. System of silkmoth sensing device

2.2 Behavior Classification

We collected 14 sets of training data (v and ω) from eight moths. In each data, a silkmoth was stimulated repetitively with the pheromone for 800 ms with a 4200-ms pause (i.e., stimulus frequency of 0.2 Hz), and the number of stimuli was 20 (data length, 100 s).

We applied a support vector machine (SVM) classifier to classify the surge from these data. The SVM can classify even high-dimensional features, and it was used for estimating the surge from electromyograms of silkmoth flight muscle [12]. The SVM classifies categorized feature vectors (**x**) into two classes using an identification function (Eq. (1)).

$$f(\mathbf{x}) = \text{sign}(\sum_i \lambda_i y_i K(x_i, \mathbf{x}) + b) \tag{1}$$

where x_i and y_i represent a support vector and a teacher vector of i-th input pattern, respectively. Each parameter, λ_i, b, is determined by solving the optimal problem. We applied the radial basis function (RBF) kernel for the kernel function K, because the RBF kernel has been reported to be better in classification performance than the polynomial kernel and sigmoid kernel [12].

We defined 1200 ms of data from the beginning of the stimulus as positive data (surge, presence of odor), and that from the end of the stimulus as negative data (zigzag turn, absence of odor). For data augmentation, the positive data that shifted from 0 to 300 ms (the increase of v and the decrease of ω began about 300 ms after the beginning of the stimulus) were added to the positive data, and the negative data that shifted from 0 to 3000 ms (including no stimulus) were also added (Fig. 4). From these 1200-ms-long data, we extracted the mean v and $|\omega|$ in every 100 ms as the feature vectors (12 feature vectors for each of v and $|\omega|$). The absolute value of the mean ω was used because the turn direction was not considered for the classification. We excluded positive data with low translational velocity (mean of $v \leq 0.2$), in which moths failed to respond to the pheromone. We finally collected 3348 positive and 2500 negative data, and split 80% for training and 20% for test data.

We subsequently standardized these feature vectors and created an SVM classifier with the RBF kernel. We tested its classification performance based on *Accuracy*, *Precision*, *Recall*, and F_1-score. *Accuracy* represents the correct prediction ratio to the whole predictions (Eq. (2)). *Precision* represents the correct positive prediction ratio to the whole positive samples (Eq. (3)). *Recall* represents the correct positive prediction ratio to the whole positive predictions (Eq. (4)). F_1-score represents the harmonic mean of *Precision* and *Recall* (Eq. (5)). These factors are often used to evaluate the classifier and are defined as the following equations:

$$Accuracy = \frac{TP + TN}{TP + TN + FP + FN} \tag{2}$$

$$Precision = \frac{TP}{TP + FN} \tag{3}$$

$$Recall = \frac{TP}{TP + FP} \tag{4}$$

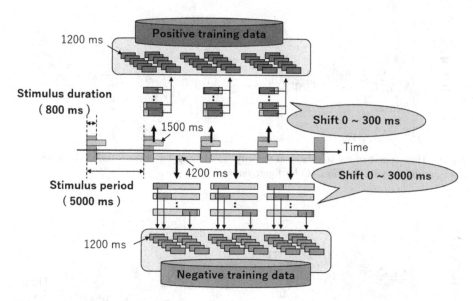

Fig. 4. Data augmentation. Blue and red squares represent positive and negative data respectively. Yellow squares represent stimulus duration of 800 ms. (Color figure online)

$$F_1\text{-score} = \frac{2 \times Precision \times Recall}{Precision + Recall} \tag{5}$$

where *TP* is the absolute number of the true positive, *TN* the true negative, *FP* the false positive, and *FN* the false negative.

2.3   Kinematic Characteristics of Behavioral Response

Figure 5 shows the time series of the translational velocity (v) and angular velocity (ω) during a repetitive stimuli. v increased after the stimulus was provided whereas ω decreased, thus indicating a surge in response to the pheromone. These observations became clearer in the overlaid plots of v and $|\omega|$ from a single stimulus sequence (Fig. 6), where v and $|\omega|$ are regarded as the magnitude of "surge" and "turn," respectively. After the onset of the stimuli, the mean v increased whereas the mean $|\omega|$ decreased. The $|\omega|$ increased again 1200 ms after the onset of the stimuli. These observations suggested that v and $|\omega|$ can be used to classify the two behaviors.

2.4   Evaluation of the SVM Classifier

We used two types of data for the performance evaluation. For the test data (behavioral response to repetitive stimuli at 0.2 Hz), all four factors were above 94% (Table 1). The confusion matrix is shown in Table 2.

Next, we tested with random data that were collected under the same condition as the test data (at 0.2 Hz, 800 ms duration) except that the stimuli were not given in a

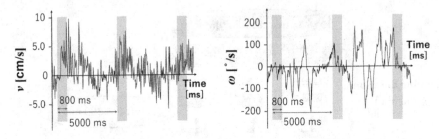

Fig. 5. Time course of the translational velocity (v) and angular velocity (ω). Yellow squares represent the stimulus duration. (Color figure online)

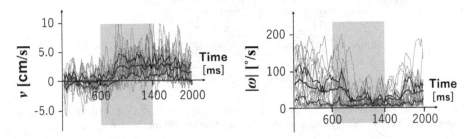

Fig. 6. Overlaid plot of v and $|\omega|$ adjusted at the onset of stimuli. Data from 20 stimuli of a single stimulus sequence (gray), mean value (red), and 25% and 75% quantiles (black) are shown. (Color figure online)

Table 1. Test data classification result.

Accuracy	Precision	Recall	F_1-score
0.964	0.943	0.984	0.963

Table 2. Confusion matrix of the test data result.

Total = 924		Actual	
		1	0
Prediction	1	True Positive = 462	False Positive = 26
	0	False Negative = 7	True Negative = 429

20% probability, the rate of 8 stimuli (800 ms) every 50 s (see Fig. 7). We prepared the random data to mimic the odor reception in a real environment. From every 1200-ms segment of random data, we predicted the odor reception in every 20 ms. If the prediction signal was raised within 5 s after a stimulus, it was defined as a true positive. If no prediction signal was raised in a step without odor stimulus, it was defined as a true negative. The results indicate that the F1-score was reduced to 0.858 compared to that of the test data (0.964, Table 1). The confusion matrix (Table 3) indicated that the overall performance decreased. However, the accuracy with the random data differed among individuals, ranging from 45 to 95% (Fig. 8, N = 8).

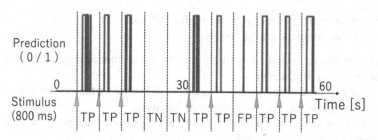

Fig. 7. Time series prediction signal when stimulated randomly (stimulated at 0.2 Hz with 80% probability). Arrowheads indicate the timing of stimuli.

Table 3. Confusion matrix of the random data result.

Total = 160	Actual	
	1	0
Prediction 1	True Positive = 103	False Positive = 17
0	False Negative = 17	True Negative = 23

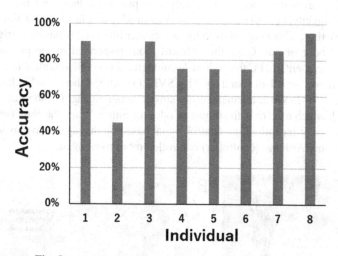

Fig. 8. Accuracy among individuals for the random data

3 Odor-Tracking Robot

3.1 Requirement Specification

To utilize odor detection using behavior for robotic odor tracking, the following specifications are required for the robots.

- Oscillation during operation is minimized to avoid unnecessary vibrations to the silkmoth and optical sensor.
- The odor extracted from an environment is delivered to the onboard moth at an arbitrary time to detect an odor-triggered behavior.
- Odor-tracking algorithms require only the timing of odor reception, whereas odor concentration is not considered.

3.2 Robot Development

Our robot consists of a mecanum wheel robot platform (10009, Nexus Robot, Hong Kong, China), trackball system (Fig. 3), and odor delivery system (Fig. 9). The mecanum wheel robot moved with little oscillation, and once the trackball system was attached at the center of the robot rotation, the robot movement did not interrupt the moth's behavior and optical sensor reading. The setups for the trackball and odor delivery system were almost the same as that used for collecting training data. The sensor of this robot was the olfactory sensor based on the silkmoth's behavior that was accomplished in the Sect. 2. The trackball was surrounded by a canopy that prevented the moth from receiving external odor directly, i.e., the moth only received an odor supplied by the delivery system at an arbitrary time. This enabled us to know whether observed behavior is triggered by the delivered odor or not. Once the onboard moth responded to the pheromone, its walking data were sent to a PC through an Arduino (reader) via Bluetooth, thus converting the optical mouse signal to v and ω. The SVM classifier subsequently classified the behavior on the PC. We implemented the simple surge-zigzagging-loop algorithm of silkmoths [6], which used only the timing of odor reception. When the classifier detected the surge, i.e., odor reception, the control signal based on the algorithm was sent to the robot and another Arduino (controller) controlled robot movement.

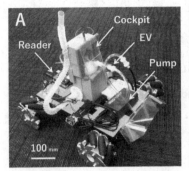 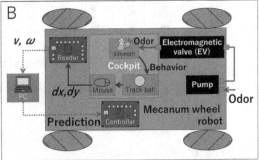

Fig. 9. Mobile robot with the insect behavior-based odor detector. (A) Appearance of the robot, (B) schematic drawing of the system.

Although we have not yet conducted odor-tracking experiments using this robot, we confirmed that training data could be collected on this platform. Hence, our robot fulfilled the requirement to utilize behavior-based odor sensing for tracking.

4 Discussion

In this study, we developed a behavior-based olfactory sensor for mobile robots with which we could fully avail an insect's ability to detect an odor. The stereotypical behavioral response of silkmoths to the sex pheromone is suitable to be applied to the SVM classifier to detect the timing of odor reception. The odor tracking robots controlled by walking or neural activity of silkmoths had been already developed [9, 10]. However, our device introduced silkmoth as a high-sensitive biosensor, which enables us to combine it with arbitrary odor searching algorithms. Our results indicated that the overall performance of our classifier was comparable to that of the previous studies in which the surge was estimated from behaviors or electromyograms [12, 13].

The F_1-score was 0.963 with the test data (the same condition as the training data, stimulated at a constant rate) while it reduced to 0.858 on the random stimulus data. This difference would be due to the training data that were obtained from moths stimulated at a constant frequency (0.2 Hz). To improve the classification performance, the training data should be collected at various stimulus frequency.

The parameters to be considered are the individual difference and system time delay. The individual difference is inevitable provided that the insect behavior is used directly; further, generating a classification model individually is the method to minimize it [13]. The time delay from stimulus onset to surge detection depends on the data length of the classifier (1200 ms in this study). We will investigate the appropriate data length and corresponding stimulus condition to minimize the delay.

In the next step, we will conduct odor-tracking tests with this robot to determine the accuracy of odor detection and the minimum time delay required for a successful orientation to the odor.

Acknowledgement. We thank NEC Corporation for their cooperative support and valuable discussions. This study was partially supported by JSPS KAKENHI (16K14192).

References

1. Murlis, J., Jones, C.D.: Fine-scale structure of odor plumes in relation to insect orientation to distant pheromone and other attractant sources. Physiol. Entomol. **6**, 71–86 (1981)
2. Elkinton, J.S., Schal, C., Onot, T., Cardé, R.T.: Pheromone puff trajectory and upwind flight of male gypsy moths in a forest. Physiol. Entomol. **12**, 399–406 (1987)
3. Wall, C., Perry, J.N.: Range of action of moth sex-attractant sources. Entomologia Experimentalis Applicata **44**, 5–14 (1987)
4. Rains, G.C., Utley, S.L., Lewis, W.J.: Behavioral monitoring of trained insects for chemical detection. Biotechnol. Progress **22**, 2–8 (2006)
5. King, T.L., Horine, F.M., Daly, K.C., Smith, B.H.: Explosives detection with hard-wired moths. IEEE Trans. Instrum. Meas. **53**, 1113–1118 (2004)

6. Kanzaki, R., Sugi, N., Shibuya, T.: Self-generated zigzag turning of *Bombyx mori* males during pheromone-mediated upwind walking. Zoolog. Sci. **9**, 515–527 (1992)

7. Namiki, S., Iwabuchi, S., Pansopha Kono, P., Kanzaki, R.: Information flow through neural circuits for pheromone orientation. Nat. Commun. **5**, 5919 (2014)

8. Kanzaki, R.: How does a microbrain generate adaptive behavior? Int. Congr. Ser. **1301**, 7–14 (2007)

9. Ando, N., Emoto, S., Kanzaki, R.: Odour-tracking capability of a silkmoth driving a mobile robot with turning bias and time delay. Bioinspiration Biomimetics **8**, 016008 (2013)

10. Takashima, A., Minegishi, R., Kurabayashi, D., Kanziki, R.: Construction of a brain-machine hybrid system to analyze adaptive behavior of silkworm moth. In: IEEE/RSJ International Conference on Intelligent Robots and Systems, pp. 2389–2394 (2010)

11. Sakurai, T., et al.: A single sex pheromone receptor determines chemical response specificity of sexual behavior in the silkmoth *Bombyx mori*. PLoS Genet. **7**, e1002115 (2011)

12. Shigaki, S., Sakurai, T., Ando, N., Kurabayashi, D., Kanzaki, R.: Time-varying moth-inspired algorithm for chemical plume tracing in turbulent environment. IEEE Robot. Autom. Lett. **3**, 76–83 (2018)

13. Chew, J.Y., Kurabayashi, D.: Quantitative analysis of the silk moth's chemical plume tracing locomotion using a hierarchical classification method. J. Bionic Eng. **11**, 268–281 (2014)

Foveated Image Processing for Faster Object Detection and Recognition in Embedded Systems Using Deep Convolutional Neural Networks

Uziel Jaramillo-Avila(✉) and Sean R. Anderson

Department of Automatic Control and Systems Engineering,
University of Sheffield, Sheffield S1 3JD, UK
{ujaramilloavila1,s.anderson}@sheffield.ac.uk

Abstract. Object detection and recognition algorithms using deep convolutional neural networks (CNNs) tend to be computationally intensive to implement. This presents a particular challenge for embedded systems, such as mobile robots, where the computational resources tend to be far less than for workstations. As an alternative to standard, uniformly sampled images, we propose the use of foveated image sampling here to reduce the size of images, which are faster to process in a CNN due to the reduced number of convolution operations. We evaluate object detection and recognition on the Microsoft COCO database, using foveated image sampling at different image sizes, ranging from 416×416 to 96×96 pixels, on an embedded GPU – an NVIDIA Jetson TX2 with 256 CUDA cores. The results show that it is possible to achieve a $4\times$ speed-up in frame rates, from 3.59 FPS to 15.24 FPS, using 416×416 and 128×128 pixel images respectively. For foveated sampling, this image size reduction led to just a small decrease in recall performance in the foveal region, to 92.0% of the baseline performance with full-sized images, compared to a significant decrease to 50.1% of baseline recall performance in uniformly sampled images, demonstrating the advantage of foveated sampling.

1 Introduction

Object detection and recognition using deep convolutional neural networks (CNNs) [10,12], has the potential to realise a step change in machine vision for embedded systems, such as in robotics, driverless cars, assistive devices and remote sensors. However, a constant driver for embedded systems is to minimise computational workload to speed up processing and reduce power consumption, noting that the processing resources for an embedded system tend to be much less than for a workstation. To this end, there has recently been a trend towards developing more compact CNNs for object detection and recognition in embedded systems, which tend to significantly improve the frame rates [13,16,21].

Computational load in CNN detection-recognition systems can also be reduced by making the size of the input image itself smaller. The reduction

© Springer Nature Switzerland AG 2019
U. Martinez-Hernandez et al. (Eds.): Living Machines 2019, LNAI 11556, pp. 193–204, 2019.
https://doi.org/10.1007/978-3-030-24741-6_17

in image size naturally leads to an increase in computational efficiency due to the reduced number of convolution operations in the CNN, but also tends to trade-off against a decrease in detection and recognition performance. Hence, the challenge is to retain detection and recognition performance whilst using small images. The solution that we investigate here is based on foveated image transformation, inspired by photoreceptor density in the human eye.

Human visual perception is dominated by the fovea, a small region of densely clustered photoreceptors in the retina, which accounts for just ~2% of the visual field [15], but as much as ~50% of the input to neurons in primary visual cortex [19]. This amplification of the visual field in neural processing is known as cortical magnification factor. In order to see with high acuity, humans actively redirect their fovea towards an object based on saliency (the perceived importance of an object). This active vision system is highly efficient compared to e.g. a passive system with photoreceptors densely distributed throughout the retina, as has been noted elsewhere:

"If the entire 160 × 175° subtended by each retina were populated by photo-receptors at foveal density, the optic nerve would comprise on the order of one billion nerve fibers, compared to about one million fibers in humans" [4].

The foveated image processing system in human vision contrasts strongly to how digital images are usually processed in computer vision, where large numbers of pixels are typically used to represent the entire field of view in dense, uniform sampling. Foveated transformation for digital image processing preserves high resolution in the foveal region, centred on an object of interest, whilst compressing the periphery, resulting in reduced image size but no reduction in the field of view.

There are a number of computational models in use in computer vision to obtain the foveated image, such as the log-polar transform [18], the reciprocal wedge-transform [17], and Cartesian foveated geometry [6]. The work in [1] has demonstrated the advantages of foveated image processing with regard to improvements in computational efficiency (but did not address CNNs). In recent models of visual saliency using CNNs, images have been applied to networks using a foveal transform [2,8]. However, those works did not investigate image size reduction and frame-rate speed-up, which is of critical importance for embedded systems. There is a current gap, therefore, in studying the speed-up effect of foveated transforms on CNNs used for detection and recognition.

The aim of this paper is to investigate quantitatively how detection, recognition and processing speed in a CNN are affected by reducing image size using a foveated transformation. The intention is to demonstrate that foveated image processing coupled with image size reduction enables a speed-up in processing, whilst retaining high performance in detection and recognition in the foveal region, and reasonable performance in detection and recognition in the periphery. This would provide the foundation for a faster, more computationally efficient object detection and recognition scheme for embedded systems.

2 Methods

This section presents the key methods used in this paper. In brief, images from the Microsoft COCO database [5], were resampled at increasingly smaller sizes using a foveated transform (Fig. 1), and used to retrain the You Only Look Once version 3 (YOLOv3) CNN for object detection and recognition [11]. This foveated approach was compared to linearly downsampled images to analyse the benefit of the foveated transform. To evaluate processing speed, YOLOv3 was implemented on an NVIDIA Jetson TX2 GPU for embedded systems (Fig. 1). In addition, as a comparison against a different type of object detection and recognition system, Faster R-CNN [12], was used with the foveated images to analyse performance (without any retraining) and also compared to YOLOv3 un-retrained. The other advantage of comparing against un-retrained CNNs was that it tests for over-specialisation to the foveated transform in object detection.

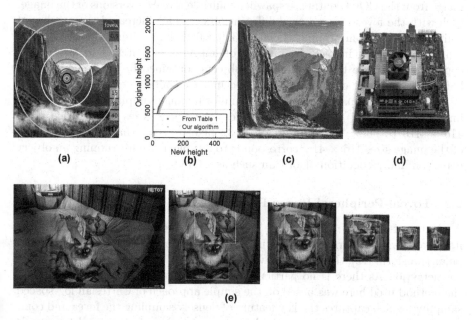

Fig. 1. (a) Representation of some key eccentricity values departing from the center of the fovea. (b) Curve representation of the logarithmic behaviour of the rows selected for the example image transformed from 2080 to 494 pixel per side. (d) NVIDIA Jetson TX2 for embedded systems (256 Pa CUDA core GPU, dual-core Denver2 processor, quad-core ARM-A57 processor, 8 GB memory, 7.5 W, 50 × 87 mm) mounted on a development board. (e) Example of typical image from the COCO dataset used for validation, from left to right, at it's original resolution of 640 × 426 pixels, at 384 × 384, 288 × 288, 192 × 192, and 96 × 96, and finally the same image normally downsampled to 96 × 96 pixels for comparison.

2.1 Image Database: Microsoft COCO

The Microsoft COCO dataset [5] was used here for training and evaluating the CNNs because it has become a standard benchmark for testing algorithms aimed at scene understanding and pixel-wise segmentation, and it also provides a rich array of relatively context-free images. Note that the COCO database is more challenging than some other standard image databases because the images tend to contain multiple objects as opposed to single objects.

To make the retraining of the CNNs more manageable, a subset of the COCO dataset was taken, considering the first 20 listed objects[1]. This dataset was chosen due to the aim of testing the hypothesis in cluttered scenarios in which the ground truth objects are not necessarily centered, having around *3.5 categories and 7.7 instances per image* [5].

The foveated transform (see next section) was applied separately to every object contained in an image in the COCO database. Therefore, a single original image from the COCO database spawned multiple foveated versions of the image, each with the fovea centred on a different object. This increased the number of training images from around 82,000 to 306,000. For retraining the CNNs with uniformly sampled images the number of images was matched to 306,000 by copying each image by the number of objects contained in the image - i.e. to balance the number of uniformly sampled images against the foveated images.

To test and compare performance of uniform image sampling versus foveated image sampling, at different image sizes, the image sizes were varied from 416×416 to 96×96, at intervals of 32 pixels[2]. Note that the upper limit of the image size, 416×416, corresponds to a typical size for running an object detection and recognition algorithm such as YOLO.

2.2 Foveal-Peripheral Image Resampling

A number of different methods have been developed to transform a standard digital image, with uniform sampling, into a foveated image. These include the log-polar transform [18], the reciprocal wedge-transform [17] and Cartesian foveated geometry [6]. As there is no particular consensus on foveated image sampling, the method used here was based on the simple approach of Cartesian log-spaced sampling, which captures the key feature of densely sampling the fovea and compressing the periphery. This method was found to be effective, and because it distorts the original uniformly-sampled image less than, e.g. a log-polar transform, it gives the additional key benefit of enabling the use of transfer learning to speed-up the training of the CNNs (i.e. initialising the CNN weights using a network pre-trained on uniformly sampled images).

The basic approach we take is to resample the uniform digital image of size $N_x \times N_y$ pixels, to a new size of $n_x \times n_y$ pixels with log-spacing, so that for the

---

[1] Person, bicycle, car, motorbike, aeroplane, bus, train, truck, boat, traffic light, fire hydrant, stop sign, parking meter, bench, bird, cat, dog, horse, sheep, cow.

[2] 96×96, 128×128, 160×160, 192×192, 224×224, 256×256, 288×288, 320×320, 352×352, 384×384 and 416×416.

upper right quadrant of the image with the fovea centred on (x_0, y_0) we have sample locations,

$$x_k = \exp(k\Delta_x) \quad \text{for } k = 0, \ldots, n_x/2 \tag{1}$$

$$y_k = \exp(k\Delta_y) \quad \text{for } k = 0, \ldots, n_y/2 \tag{2}$$

where

$$\Delta_x = 2n_x^{-1}\log(N_x/2) \tag{3}$$

$$\Delta_y = 2n_y^{-1}\log(N_y/2) \tag{4}$$

To illustrate the performance of this model, a uniformly sampled image of 2080×2080 pixels is shown in Fig. 1(a): if we use the eccentricity/data field values in Table 1 from [20], we observe that the sampling model given above fits well to this data Fig. 1(b), and produces the foveated image of 494×494 pixels shown in Fig. 1(c).

To illustrate the foveal sampling algorithm an example of an image downsampled logarithmically, at different resolutions, can be found in Fig. 1(e), where the fovea is focused in a cat in the lower half of the image.

Table 1. Relationship between the eccentricity angle in the eye and the number of data fields [20], where they represent retinal regions over which stimulus is collected in cell sub-assemblies from thousands of input fibers and overall properties are calculated over them. Data reproduced from [20].

Eccentricity	0.5	1	2	5	10	30	45	60	70	90
Number of data fields	256	552	848	1239	1534	2003	2176	2299	2365	2472

2.3   Object Recognition with YOLO

The foveated image processing method was tested and evaluated here using the object detection and recognition algorithm based on You Only Look Once (YOLO) [10], specifically using the current latest version of the algorithm (YOLOv3) known as Darknet-53 [11], as found in its original repository [9]. This algorithm was selected because it has become well established since its inception.

In brief, the YOLOv3 network is a CNN with 53 layers (hence the label Darknet-53). The network is designed with successive blocks, where each block is composed of a 1×1 convolutional layer, followed by a 3×3 convolutional layer, and a residual layer. Blocks are repeated numerous times with occasional shortcut connections, followed by average pooling then a fully connected layer with softmax output.

YOLOv3 uses dimension clusters as anchor boxes to predict the object bounding boxes along with the class label [11]. The system outputs 4 coordinates to define each bounding box: the centre coordinates of the box (x, y), the width, w, and height, h. The loss function for each of these variables is defined as the sum-of-squared error. The class label prediction is done for the objects contained in each bounding box using multilabel classification, which is trained using a binary cross-entropy loss function.

Training was performed here on an NVIDIA GeForce GTX 1070 GPU (with 1,920 Pa CUDA cores), using 306,000 images (derived from the COCO database), with a batch size of 32, and subdivision of 16. Stochastic gradient descent with momentum was used as the training algorithm, with learning rate of 0.001, momentum of 0.9 and weight decay of 0.0005. Network weights were initialised using the pre-trained network obtained from [9]. The training process was iterated for 200,000 steps ($\sim 9,500$ iterations per epoch, i.e. for 20 epochs), repeating the entire process for the 11 image sizes listed in Sect. 2.1, where each CNN was restructured to match the size of the input images. Testing was done on a reserved validation data set of 6000 images.

Frame-rate was evaluated by processing all test images and averaging the result on an NVIDIA Jetson TX2 board, with a 256-core Pascal GPU, using CUDA Toolkit 8.0 and cuDNN 5.1, with the images saved on internal memory but ignoring the time required to load or display them.

2.4 Object Recognition with Faster R-CNN

Faster-RCNN is an object detection and recognition system that uses a region proposal network (RPN) to generate region proposals for object detection and recognition by a subsequent CNN [12]. Faster-RCNN is particularly efficient because the RPN shares convolutional features with the detection/recognition CNN. In this paper, Faster-RCNN is used without retraining as a comparison to YOLO for processing foveated images. The specific implementation used is the current version developed by the original authors [7].

2.5 Analysis and Evaluation

Performance is evaluated here using the averaged precision and recall metrics [14],

$$\text{Precision} = \frac{\sum_{i=1}^{n} \text{TP}_i}{\sum_{i=1}^{n} (\text{TP}_i + \text{FP}_i)} \quad \text{and} \quad \text{Recall} = \frac{\sum_{i=1}^{n} \text{TP}_i}{\sum_{i=1}^{n} (\text{TP}_i + \text{FN}_i)}$$

where TP are the true positives, FP are the false positives, and FN are the false negatives. A true positive is only counted if the CNN predicts the correct class label *and* the object location, as measured by an Intersection over Union (IoU) value [10], is over a threshold, set to 0.5 as in [10,11], a ratio of the between the area of overlap and the area of union between the prediction and the ground-truth. It is important to differentiate that, while it is assumed that the fovea is centered in the object, object localization still needs to be evaluated as passing the bounding box IoU threshold.

Performance is evaluated separately in the fovea and the fovea-periphery (to explicitly quantify performance in the foveal region where detection-recognition should be accurate, and in the periphery where we expect accuracy to decrease).

3   Results

To recap, the aim of this paper was to analyse the object detection and recognition performance of CNNs using foveated images, with reduced image size to enable speed-up in processing. Varying image sizes were evaluated along with two CNNs: YOLOv3 and Faster-RCNN. The CNN frame rates were analysed from implementation on an NVIDIA Jetson TX2 – a GPU designed for embedded systems.

The results are analysed in this section in three parts: 1. foveal performance on retrained YOLOv3 (with 20 object classes); 2. foveal-peripheral performance on retrained YOLOv3 (with 20 object classes); 3. foveal and foveal-peripheral performance on un-retrained Faster-RCNN versus un-retrained YOLOv3 (both with 80 object classes). Comparing against un-retrained systems also tests for over-specialisation to the foveated transform itself in object detection.

3.1   Foveal Analysis on YOLO with Re-Training

The foveal analysis performed in this section assumes that a saliency step has already been performed that crudely aligns the fovea with a point of interest. The CNN still has to detect the object precisely, in terms of the bounding box, and also recognise the object using classification.

Baseline recall performance of YOLO using foveated and uniformly sampled images at the largest image size tested, 416 × 416 pixels, was similar at 35.20% and 34.57% respectively (Fig. 2 and Table 2). The framerate on the Jetson TX2 at this image size was just 3.59 FPS.

The recall at size 128 × 128 using foveated images decreased only slightly to 32.38% (92.0% of the baseline result) but for uniformly sampled images decreased to 17.33% (50.1% of the baseline result) - Table 3. The key additional point is that frame rate increased to 15.24 FPS at an image size of 128 × 128 - this is over a 4× speed-up.

Interestingly, the precision performance increased for the foveated images as image size reduced, but decreased for the uniformly sampled images (Fig. 2 and Table 2). The increase in precision performance for foveated images is likely a benefit of the fact that the object of interest takes up more of the visual scene, reducing the false positives.

3.2   Foveal-Peripheral Analysis on YOLO with Re-training

The foveal-peripheral recall performance was similar to the foveal-only performance at the largest image size, 416 × 416 pixels, for foveated images (35.20%)

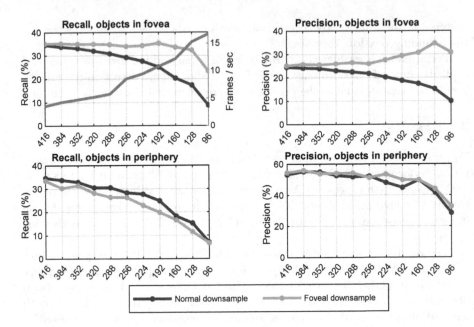

Fig. 2. Recall and precision performance for the YOLO network trained at different resolutions. Top row: objects in the fovea. Bottom row: objects in the periphery. Top left also shows the average frame rate for processing each image size.

and uniformly sampled images (34.57%) (Fig. 2). As image size was reduced to 128 × 128 pixels, recall performance for both foveal and uniformly sampled images decreased significantly, to 34.3% of baseline for foveated images and 45.3% of baseline for uniform images (Fig. 2 and Table 3). The decrease in precision is less pronounced across the same range (to about ~30% for both image types), indicating that precision is less sensitive to the reduction in image size in the periphery. The precision-recall curve for the smaller networks is shown in Fig. 4.

3.3   Comparison Between Faster R-CNN and YOLO Un-retrained

To corroborate the previous observations, Faster-RCNN was also tested with the foveated images and uniformly sampled images at varying sizes. Due to the lengthy training process, retraining was avoided here for Faster-RCNN, and to provide a consistent comparison an un-retrainined version of YOLOv3 was also used in this section. Both networks were used with all 80 object classes from their original versions. The behaviour was remarkably similar to that obtained in the previous sections, for both YOLO and Faster R-CNN. (Fig. 3). A 4× speed-up in frame rate was still observed for YOLOv3, from 3.31 FPS to 14.63 FPS at 416 × 416 and 128 × 128 respectively (Fig. 3). This serves as some confirmation that the approach of using foveated images with reduced size is beneficial to wider CNN designs used in object detection and recognition. These results also provide

Table 2. Comparison of the precision and recall (%) for only the object centered in the fovea, with image and network at varying resolutions, from 416 to 96 (per side), along with the frame-rate average on a Jetson TX2 board.

Network size	416	384	352	320	288	256	224	192	160	128	96
Foveal recall	35.20	35.27	35.03	34.30	34.83	33.98	34.30	35.33	33.62	32.38	23.32
Normal recall	34.57	33.75	33.15	31.89	30.82	29.29	27.60	25.07	20.30	17.33	6.42
Foveal precision	25.09	25.66	25.51	25.36	26.47	25.95	27.58	29.43	30.70	34.70	30.80
Normal precision	24.45	24.09	23.85	23.14	22.42	21.72	20.19	18.71	17.41	15.15	8.31
20 object frame-rate	3.59	4.29	4.75	5.21	5.76	8.52	9.40	10.76	12.14	15.24	16.65
80 object frame-rate	3.31	4.02	4.53	4.87	5.34	8.04	8.91	10.36	11.70	14.63	15.75

Table 3. (Left) Recall for objects in the fovea, proportional to the performance at 416 × 416, with foveal and normal downsamples, along with the speed-up for detection of 20 objects on a Jetson TX2. **(Right)** Recall comparison for objects in the periphery, proportional to the performance at 416 × 416.

Size	416	192	160	128	96
Foveal	1	1.003	0.955	0.919	0.663
Normal	0.982	0.712	0.577	0.492	0.182
Speed-up	1	2.997	3.381	4.245	4.637

Size	416	192	160	128	96
Foveal	1	0.591	0.494	0.343	0.200
Normal	1.034	0.739	0.543	0.453	0.157

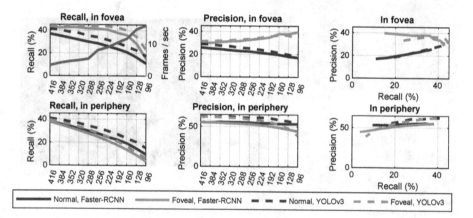

Fig. 3. Comparison of performance changes using the un-retrained YOLOv3 and un-retrained Faster R-CNN neural networks as they were trained by their initial contributors on 80 object classes. Note that frames per second in the top panel is for YOLOv3 only.

evidence that the advantages of foveation in object detection are not simply due to an effect of detecting image distortion due to the foveated transform itself.

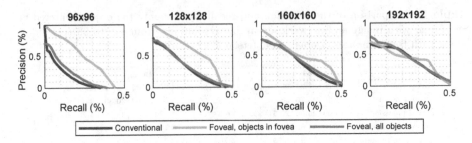

Fig. 4. Precision and recall performance curves for the network at small resolutions (96 × 96, 128 × 128, 160 × 160 and 192 × 192). The foveal advantage is much more evident for the smaller networks, where the speed-up is also larger. In all cases, the performance is very similar between the normal downsample and the average of all objects present in the foveated image. For the larger networks, the prospect of detecting objects in the periphery increases, which affects the precision measurements when only the foveal object is considered as a true positive.

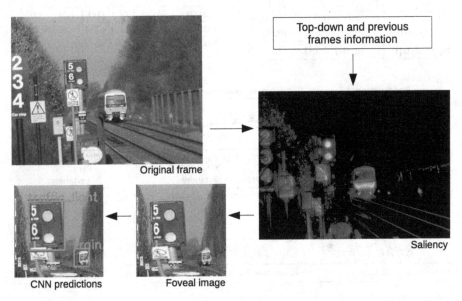

Fig. 5. Example of an image from the Coco dataset run through the Vocus2 bottom-up saliency algorithm [3], then taking the most salient point as the center of the fovea. In this example the original image is 640 × 480 pixels, which in this case is downsampled to 160 × 160 pixels.

4   Discussion

4.1   Implication of Results

The motivation for this study was to make object detection and recognition with CNNs more efficient for embedded GPU systems. The aim was to investigate quantitatively how detection, recognition and processing speed in a CNN were affected by reducing image size using a foveated transformation. The results demonstrated that images could be reduced in size from 416×416 to 128×128 pixels, with only a small decrease, 8.0%, in recall using foveated sampling. A limitation of the approach was the decrease in object detection and recognition in the periphery, which was to be expected given the downsampling of pixels.

The key benefit observed here was the processing speed-up for reduced size images, specifically a $4\times$ speed-up with 128×128 pixel images. The increase in processing speed observed here is advantageous for future embedded systems: in the short term embedded systems with limited GPU processing power can more readily exploit the latest advanced algorithms, whilst in the long term as GPUs advance, less resource will be needed for object detection and recognition, maximising resources and energy efficiency.

4.2   Future Work

The foveation method investigated here, in practice, would be part of a wider active vision system, incorporating saliency to re-direct the fovea to objects of interest. This is a key area to develop in future work. In order to illustrate how visual saliency and foveated object detection-recognition might function in practice, we have demonstrated the method developed here in combination with a well established bottom-up saliency algorithm [3] (Fig. 5).

Several methods have been developed to build-in saliency into the structure of the CNN itself [22]. It may be possible, therefore, to realise improved computational efficiency if saliency and object detection-recognition layers in the CNN are shared. This would be an interesting area of future work.

References

1. Akbas, E., Eckstein, M.P.: Object detection through search with a foveated visual system. PLoS Comput. Biol. **13**(10), e1005743 (2017)
2. Almeida, A.F., Figueiredo, R., Bernardino, A., Santos-Victor, J.: Deep networks for human visual attention: a hybrid model using foveal vision. In: Ollero, A., Sanfeliu, A., Montano, L., Lau, N., Cardeira, C. (eds.) ROBOT 2017. AISC, vol. 694, pp. 117–128. Springer, Cham (2018). https://doi.org/10.1007/978-3-319-70836-2_10
3. Frintrop, S., Werner, T., Martin Garcia, G.: Traditional saliency reloaded: a good old model in new shape. In: Proceedings of the IEEE Conference on Computer Vision and Pattern Recognition, pp. 82–90 (2015)
4. Itti, L.: Automatic foveation for video compression using a neurobiological model of visual attention. IEEE Trans. Image Process. **13**(10), 1304–1318 (2004)
5. Lin, T.-Y., et al.: Microsoft COCO: common objects in context. In: Fleet, D., Pajdla, T., Schiele, B., Tuytelaars, T. (eds.) ECCV 2014. LNCS, vol. 8693, pp. 740–755. Springer, Cham (2014). https://doi.org/10.1007/978-3-319-10602-1_48
6. Martinez, J., Altamirano, L.: A new foveal cartesian geometry approach used for object tracking. In: Proceedings of the IASTED International Conference on Signal Processing, Pattern Recognition, and Applications, SPPRA 2006, Innsbruck, Austria, pp. 133–139 (2006)

7. Paszke, A., et al.: Automatic differentiation in PyTorch. In: NIPS-W (2017). Accessed 20 Oct 2018
8. Recasens, A., Kellnhofer, P., Stent, S., Matusik, W., Torralba, A.: Learning to zoom: a saliency-based sampling layer for neural networks. arXiv preprint arXiv:1809.03355 (2018)
9. Redmon, J.: Darknet: open source neural networks in C (2016). http://pjreddie.com/darknet/. Accessed 25 Aug 2018
10. Redmon, J., Divvala, S., Girshick, R., Farhadi, A.: You only look once: unified, real-time object detection. In: Proceedings of the IEEE Conference on Computer Vision and Pattern Recognition, pp. 779–788 (2016)
11. Redmon, J., Farhadi, A.: YOLOv3: an incremental improvement. arXiv preprint arXiv:1804.02767 (2018)
12. Ren, S., He, K., Girshick, R., Sun, J.: Faster R-CNN: towards real-time object detection with region proposal networks. In: Advances in Neural Information Processing Systems, pp. 91–99 (2015)
13. Shafiee, M.J., Chywl, B., Li, F., Wong, A.: Fast YOLO: a fast you only look once system for real-time embedded object detection in video. arXiv preprint arXiv:1709.05943 (2017)
14. Sokolova, M., Lapalme, G.: A systematic analysis of performance measures for classification tasks. Inf. Process. Manage. **45**(4), 427–437 (2009)
15. Strasburger, H., Rentschler, I., Jüttner, M.: Peripheral vision and pattern recognition: a review. J. Vision **11**(5), 1–82 (2011)
16. Tijtgat, N., Van Ranst, W., Volckaert, B., Goedemé, T., De Turck, F.: Embedded real-time object detection for a UAV warning system. In: The International Conference on Computer Vision, ICCV 2017, pp. 2110–2118 (2017)
17. Tong, F., Li, Z.N.: Reciprocal-wedge transform for space-variant sensing. IEEE Trans. Pattern Anal. Mach. Intell. **17**(5), 500–511 (1995)
18. Traver, V.J., Bernardino, A.: A review of log-polar imaging for visual perception in robotics. Rob. Autonom. Syst. **58**(4), 378–398 (2010)
19. Wässle, H., Grünert, U., Röhrenbeck, J., Boycott, B.B.: Cortical magnification factor and the ganglion cell density of the primate retina. Nature **341**(6243), 643–646 (1989)
20. Wilson, S.W.: On the retino-cortical mapping. Int. J. Man Mach. Stud. **18**(4), 361–389 (1983)
21. Wu, B., Iandola, F.N., Jin, P.H., Keutzer, K.: SqueezeDet: unified, small, low power fully convolutional neural networks for real-time object detection for autonomous driving. In: CVPR Workshops, pp. 446–454 (2017)
22. Zhang, X., Gao, T., Gao, D.: A new deep spatial transformer convolutional neural network for image saliency detection. Des. Autom. Embed. Syst. 1–14 (2018)

Design, Optimization and Characterization of Bio-Hybrid Actuators Based on 3D-Bioprinted Skeletal Muscle Tissue

Rafael Mestre[1], Tania Patiño[1], Maria Guix[1], Xavier Barceló[1], and Samuel Sanchez[1,2(✉)]

[1] Institute for Bioengineering of Catalonia (IBEC), The Barcelona Institute of Science and Technology, Baldiri Reixac 10-12, 08028 Barcelona, Spain
{rmestre, tpatino, mguix, ssanchez}@ibecbarcelona.eu
[2] Institució Catalana de Recerca i Estudis Avancats (ICREA), Barcelona, Spain

Abstract. The field of bio-hybrid robotics aims at the integration of biological components with artificial materials in order to take advantage of many unique features occurring in nature, such as adaptability, self-healing or resilience. In particular, skeletal muscle tissue has been used to fabricate bio-actuators or bio-robots that can perform simple actions. In this paper, we present 3D bioprinting as a versatile technique to develop these kinds of actuators and we focus on the importance of optimizing the designs and properly characterizing their performance. For that, we introduce a method to calculate the force generated by the bio-actuators based on the deflection of two posts included in the bio-actuator design by means of image processing algorithms. Finally, we present some results related to the adaptation, controllability and force modulation of our bio-actuators, paving the way towards a design- and optimization-driven development of more complex 3D-bioprinted bio-actuators.

Keywords: Muscle-based bio-actuators · 3D bioprinting · Bio-hybrid robotics

1 Introduction

The integration of biological entities and artificial components has been gaining increasing attention over the past few years, mainly due to the development of tissue engineering techniques that can reproduce the behavior and characteristics of intricate human or animal tissue. Complex features inherently present in natural systems, such as self-healing, adaptability to harsh environment, response to different stimuli, resilience and efficiency are amongst the most desired features in robotics, particularly in soft robotics, which tries to bio-mimic soft and compliant materials similar to those found in living systems. However, in reality, matching the high degree of complexity, efficiency and effectiveness present in nature through bio-mimicry or biological engineering has proven to be a difficult task [1–4].

Nowadays, the discipline of bio-hybrid robotics aims at reducing the gap between man-made and natural systems by integrating living tissue, such as muscle, to fabricate hybrid systems that can perform complex tasks powered by their contractions.

© Springer Nature Switzerland AG 2019
U. Martinez-Hernandez et al. (Eds.): Living Machines 2019, LNAI 11556, pp. 205–215, 2019.
https://doi.org/10.1007/978-3-030-24741-6_18

Particularly, dorsal vessel tissue [5], cardiomyocytes [6] and skeletal muscle [7, 8] are amongst the most used types of muscular tissue. In the literature, several research groups have presented different examples of bio-actuators powered by these types of tissue that can perform tasks such as gripping [5, 9], crawling [10], swimming [11, 12], or can be used as a bio-sensing platform [13]. Skeletal muscle tissue from commercial cell lines provides a very suitable option for groups aiming to research these kinds of bio-hybrid devices. Although more powerful force strokes can be achieved with primary cardiomyocytes or myoblasts [9], and harsher environmental conditions can be sustained by dorsal vessel tissue, the techniques or facilities required are not always available. Therefore, there is a crescent need to improve the bio-fabrication of bio-hybrid robots or actuators based on skeletal muscle to achieve efficiency levels comparable to those of native tissue.

In this paper, we develop a full optimization and characterization of bio-hybrid actuators based on two PDMS posts surrounded by a 3D-bioprinted skeletal muscle tissue. Although force measurement of muscle tissue using micro-posts has already been used by the gel-casting technique [14], we propose a fully 3D-printed approach to study and tailor the performance of bio-hybrid actuators towards more complex custom-made bio-robots. We start by describing the fabrication process by 3D bioprinting, which can print both the artificial skeleton and the cell-laden hydrogel in the same process. Then, we show the importance of optimizing the designs to obtain the best performance and we describe a method of computing force generation based on the deflection of the posts during electrical stimulation. Finally, we summarize some of our findings related to the controllability, adaptability and force modulation of these bio-actuators.

2   Fabrication of 3D-Bioprinted Bio-Actuators

The biological actuators were fabricated using the 3D bioprinting technique. A commercial cell line of mouse myoblasts (C2C12) were encapsulated in a hydrogel consisting of fibrinogen, gelatin and hyaluronic acid (Fig. 1A) in Dubelcco's Modified Eagle Medium (DMEM), as reported elsewhere [4, 15]. The combination of these materials allows for a proper cell environment, mimicking their natural extracellular matrix, as fibrinogen and gelatin present cell attachment sites. Gelatin forms a gel at low temperatures and hyaluronic acid provides the desired shear-thinning properties, therefore allowing the bioprinting of the hydrogel with controllability and no dripping. Moreover, fibrinogen can be cross-linked to form fibrin by the addition of thrombin after bioprinting. In this way, the bioprinted construct can retain the shape when it is incubated in cell growth medium in culture conditions (37 °C).

Our bio-actuators consisted on two posts made of PDMS and a square of bioprinted cell-laden hydrogel around it. With such architecture, the muscle construct could bend the soft posts and, by video recording, we could estimate the forces being generated at different stimulation conditions, as well as other parameters (i.e. response times). For this purpose, we used the extrusion-based CELLINK's Inkredible+ bioprinter, which has two printing heads that allow a consecutive printing of the posts and the cell-laden hydrogel within the same process (Fig. 1B). Figure 1C shows four snapshots of a bioprinting

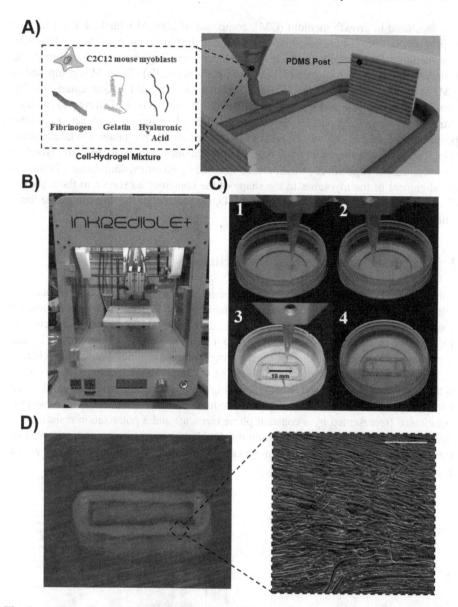

Fig. 1. (A) Schematic of the composition of the cell-laden hydrogel and the bioprinting process. (B) 3D bioprinter used to fabricate bio-actuators. (C) Snapshots of the fabrication process of a bio-actuator. (D) Image of a 3D-bioprinted bio-actuator after several days in differentiation medium, when the tissue has compacted and is able to pull the posts. The zoomed-in image corresponds to an SEM image showing aligned myotubes in the 3D cell-laden scaffold (scale bar = 50 μm).

process, where one can observe that the hydrogel is located 2 mm away from the posts. After this process, the construct is submerged in a thrombin solution, washed with PBS and incubated in growth medium (GM), composed of DMEM with 10% Fetal Bovine Serum (FBS), 200 nM L-Glutamine and 1% Penicilin/Streptomycin. Then, differentiation medium (DM) is added, which activates cell signaling pathways resulting in the fusion of myoblasts, forming myotubes (multi-nucleated cells). This DM is composed of DMEM supplemented with 10% Horse Serum (HS), 200 nM L-Glutamine and 1% Penicilin/Streptomycin and Insuline-like Growth Factor 1 (IGF-1). During this process, extracellular matrix remodeling causes the cell-laden hydrogel to compact around the posts, which have been slowly cured at 37 °C while cell differentiation was taking place (Fig. 1D). After approximately 5–7 days of differentiation, the newly formed myotubes show contractile capabilities, which can be induced by electrical stimulation. Thanks to the alignment of the myotubes to the shape of the construct, as shown in the scanning electrode microscopy (SEM) image of Fig. 1D, we can ensure that the contractile force will be generated along that axis.

3   Electrical Stimulation of Bio-Actuators

Contractions in skeletal muscle tissue can be induced by electrical pulse stimulation (EPS). Since the bio-actuators are static and fabricated in bottom-glass Petri dishes, we designed a stimulation setup consisting on a pair of carbon rod electrodes attached to the cover of the dish. In this manner, we could ensure sterility of the sample by not being exposed to outer conditions during long stimulation times. Impedance characterization of the electrodes are presented in Fig. 2. The bode plot of Fig. 2A was fitted to the equivalent circuit (inset schematic in Fig. 2A), consisting on a series resistance that correspond to the resistance of growth medium and cables, together with a pseudo-capacitance (represented by a constant phase element) and a polarization resistance in parallel. This last part takes into account the double layer capacitance and reversible or irreversible Faradaic reactions that might occur at the carbon-medium interface, which might cause corrosion or hydrolysis.

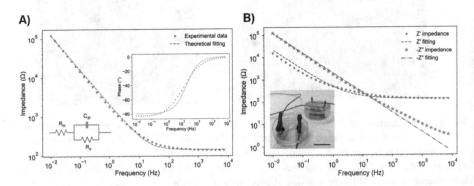

Fig. 2. (A) Bode plot of the carbon electrodes with phase plot and equivalent circuit as insets. (B) Z' and Z'' plots with their respective fittings and a picture of the electrodes as an inset.

The fitting to the bode plot was accurate and gave results of $R_m = 143 \pm 3\Omega$, $C_{dl} = 9.4 \cdot 10^{-5} \pm 0.2 \cdot 10^{-5}$ F $\cdot s^{n-1}$, and $n = 0.887 \pm 0.009$ (index of constant-phase element). This indicates that the electrodes effectively behave as a very small medium resistance in series with a pseudo-capacitance that represents the double-layer capacitance. At this frequency range, the polarization resistance, R_p, could not be fitted as part of this model. This is most likely due to its value being too large, since one would expect a plateau at low frequencies reaching this value of impedance. Therefore, we can assume that the equivalent circuit for these electrodes has such a high polarization resistance that it can be omitted, meaning that the reactions that occur at the interface do not cause severe corrosion or hydrolysis, which might damage the bio-actuators and the electrodes themselves in the long term. The phase of the impedance (inset of Fig. 2A) and the resistance (Z') and reactance (Z'') are not perfectly fitted, which might indicate small deviations of this model, but it is observed that the trend is generally well maintained.

4 Geometry Optimization for Force Measurement

One of the biggest advantages of using 3D bioprinting for the fabrication of bio-hybrid actuators based on muscle tissue is its versatility to implement multiple designs. By using a computer-aided design (CAD) software, we can easily sketch multiple configurations, which can be later sliced into filaments by a specialized software (e.g. Slic3r) and then translated into G-Code, which can be used by the bioprinter to fabricate the desired shapes. We took advantage of this versatility to optimize the geometry of the bio-actuator's posts, without the need to fabricate the whole bio-actuator and check, by trial and error, if the geometric stiffness was too high for the bioprinted muscle to bend.

We considered two types of design, a flat slab and a post (Fig. 3A). With COMSOL Multiphysics, we simulated the effect of the tissue construct by applying an edge load at a distance of 2 mm from the bottom of the post, which had a total height of 3 mm (Fig. 3B). Even though a thin and hollow cylinder could have been less stiff than a flat slab, we found that, due to the constraints imposed by the sensitivity of the bioprinting nozzle, we could achieve better results with the flat slab. Figure 3C shows the displacement of the two kinds of posts after applying a total edge force in a range of 0–50 μN, which were values similar to those reported in the literature [7].

Finally, by applying Euler-Bernoulli's beam bending theory to the geometry of the flat slab, and assuming that such small deformations can be considered linear, we related the displacement of the posts to the applied force as:

$$y(x) = \frac{Px^2}{6EI_z}(3a - x) \qquad \text{for } 0 < x < a$$

$$y(x) = \frac{Pa^2}{6EI_z}(3x - a) \qquad \text{for } a < x < h, \tag{1}$$

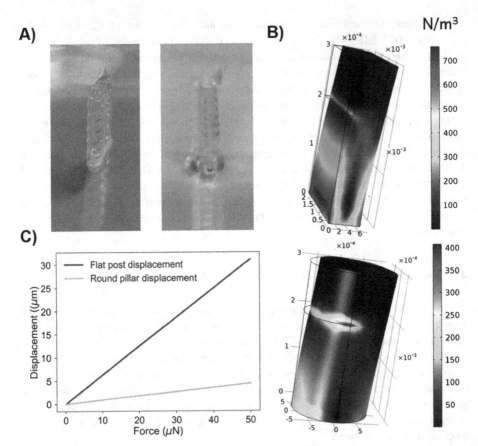

Fig. 3. (A) Two images of posts designed as a flat slab (left) and a hollow pillar (right). (B) Stresses generated by a simulated edge force on the two designs, leading to deformation (a scaling factor has been applied to make the deformations visible). (C) Displacement of the top part of the post for different applied forces and for each design.

where P is the applied force, a is the height at which the force is being applied, E is the Young's modulus of the post (measured by tensile mechanical testing), and I_z is the second moment of area of the post around the z-axis.

5   Force Measurement and Adaptability of Bio-Actuators

Having obtained a relationship between the post displacement and the applied force, we developed a protocol to characterize the performance of the bio-actuators in order to better understand their behavior and optimize future designs. During electrical stimulation, the samples were being recorded with an inverted microscope with a micrometric z-axis stage. Firstly, the exact position of the tissue with respect to the bottom of the Petri dish was calculated by performing a z-stack. Secondly, the video was focused at the point of the applied force to record the deformations of the post.

After acquisition, a home-made Python script based on image processing and computer vision algorithms was used to track the displacement of the posts. At the beginning, a Sobel operator was applied to find the edges of the image, which were binarized afterwards (Fig. 4A). The threshold of the Sobel operator could be modified online in order to account for different brightness in the videos. The user was then asked to draw a straight, perpendicular line, to one of the outer edges of the post (Fig. 4B). A Bresenham's line algorithm was then applied to approximate the drawn line to a set of pixels. As depicted in Fig. 4C, the intersection between the edge pixels (grey squares) with the Bresenham's approximation (pink squares) would define the location of the edge. A profile along the Bresenham's line would reveal a square jump at the position of the edge. This profile was then fitted to a Gaussian function and its mean was computed. For each frame of the video, the line coordinates were kept constant, while the position of the edge was moving along it. Time evolution of the Gaussian means of the profile projection could be used to compute the displacement of the posts due to the contractions and, by using Eq. (1), the force generated by the muscular tissue could be measured.

As a result of this measurement platform and algorithm, we were able to characterize in depth the performance of these bio-actuators under different conditions. For instance, we were able to see that they were always responding to the applied frequency of stimulation, as expected (Fig. 5A). We could also estimate the response by measuring the time it took to reach the peak from the baseline at each stimulation, obtaining a value of $t_{raise} = 0.17 \pm 0.07$ s and, equivalently for the falling time, $t_{falling} = 0.35 \pm 0.08$ s. Moreover, we observed adaptability of the tissue according to the training conditions. If a bio-actuator was stimulated during 1 h a day for 4 consecutive days at different frequencies, we could see a force increment with respect to a control, non-stimulated sample (Fig. 5B). In fact, there was a proportional increment in the 0.1–5 Hz range. In contrast, using high frequencies of about 10 Hz (high enough to produce tetanic contractions) had a detrimental effect, probably due to tissue damage after being exposed to such extreme conditions. Furthermore, we could modulate the amount of force generated by modifying the pulse width and applied voltage (Figs. 5C and D). As one would expect, increasing the voltage and the pulse width resulted in a higher force output, because a larger number of muscular fibers being recruited for contraction. Nevertheless, any value between the peak force and 0 N could be achieved by just modifying these parameters. Surprisingly, the maximum force was not obtained with the maximum pulse width, but there is an optimal width which yields the highest force. This could be related to the relaxation of the cells after applying stimulation, since high pulse widths might not leave enough time to achieve full relaxation and a strong contraction.

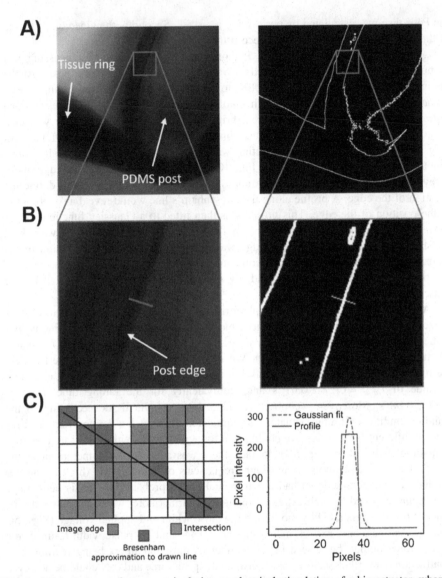

Fig. 4. (A) Left: Image from a movie during an electrical stimulation of a bio-actuator, where the tissue (darker section) and the post (lighter section) are shown. Right: Binarization after edge detection of the left image. (B) Left and right: zoomed-in sections of the respective images where the user has drawn a line. (C) Left: schematic representing the Bresenham's line algorithm. Right: profile along the line showing the detection of the edge and the fitting to a Gaussian function.

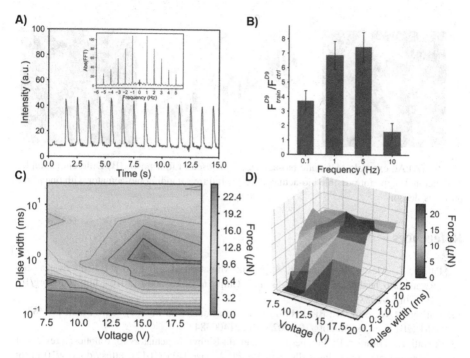

Fig. 5. (A) Response of an electrically stimulated bio-actuator in arbitrary units. The fast Fourier Transform of the inset shows that that the frequency of stimulation is 1 Hz. (B) Force increment of trained bio-actuators at different frequencies compared to untrained ones (control). (C) Heatmap of the force generated by a bio-actuator when the pulse width and the voltage are modified. (D) Surface plot of the force generated vs. the voltage and pulse width, showing how modulation can be achieved from 0 N to the peak force (25 µN).

6 Conclusions and Future Prospects: Towards More Complex Bio-Hybrid Robots

As a conclusion, we have demonstrated that 3D bioprinting is a powerful technique for the fabrication of biological actuators based on skeletal muscle tissue. Due to the versatility and ease of design, one can easily optimize the geometry and architecture of the devices. We have also described how a proper characterization of the performance of the bio-actuators is crucial to demonstrate, validate and understand certain aspects, such as controllability, adaptability and force modulation. With this design- and optimization-driven mindset, one can envision many different compositions, ranging from static constructs, similar to the one proposed in this paper (Fig. 6A), to more sophisticated and carefully designed free-standing skeletons (Fig. 6B), which can possess inherent asymmetries that might lead to more complex behavior (Fig. 6C).

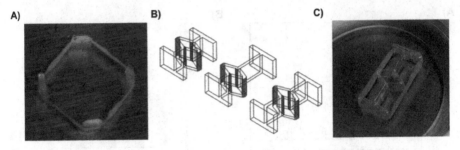

Fig. 6. (A) An example of a static bio-actuator composed of four posts. (B) Different examples of skeleton designs for possible bio-actuators (C) A full free-standing bio-actuator with one of the previous designs.

References

1. Patino, T., Mestre, R., Sánchez, S., et al.: Miniaturized soft bio-hybrid robotics: a step forward into healthcare applications. Lab Chip **16**, 3626–3630 (2016). https://doi.org/10.1039/C6LC90088G
2. Carlsen, R.W., Sitti, M.: Bio-hybrid cell-based actuators for microsystems. Small **10**, 3831–3851 (2014). https://doi.org/10.1002/smll.201400384
3. Ricotti, L., Trimmer, B., Feinberg, A.W., et al.: Biohybrid actuators for robotics: a review of devices actuated by living cells. Sci. Robot. **2**, eaaq0495 (2017). https://doi.org/10.1126/scirobotics.aaq0495
4. Mestre, R., Patiño, T., Barceló, X., et al.: Force modulation and adaptability of 3D bioprinted biological actuators based on skeletal muscle tissue. Adv. Mater. Technol. **4**, 1800631 (2018)
5. Akiyama, Y., Sakuma, T., Funakoshi, K., et al.: Atmospheric-operable bioactuator powered by insect muscle packaged with medium. Lab Chip **13**, 4870–4880 (2013). https://doi.org/10.1039/c3lc50490e
6. Feinberg, A.W., Feigel, A., Shevkoplyas, S.S., et al.: Muscular thin films for building actuators and powering devices. Science **317**, 1366–1370 (2007). https://doi.org/10.1126/science.1146885
7. Cvetkovic, C., Raman, R., Chan, V., et al.: Three-dimensionally printed biological machines powered by skeletal muscle. Proc. Natl. Acad. Sci. U.S.A. **111**, 10125–10130 (2014). https://doi.org/10.1073/pnas.1401577111
8. Mestre, R., Patiño, T., Barceló, X., Sanchez, S.: 3D bioprinted muscle-based bio-actuators: force adaptability due to training. In: Vouloutsi, V., et al. (eds.) Living Machines 2018. LNCS (LNAI), vol. 10928, pp. 316–320. Springer, Cham (2018). https://doi.org/10.1007/978-3-319-95972-6_33
9. Morimoto, Y., Onoe, H., Takeuchi, S.: Biohybrid robot powered by an antagonistic pair of skeletal muscle tissues. Sci. Robot. **3**, eaat4440 (2018). https://doi.org/10.1126/scirobotics.aat4440
10. Pagan-Diaz, G.J., Zhang, X., Grant, L., et al.: Simulation and fabrication of stronger, larger, and faster walking biohybrid machines. Adv. Funct. Mater. **1801145**, 1–13 (2018). https://doi.org/10.1002/adfm.201801145
11. Nawroth, J.C., Lee, H., Feinberg, A.W., et al.: A tissue-engineered jellyfish with biomimetic propulsion. Nat. Biotechnol. **30**, 792–797 (2012). https://doi.org/10.1038/nbt.2269

12. Park, S.-J., Gazzola, M., Park, K.S., et al.: Phototactic guidance of a tissue-engineered soft-robotic ray. Science **353**, 158–162 (2016). https://doi.org/10.1126/science.aaf4292
13. Lind, J.U., Busbee, T.A., Valentine, A.D., et al: Instrumented cardiac microphysiological devices via multimaterial three-dimensional printing. Nat. Mater. 1 (2016). https://doi.org/10.1038/nmat4782
14. Legant, W.R., Pathak, A., Yang, M.T., et al.: Microfabricated tissue gauges to measure and manipulate forces from 3D microtissues. Proc. Natl. Acad. Sci. **106**, 10097–10102 (2009). https://doi.org/10.1073/pnas.0900174106
15. Kang, H.-W., Lee, S.J., Ko, I.K., et al.: A 3D bioprinting system to produce human-scale tissue constructs with structural integrity. Nat. Biotechnol. **34**, 312–319 (2016). https://doi.org/10.1038/nbt.3413

Chemotaxis Based Virtual Fence
for Swarm Robots in Unbounded Environments

Simon O. Obute[1]([⊠]), Mehmet R. Dogar[1], and Jordan H. Boyle[2]

[1] School of Computing, University of Leeds, Leeds, UK
{scsoo,M.R.Dogar}@leeds.ac.uk
[2] School of Mechanical Engineering, University of Leeds, Leeds, UK
J.H.Boyle@leeds.ac.uk

Abstract. This paper presents a novel swarm robotics application of chemotaxis behaviour observed in microorganisms. This approach was used to cause exploration robots to return to a work area around the swarm's nest within a boundless environment. We investigate the performance of our algorithm through extensive simulation studies and hardware validation. Results show that the chemotaxis approach is effective for keeping the swarm close to both stationary and moving nests. Performance comparison of these results with the unrealistic case where a boundary wall was used to keep the swarm within a target search area showed that our chemotaxis approach produced competitive results.

Keywords: Chemotaxis · Swarm robots · Exploration ·
Distributed robot systems

1 Introduction

Swarm robotics is a bio-inspired multi-robot research theme focused on the actualization of swarm intelligence observed in nature on robotic platforms. Biological swarms like bees, ants and termites are able to accomplish complex tasks, such as finding food and building nests, through local interaction with each other and/or their environments. These tasks are beyond the capabilities of a single agent and, in general, unattainable without cooperation among swarm members. By mimicking nature, swarm robotics emphasizes local interactions and autonomous decision making of agents to develop simple, flexible, scalable and robust algorithms for multi-robot platforms [2, 16]. Typical swarm behaviours include foraging, aggregation, exploration, clustering, assembly and flocking [2]. A major concern for swarm robotics applications is development of effective means for keeping swarm robots within the desired work area while they perform their tasks. This is important for real world deployment of swarm robotics systems, where they encounter unknown and unstructured environments that are, in many cases, unfenced. Much work has been done that assumed the presence of a boundary (or fence) [1,5,9]

Supported by National Information Technology Development Agency, Nigeria. Simulations were undertaken on ARC3, part of the High Performance Computing facilities at the University of Leeds, UK.

U. Martinez-Hernandez et al. (Eds.): Living Machines 2019, LNAI 11556, pp. 216–227, 2019.
https://doi.org/10.1007/978-3-030-24741-6_19

that keeps the swarm from drifting over time from the work area - an approach we believe to be unrealistic because such a structure will not be available in many applications and in some cases the swarm working area must change over time. Thus, a main contribution of this work is to provide a means for keeping swarm robots within a work area by introducing a simple, hardware-grounded means of communication between robots and their nest (or guide robot). Our approach is effective for both static and dynamic work area for swarm robots. We make use of a nest robot that broadcasts a range-limited signal that degrades with distance, which swarm members listen to. When they sense that intensity of nest signal drops below a threshold, they use this sensory information to perform a chemotaxis-based search for the work area.

This simple bio-inspired search algorithm is based on the chemotaxis behaviour observed in the nematode worm *Caenorhabditis elegans* [8, 12] in response to chemical attractants, which is one of the primary methods the worm uses to navigate towards favourable conditions. The worm's small size and limited neural circuit preclude the use of 'stereo' sensing to detect the spatial gradient of the chemical cue, so the behaviour is instead based on the temporal gradient sensed by the worm as it moves, which requires only a single sensory receptor. By default the worm performs a random walk consisting of runs of relatively straight, forwards motion, interspersed by large turns called pirouettes at random intervals. If the temporal gradient of a chemical attractant is positive, the probability of performing a turn is reduced so the worm is more likely to keep moving in a beneficial direction. Conversely, a negative temporal gradient increases the turn probability so it is more likely to reorient to a more favourable direction.

The results we present in this paper study the relationship between nest signal threshold and work area size, selection of good chemotaxis parameters for stationary and moving nests, and how nest velocity affects target search efficiency of swarms.

Section 2 reviews swarm algorithms in literature, with a focus on mechanisms used to keep robots within work area. In Sect. 3 we detail the chemotaxis-based algorithm for keeping robots within a designated work area for both stationary and moving nest (or guide robot). The details of how we model our swarm communication is presented in Sect. 4. In Sects. 5 and 6 we present simulation and real robot experimental results respectively, then conclude in Sect. 7.

2   Review of Similar Works

The two extremes in multi-robot exploration algorithms are: random search and systematic exploration [11]. In random search, robots use Brownian-like motion to explore the environment until they perceive a feature of interest. This approach is sufficient for bounded environments because it will typically explore all regions of the environment when given sufficient time. It is unsuitable for large or open (unbounded) environments because robots will drift away from the work area and lose contact with other swarm members. In the systematic approach, robots use a priori knowledge of the environment's structure to methodically explore it. Although this approach optimizes exploration time and prevents oversampling of regions in the environment, its memory requirements become excessive for large environments. Its localization, mapping and planning algorithms do not scale well with increase in swarm and environment sizes. Most swarm robotics exploration algorithms propose balance between these two approaches to develop robust, flexible and scalable algorithms.

The Gradient Algorithm in [4] is based on the gas expansion approach, where robots try to maintain communication links with their neighbours while maximizing the distance between themselves. Also in [4], the Sweeper Algorithm made the interconnected robots form a 1D chain, which rotates about the nest (like the hand of the clock, where the nest is the centre). This extends the area covered by the swarm beyond what is attainable by the Gradient Algorithm. In these algorithms, the size of environment the swarm can cover is dependent on the number of robots, since maintaining communication links is paramount for the swarm to keep robots within work area. The success of these approaches also requires formation of *ad hoc* networks where such infrastructure is unavailable [13]. The work in [3] and hierarchical swarm in [7] also require the swarm to maintain communication networks for their task. In [10], swarms of robots deployed underwater kept track of their initial deployment region using a scheme termed virtual tether search. The robots used random walk to search for targets, while using dead reckoning to constrain their distance from their initial deployment point. Another dead reckoning approach, which kept track of a stationary nest location within the context of foraging swarm was implemented in [6]. Dead reckoning is unsuited for large work areas because it becomes less accurate over time or distance travelled, and is terrain dependent. It is also unusable for applications where the nest is mobile. Pheromone-based approaches, as in [5] and [16] are difficult to realise in hardware. The various attempts to provide hardware implementations have resulted in the use of beacon robots [4], LCD platform [1], RFID and other technologies [15]. Such approaches do not scale well when increasing size of the environment.

Our approach does not require network connectivity among swarm robots or dead reckoning, thus freeing them to autonomously explore the work area. Our robots only need to sense the intensity of a nest signal (we use sound in the present work) in their current location to make autonomous decision on whether they are within or outside the desired work area. This approach greatly simplifies our swarm algorithm and communication strategy. Furthermore, we demonstrate that our implementation is effective for a moving nest and easily realizable on hardware platforms.

3   Unbounded Exploration

3.1   Robot Exploration with Chemotaxis Activation

In our design, the region surrounding the nest (or guide robot) is divided into a work area ($<d_c$) and a chemotactic region ($>=d_c$), where d_c is the distance that corresponds to chemotaxis activation threshold, $A(d_c)$. Within the work area, the robots perform their expected swarm task, which we abstract as random exploration of the region. Beyond this area, there is the chemotactic region, which serve as an effective wall for keeping robots within the work area. Robots within the chemotactic region make use of a *C. elegans*-inpsired 'chemotaxis' behaviour (using sound intensity in place of a chemical signal) to search for the work area. Algorithm 1 represents the steps executed by each exploration robot in the swarm within each time step.

The robot first senses the nest signal, A_t from its current location and initializes its turn probability, P_t, to a pre-determined base probability, P_b. If A_t is less than a pre-determined threshold, $A(d_c)$, it updates P_t based on whether nest signal has increased or decreased since the last time step. M and D are probability multipliers and divisors for increasing or decreasing the robot's turn probability. The robot uses P_t to decide whether to make a turn or continue linear, straight motion at constant velocity, v_r.

Algorithm 1. Random Walk with chemotaxis activation.

1: Sense nest signal, A_t
2: Initialize $P_t = P_b$ to default value
3: **if** $A_t < A(d_c)$ **then**
4:     **if** $A_t < A_{t-1}$ **then**
5:         $P_t = P_b \times M$
6:     **else if** $A_t > A_{t-1}$ **then**
7:         $P_t = P_b \div D$
8: **if** rand(0,1) $< P_t$ **then**
9:     make random turn of $\mathcal{N}(180^0, 90^0)$
10: **else**
11:     make straight motion

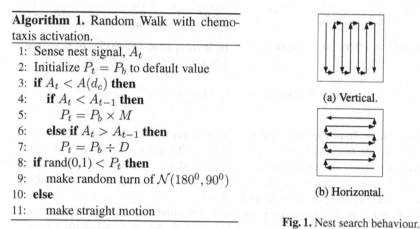

(a) Vertical.

(b) Horizontal.

Fig. 1. Nest search behaviour.

3.2 Moving the Nest

In the basic form of our approach, the nest is stationary. However, with the absence of a physical boundary to restrict the swarm's work area, the nest itself can be free to move within the unbounded environment, thereby guiding exploration of the swarm as it makes its motion. The basic form of this moving nest is a linear motion from a starting location to destination point by moving at a constant velocity that is a fraction of the exploration robots' velocity v_n. The nest waits (stops briefly) whenever it senses robot(s) within d_n metres of its front region to avoid collisions. We extend the nest's motion to cover a 2D search area by following a sequence of checkpoints that causes it to perform vertical then horizontal sweeps of the environment (as shown in Fig. 1). These sweeps are repeated continuously for a maximum simulation time, t_{max}. The introduction of a moving nest extends the search area of the swarm of robots by guiding them to regions where they can execute their tasks. However, it also brings up questions regarding the optimal nest velocity that will give the best balance between exploration speed, accuracy (or efficiency) and minimization of the number of robots that lose track of the nest signal and get left behind. We investigate these questions in upcoming sections.

4   Development of Communication Model

The successful deployment of our swarm in unbounded environments is dependent on a realistic communication model between the nest (or guide) and other swarm members. We implemented this communication using white noise broadcast from a speaker

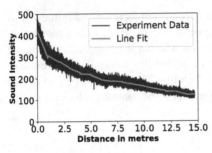

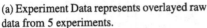

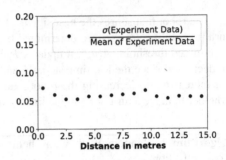

(a) Experiment Data represents overlayed raw data from 5 experiments.

(b) Ratio of standard deviation of experiment data to mean value of line fit segment.

Fig. 2. Developing noise model for simulation.

attached to the nest. To model the noise accurately in our simulations, we first collected sound intensity data from real robot experiments. In the setup, a Turtlebot2 robot was placed 15 m away from the speaker and programmed to move towards the sound source at a velocity of 0.1 m/s while logging the sound intensity perceived on its attached microphone. This experiment was repeated 5 times.

In the second step, we computed parameters for sound degradation with distance. We used Eq. 1 for the sound model [14], where $A(d)$ is the sound intensity d metres away from a speaker. A_0 is the sound intensity at the speaker, α is the attenuation factor and the A_e term was added to account for ambient noise. The model parameters were computed by evaluating the least square error fit between the collected data and Eq. 1 using MATLAB's nonlinear curve-fitting function. The values computed were $A_0 = 140.5193$, $\alpha = 0.1193$ and $A_e = 48.1824$.

$$A(d) = A_0 e^{-\alpha d} + A_e \tag{1}$$

The third step involved quantifying the noise in the recorded data. To do this, the logged data was broken into 1 m segments; a line was fitted to each segment (as shown in Fig. 2a); and the means and standard deviations of the sound data from the fitted line segments were computed. It was observed that, though the deviation increased with increasing mean sound intensity, the ratio between each mean and the corresponding standard deviation remained fairly constant at 0.06 (Fig. 2b). Thus, noise was modelled as random deviation with standard deviation of 0.06 from the mean intensity perceived from a sound source. Equation 2 represents the noisy sound intensity d metres away, at the i-th time step.

$$A_i(d) = A(d)(1 - \mathcal{N}(0, 0.06)) \tag{2}$$

In order to help the robots detect the underlying gradient despite the substantial noise, we added a filtering system to the behavioural algorithm. We implemented an averaging filter, shown in Eq. 3, where t is the current time step and $n = 40$ time steps. A time step in our experiments was 0.0025 s, which means that a robot's sensed nest signal is updated at 1 Hz (40 time steps make 1 s).

$$A_f(d) = \frac{\sum_{i=t-n}^{t} A_i(d)}{n} \tag{3}$$

Table 1. Chemotaxis activation distance d_c versus robots distances from nest d_r. Each value represents the mean number of robots within d_r of the nest and the 95% confidence interval of this value over 30 repetitions of each simulation. Simulation time was 1500 s, $M = 10$ and $D = 1000$.

d_r	d_c				
	6 m	8 m	10 m	12 m	14 m
6	4.4 ± 0.03	-	-	-	-
8	7.9 ± 0.02	5.3 ± 0.04	-	-	-
10	9.4 ± 0.01	8.3 ± 0.02	6.0 ± 0.04	-	-
12	9.8 ± 0.01	9.5 ± 0.01	8.6 ± 0.02	6.5 ± 0.04	-
14	10.0 ± 0.00	9.8 ± 0.01	9.6 ± 0.01	8.8 ± 0.02	6.7 ± 0.04
16	10.0 ± 0.00	10.0 ± 0.00	9.9 ± 0.01	9.7 ± 0.01	8.7 ± 0.03
18	10.0 ± 0.00	10.0 ± 0.00	10.0 ± 0.00	9.9 ± 0.00	9.6 ± 0.01
20	10.0 ± 0.00	10.0 ± 0.00	10.0 ± 0.00	10.0 ± 0.00	9.9 ± 0.01
22	10.0 ± 0.00	10.0 ± 0.00	10.0 ± 0.00	10.0 ± 0.00	10.0 ± 0.00

5 Simulation Results

5.1 Simulation Setup

We used the Gazebo simulation platform to investigate the performance of our approach. A swarm size of 10 robots moving at $v_r = 0.605$ m/s was used. The robot's base turn probability for all simulations was $P_b = 0.0025$ per time step. Nest velocity v_n is expressed relative to v_r for all experiments and the nest stops when it senses a robot is within $d_n = 0.1$ m from its front region.

5.2 Determining the Chemotactic Region

To be able to determine the chemotaxis activation intensity, $A(d_c)$, needed to keep swarm robots within a specified distance of a stationary nest, d_r, we conducted simulation experiments where chemotaxis activation distance, d_c was varied from 6 m to 14 m from the nest. The robots were made to perform a random walk for 1500 s around the nest for each d_c. Each simulation was repeated 30 times and we analysed the average number of robots within varied distances from the nest. Results are presented in Table 1. This shows that the chemotactic region is effective in keeping more than 95% of robots within $d_c + 4$ of the nest in all distance ranges tested. Thus, for design purposes, to keep at least 95% of swarm members within d_w metres of a stationary nest, the chemotaxis activation distance can be computed using Eq. 4.

$$d_c = d_w - 4 \qquad (4)$$

5.3 Effects of Base Probability Multiplier and Divisor

Important factors that change the effectiveness of the chemotactic region in keeping the swarm together include the nest's relative velocity v_n, and the probability multiplier

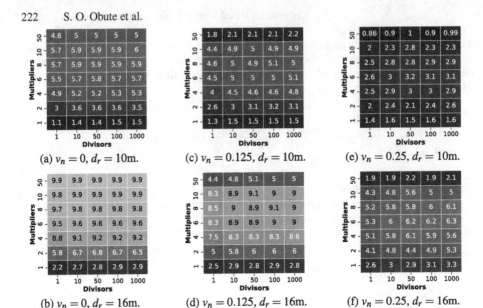

Fig. 3. Heat map of the effects of nest relative velocity, v_n, probability multiplier, M, and divisor, D, on the average number of robots within a specific distance, d_r from the nest/guide robot. Chemotaxis activation distance, $d_c = 10\,\text{m}$, for all simulations.

M and divisor D. We investigate the effects of these values in Fig. 3. The chemotaxis activation distance was 10 m for these simulations. Each value in Fig. 3 represents the mean number of robots within a distance d_r of the nest, averaged across 30 independent simulation repetitions. When $v_n > 0$, the nest moved for 100 m along a straight path.

The results in Fig. 3 indicate that the probability multiplier, M, and divisor D play a major role in the effectiveness of using chemotaxis to keep robots within the work area. A small value of M made the robots less responsive to decreasing nest signal when in the chemotactic region, thus causing them to move further away from the work area, indicating a high flexibility of the 'chemotactic wall'. Large values for M made the robots more responsive to negative temporal gradients of the nest signal, preventing them from going further into the chemotactic region. However, a very high probability multiplier, $M = 50$, caused the robots to turn too frequently in the chemotactic region, thus, preventing them from making sufficient linear motion to compute a reliable temporal gradient from the noisy nest signal.

The probability divisor, D, has a lesser effect than M on the swarm's ability to remain within the work area. The results show a general trend, where increasing D results in slightly more robots remaining within the work area. Low values of D made robots less responsive to positive temporal gradients of nest signal when in the chemotactic region, making robots' suppression of turns less effective during chemotaxis. Increasing D caused robots performing chemotaxis to suppress turns better when they sense positive temporal gradient from the nest signal.

Figure 3 also shows that fewer robots are able to remain within the work area as the nest's relative velocity, v_n, increases, which is unsurprising. However, there is a variation in the best performing M and D as the nest's velocity increases. In general, as the nest becomes faster, smaller M and larger D gave better performance. Thus, when

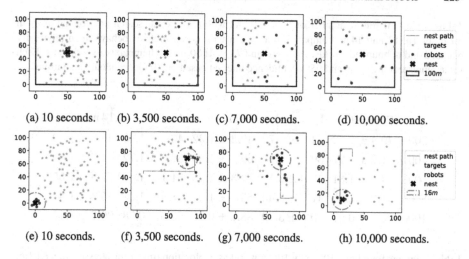

(a) 10 seconds.   (b) 3,500 seconds.   (c) 7,000 seconds.   (d) 10,000 seconds.

(e) 10 seconds.   (f) 3,500 seconds.   (g) 7,000 seconds.   (h) 10,000 seconds.

Fig. 4. Sample simulation showing swarm searching for 100 targets uniformly distributed within 100 m by 100 m search area. (a-d) are for $v_n = 0$ and robots perform random walk within a bounded search area. (e-h) are for moving nest within unbounded search area, where $v_n = 0.167$, $M = 6$ and $D = 1000$. x and y axis are environment coordinates in metres.

$v_n = 0$, $M = 10$ performed best, while when $v_n = 0.25$, $M = 6$ and $D = 1000$ gave good results. These indicate that an equivalent of Eq. 4 for the moving nest case is more complex, needing a relationship that relates nest velocity, rate of robots getting 'lost' and distribution of robots within the work area.

5.4   Investigating Exploration Effectiveness

It is important that the swarm effectively explores the work area, and are able to minimize time spent in the chemotactic region. We tested the swarm's ability to explore the work area using a target search task for both the stationary and moving nest setups. In each simulation, the task is for 10 swarm robots to locate 100 targets that are randomly but uniformly distributed within the search area. Robots were able to detect targets beneath them i.e. when the robot's distance from the target was less than robot's radius. Detected targets were removed from the world and 30 independent simulations were repeated for each simulation setup. Our approach was compared with two environment setups as baseline: when a wall was used to keep robots within search area (*Bounded*); and when the wall was removed (*Unbounded*), thus removing any mechanism to restrict the robots to the search area.

In the stationary nest simulation setup, 100 targets were uniformly distributed within 14 m radius search area around the nest. Number of found targets by the swarm at different time steps till 1000 simulated seconds, averaged for 30 independent simulation repetitions are shown in Table 2. The result indicates that the exploration ability of the swarm when using chemotaxis to keep robots within the target search area is effective. Perfect restriction of the robot's movement to within the search area using a wall (*Bounded*) caused the swarm to find 95.2% of targets after 1000 s, while removal of the wall (and no chemotaxis) caused performance to drop to 50.5% (*Unbounded*). The presence of nest signal improved the swarm's performance in absence of a wall,

Table 2. Comparison of number of targets found within a circular search area of radius 14 m for d_c of 10, 12 and 14 m, compared to a swarm with no chemotaxis behaviour in physically bounded and unbounded worlds. $M = 10$ and $D = 1000$ in all chemotaxis experiments. Each value represents the mean and 95% confidence interval based on 30 independent simulations.

t	d_c				
	Bounded	Unbounded	10 m	12 m	14 m
200	49.4 ± 2.32	34.0 ± 1.72	49.2 ± 1.32	46.7 ± 1.43	45.3 ± 1.12
400	71.2 ± 2.27	39.0 ± 2.18	69.1 ± 1.66	68.3 ± 1.72	64.7 ± 1.50
600	84.5 ± 1.81	43.9 ± 3.11	79.3 ± 1.33	81.1 ± 1.40	77.0 ± 1.55
800	91.2 ± 1.25	47.0 ± 3.43	85.5 ± 1.07	88.4 ± 1.27	85.7 ± 1.47
1000	95.2 ± 0.97	50.5 ± 3.79	88.7 ± 0.98	93.5 ± 0.78	90.7 ± 1.17

Table 3. Targets found in a 100 m by 100 m world as exploration time, t, progresses. $d_c = 12$ m, $M = 6$ and $D = 1000$ for the chemotaxis based approach. $v_n = 0$ for Bounded and Unbounded cases. Each value represents the mean and 95% confidence interval based on 30 independent simulations.

t	v_n					
	Bounded	Unbounded	0.1	0.125	0.167	0.25
2000	35.1 ± 1.21	21.3 ± 1.57	17.9 ± 0.84	19.3 ± 1.29	22.9 ± 1.30	21.9 ± 1.45
4000	56.0 ± 1.65	27.0 ± 2.02	34.8 ± 0.87	38.9 ± 1.45	45.2 ± 1.79	41.3 ± 2.06
6000	69.0 ± 1.69	31.4 ± 2.28	51.7 ± 1.11	57.9 ± 1.60	61.9 ± 2.03	55.2 ± 2.18
8000	78.6 ± 1.37	34.3 ± 2.45	72.5 ± 1.38	71.3 ± 1.75	72.4 ± 1.87	62.8 ± 2.62
10000	86.1 ± 1.30	36.9 ± 2.53	80.8 ± 1.09	78.4 ± 1.61	79.1 ± 1.53	70.9 ± 2.68

causing them to locate 93.5% when $d_c = 12$ m. When $d_c = 10$ m, the robots where able to effectively locate targets close to the nest at the early stages of the simulation, but the chemotactic region beyond 10 m from the nest reduced the swarm's ability to locate targets in that region. Overall, $d_c = 12$ m gave best balance between searching for targets within the chemotactic region (12 m - 14 m from nest) and the work area (0 m–12 m), making it almost as good as the *Bounded* case.

The last set of simulations investigates the swarm's ability to perform a similar exploration task within a 100 m by 100 m target search area, guided by a moving nest. As stated earlier, this is one of the main advantages of our approach, where swarms are able to follow a guide robot (or moving nest) while performing their tasks. In this setup, 100 targets were uniformly distributed within the world and the guide robot was used to perform a sweep of the environment using the search behaviour shown in Fig. 1. A value of $d_c = 12$ m was used in all cases, while v_n varied from 0.1 to 0.25. Simulations were stopped after 10,000 s. Table 3 gives the average number of targets found by the swarm, while snapshots of sample simulations of the swarm performing the target search task are shown in Fig. 4.

After 10,000 simulation seconds, the swarm within a bounded search area was able to locate 86.1% of targets (see Table 3). Removal of the wall caused swarm's performance to drop to 36.9% of targets found. Using our chemotactic approach with a

(a) Experiment robots.   (b) White line is approximately 10 metres.

Fig. 5. Robots used for the experiment and snapshots of exploration robot following the moving nest. Experiment video is available at https://youtu.be/ua0w3aXOYJI.

moving nest that guided exploration within the 100 m by 100 m search area, the swarm was able to give competitive target detection ability (80.1% when $v_n = 0.1$). This is a significant contribution because it is a realistic approach to swarm robot deployment in open space (boundless) application areas, where it can be impractical to build fences around such regions or make the fence mobile to guide the swarm's work area.

In some applications (for example in foraging), it is important to find a balance between maximizing the number of robots close to the nest and fast exploration of the search area. A slow moving nest maximises robots close to the nest, resulting in thorough exploration of the work area. A fast moving nest, however, will result in the search area being covered quicker by the nest at the expense of the number of robots that are able to remain within the nest's work area. This causes the search to be less thorough. Multiple sweeps of the environment by the fast moving nest can compensate for this poor search. We will investigate in more detail the question of maximising the number of robots close to the nest while minimising search time in future work.

6 Real Robot Experiments

To validate that our simulation model can be realised on hardware, we conducted experiments with two Turtlebot2 robots[1] where one robot acted as the nest and the second was used as the exploration robot. For this experiment, $v_r = 0.1$ m/s, $M = 6$, $D = 1000$ and $P_b = 0.0025$ per time step. The nest robot used a speaker to broadcast white noise upwards, which was then reflected radially outwards using an inverted, 3D printed cone as shown in Fig. 5a. The exploration robot used an omnidirectional microphone to perceive the sound signal. Work done by other researchers used multiple microphones on the robot to measure sound intensity [1]. We show that our algorithm works well with a single microphone. Thereby simplifying the hardware implementation. Chemotaxis activation intensity, $A(d_c) = 180$ was used for these experiments.

For stationary nest experiments ($v_n = 0$) the nest was centred within a 3 m by 6.4 m space. The exploration robot was then left to perform random walk within the arena for 600 s. Figure 6a compares the distance of the exploration robot from nest for random walk and our chemotaxis approach, averaged for 5 consecutive repetitions of the experiment. Results show that our approach was reasonably successful in keeping the exploration robot close to the nest's location, with mean distance being 0.9 m within

---

[1] Two robots were used due to availability of robot hardware. Validation with more robots will be done in future work.

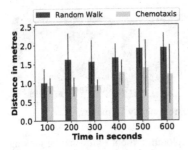
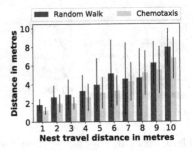

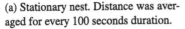

(a) Stationary nest. Distance was averaged for every 100 seconds duration.

(b) Moving nest. Distance was averaged for every 1m of nest's journey.

Fig. 6. Real robot validation of chemotaxis behaviour to remain close to nest. Experiments were repeated 5 times, and error bars represent 95% confidence interval.

the first 100 s and 1.2 m between 500–600 s of the experiment. This validates that the exploration robot was using the chemotaxis approach to remain close to the nest, and not just performing random exploration of the environment.

The second phase of the experiment measures the exploration robot's ability to remain close to a moving nest, when $v_n = 0.125$ and the distance travelled by nest is 10 m. In this setup, the arena's width was 3 m and one short edge of the arena was left open to allow the nest to make the 10 m journey. Figure 5b shows snapshots of the experiment as the nest makes its 10 m journey. The average distance of exploration robot from the moving nest is shown in Fig. 6b for different distance ranges of the nest's journey. In comparison to the random walk, in which the exploration robot did not listen to the nest's signal, our chemotaxis approach indicates good nest following ability for the first 6 m of the nest's journey. Beyond 6m, the chemotaxis became less effective. It is good to appreciate that echoes from the walls, intensity of sound source, ambient noise (including noise from the robots drive systems) and furniture in the environment can have a significant impact on the exploration robot's ability to compute a reliable temporal gradient when performing chemotaxis. These factors were the major contributors to poorer performance of our chemotaxis validation experiments compared to the simulations. In future research, we will work on minimising these environmental factors by conducting experiments in outdoor environments to eliminate effects of echoes and optimising the audio hardware for better signal-to-noise ratio.

7 Conclusion

This paper has presented a simple, yet effective, means for deploying swarm robots in open (or boundless) environments. The biological inspiration for our algorithm is the chemotaxis behaviour used by the nematode *C. elegans* to find high concentrations of chemical attractants. We have used sound experiments to provide a realistic, hardware verifiable model of the communication used in our simulations. Extensive simulation experiments were conducted to investigate effects of our algorithm's parameters on the swarm's ability to use chemotaxis to return to the work area near the nest's location. Furthermore, we show that our algorithm is also effective in scenarios where the nest moves to guide the exploration robots to cover wider areas in a target search challenge, showing the interplay between nest velocity and number of robots that are able to keep up with it. Finally, we validated our algorithm using real robot experiments, showing that it is viable on hardware but would benefit from further optimisation. In the future, we will extend the work to swarm foraging and investigate deployments on large scale swarm sizes on hardware platforms. We will also investigate other technologies, such as Wi-Fi, Zigbee and ultrasound for nest-robots communication.

References

1. Arvin, F., et al.: φ clust: Pheromone-based aggregation for robotic swarms. In: 2018 IEEE/RSJ International Conference on Intelligent Robots and Systems (IROS), pp. 4288–4294. IEEE (2018)
2. Bayindir, L.: A review of swarm robotics tasks. Neurocomputing **172**, 292–321 (2016)
3. Couceiro, M.S., Figueiredo, C.M., Rocha, R.P., Ferreira, N.M.: Darwinian swarm exploration under communication constraints: initial deployment and fault-tolerance assessment. Robot. Auton. Syst. **62**(4), 528–544 (2014)
4. Hoff, N., Wood, R., Nagpal, R.: Distributed colony-level algorithm switching for robot swarm foraging. In: Martinoli, A., et al. (eds.) Distributed Autonomous Robotic Systems. STAR, vol. 83, pp. 417–430. Springer, Berlin (2012). https://doi.org/10.1007/978-3-642-32723-0_30
5. Lima, D.A., Oliveira, G.M.B.: A probabilistic cellular automata ant memory model for a swarm of foraging robots. In: 2016 14th International Conference on Control, Automation, Robotics and Vision, ICARCV 2016, pp. 1–6. IEEE, November 2017
6. Lu, Q., Hecker, J.P., Moses, M.E.: Multiple-place swarm foraging with dynamic depots. Auton. Robot. **42**(4), 909–926 (2018)
7. Ngo, T.D., Hung, P.D., Pham, M.T.: A Kangaroo inspired heterogeneous swarm of mobile robots with global network integrity for fast deployment and exploration in large scale structured environments. In: 2014 IEEE International Conference on Robotics and Biomimetics (ROBIO 2014), pp. 1205–1212. IEEE, December 2014
8. Pierce-Shimomura, J.T., Dores, M., Lockery, S.R.: Analysis of the effects of turning bias on chemotaxis in C. elegans. J. Exp. Biol. **208**(24), 4727–4733 (2005)
9. Schmickl, T., Hamann, H.: BEECLUST: a swarm algorithm derived from honeybees. In: Bio-Inspired Computing and Communication Networks, pp. 95–137 (2011)
10. Tolba, S., Ammar, R.: Virtual Tether Search: a self-constraining search algorithm for swarms in an open ocean. In: 2017 IEEE Symposium on Computers and Communications (ISCC), pp. 1128–1135. IEEE, July 2017
11. Trianni, V., Campo Alexandre, A.: Fundamental collective behaviors in swarm robotics. In: Kacprzyk, J., Pedrycz, W. (eds.) Springer Handbook of Computational Intelligence, pp. 1377–1394. Springer, Heidelberg (2015). https://doi.org/10.1007/978-3-662-43505-2_71
12. Ward, S.: Chemotaxis by the nematode Caenorhabditis elegans: identification of attractants and analysis of the response by use of mutants. Proc. Natl. Acad. Sci. U.S.A. **70**(3), 817–21 (1973)
13. Winfield, A.F.T., Liu, W., Nembrini, J., Martinoli, A.: Modelling a wireless connected swarm of mobile robots. Swarm Intell. **2**(2–4), 241–266 (2008)
14. Yu, P., Yan, R., Yao, L.: Measurement of acoustic attenuation coefficient of stored grain. In: 3rd International Conference on Control, Automation and Robotics, pp. 551–554 (2017)
15. Zedadra, O., Jouandeau, N., Seridi, H., Fortino, G.: Multi-Agent Foraging: state-of-the-art and research challenges. Complex Adapt. Syst. Model. **5**(1), 3 (2017)
16. Zedadra, O., Seridi, H., Jouandeau, N., Fortino, G.: An energy-aware algorithm for large scale foraging systems. Scalable Comput. **16**(4), 449–466 (2015)

Design of a Canine Inspired Quadruped Robot as a Platform for Synthetic Neural Network Control

Cody Scharzenberger$^{(\boxtimes)}$, Jonas Mendoza, and Alexander Hunt

Portland State University, Portland, OR 97207, USA
cscharz2@pdx.edu

Abstract. Legged locomotion is a feat ubiquitous throughout the animal kingdom, but modern robots still fall far short of similar achievements. This paper presents the design of a canine-inspired quadruped robot named DoggyDeux as a platform for synthetic neural network (SNN) research that may be one avenue for robots to attain animal-like agility and adaptability. DoggyDeux features a fully 3D printed frame, 24 braided pneumatic actuators (BPAs) that drive four 3-DOF limbs in antagonistic extensor-flexor pairs, and an electrical system that allows it to respond to commands from a SNN comprised of central pattern generators (CPGs). Compared to the previous version of this robot, DoggyDeux eliminates out-of-plane bending moments on the legs, has biologically realistic joint range of motion for walking, and eliminates buckling of the BPAs by utilizing a biologically inspired muscle attachment approach. A simple SNN comprised of a single isolated CPG for each joint is used to control the front left leg on DoggyDeux and joint angle data from this leg is collected to verify that the robot responds correctly to inputs from its SNN. Future design work on DoggyDeux will involve further improving the muscle attachment mechanism, while future SNN research will include expanding the robot's SNN to achieve coordinated locomotion with all four legs utilizing sensory feedback.

Keywords: Quadruped robot · Synthetic neural network · Central pattern generator

1 Introduction

Although animals are able to effortlessly achieve complex locomotion in unstructured environments, similar accomplishments still prove elusive for modern robots. In particular, legged locomotion is a versatile ambulatory technique that is ubiquitous in the animal kingdom from insects and small mammals to humans; yet current control methods are not robust nor adaptable enough to deliver

Supported by Portland State University, NIH grants UL1GM118964, RL5GM118963, and TL4GM118965, and NSF grant IIS-1608111.

© Springer Nature Switzerland AG 2019
U. Martinez-Hernandez et al. (Eds.): Living Machines 2019, LNAI 11556, pp. 228–239, 2019.
https://doi.org/10.1007/978-3-030-24741-6_20

similar results in artificial systems. One increasingly important approach for addressing the problem of achieving legged locomotion in robots has therefore been to turn to biology for inspiration. The field of biologically inspired robotics casts a wide net, including approaches that draw loosely from biological observations to strict biological realism [10]. However, as the fields of neurobiology and computational neuroscience have matured, more details about the underlying biological neural circuits used by animals for motor control have become available to roboticists [3]. Beyond capturing merely the biological details of structure and form, roboticists are able to study and apply the fundamental mechanisms of biological control. It is for the purpose of better understanding these biological control systems and applying them to robotics that the Biologically Inspired Robotics Lab at Case Western Reserve University (CWRU) developed the canine inspired quadruped robot named Puppy pictured in Fig. 1a [2,7,9]. While the physical design of Puppy agrees with biological data taken from dogs, more importantly, it serves as a platform for testing biologically inspired synthetic neural networks (SNNs) for locomotion control. Toward these same goals, the work herein details the design of an updated version of Puppy as a test bed for SNN and controls research at Portland State University (PSU). This paper describes what was accomplished with Puppy at CWRU and the limitations of this robot before discussing how these problems are resolved on DoggyDeux, the preliminary results we have obtained, and the future work we intend to do with this robot.

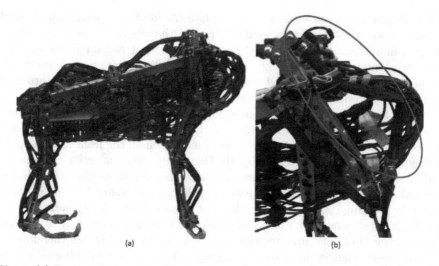

(a)   (b)

Fig. 1. (a) Puppy robot at Case Western Reserve University. (b) Severe buckling of the front right elbow extensor muscle (circled) on Puppy robot at Case Western University.

1.1   Background

The Puppy robot at CWRU was built for the purpose of researching legged loco-motion and was later adapted to be controlled via SNNs [2]. The most notable difference between the neural network implemented on this robot and those being applied to most other areas in modern robotics, such as computer vision, is the degree of biological plausibility of these models. While modern approaches in machine learning apply deep neural networks with largely unconstrained topolo-gies and massive parameter spaces, Puppy's neural network contains relatively few neurons arranged into an architecture directly informed by neurobiology [7]. For instance, Puppy's neural network features populations of neurons organized into central pattern generators (CPGs) and biologically relevant proprioceptive feedback pathways (joint angle, muscle tension, etc.). As a result, Puppy is able to achieve a stepping motion with emergent coordination among its hide legs without a central controller to dictate timing. At the same time, work has also been done on Puppy related to the mathematical characterization of braided pneumatic actuators (BPAs), which are compliant actuators with similar prop-erties to real muscles [1]. While the compliance and nonlinear behavior of these types of actuators make them more challenging to control, their similarity to real muscles makes them more biologically plausible and therefore more amenable to SNN research.

1.2   Limitations of Existing Design

While Puppy has been successful as a platform for SNN locomotion control research, there are several notable limitations of the robot. The most important of these limitations are the limited range of motion at certain joints and the persistent kinking of the BPAs [2]. The range of motion restrictions of the robot are primarily due to the limited draw length of the BPAs, which is determined by both their resting length and the maximum available supply pressure [1]. Similarly, kinking of the BPAs occurs due to interference with nearby compo-nents (in the case of the scapula/hip muscles) and the fact that the BPAs are pinned at both ends. Both of these effects can be seen on the front right scapula of Puppy at CWRU pictured in Fig. 1b. Due to the pin connections, whenever both extensor-flexor muscle pairs are fully lengthened (such as when the robot is powered off), the muscles have no space to expand and therefore buckle. Not only does this buckling damage the muscles, but it also affects the dynamic behav-ior of the robot whenever the muscles are not explicitly controlled to remove the resulting kink. The primary goals of the redesigned robot are therefore to address these issues in order to improve the utility of the new robot as a tool for SNN research.

2   Methodology and Materials

Cognizant of the aforementioned limitations, the following sections detail the design methodology and materials for various aspects of the new version of the robot, focusing on the robot's structure, actuation system, and electrical system. In addition to addressing the primary limitations of the previous robot as discussed above, we seek to achieve several additional goals with the new robot design, including using a fully 3D printable frame in order to simplify future modifications. As will be explained in the following sections, these goals are largely accomplished via localized redesign of the structural components and large scale modifications to the muscle attachment scheme.

2.1 Structural Design

Design efforts on the new frame were focused on maintaining the biologic realism of the original robot while making the frame 3D printable and increasing the range of motion of the joints by moving muscle attachment points.

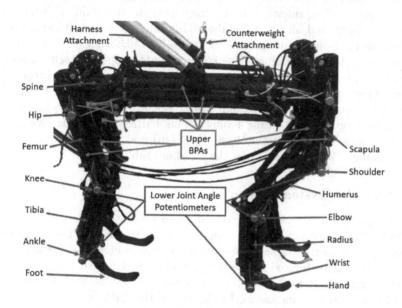

Fig. 2. DoggyDeux robot frame at Portland State University.

Creating 3D printable structural components required that many parts be redesigned to accommodate minimum stiffness and fastening requirements. At the same time, however, 3D printing also allowed for greater design flexibility, which facilitated a significant reduction in the total number of components used on the robot. By combining parts, we were able to reduce the complete frame assembly from approximately 500 components to approximately 360 components. As a result, the complete frame with the BPAs was reduced in weight from approximately 6.8 kg (15 lbs) to approximately 2 kg (4.4 lbs).

Another aspect of the frame design that was improved was the placement of muscle attachment points. By utilizing more complex geometries at the joints, the muscle attachment points were moved farther apart while maintaining the same limb lengths. For example, the front wrist extensor was lengthened by raising its upper attachment point up the back of the leg. Similarly, the scapula/hip muscles of the robot were nearly doubled in length by redesigning the harness attachment components and moving the scapula/hip muscle attachment points such that the scapula/hip muscles could extend across the entire body. These modifications allowed for the universal use of longer muscles on the newly designed robot and therefore improved the range of motion of each joint to be within a biologically relevant range for walking.

2.2 Harness Design

Like its predecessor, DoggyDeux is limited to sagittal plane motion. As a result, we also designed a harness that is compatible with DoggyDeux's frame to prevent the robot from falling sideways during testing on our treadmill. This harness is a counter weight and slider mechanism built into the upper structure of the treadmill using T-slot framing components, pulleys, 6.35 mm (0.25 in) diameter nylon rope, and linear bearings. The counterweight support attaches to an eye bolt mounted on the back of the robot, while the slider mechanism attaches via 25.4 mm (1 in) diameter aluminum tubing and roller bearings (see Fig. 2). The upper sliding mechanism moves along two T-slot frames using two roller wheel brackets and two linear bearing mounts. This harness allows for forward and backward motion of approximately 61 cm (24 in) and vertical movement up to approximately 25.4 cm (10 in) from the treadmill table band.

2.3 Actuation System Design

Both Puppy and DoggyDeux rely on BPAs to generate motion. BPAs are an excellent actuator for bio-mimetic applications due to the fact that they exhibit force-length curves that closely resemble those seen in biological systems [1,11]. However, they have limited stroke lengths and are damaged by kinking. The primary design effort for this robot with respect to the actuation system was therefore dedicated to increasing the length of the BPAs such that we could achieve a biologically realistic range of motion during walking and eliminating the BPA kinking found in the original robot.

In our discussion of the frame, we already noted that the resting muscle lengths were increased; as such, we now focus on the design decisions taken to eliminate the buckling of the BPAs. The original robot experienced muscle kinking primarily due to the fact that the muscles were pinned at both ends. Our new design eliminates this root cause by pinning down only the upper end of each muscle and using a string embedded in the lower joint component to tie down the other end. To do this, we first set the resting muscle length of the muscle of interest to be the longest possible that avoids collision with the surrounding components, and then we set the associated string length so that the joint is able to achieve its full range of motion. This method eliminates muscle kinking when extensor-flexor muscle pairs are both simultaneously lengthened by allowing the strings to carry the slack. An example of this technique applied to the back right knee is shown in Fig. 3ab.

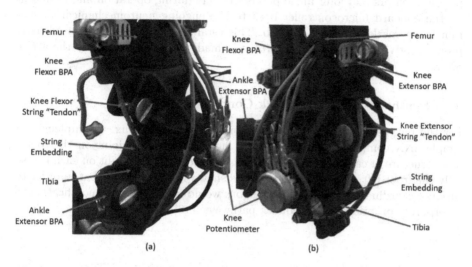

Fig. 3. (a) Rear view of the extended back right knee. (b) Front view of the flexed back right knee.

The new muscle-string design has the additional benefit of allowing greater flexibility in the location of lower muscle attachment points. Since the strings are thin, approximately 3.175 mm (0.125 in), the muscle attachment points can be moved closer to one another and closer to the center of rotation of the joint, which allows smaller muscle draw lengths to be translated into larger limb angle changes. Thus we can achieve a larger range of motion at any given joint with the same muscle draw length. Beyond these practical benefits, the muscle-string design is also more biologically realistic, since the string acts as a tendon in the way it allows the artificial muscles to wrap around joints.

2.4   Electrical System Design

Having completed the redesign of the robot's structural and actuation mechanisms, we are currently developing a new electrical system for the robot. This electrical system and the accompanying software are similar to that of the original robot in that their primary purpose is to transmit information between the robot and its SNN. Since the SNN is simulated in Animatlab (a neuromechanical simulation software) on a desktop computer, the electrical system routes muscle activation information from an active Animatlab simulation to DoggyDeux's onboard microcontroller [4] via Matlab. Animatlab first computes desired muscle tensions by simulating DoggyDeux's SNN, and Matlab then converts these tension values into associated BPA pressures values before passing them off to the onboard microcontroller. This microcontroller implements a local pressure control algorithm and routes the necessary BPA control signals to the appropriate valve on the manifold. Sensory information is collected from the BPA pressure sensors and joint angle potentiometers during operation and then sent by the onboard microcontroller back to the ongoing neuromechanical simulation in Animatlab through Matlab. This establishes a feedback loop whereby proprioceptive feedback from the robot is made available for use by the active SNN.

2.5   Synthetic Neural Network Controller Design

For the purpose of verifying the functionality of DoggyDeux, we implement a simple SNN comprised of isolated CPG networks for each joint on the robot. The structure of each of these networks is identical for each joint on each leg, so only the front left scapula/hip network is shown in Fig. 4. Note that in order to produce coordinated walking, this network would need extensive modification to incorporate proprioceptive feedback pathways [6,8].

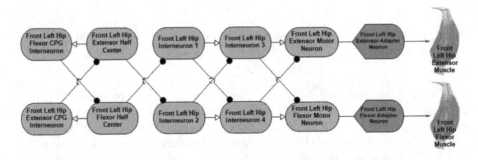

Fig. 4. Front left scapula synthetic neural network on DoggyDeux at Portland State University.

Since the outputs of the SNN are desired tensions for each muscle on the robot, these values must be converted to desired BPA pressure values and implemented via local pressure controllers for each muscle. Past experimental work characterizing the tension, pressure, and strain relationship of the BPAs provides a method of computing the requisite BPA pressure necessary to achieve a desired muscle tension given the current muscle length via an empirically derived relationship [1]. The previous robot used a bang-bang control scheme wherein the BPA valves were set to fill/exhaust if the pressure was beyond a certain threshold below/above the desired BPA pressure. This is the same strategy that we implement here with the addition of a flow rate limiter to reduce the steady state pressure fluctuations in the muscles. As one might expect, the steady state pressure bound can be arbitrarily reduced by reducing the flow rate to and from the valve manifold. However, beyond a certain threshold, the system rise time begins to drop precipitously.

3   Results

In order to demonstrate the ability of DoggyDeux to serve as a platform for SNN research, the simple SNN described above has been implemented and tested on the robot along with a bang-bang controller for local pressure control. The results presented next are based on data collected from the front left leg while running this network.

3.1   Mechanical Design Results

Many of the objectives that we set out to achieve for DoggyDeux are related to its mechanical design. For instance, in accordance with our design objectives, DoggyDeux features a fully 3D printed frame and in-plane muscle alignment while eliminating buckling of the braided pneumatic actuators (BPAs). At the same time, DoggyDeux has biologically realistic limb length proportions and joint range of motion compared to canines during walking. The exact dimension of each of DoggyDeux's limbs along with their proportions are compared to typical canine limb proportions in Table 1. Similarly, the range of motion of each of DoggyDeux's joints is compared to the typical range of motion for these joints on canines during walking in Table 2.

Table 1. Limb lengths and proportions for DoggyDeux at Portland State University compared to typical canine limb proportions [5].

Limb	Length (Robot)	Proportion (Robot)	Proportion (Canines)
[-]	[cm]	[%]	[%]
Spine	50.8	-	-
Scapula	18	26.47	28 ± 2.2
Humerus	18.1	26.62	27 ± 0.6
Radius	21.0	30.88	30 ± 2.5
Hand	10.9	16.03	16 ± 1.0
Femur	20.5	36.48	37 ± 1.3
Tibia	21.0	37.37	37 ± 1.3
Foor	14.7	26.16	26 ± 1.5

3.2   Local Pressure Controller Results

The SNN driving our robot generates desired muscle tensions, but these muscle tensions must be converted to pressures and enforced by a local pressure controller in order to actually achieve these target values on the robot. As a simple solution to this problem, we utilize a bang-bang control algorithm via our onboard microcontroller. Figure 5 shows the pressure response of the front left wrist extensor BPA given a sinusoidal input for (a) only the valve manifold and (b) the valve manifold with a flow rate limiting device. From Fig. 5a we see

Table 2. Range of motion of DoggyDeux joints compared to typical canine range of motion during walking [5].

Joint	ROM (Robot)	ROM (Canines)
[-]	[deg]	[deg]
Scapula	60	30
Shoulder	60	55
Elbow	60	40
Wrist	80	45
Hip	60	37
Knee	80	32
Ankle	80	48

that pressure fluctuations of approximately 2.4 bar (35 psi) occur in the system when the flow rate from the valve manifold is left unrestricted. These pressure fluctuations are due to the combined effects of our bang-bang control algorithm and the maximum switching frequency of the valve manifold. Since the valve manifold has a maximum switching frequency of approximately 100 Hz, every time the valve is opened or closed it takes approximately 10 ms before the valve is able to switch back to its previous position, allowing air to rush into or out of the BPAs. Fortunately, limiting the flow rate to and from the valve manifold offers a simple solution. While this method does reduce the rise time of the BPA pressure response, Fig. 5b shows how this technique significantly reduces the pressure fluctuations present in the unconstrained system. As such, we can limit the flow rate from the valve manifold to improve the accuracy of our BPA pressure system during walking.

3.3   Synthetic Neural Network Control Results

With a sufficient local pressure controller in place, we can now test DoggyDeux with a SNN. The CPG half-center neuron membrane voltages, commanded muscle tensions, and the resulting BPA pressures are shown in Fig. 6a-d. These plots indicate that the BPA pressures on the physical robot respond correctly to the muscle tension values dictated by the SNN. Both the half-center neuron membrane voltages and muscle tensions are computed by Animatlab simulations of our SNN, while the front left scapula BPA pressure and joint angle are measurements taken from the robot's sensors during operation. Note that the CPG membrane voltage amplitude shown in Fig. 6a is quite small. This membrane voltage amplitude is scaled up by the interneurons connecting the CPG and the motor neurons, causing the muscles to alternate between states of minimum and maximum tension. Figure 6a also shows the characteristic transient behavior associated with CPG oscillations wherein the membrane voltage increases sharply and then decreases slightly to a temporary equilibrium value. These same transients are not present in the muscle tension plot, and hence also the BPA pressure and joint angle plots, because in this example the interneurons map the CPG equilibrium values to the maximum and minimum muscle tensions.

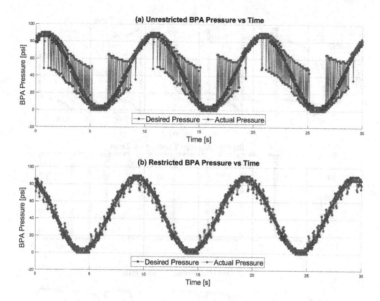

Fig. 5. (a) BPA pressure sinusoidal response without flow rate restriction. (b) BPA pressure sinusoidal response with flow rate restriction.

4 Discussion

Herein we have presented the design of a new canine inspired quadruped robot named DoggyDeux as a platform for SNN locomotion control research that builds upon the previous version constructed at CWRU. The structural and actuation mechanisms of the new robot have been redesigned in such a way as to ensure that we are able to achieve a biologically realistic range of motion during walking and to eliminate buckling of the BPAs. At the same time, this new robot utilizes a fully 3D printable frame, eliminates out-of-plane bending of the leg members, reduces component count and weight, and uses a new muscle-tendon feature that makes the muscle attachments more biologically realistic. We have also demonstrated the ability of this robot to be controlled via a simple SNN in combination with a local pressure controller. Further improvements could be made to the robot by upgrading the muscle-tendon feature to utilize a tensioning mechanism and developing a more sophisticated local BPA pressure control scheme. At the same time that we continue to improve the robot itself, we can continue to build on past SNN research by expanding the capabilities of our SNN to include coordination of all four limbs. In particular, we want to explore using more biologically realistic neuron models (e.g. spiking neural networks), to incorporate more diverse types of sensory feedback (e.g. visual and vestibular feedback), and to investigate the effect of descending commands. DoggyDeux will serve as an effective test platform for these future research efforts.

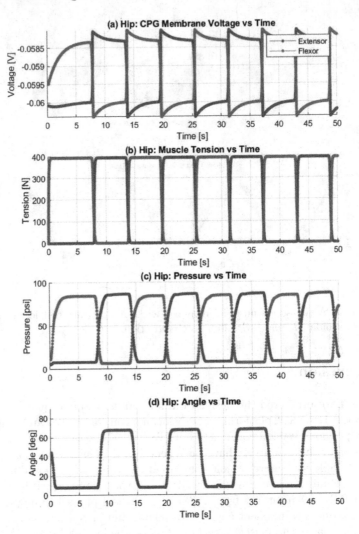

Fig. 6. Front left scapula data during operation of DoggyDeux with a simple SNN. (a) Front left scapula CPG membrane voltages. (b) Front left scapula muscle tensions. (c) Front left scapula BPA pressure. (d) Front left scapula joint angle.

Acknowledgements. The authors would like to acknowledge support by Portland State University, the National Science Foundation under award IIS-1608111, and the National Institutes of Health Common Fund and Office of Scientific Workforce Diversity under awards UL1GM118964, RL5GM118963, and TL4GM118965, administered by the National Institute of General Medical Sciences. The work is solely the responsibility of the authors and does not necessarily represent the official view of the National Institutes of Health.

References

1. Hunt, A.J., Graber-Tilton, A., Quinn, R.D.: Modeling length effects of braided pneumatic actuators. In: IDETC/CIE 2017, Cleveland, OH. ASME, August 2017. https://asme.pinetec.com/detc2017/data/pdfs/trk-8/DETC2017-67458.pdf
2. Aschenbeck, K.S.: Design of a quadruped robot driven by air muscles, Master's thesis. Ph.D. thesis, Case Western Reserve University (2006)
3. Buschmann, T., Ewald, A., von Twickel, A., Büschges, A.: Controlling legs for locomotion-insights from robotics and neurobiology. Bioinspir. Biomim. 10(4), 041001 (2015). http://stacks.iop.org/1748-3190/10/i=4/a=041001
4. Cofer, D.W., Cymbalyuk, G., Reid, J., Zhu, Y., Heitler, W.J., Edwards, D.H.: AnimatLab: a 3D graphics environment for neuromechanical simulations. J. Neurosci. Methods 187(2), 280–288 (2010)
5. Fischer, M.S., Lilje, K.E.: Dogs in Motion, 2nd edn. Bonifatius GmbH, Germany (2014)
6. Hiebert, G.W., Pearson, K.G.: Contribution of sensory feedback to the generation of extensor activity during walking in the decerebrate cat. J. Neurophysiol. 81(2), 758–770 (1999)
7. Hunt, A., Szczecinski, N., Quinn, R.: Development and training of a neural controller for hind leg walking in a dog robot. Front. Neurorobot. 11 (2017). http://journal.frontiersin.org/article/10.3389/fnbot.2017.00018/full
8. Hunt, A.J., Szczecinski, N.S., Andrada, E., Fischer, M., Quinn, R.D.: Using animal data and neural dynamics to reverse engineer a neuromechanical rat model. In: Wilson, S.P., Verschure, P.F.M.J., Mura, A., Prescott, T.J. (eds.) LIVINGMACHINES 2015. LNCS (LNAI), vol. 9222, pp. 211–222. Springer, Cham (2015). https://doi.org/10.1007/978-3-319-22979-9_21
9. Hunt, A.J.: Neurologically based control for quadruped walking. Ph.D. thesis, Case Western Reserve University (2016). https://etd.ohiolink.edu/pg_10?214907849232972::NO:10:P10_ETD_SUBID:108686
10. Iida, F., Ijspeert, A.J.: Biologically inspired robotics. In: Siciliano, B., Khatib, O. (eds.) Springer Handbook of Robotics, pp. 2015–2034. Springer, Cham (2016). https://doi.org/10.1007/978-3-319-32552-1_75
11. Kelasidi, E., Andrikopoulos, G., Nikolakopoulos, G., Manesis, S.: A survey on pneumatic muscle actuators modeling. In: 2011 IEEE International Symposium on Industrial Electronics, pp. 1263–1269. IEEE (2011). http://ieeexplore.ieee.org/xpls/abs_all.jsp?arnumber=5984340

Heads or Tails? Cranio-Caudal Mass Distribution for Robust Locomotion with Biorobotic Appendages Composed of 3D-Printed Soft Materials

Robert Siddall[1]([✉]), Fabian Schwab[2], Jenny Michel[1,4],
James Weaver[2,3], and Ardian Jusufi[1]

[1] Max Planck Institute for Intelligent Systems, Stuttgart, Germany
{rob,ardian}@is.mpg.de
[2] Wyss Institute for Biologically-Inspired Engineering, Harvard University,
Cambridge, USA
[3] School of Engineering and Applied Sciences, Harvard University, Cambridge, USA
[4] University of Hohenheim, Schloß Hohenheim 1, Stuttgart, Germany

Abstract. The addition of external mass onto an organism can be used to examine the salient features of inherent locomotion dynamics. In this biorobotics study general principles of systems in motion are explored experimentally to gain insight on observed biodiversity in body plans and prevalent cranio-caudal mass distributions. Head and tail mass can make up approximately 20% of total body mass in lizards. To focus on the effect of differential loading of the 'head' and the 'tail' we designed an experiment using weights of 10% total body mass connected to the front and rear at varying distances to simulate biological mass distribution. Additive manufacturing techniques with compliant materials were utilized to make the biomimetic limbs. Obstacle traversal performance was evaluated over 126 trials in a variety of Moment of Inertia (MOI) configurations, recording pitch angles. Results showed that a forward-biased MOI appears useful for regaining contact in the front wheels during obstacle negotiation, while large passive tails can have a destabilising effect in some configurations. In our robophysical model, we explore both wheeled and legged locomotion ('whegs'), and additionally examine damping the motion of the chassis by utilizing soft non-pneumatic tires ('tweels') which reduce body oscillations that arise from locomotion on irregular terrain.

Keywords: Bioinspired robot · Soft robotics · Additive manufacturing

1 Introduction

Taxa comprising the animal kingdom exhibit diverse body plans, often with specialized morphological structures facilitating traversal of irregular terrain to

Supported by the Swiss National Science Foundation, the Max Planck Society, and the Cyber Valley Initiative.

© Springer Nature Switzerland AG 2019
U. Martinez-Hernandez et al. (Eds.): Living Machines 2019, LNAI 11556, pp. 240–253, 2019.
https://doi.org/10.1007/978-3-030-24741-6_21

which organisms appear to be adapted. Many ecological situations can disrupt animals' balance through temporary changes in weight and mass distribution. Gravidity, carrying offspring, transporting captured prey or the consumption of large meals are common situations in nature that add irregular mass to an animal's body. Additionally, some animals possess extreme morphological features that result in larger MOIs of the head and/or the tail. The specialized anatomy of the giraffe provides feeding advantages, but necessitates adaptations of physiological structures and locomotion, like the specialized blood pumping mechanisms, higher respiration rates and the selection of very specific stride frequencies [5,26,33].

When running, giraffes are able to oscillate their long neck in order to reduce the load on the forelimbs and also to conserve energy which is needed to support the head and neck [5]. Hyenas, with their long neck and forelimbs, are adapted for carrying large and heavy carcasses, but are limited in their running abilities [31]. Animals with massive tails, such as kangaroos or alligators also possess special adaptations for locomotion. Kangaroos use their tail for body weight support during walking and for balance during running and jumps [11,21]. Alligator tails make up 28% of their body mass, which is why the hindlimbs need to generate higher propulsive forces, which is reduced by inverse pendulum mechanics of the tail [34]. Caudal autotomy in lizards results in an anteriorly directed shift in the animal's center of mass [14], leading to impairment [4,8,17,25] or enhancement [6,9,10] of locomotor performance. Despite the locomotor functions of tails in multiple modes of locomotion demonstrated in Jusufi et al. [18–20], we consider multi-functionality and that the tail shapes present in extant taxa do not necessarily allow us to directly infer that these shapes are optimal in their mass distribution for a particular task. Specifically, of all the tail shapes that a parameter sweep could yield, we would expect different task-dependent optima for shape and distributions of mass for inertial appendages, if we consider what tail morphologies are expressed in extant taxa are constrained to a subset of phenotypes by evolutionary history. Perhaps more importantly, multiple selection pressures act to determine the length, shape and mass distribution of tails.

Reptile tails have been shown to affect running speed [3,9,24], maneuverability [7], and endurance [8] on level ground. In arboreal environments, prehensile tails [12] facilitate resting balance and slow climbing. However, tail function during rapid climbing, aerial descent and gliding is largely unknown [6,8,13].

Head and tail mass can make up to 20% of total body mass in lizards [18], and far greater extremes are found in the fossil record. Biorobotics can help to extend the range of control experiments of differential loading. In a previous study the elastic decoupling of mass atop a robot traversing an obstacle-laden path was shown to increase speed while reducing energy consumption [1]. In another experiment locomotion induced oscillations of torso mass were shown to have implications for the origin of avian flight [32]. To experimentally address the effect of differential loading of 'head' versus 'tail' we evaluated the obstacle traversal performance of a bioinspired robot over 126 trials as a function of several MOI configurations. To simulate biological mass distribution, weights comprising 10% of total body mass were connected to the front and rear of a robot at different positions. The effect was examined for locomotion with rigid wheels, soft tweels and whegs.

The gecko has been identified as a model system of value inform the design of climbing appendages in agile mobile robots. Measurements of kinematics and forces reveal that lizards have a repertoire of disturbance rejection mechanisms used in climbing on natural surfaces. Though the remarkable climbing performance of geckos has traditionally been attributed to specialized feet with dry fibrillar adhesives [2], it was found that a gecko's tail functions as an emergency fifth leg to prevent falling during rapid climbing [19]. A response initiated by slipping causes the tail tip to push against the vertical surface, to prevent pitch-back of the head and upper body. When pitch-back cannot be avoided, geckos avoid falling by placing their tail in a posture similar to a bicycle's kickstand. These experiments revealed that the secret to the gecko's arboreal acrobatics includes an active tail, which functions as a highly active control appendage improving disturbance rejection and climbing abilities [19]. Further research revealed that tails are also beneficial to stabilize the gecko's body [23], to allow mid-air reorientation [18,20], or for maneuvering terrestrial robots at high-speed [27].

Conversely, robotics-inspired studies of animal locomotion can allow the use of biological control principles in robots. As part of the climbing robot developed within the framework of the Robots in Scansorial Environments (RiSE) project [29], designed for statically stable vertical locomotion, passive tails were shown to enhance performance and quasi-static climbing stability. In the hexapedal running robot RHEX, distributed mechanical feedback inspired by multi-legged organisms [28] was shown to simplify control of locomotion even on substrates with 90% of contact area removed.

Although great advances in our understanding of the biomechanics of steady-state locomotion have been made thanks to the studies of living organisms, there are limitations to this comparative method stemming from a large number of interspecific differences in morphology and mass distribution. Despite the significant efforts from the comparative method, our inability to control for multiple parameters necessarily constrains the reach of conclusions.

The experimental challenges to make consistent, repetitive experiments with living organisms brought forth a new strategy to examine principles of animal locomotion techniques: Robophysics (sensu Goldman), in which experimental robotics utilizes animated physical models to analyze specific aspects of movements and tries to determine underlying control principles of locomotion [30].

In this paper, we present a bio-inspired robot, which can be utilized to address the biomechanical effect of mass distribution on locomotion dynamics. The robot leverages state of the art multimaterial additive manufacturing processes to create non-pneumatic wheels ('tweels') in a single print cycle. We are able to eliminate the relatively large body oscillations of legged robots with the use of non-pneumatic wheels, which facilitate study of the robot's locomotion. We focus on fabrication and experimental verification of the added features. We then use the robot to experimentally examine the role of inertia distribution in dynamic locomotion.

The results provide new insights into effective shape and mass distribution for locomotion, and thereby how we can improve the operation of current mobile robots, particularly in unstructured environments. We hypothesize that asymmetrically distributed body mass will have a strong impact on inertia and therefore impair the ability to traverse the obstacle, resulting in an increase of the pitch response. Additionally, the extent of the pitch changes will increase while using higher speeds and will most likely decrease when using the compliant tweels.

2 Materials and Methods

We investigated traversal of a simple object under various conditions using a small mobile wheeled robot platform. This included changes in the robot's distribution of mass, locomotion appendages and movement speed. In this experiment we aim to examine the effect of cranio-caudal inertia isolated from the contact and traction roles tail appendages often play [19].

2.1 Mobile Robot Platform

The platform adapted for the locomotion experiments is a custom built four wheeled robot from TRIC Robotics (Newark, USA), which uses two drive motors to power pairs of wheels on either side, with each wheel pair geared together by a chain. A battery (11.1 V, 2700 mAh) is used for power, and an ATMega328p is used for processing (Arduino Nano). The robot is connected by a wireless link (Xbee Series 1) to Matlab, which is used to record serial data. This data comprises of current measurements from the drive motors and readings from an inertial Measurement Unit (Bosch BNO055) which is used to record pitch angles. Measurements are recorded at a frequency of 180 Hz, limited by the serial data rate and processor speed.

Cranio-caudal mass distribution is altered by placing masses on 300 mm long aluminium tubes, mounted on elastic suspensions pointing upwards at an angle of 30° from the robot chassis (Fig. 1A, B). A pair of 126 g weights (252 g total, 10% of the base robot's 2.56 kg body mass) are placed along these tubes at different positions, to create symmetric and asymmetric mass distributions (Table 1). A proximity sensor (Sharp GP2Y0A21) is mounted at the tip of the rear tube to monitor the occurrence of tail strikes. The robot was fitted with three different wheel types: a set of rigid plastic wheels, soft airless 'tweels' and a set of compliant whegs (Fig. 1B), allowing the experiments to explore the effect of contact compliance and legged locomotion oscillations on obstacle traversal. The weights were placed in a way that would represent naturally occurring situations in the ecology of animals. Distributing the weights symmetrically on the head and the tail represents animals that have similar head and tail masses (e.g. Platypus), whereas placing them in the center of the robot depicts a situation that can be observed for tortoises, as they carry their heavy shells during locomotion. Ecologically relevant scenarios of adding 10% of body mass on the anterior of the

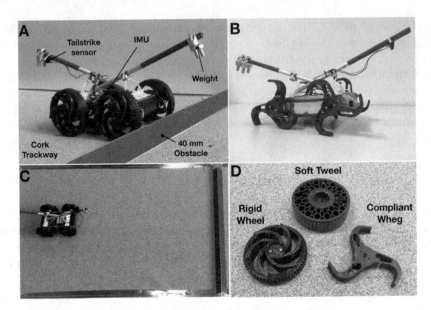

Fig. 1. Experimental apparatus and robot components. (A) Robot Platform showing head an tail masses. (B) Robot fitted with whegs, with both masses placed in the tail. (C) Different wheels used in experiments. (D) Section of the cork trackway showing the robot and the obstacle.

robot serve to approximately model mass distribution in a hyena in pursuit of prey on uneven terrain. By contrast, the situation of a long-tailed grass lizard fleeing from a predator could be explored with a robot with a large tail MOI.

Table 1. Key parameters for the robot platform.

Parameter	Value	Parameter	Value
Obstacle Height (mm)	40	Added Mass (g)	252
Chassis Length (mm)	240	Mass position 1 (mm)	200
Robot Weight (g)	2560	Mass position 2 (mm)	300

2.2 Obstacle Traversal Experiments

Experiments were performed on a trackway with an obstacle placed midway along the robot's path. The trackway was 3 m long to ensure that the robot reached a constant speed before encountering the obstacle. The trackway was covered with a 5 mm thick sheet of natural cork, to simulate a more natural surface and provide adequate and consistent traction during the experiment. The obstacle was formed from a right angled triangular prism, with the long face down. The exterior of the obstacle was covered by sandpaper with a mean particle size of 0.5 mm (Fig. 1C). For each experiment, the robot was placed at the same starting position, and driven at a constant forward power over the obstacle, with sensor readings recorded on a laptop. In total, obstacle traversal recordings were taken 126 times, repeating each combination of parameters 3 times.

2.3 Soft Tweels

The honeycomb structure in the fully 3d-printed, soft, non-pneumatic wheel as shown in Fig. 2 is arranged radially around the hub.

Fig. 2. (a) The honeycomb structure adapts to various rough terrains creates a large contact are over uneven terrain. (b) A view of the tweel showing the undeflected honeycomb structure.

The following fabrication method allows us to produce, in a single print, a multi-material compliant structure with non-compliant features. The wheel hub was fabricated from a rigid photopolymer (Stratasys VeroClear) with a modulus of approximately 1 GPa, while the tire and honeycomb structure was fabricated from a rubber-like material (Stratasys TangoBlack) with a modulus of approximately 1 MPa.

When the printed part is in contact with terrain during locomotion, this honeycomb geometry will permit a uniform force propagation between the outer surface and the hub, resulting in an even load distribution in the contact area.

Compression tests of the tweel (Fig. 3A) were performed on a materials testing machine (Instron) to demonstrate the capability of the honeycomb structure in the tweel to adapt to high forces. The shallow linear trend shows the high adaptability to external forces and pressures up to 100 N.

Drop tests revealed that the tweel is able to absorb large impulses as illustrated in Fig. 3B. When the tweel was dropped from 50 cm height, it only separated from the ground by approximately 0.8 cm. Even drops from a height of 100 cm resulted in separation of under 2 cm. This equivalent to a 14% coefficient of restitution. This suggests that obstacles encountered during climbing will be dampened out to a greater degree than could occur with legged robots (such as RHeX in [28]).

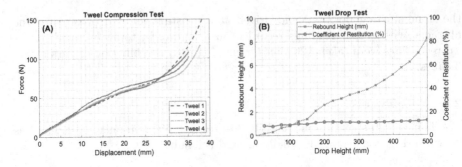

Fig. 3. Soft Tweel Mechanical Performance: (a) Instron compression tests show the tweel's ability to be compressed in a linear, coordinated fashion and therefore provide greater stability to the robotic platform. (b) Drop test from various heights show that the bounce height stays minimal, even with high falls. This is a feature of the high damping ability of the tweels, which enable a steady locomotion.

To show the benefit of highly compliant tweels for mobile robot applications, we examined typical unstructured outdoor terrain. The tweels are able to drive on various substrates and show great adaptability to sudden disturbances. Figure 2A shows how adaptive the tweel is. Owing to its structure, the tweel is able to maneuver over sharp corners and conforms to rough terrain.

2.4 Whegs

The traversal experiments were also carried out using compliant whegs to examine the mass distribution effects on legged locomotion and provide a basic comparison point against the oscillation suppressing effect of the tweels. Whegs were produced using a Markforged 3D printer, using Onyx filament (chopped carbon fibre filled nylon). Each wheg has three equally spaced feet (Fig. 1D), with a hollow section to create compliance, but with a limited maximum deflection to prevent damage. The whegs are mounted onto the robot such that the pairs on each side are 60° out of phase with each other.

3 Obstacle Traversal Results

The pitch response resulting from obstacle traversal was recorded for various values of inertia, speed and with different wheel types (Fig. 4). Each set of results includes runs with all masses placed in the centre of the robot, to give a control with minimal inertia. Each run configuration was repeated three times. Full results for all runs are displayed in Figs. 5A–D, 6A–D and 7A–D. Where a line is plotted, it indicates a successful traversal of the obstacle; in one configuration (whegs, tail mass only at 300 mm and 100% power, Fig. 7D) traversal was not possible and no data is plotted. For the case where the mass is placed at the centre of the robot, results are plotted in both the figures for 200 mm and 300 mm mass placement, for the sake of comparison. The total mass added to the robot is the same across all trials, only the positions of the masses are changed.

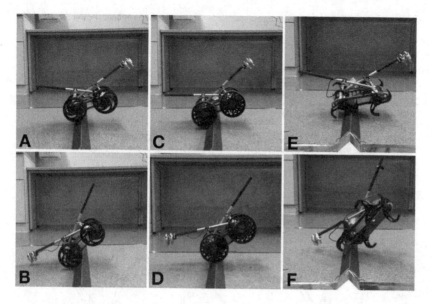

Fig. 4. Stills from obstacle traversal tests. (A) Robot passing obstacle at 100% power with rigid wheels and cranial mass. (B) Robot passing obstacle at 100% power with rigid wheels and caudal mass. (C) Robot passing obstacle at 100% power with soft tweels and cranial mass. (D) Robot passing obstacle at 100% power with soft tweels and caudal mass. (E) Robot passing obstacle at 100% power with compliant whegs and cranial mass (F) Robot passing obstacle at 100% power with compliant whegs and caudal mass; test ends in catastrophic failure.

3.1 Effect of Inertia

Using wheels (rigid and soft) at low speed, little dependency on inertia was observed, other than a fractionally higher pitch response with mass distributed toward the rear of the robot, and a consistently slightly quicker recovery with all mass at the centre, which is expected from the reduced moment of inertia. At higher speed, a far more significant difference was apparent, and the obstacle caused a larger initial pitchback, which meant that the robot cleared the obstacle completely before pitching forward, resulting in a short leap (Fig. 4C–D). This was true in all cases except where mass was placed at the head, where initial pitchback was reduced and the robot rotates nose down as the rear wheels clear the obstacle.

In the symmetric mass case the effect of distributing the mass outward and increasing the MOI was a small but observable increase in recovery time and maximum pitch angle. With masses in the 200 mm position little difference was observed between tail and symmetric mass cases, suggesting that rearward asymmetry has little effect.

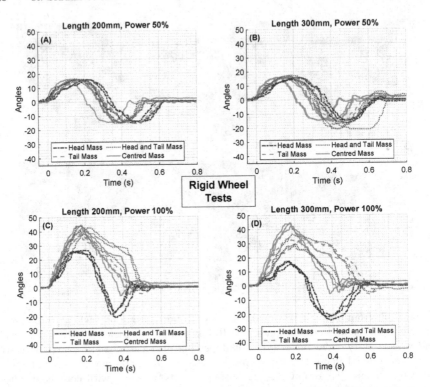

Fig. 5. Obstacle traversal experiments, showing the pitch changes as the robot traverses a 40 mm obstacle in a variety of conditions using rigid wheels. (A) Obstacle traversal at 50% power with a 200 mm mass suspension length. (B) Obstacle traversal at 50% power with a 200 mm mass suspension length. (C) Obstacle traversal at 100% power with a 200 mm mass suspension length. (D) Obstacle traversal at 100% power with a 300 mm mass suspension length

3.2 Effect of Soft Wheels

As shown in Sect. 2.3, the soft tweel exhibits significant damping (drop test restitution coefficient 14%, or a kinetic energy recovery of 1%) and creates a large contact area due to its compliance. The use of these tweels accordingly had a strong effect on the obstacle traversal dynamics, by increasing both contact damping and traction. The compliance of the wheels and the resulting large deflections meant that the robot was more sensitive to initial conditions, and larger scatter was observed in the data.

The effect of increased contact damping can be observed most markedly in comparison with rigid wheel runs with a forward mass distribution (i.e. comparing head mass results in Figs. 5C, D with those in Figs. 6C, D). In this case the rigid wheeled robot pitches forward once the front wheels clear the obstacle, and ultimately over rotates and is nose-down for a period as the rear wheels pass the obstacle. However, where the soft wheels are used no over rotation occurs.

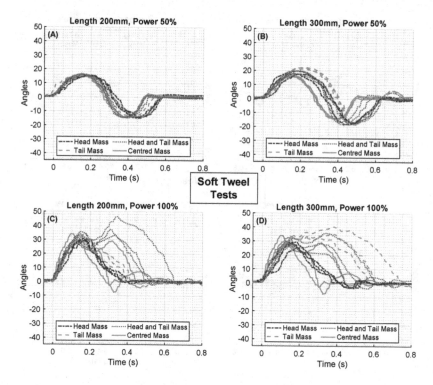

Fig. 6. Obstacle traversal experiments, showing the pitch changes as the robot traverses a 40 mm obstacle in a variety of conditions using soft tweels. (A) Obstacle traversal at 50% power with a 200 mm mass suspension length. (B) Obstacle traversal at 50% power with a 200 mm mass suspension length. (C) Obstacle traversal at 100% power with a 200 mm mass suspension length. (D) Obstacle traversal at 100% power with a 300 mm mass suspension length

This is due both to the damping of the wheel impacts on the far side of the obstacle, and by the contact damping of the rear wheels, which dissipates rotational energy and limits the tendency of the robot to rotate about its rear wheels when nose up with the front wheels off the ground.

3.3   Effects on Legged Locomotion

Experiments with whegs showed the changes in mass distribution to have a far more dramatic effect on locomotion. With the largest tail moment of inertia (mass placed at 300 mm) and maximum power (Fig. 7D), the robot was unable to traverse the obstacle without a catastrophic pitch back (Fig. 4F). In all other configurations traversal was possible, but significant variation in maximum pitch was observed, depending strongly on the way in which the whegs struck the obstacle. In symmetric mass cases the robot was generally barely perturbed by the obstacle (Fig. 7A–D), but in asymmetric configurations large changes

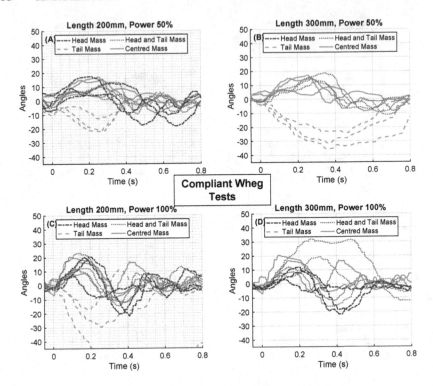

Fig. 7. Obstacle traversal experiments, showing the pitch changes as the robot traverses a 40 mm obstacle in a variety of conditions using compliant whegs. (A) Obstacle traversal at 50% power with a 200 mm mass suspension length. (B) Obstacle traversal at 50% power with a 200 mm mass suspension length. (C) Obstacle traversal at 100% power with a 200 mm mass suspension length. (D) Obstacle traversal at 100% power with a 300 mm mass suspension length

in heading and up to 80° pitchback was observed. Tail mass was particularly destabilizing, as can be seen in Figs. 7B and C. But with a symmetric mass distribution, the robot was largely unaffected by changes in inertia or speed, and the obstacle caused only a slight perturbation.

4   Conclusions and Future Work

In this paper, we have demonstrated that the symmetry of mass distribution has a strong effect on locomotion over uneven terrain, and is a promising area of inquiry. Animals as well as our study have shown that an additional mass on the cranial or caudal side can bring advantages or disadvantages, when confronted with certain tasks in terms of locomotion. As hypothesized, the asymmetrical distribution overall had a strong influence on the ability to traverse the obstacle. This was particularly noticeable when adding mass to the caudal site, which made it impossible to traverse the obstacle when using full power and the 'whegs' wheel type and resulted in greater leaps for the other situations. However, putting the additional body mass on the cranial site resulted in an advantage for this specific setup, leading to a reduced initial pitchback. We observed that changes in pitch response are elevated with the mass being more outward (300 mm), which suggests that animals with long and heavy necks or tails are especially affected by large inertia. Particularly higher speeds are bound to influence maneuverability and energy consumption, which is supported by the fact that respective animals use elastic body elements [5, 11] and pendulum-like movements [34] for energy recovery. Also, the selection of very specific stride frequencies [5] and velocities [11, 21] and even a specialized bone and muscle morphology [31] can be observed in such animals and are said to compensate for the asymmetrically distributed mass. In the natural world, animals are able to dynamically reconfigure their mass distribution through movement of heads, tails and other structures. This way, animals with large cranial or caudal mass traversing an obstacle may use this trait to their advantage by repositioning in a certain direction depending on the objective, as is indicated by our results. Future work will explore the effect of active mass distribution on movement, and the way in which locomotion perturbations can be reflexively or mechanically rejected; Destabilising movement of mass can potentially enhance maneuverability, and stabilising movement can provide robustness in the face of perturbations.

We have also introduced a design for airless tweels that show several advantages in maneuvering over uneven terrain. Increased flexibility in the vertical direction extends the contact area with the surface and therefore the maximum traction, while the significant damping capacity of the robot allows the rejection of perturbations to locomotion, and makes the system less sensitive to mass distribution, allowing for a broader space of configuration, and potentially the addition of sensing and interaction appendages.

Physical models of the kind employed here with our robot are critical because they meet the real environment [22] and can inform our mathematical models, explore new parameters and serve to test specific neuromechanics hypotheses [15] about the salient features of natural motion patterns.

Based on the results in this paper future work can address hypotheses of neuromechanics of locomotion, such as how sensory feedback from the anterior part of the animal (i.e. optic flow) can relay state information and trigger reflexes so as to improve perturbation rejection. Other types of sensory feedback, such as mechanosensors capturing loss of traction on the front propulsive units or foot slippage, could also serve in this manner. The emerging field of biorobotics facilitates investigation of locomotion by using robots with more life-like capabilities [16]. Advances in experimental robotics provide novel instruments that exhibit great promise for testing biological hypotheses.

References

1. Ackerman, J., Seipel, J.: Energy efficiency of legged robot locomotion with elastically suspended loads. IEEE Trans. Rob. **29**(2), 321–330 (2013)
2. Autumn, K., et al.: Evidence for van der Waals adhesion in gecko setae. Proc. Nat. Acad. Sci. **99**(19), 12252–12256 (2002)
3. Ballinger, R.E., Nietfeldt, J.W., Krupa, J.J.: An experimental analysis of the role of the tail in attaining high running speed in Cnemidophorus sexlineatus (Reptilia: Squamata: Lacertilia). Herpetologica **35**, 114–116 (1979)
4. Ballinger, R.E., Tinkle, D.W.: On the cost of tail regeneration to body growth in lizards. J. Herpetology **13**(3), 374–375 (1979)
5. Basu, C., Wilson, A.M., Hutchinson, J.R.: The locomotor kinematics and ground reaction forces of walking giraffes. J. Exp. Biol. **222**(2), jeb159277 (2019)
6. Brown, R.M., Gist, D.H., Taylor, D.H.: Home range ecology of an introduced population of the European wall lizard podarcis muralis (Lacertilia; Lacertidae) in Cincinnati, Ohio. Am. Midl. Nat. **133**, 344–359 (1995)
7. Carrier, D.R., Walter, R.M., Lee, D.V.: Influence of rotational inertia on turning performance of theropod dinosaurs: clues from humans with increased rotational inertia. J. Exp. Biol. **204**(22), 3917–3926 (2001)
8. Chapple, D., Swain, R.: Effect of caudal autotomy on locomotor performance in a viviparous skink, niveoscincus metallicus. Funct. Ecol. **16**(6), 817–825 (2002)
9. Daniels, C.B.: Running: an escape strategy enhanced by autotomy. Herpetologica **39**, 162–165 (1983)
10. Daniels, C.B., Flaherty, S.P., Simbotwe, M.P.: Tail size and effectiveness of autotomy in a lizard. J. Herpetology **20**(1), 93–96 (1986)
11. Dawson, T.J., Taylor, C.R.: Energetic cost of locomotion in kangaroos. Nature **246**(5431), 313 (1973)
12. Emmons, L.H., Gentry, A.H.: Tropical forest structure and the distribution of gliding and prehensile-tailed vertebrates. Am. Nat. **121**(4), 513–524 (1983)
13. Essner, R.L.: Three-dimensional launch kinematics in leaping, parachuting and gliding squirrels. J. Exp. Biol. **205**(16), 2469–2477 (2002)
14. Gillis, G., Higham, T.E.: Consequences of lost endings: caudal autotomy as a lens for focusing attention on tail function during locomotion. J. Exp. Biol. **219**(16), 2416–2422 (2016)
15. Ijspeert, A.J., Crespi, A., Ryczko, D., Cabelguen, J.M.: From swimming to walking with a salamander robot driven by a spinal cord model. Science **315**(5817), 1416–1420 (2007)
16. Ijspeert, A.J.: Biorobotics: using robots to emulate and investigate agile locomotion. Science **346**(6206), 196–203 (2014)
17. Jagnandan, K., Higham, T.E.: Lateral movements of a massive tail influence gecko locomotion: an integrative study comparing tail restriction and autotomy. Sci. Rep. **7**(1), 10865 (2017)
18. Jusufi, A., Kawano, D.T., Libby, T., Full, R.J.: Righting and turning in mid-air using appendage inertia: reptile tails, analytical models and bio-inspired robots. Bioinspiration Biomimetics **5**(4), 045001 (2010)
19. Jusufi, A., Goldman, D.I., Revzen, S., Full, R.J.: Active tails enhance arboreal acrobatics in geckos. Proc. Nat. Acad. Sci. **105**(11), 4215–4219 (2008)
20. Jusufi, A., Zeng, Y., Full, R.J., Dudley, R.: Aerial righting reflexes in flightless animals. Integr. Comp. Biol. **51**(6), 937–943 (2011)

21. Kram, R., Dawson, T.J.: Energetics and biomechanics of locomotion by red kangaroos (Macropus rufus). Comp. Biochem. Physiol. B: Biochem. Mol. Biol. **120**(1), 41–49 (1998)
22. Li, C., Zhang, T., Goldman, D.I.: A terradynamics of legged locomotion on granular media. Science **339**(6126), 1408–1412 (2013)
23. Libby, T., et al.: Tail-assisted pitch control in lizards, robots and dinosaurs. Nature **481**(7380), 181–184 (2012)
24. Lin, Z.H., Qu, Y.F., Ji, X.: Energetic and locomotor costs of tail loss in the Chinese skink, Eumeces chinensis. Comp. Biochem. Physiol. A **143**(4), 508–513 (2006)
25. Martin, J., Avery, R.: Effects of tail loss on the movement patterns of the lizard, Psammodromus algirus. Funct. Ecol. **12**(5), 794–802 (1998)
26. Mitchell, G., Skinner, J.: How giraffe adapt to their extraordinary shape. Trans. R. Soc. S. Afr. **48**(2), 207–218 (1993)
27. Patel, A., Braae, M.: Rapid turning at high-speed: inspirations from the cheetah's tail. In: IEEE/RSJ International Conference on Intelligent Robots and Systems (IROS), pp. 5506–5511 (2013)
28. Spagna, J.C., Goldman, D.I., Lin, P.C., Koditschek, D.E., Full, R.J.: Distributed mechanical feedback in arthropods and robots simplifies control of rapid running on challenging terrain. Bioinspiration Biomimetics **2**(1), 9–18 (2007)
29. Spenko, M.J., et al.: Biologically inspired climbing with a hexapedal robot. J. Field Robot. **25**(4–5), 223–242 (2008)
30. Sponberg, S.: The emergent physics of animal locomotion. Phys. Today **70**(9), 34–40 (2017)
31. Spoor, C., Badoux, D.: Descriptive and functional morphology of the locomotory apparatus of the spotted hyaena. Anat. Anz **168**, 261–266 (1989)
32. Talori, Y.S., Zhao, J.S., Liu, Y.F., Lu, W.X., Li, Z.H., O'Connor, J.K.: Identification of avian flapping motion from non-volant winged dinosaurs based on modal effective mass analysis. PLoS Comput. Biol. **15**(5), e1006846 (2019)
33. Warren, J.V.: The physiology of the giraffe. Sci. Am. **231**(5), 96–105 (1974)
34. Willey, J.S., Biknevicius, A.R., Reilly, S.M., Earls, K.D.: The tale of the tail: limb function and locomotor mechanics in alligator mississippiensis. J. Exp. Biol. **207**(3), 553–563 (2004)

Tuning a Robot Servomotor to Exhibit Muscle-Like Dynamics

Nicholas S. Szczecinski[✉][iD], Clarissa A. Goldsmith,
Fletcher R. Young, and Roger D. Quinn

Case Western Reserve University, Cleveland, OH 44106, USA
nicholas.szczecinski@case.edu

Abstract. This work shows one way to tune a servomotor controller to make it perform in a similar way to a biomechanical model of an insect leg joint. Three key metrics were considered: the equilibrium angle of the joint as a function of antagonistic inputs; the dynamics of the free response when perturbed; and the dynamics of active motions. We model an insect leg joint as a hinge actuated by a pair of antagonistic linear Hill muscles that drive a rigid distal leg segment. Passive forces from the exoskeleton are also modeled as passive viscoelastic elements (PVE). We approximate parameter values for the model based on the biomechanics literature, and then dynamically scale them to the scale of our robot, Drosophibot. We show how to tune the servo's control mapping and feedback gain to mimic the dynamically scaled model of the animal joint.

Keywords: Dynamic scale · Hill muscle model · Legged robot · Passive compliance · Servomotor

1 Introduction

Insects have served as inspiration for legged robots for decades (for reviews, see [3,14]). Oftentimes such robots are used to test animal-like locomotion control systems [5,12,15,18,19]. The benefit of this approach is that the performance of the robot may suggest further refinements to biological models of motor control, or provide direction for future biological experiments [14]. However, the applicability of results from robotics to neuroscience may depend strongly on the dynamics of the control plant, that is, the robot's body [10].

A robot's dynamic scale may match that of an insect even if its length scale does not. One might reasonably insist that only insect-sized robots could provide insight into the motor control of insects. However, many technologies for robot miniaturization, such as smaller actuators and batteries, are still under development. Therefore, it is more practical in the short term to design a meso-scale robot that dynamically behaves like a centi- or milli-scale animal by scaling the inertia, damping, and elasticity of the body. This consideration is not often made when designing robots, and represents a novel contribution of this work.

Funding for this work was provided by NSF Grant 1704436 to RDQ.

© Springer Nature Switzerland AG 2019
U. Martinez-Hernandez et al. (Eds.): Living Machines 2019, LNAI 11556, pp. 254–265, 2019.
https://doi.org/10.1007/978-3-030-24741-6_22

Reducing an animal's dynamic scale inherently increases the elastic forces from muscles and other tissue relative to inertial forces from limb and body mass [10,11]. Inertia scales with length cubed, but elastic forces scale with length squared, meaning that if an animal that is 1/10 the scale of a human were scaled up to human proportions, it would have muscles and joints that were 10 times as stiff as ours, given our same mass [10,11]. This has significant effects on motor control. While large animals like horses and humans rely on momentum to swing their legs forward after an initial torque at the hip joint at the start of the swing phase, small animals must maintain persistent motor activity throughout the entirety of swing phase [11]. Experiments with locusts show that single motor neuron action potentials in leg motor neurons cause transient joint rotations, after which the leg segment returns to its original rest angle [1], which is gravity independent in many insects [11]. This suggests that the steady-state deflection of the leg depends on the firing frequency of the legs' motor neurons.

This mapping from motor neuron firing frequency to joint rotation angle suggests that an insect leg joint may operate similarly to a servomotor. The firing frequency of motor neurons that innervate antagonistic muscles determine the steady state rotation of the joint. The stiffness of the muscles and skin provide a restoring force to this angle, akin to the proportional negative feedback of a servomotor. Understanding the relationship between these two systems, "muscle-actuated" and "servomotor-actuated," would enable engineers to tune the dynamics of a robot such that robot's legs would move in a comparable way to an insect's, given the same motor neuron activity.

In this work, we model an insect leg joint an antagonistic pair of Hill muscles, in parallel with a torsional spring. The spring represents the elasticity of the insect's skin across the joint. We show how to scale this model up by a factor of 10, and then show one way to map between the parameters in the biomechanical model, and those of a robot joint actuated by a servomotor working in parallel to a torsional spring, as in our insect-like robot, Drosophibot [8]. Results from a simulation of each system are presented and discussed.

2 Methods

The goal of this work is to identify analogous parameters, or combinations of parameters, between an insect leg joint actuated by a pair of antagonistic Hill muscles with additional viscoelastic forces from skin across the joint, and a robot leg joint actuated by a servomotor with additional viscoelastic forces acting in parallel to the servomotor. Both of these configurations are illustrated in Fig. 2. In the rest of this section, we will present the models used and other equations that will aid in the analysis in the Results.

2.1 Actuator and Mechanical Models

Linear Hill Muscle Model. The linear Hill muscle model abstracts the complicated mechanics of muscle contraction into an assembly of an active contractile

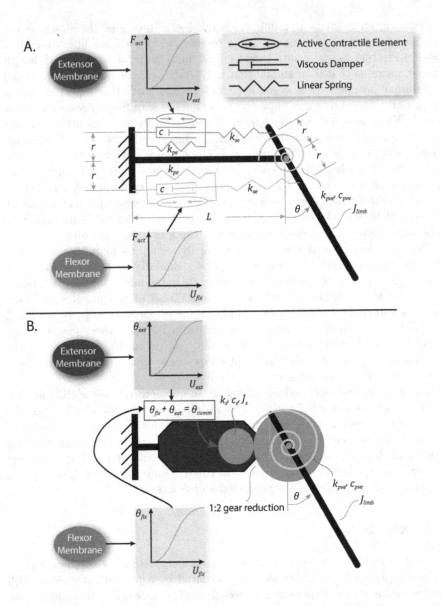

Fig. 1. Diagrams of the two actuator models used in this work. In both cases, the distal limb segment is modeled as a rigid rod, attached to the proximal segment, with a torsional spring and dashpot between them (termed "passive viscoelastic element" (PVE), green spiral). The actuators work in parallel to these components. (A) The limb is actuated by an antagonistic pair of linear Hill muscles. Each muscle's active contractile element applies force as a sigmoidal function of that muscle's membrane voltage. (B) The limb is actuated by a model of a Dynamixel smart servo. The commanded position is given by Eq. 16. The servo applies torque proportional to the difference between the commanded and instantaneous angle of the joint. (Color figure online)

unit, a dashpot, and two springs [7]. These are drawn in cyan and blue in Fig. 2. The active contractile unit produces a force proportional to a muscle membrane, as explained below (Subsects. 2.3 and 2.4). The contractile speed and distance of the muscle are controlled by the dashpot and the parallel spring, respectively. The series spring represents the muscle's apodeme, the arthropod analogue to vertebrate tendon. The apodeme is very stiff compared to the other passive elements, typically 20–40 times stiffer than mammalian tendon tissue [6]. A muscle's tension T evolves according to the differential equation (Eq. 1)

$$\frac{dT}{dt} = \frac{k_{se}}{c} \cdot \left(- \left[1 + \frac{k_{pe}}{k_{se}} \right] \cdot T + k_{pe} \cdot (l - l_{rest}) + c \cdot \frac{dl}{dt} + F \right), \tag{1}$$

where k_{se} is the series element stiffness; k_{pe} is the parallel element stiffness; c is the damping coefficient; l is the instantaneous length of the muscle; l_{rest} is the resting length of the muscle, i.e., its length when generating no tension, active or passive; and F is the force supplied by the active contractile unit [17].

When a muscle is at equilibrium, its tension and length are constant. The tension can be solved as a function of F and its length l,

$$T_{ss}(F, \theta) = \frac{k_{se}}{k_{se} + k_{pe}} \cdot \left(F + k_{pe} \cdot \left(l(\theta) - l_{rest} \right) \right). \tag{2}$$

The antagonistic muscles' lengths change when the joint angle, θ, changes. If contracting the extensor causes positive joint rotation,

$$l_{ext}(\theta) = \sqrt{2 \cdot r^2 \cdot (1 - cos(\theta)) + L^2 - 2 \cdot r \cdot L \cdot sin(\theta)}, \tag{3}$$

$$l_{flx}(\theta) = \sqrt{2 \cdot r^2 \cdot (1 - cos(\theta)) + L^2 + 2 \cdot r \cdot L \cdot sin(\theta)}. \tag{4}$$

Equation 2 reveals that k_{pass}, the passive stiffness of the muscle, equals

$$k_{pass} = \frac{dT_{ss}}{dl} = \frac{k_{se} \cdot k_{pe}}{k_{se} + k_{pe}}. \tag{5}$$

Thus k_{pass} simply how two springs add in series. This is to be expected, because when $F = 0$, the muscle reduces to the series and parallel elements in series with one another.

Servomotor Model. The servomotor model is based on the AX-12 Dynamixel smart servo (Robotis, Seoul, South Korea). In [8] we experimentally measured the inertia of the motor's rotor and the viscous damping coefficient of the motor. The torque applied by the servo to the shaft is

$$\tau_s = k_s \cdot (\theta_{comm} - \theta), \tag{6}$$

where k_s is the feedback gain of the servo's P controller, θ_{comm} is the commanded equilibrium angle, and θ is the instantaneous angle.

Table 1. Data from the literature that provides approximate values for the insect-scale model parameters in this study.

Model parameter	Approximate value	Source in literature
k_{pe} (via k_{total})	8 N/m	[9] Fig. 6B
k_{se}	1000 N/m	[2] Fig. 4C
c	10 N · s/m	Approx. from [2] Fig. 3A
F_{max}	100×10^{-3} N	[2] Fig. 5B
k_{pve}	1×10^{-6} N · m/rad	[16]
c_{pve}	1×10^{-6} N · m · s/rad	
r	500×10^{-6} m	[9] Fig. 5
L	10×10^{-3} m	[9] Fig. 5
J_{limb}	320×10^{-12} kg · m^2	[11] Appendix

2.2   Mechanical Analysis and Tuning

We wish to tune our model by estimating parameter values from the insect literature, scaling those parameters up to the size of our robot Drosophibot [8], and tuning the robot's joint controllers to be dynamically similar. The values and sources used for each parameter are listed in Table 1.

The dynamic scaling of these parameters can be explored through the equation of motion of a spring-mass-damper system [13],

$$m \cdot \ddot{x} + c \cdot \dot{x} + k \cdot x = 0, \tag{7}$$

where x is the displacement of a mass from equilibrium, m is the mass, c is the damping constant, and k is the spring stiffness. The stiffness of tissue scales with the cross sectional area, which is proportional to the length-scale squared, and the mass of objects scales with the length-scale cubed [10]. We can calculate how the damping coefficient scales, using the expression for the mass-normalized damping [13],

$$c = 2 \cdot \zeta \cdot \sqrt{k} \cdot \sqrt{m} \propto \sqrt{L^2} \cdot \sqrt{L^3}. \tag{8}$$

This shows that the damping scales by the length-scaled to the 2.5 power. Using the principle of equivalent energy [13], we know that a linear spring attached to a rotating member (i.e. the muscles attached to the distal limb segment) can be treated as a torsional spring when scaled by their attachment radius squared. These rules enable us to scale up the values in Table 1, shown in Table 2.

To compare the scaled-up muscular system to the servo system, we need to convert the linear stiffness of the muscles to a rotational stiffness and add the contribution of the PVE:

$$k_{total,musc} = 2 \cdot \frac{k_{se} \cdot k_{pe}}{k_{se} + k_{pe}} \cdot r^2 + k_{pve}. \tag{9}$$

Table 2. Scaled values from Table 1 that describe the parameter values appropriate for an insect that is the scale of our robot Drosophibot.

Model parameter	Scaling factor	Scaled approximate value
k_{pe}	10^2	800 N/m
k_{se}	10^2	100×10^3 N/m
c	$10^{2.5}$	3.16×10^3 N $\cdot$ s/m
F_{max}	10^3	100 N
k_{pve}	10^4	10×10^{-3} N $\cdot$ m/rad
c_{pve}	$10^{4.5}$	31.6×10^{-3} N $\cdot$ m $\cdot$ s/rad
r	10	5×10^{-3} m
L	10	100×10^{-3} m
J_{limb}	10^5	32.0×10^{-6} kg $\cdot$ m^2

Table 3. Comparison of values between Table 2 and values for the servo from [8]

Model parameter	Muscular value (Torsional equivalent)	Robot value
k_{pve}	$k_{pve} = 10 \times 10^{-3}$ N $\cdot$ m/rad	$k_{pve} = 612 \times 10^{-3}$ N $\cdot$ m/rad
$k_{actuator}$	$k_{pass} = 39.7 \times 10^{-3}$ N $\cdot$ m/rad	$k_s = 9.17$ N $\cdot$ m/rad
k_{total}	$k_{total} = 50.0 \times 10^{-3}$ N $\cdot$ m/rad	$k_{total} = 9.78$ N $\cdot$ m/rad
c_{total}	$c_{pve} = 31.6 \times 10^{-3}$ N $\cdot$ m $\cdot$ s/rad	$c_{pve} + c_s = 31.3$ N $\cdot$ m $\cdot$ s/rad
J_{total}	$J_{limb} = 32.0 \times 10^{-6}$ kg $\cdot$ m^2	$J_{limb} + J_{servo} = 4 \times 10^{-3}$ kg $\cdot$ m^2

For the servo, we simply add the feedback gain of the servo to the elastic force from the PVE:

$$k_{total,servo} = k_s + k_{pve}. \tag{10}$$

The damping requires similar treatment. Since $k_{se} \gg k_{pe}$, the velocity of the damping element is approximately equal to the total contraction velocity of the muscle. Thus, each muscle also acts as a damper, which must be converted to a rotational damper and added to the contribution of the PVE:

$$c_{total,musc} \approx 2 \cdot c \cdot r^2 + c_{pve}. \tag{11}$$

For the servo, we add the servo's viscous damping coefficient and that of the c_{pve}:

$$c_{total,servo} = c_s + c_{pve}. \tag{12}$$

It should be noted that the value of c_s used in this work is about 25 times larger than that measured for the servo [8]. However, this difference can be accounted for via derivative feedback in the servo's controller, which acts like a damping force. Finally, the servo has additional inertia due to its motor's rotor and the large gear ratio. All of these total dynamic parameter values are summarized in

Table 4. Comparison of dynamic scaling variables among all three models.

Model parameter	Insect Scale + Muscles	Robot Scale + Muscles	Robot Scale + Servo
ω_n	125 rad/s	39.4 rad/s	49.3 rad/s
ω_n, time-scaled	39.4 rad/s	39.4 rad/s	49.3 rad/s
ζ	75.2	75.2	78.9

Table 3. The absolute values of the total stiffness, damping, and inertia of each model are quite different. However, we primarily want to match the dynamic scale, that is: the nondimensional damping ratio ζ should be the same no matter the size, and the natural frequency $\omega_n = \sqrt{k/J} \propto \sqrt{1/L}$. Table 4 shows that these values are in agreement across all three models.

2.3 Nonspiking Muscle Membrane Model

Here we focus on modeling slow muscle fibers which, like most arthropod muscle fibers, rarely fire action potentials [20]. Therefore, the muscle membranes (MMs) are modeled as nonspiking leaky compartments, whose voltage changes as a function of the currents passing through the membrane:

$$C_m \cdot \frac{dV}{dt} = G_m \cdot (E_{rest} - V) + I_{app}. \tag{13}$$

In this equation, C_m is the capacitance of the MM, G_m is the conductance of the MM, V is the voltage of the MM, E_{rest} is the rest potential of the MM, and I_{app} is the current injected through the MM. For the rest of this work, we will refer to $U = V - E_{rest}$, that is, the voltage above the rest potential.

2.4 Mapping Neural Activity to Actuator Commands

For the muscle-actuated model, the voltage of each MM maps to the active contractile force of the respective muscle. This relationship is known to be sigmoidal [9,17]. We generate this sigmoidal curve with the function

$$F = \frac{F_{max}}{1 + e^{S \cdot (E-U)}}, \tag{14}$$

where F_{max} is the maximum active contractile force of the muscle, S is the maximum slope of the sigmoid function and E is an x-axis offset. Examples of this function are illustrated in the shaded areas of Fig. 2.

The equilibrium joint angle θ_{eq} given the activation of the extensor and flexor muscles cannot be solved explicitly. Instead, it must be calculated numerically by solving the equation

$$\sum M_{joint} = 0 = \vec{u}_{joint}^T \left(\vec{r}_{ext} \times \vec{T}_{ext,ss}(F_{ext}, \theta_{eq}) \right.$$
$$\left. + \vec{r}_{flx} \times \vec{T}_{flx,ss}(F_{flx}, \theta_{eq}) \right) - k_{pve} \cdot \theta_{eq}, \tag{15}$$

where $\vec{u}_{joint}$ is a unit vector along the hinge joint; $\vec{r}_x$ is the vector of muscle x's attachment to the distal segment relative to the joint, as rotated by θ; $\vec{T}_{x,ss}(F_x, \theta_{eq})$ is the vector of muscle x's tension in steady state, whose magnitude is calculated via Eq. 2.

For the servomotor-actuated model, the voltage of each MM maps to the commanded angle for the servo, and then the sum of the two commanded angles is sent to the servomotor (as illustrated in Fig. 2). Each MM's contribution to the commanded angle θ_{comm} is analogous to Eq. 14 for the active contractile force of one muscle:

$$\theta_{comm} = \frac{A \cdot \theta_{max}}{1 + e^{S \cdot (E-U)}}, \tag{16}$$

where θ_{max} is the maximum joint angle in one direction. The parameters A and S can be tuned with gradient-based optimization to match the solution to Eq. 15 closely.

These models differ in that the control inputs determine the muscle *force* in the muscle-actuated system, but the servo *position* in the servo-actuated system. However, due to the elasticity present in both systems, the contractile force of the muscle also sets its length; likewise, the commanded position of the servo determines its output force (more specifically, its torque). Therefore, these two systems have several input-output parallels which are explored in the next section.

3 Results

Equilibrium Positions. The two joint control schemes shows in Fig. 2 can be tuned to produce nearly identical equilibrium joint angles, given the same inputs (U_{ext}, U_{flx}). Figure 2 shows the equilibrium angle for the robot-scale muscle system, the servo system, and the insect-scale muscle system. For the muscle systems, these positions arise because the elastic forces in the antagonistic muscles come to equilibrium with one another. For the servo system, this is the commanded joint angle.

One can see that if the MM voltages are equal, then the equilibrium angle is $\theta = 0$ rad. When the MM voltages are not equal, the equilibrium angle biases towards the direction of the more active MM (i.e. $U_{ext} > U_{flx}$ increases the equilibrium angle). As the sum $U_{sum} = U_{ext} + U_{flx}$ increases, the difference $U_{diff} = U_{ext} - U_{flx}$ causes a larger change in the equilibrium joint angle. Thus, when U_{sum} is small, the equilibrium angle can be controlled precisely with feedforward muscle activation. When U_{sum} is large, the angle cannot be precisely controlled, but this increase in gain is ideal for feedback control of the joint angle.

Even when an elastic element is placed across the joint, in parallel with the actuators, the equilibrium angles are largely unaffected. Repeating the analysis with such springs is important because the joint membranes of small animals exert large forces on the body. In fact, in some arachnids and insect leg joints, some muscles do not have antagonists, but instead rely on passive elastic forces

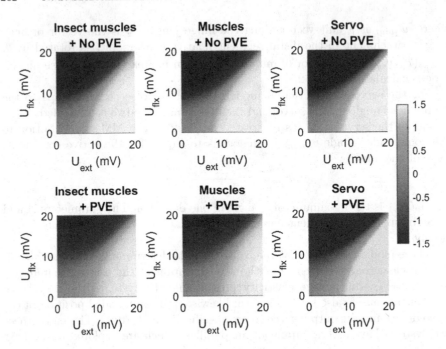

Fig. 2. Equilibrium angle of the joint given the MM voltages. In the top row, the joint's PVE has been removed. The insect-scale muscular system (top left), the robot-scale muscular system (top center), and servo system (top right), all show the same type of relationship. In the bottom row, the joint's PVE has been reintroduced, without retuning. Each plot is still nearly identical, although some subtle differences arise. (Color figure online)

from the exoskeleton to help them actuate their limbs [1,4,16]. If a robot were to be used to explore motor control in insects, it would require elastic elements in parallel with the actuators.

Figure 2 also shows the equilibrium joint angles after the parallel element has been added to each joint model. This has the effect of "smoothing" the surfaces. The effect is not stark because the elasticity of the parallel element is low relative to the stiffness of the muscular and servo systems. However, more accurate measurements of the stiffness of insects' joint membranes may reveal them to be much stiffer than assumed in this study, causing them to significantly affect motor output.

Passive Responses. The passive responses of the servo system, robot-scaled muscular system, and insect-scaled muscular system are all dynamically similar. Figure 3 shows data from the models in multiple scenarios, in which an external moment was applied to the joint, the joint came to equilibrium, and then was released. The timecourses of each scenario are nearly identical, due to the tuning carried out in Sect. 2.2. However, there are two differences. First, the time axis on the insect-scale data has been scaled by $\sqrt{10}$, to account for the dynamic scaling of the systems. Second, the muscular systems are not linear like the servo system, and therefore show reduced stiffness (e.g. slower timecourse) when displaced to larger angles.

Active Motions. The active motions generated by the servo system, robot-scaled muscular system, and insect-scaled muscular system are all dynamically similar. Figure 4 shows data from multiple trials, in which the U_{ext} MM was stimulated to increasing levels. In the first three rows, the timecourses are similar. However, in the fourth row, the muscular systems do not quite reach the same range of motion, because the stiffness of the muscles (which depends on the angle) decreases, while the stiffness of the PVE (which does not depend on the angle) does not decrease. The servo system does not have this issue because while all three systems have the same total joint stiffness for their scale, more of the servo system's stiffness comes from the actuator than from the joint's PVE. Therefore, it can more easily overcome the torque applied by the PVE, and rotate further.

4 Discussion

In this work, we showed that it is possible to configure a servomotor to behave similarly to a biomechanical model of an insect leg joint. We started with parameter values from insects, then scaled them to the size of our robot, and used them as constraints on the way that "muscle membrane" voltage was mapped to the servo's commanded position. Such work will guide our future development of the neural control of locomotion for our robot Drosophibot, which is a dynamically scaled model of the insect [8].

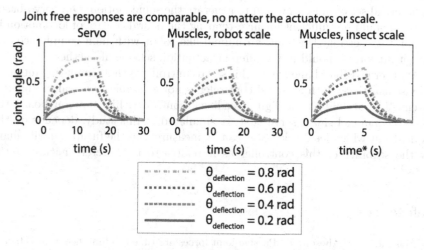

Fig. 3. For each model, multiple external moments were applied to rotate the joint to a new position, and then allowed to freely return to rest. In each row, the three models show the same transient activity. Note the difference in x-axis scale in the rightmost column, to account for the different scale of the system.

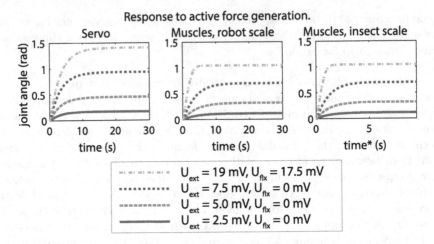

Fig. 4. For each model, multiple MM currents were applied to cause the actuators to rotate the joint to a new position. For small motions, all three responses are nearly identical. At larger angles, the stiffness of the muscles relative to the PVE decreases, reducing the range of motion.

We also observed differences in performance between the systems. First, the muscular systems are nonlinear whereas the servo system is not. Therefore, the joint angle timecourse is not always the same among the systems, especially when the joint angle is far from 0 rad. Additionally, the total stiffness of the robot-scale muscular system is much lower than the servo system, even though the dynamic scales are nearly identical. This requires the servo to apply more torque than a hypothetical set of muscles would to generate the same motion. Our servo-based solution should be sufficient for investigating the neural control of locomotion in a laboratory setting. However, an animal-like robot with high compliance and low output forces should use a different actuation scheme altogether.

Another possible challenge for this servo controller is that simulating mechanical viscoelasticity with a digital controller is not as stable as a real mechanical system. The stability of a digital feedback controller, like that on board the AX-12 Dynamixel smart servo that we simulated in this study, depends on the frequency at which feedback states can be measured. In the future we will quantify the stability of this controller as it relates to the discrete nature of the controller.

References

1. Ache, J.M., Matheson, T.: Passive joint forces are tuned to limb use in insects and drive movements without motor activity. Curr. Biol. 23(15), 1418–1426 (2013)
2. Blümel, M., Hooper, S.L., Guschlbauer, C., White, W.E., Büschges, A.: Determining all parameters necessary to build hill-type muscle models from experiments on single muscles. Biol. Cybern. 106(10), 543–558 (2012)

3. Buschmann, T., Ewald, A., Twickel, A.V., Büschges, A.: Controlling legs for locomotion - insights from robotics and neurobiology. Bioinspiration Biomimetics **10**(4), 41001 (2015)
4. Carbonell, C.S.: The thoracic muscles of the cockroach Periplaneta americana (L.). Smithsonian miscellaneous collections (1947)
5. Espenschied, K.S., Quinn, R.D., Beer, R.D., Chiel, H.J.: Biologically based distributed control and local reflexes improve rough terrain locomotion in a hexapod robot. Robot. Auton. Syst. **18**(1-2), 59-64 (1996)
6. Full, R., Ahn, A.: Static forces and moments generated in the insect leg: comparison of a three-dimensional musculo-skeletal computer model with experimental measurements. J. Exp. Biol. **198**(Pt 6), 1285-1298 (1995)
7. Gasser, H.S., Hill, A.V.: The dynamics of muscular contraction. Proc. R. Soc. B **96**, 398-437 (1924)
8. Goldsmith, C., Szczecinski, N., Quinn, R.: Drosophibot: a fruit fly inspired biorobot. In: Submitted to Conference on Biomimetic and Biohybrid Systems, pp. 1-12 (2019)
9. Guschlbauer, C., Scharstein, H., Buschges, A.: The extensor tibiae muscle of the stick insect: biomechanical properties of an insect walking leg muscle. J. Exp. Biol. **210**(6), 1092-1108 (2007)
10. Hooper, S.L.: Body size and the neural control of movement. Curr. Biol. **22**(9), R318-R322 (2012)
11. Hooper, S.L., et al.: Neural control of unloaded leg posture and of leg swing in stick insect, cockroach, and mouse differs from that in larger animals. J. Neurosci. **29**(13), 4109-4119 (2009)
12. Manoonpong, P., Parlitz, U., Wörgötter, F.: Neural control and adaptive neural forward models for insect-like, energy-efficient, and adaptable locomotion of walking machines. Front. Neural Circuits **7**, 314-341 (2013)
13. Rao, S.S., Yap, F.F.: Mechanical Vibrations, vol. 4. Prentice Hall, Upper Saddle River (2011)
14. Ritzmann, R.E., Quinn, R.D., Watson, J.T.: Insect walking and biorobotics: a relationship with mutual benefits. Bioscience **50**(1), 23-33 (2000)
15. Schneider, A., Paskarbeit, J., Schaeffersmann, M., Schmitz, J.: HECTOR, a new hexapod robot platform with increased mobility - control approach, design and communication. In: Rückert, U., Joaquin, S., Felix, W. (eds.) Advances in Autonomous Mini Robots, pp. 249-264. (2012). https://doi.org/10.1007/978-3-642-27482-4_24
16. Sensenig, A.T., Schultz, J.W.: Mechanics of cuticular elastic energy storage in leg joints lacking extensor muscles in arachnids. J. Exp. Biol. **206**(4), 771-784 (2003)
17. Shadmehr, R., Arbib, M.A.: A mathematical analysis of the force-stiffness characteristics of muscles in control of a single joint system. Biol. Cybern. **66**(6), 463-477 (1992)
18. Szczecinski, N.S., Getsy, A.P., Martin, J.P., Ritzmann, R.E., Quinn, R.D.: Mantisbot is a robotic model of visually guided motion in the praying mantis. Arthropod Struct. Dev. **46**, 736-751 (2017)
19. von Twickel, A., Hild, M., Siedel, T., Patel, V., Pasemann, F.: Neural control of a modular multi-legged walking machine: simulation and hardware. Robot. Auton. Syst. **60**(2), 227-241 (2011)
20. Wolf, H.: Inhibitory motoneurons in arthropod motor control: organisation, function, evolution. J. Comp. Physiol. A **200**(8), 693-710 (2014)

Manufacturing Artificial Wings Based on the *Manduca sexta* Hawkmoth

Matthias Weisfeld[1(✉)], Kenneth Moses[1], David Prigg[1], Richard Bachmann[1], Mark Willis[2], and Roger Quinn[1]

[1] Department of Mechanical and Aerospace Engineering, Case Western Reserve University, Cleveland, OH 44106-7222, USA
msw94@case.edu
[2] Department of Biology, Case Western Reserve University, Cleveland, OH 44106-7080, USA

Abstract. This work includes the analysis and evaluation of surgically removed wings from *Manduca sexta* hawkmoth and the fabrication and testing of moth-like wings for the eventual goal of developing a flapping wing micro air vehicle. The natural and manufactured wings are compared in three main characteristics, their distribution of mass, their flexural stiffness, and their camber. Previous results indicate that if these three properties can be mimicked, manufactured wings could produce similar flight properties to the natural wings. Wings are manufactured based on templates created from three different moths. Additionally, three different materials are used for fabricating the membrane, Icarex Ripstop Fabric, Mylar Film, and Kapton Film. Strips of unidirectional carbon fiber are used to mimic the venation structure. Wings manufactured from Icarex and Kapton replicated the mass of the natural wings. However, all manufactured wings are far stiffer than the natural ones. Icarex retains its camber the best.

Keywords: Flapping-wing micro aerial vehicle · Hawkmoth · Wing camber · Wing stiffness

1 Introduction

The work presented in this paper is part of a larger project that seeks to develop a flapping wing micro air vehicle (FWMAV) based on the *Manduca sexta* hawkmoth. This work focuses on the analysis of the moth's wings and manufacturing processes to create artificial ones. The project has been active for a number of years [1–3].

FWMAVs are generally based on birds, bats, or insects. Much work has been done in all three of these categories [4–11]. There are some advantages to mimicking insects: they have entirely passive wings and are capable of carrying a considerable payload as measured as a fraction of their body weight [4]. Among them, the *Manduca sexta* hawkmoth is particularly promising as a subject for replication. *M. sexta* are relatively large insects, are capable of flight with exclusively their forewings, can carry payloads of at least 50% of their bodyweight, and can be reared in biology labs.

© Springer Nature Switzerland AG 2019
U. Martinez-Hernandez et al. (Eds.): Living Machines 2019, LNAI 11556, pp. 266–276, 2019.
https://doi.org/10.1007/978-3-030-24741-6_23

Much work has gone into researching the flight dynamics of the *M. sexta*. Combes and Daniel investigated the relationship between inertial elastic forces and aerodynamic forces, leading them to the controversial conclusion that inertial-elastic forces play a larger effect than aerodynamic ones [12–14]. Mountcastle investigated how flexural stiffness was related to flight ability, concluding that more flexible wings could generate more lift [15–17]. It was felt that if the mass distribution and flexural stiffness could be replicated, then the wings may be able to produce a similar amount of lift.

A number of researchers have investigated building a FWMAV based on *M. sexta*. Some notable contributions come from O'Hara and Palazotto. Palazotto oversaw much of the work done at the Air Force Institute of Technology [18–22]. O'Hara's research served as the basis for much of the work presented here [18, 19]. O'Hara's wings were constructed using Icarex fabric for the membrane and unidirectional carbon fiber for the venation structure [18]. These wings were found to be too heavy, and therefore further examination was required.

2 Wing Morphology

It is believed that both inertial-elastic forces and flexural stiffness play important roles in the flight dynamics of *M. sexta* hawkmoth [12]. It was felt that in order to better understand these properties, the wings must first be studied in depth.

M. sexta wings are composed of three distinct sections: the outer scales, the venation structure, and the membrane. The outer scales appear almost like fur, providing a thin covering for the wings. Their role in flight dynamics is still uncertain [22]. Scales can be removed with ease from the extracted wings simply by gently rubbing them.

The venation structure gives the wings rigidity. The structure follows a consistent pattern throughout most wings. The venation structure carries hemolymph and nerves throughout the wings, although not all do either or both of these [22]. The leading edges are generally thicker and heavier than the trailing edge veins. They vary in diameter from approximately 500 μm to 60 μm [19]. Veins are rarely perfectly circular, normally, they are more ellipsoid in shape [18]. The accepted method of venation labeling is shown in Fig. 1.

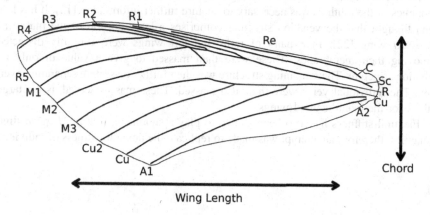

Fig. 1. Naming scheme for the venation structure of *M. sexta*

The membrane connects the veins of the venation structure. It is considerably thinner, estimated to be approximately 5 μm in thickness [18]. Once scales have been removed, the venation structure and membrane may be distinguished visually. Wings based on work done by O'Hara using the Comstock-Needham method [18].

3 Methods

3.1 Wing Removal

Initially, a number of wings were extracted from *M. sexta* hawkmoths reared in the Willis Lab at Case Western Reserve University. Wings were extracted with a pair of tweezers and either a scalpel or dissection scissors. Following surgical removal of the wings, they were massed. The outer scales were then carefully rubbed off, revealing the membrane and venation structure below. It was then re-massed. In many cases, a significant portion of scales were difficult to remove and other action was taken. Wings were dipped into a bath of undiluted bleach and left to sit for no more than three minutes. They were turned and prodded throughout. The wings were then removed and dried with a foam brush or paper towel. This process was conducted on twenty-three different *M. sexta* moths. Wings were massed before and after to ensure no bleach was absorbed.

3.2 Wing Analysis

After the wings were removed and cleaned, they were scanned at 12800 dots per inch (DPI). From these images, estimates of length and thickness were calculated given the DPI. With a measured thickness and estimated density, the mass of the veins was calculated. The assumption was made that the veins were circular in cross section, an undoubtedly false assumption, but which provided an estimate of the venation mass. Additionally, some of these scans were converted into templates used for later manufacturing processes. The scans were run through a MATLAB program which converted them into purely black and white images, showing only the venation structure and an outline of the overall wing.

As the distribution of mass is thought to have a considerable effect on the flight dynamics of the moth, it was necessary to acquire further information [12]. It has long been thought that the venation structure comprises a large portion of the mass of a *M. sexta* wing [22]. Five pairs of right and left wings were carefully dissected, removing their membranes. These were then massed to give a value of only the venation structure. The remaining structure was then further dissected, separating every vein. The individual veins were then also massed. These masses served as the target values for the manufactured wings.

Flexural stiffness has also been shown to play a significant role in *M. sexta* flight dynamics, therefore an attempt was made to replicate the flexural stiffness of individual moth's wings [17]. The wings are assumed to behave similarly to a simple cantilever beam, most likely a simplified assumption. Flexural stiffness was tested by placing the extracted wing in a clamp. This was then put onto a scale in a CNC mill. The CNC acted to precisely move a 1/8 in. diameter steel rod which was positioned such that it applied a force at a point 70% along the span. By varying the displacement caused by the rod on the wing and recording the force, flexural stiffness was calculated. The following equation gives this relationship.

$$EI = \frac{FL^3}{3\delta} \tag{1}$$

Where E is Young's Modulus, I is the area moment of inertia, F is the applied force, L is the length, and δ is the displacement. Three tests were run on each wing applying the force from the dorsal side. Another three tests were run with the force applied on the ventral side. Each test was composed of six data points. The steel rod was initially positioned to not apply any force while still touch the wing, this is the first data point. The displacement was then increased from 0 mm to 2.5 mm in 0.5 mm increments for the remaining data points. A Hurco VM1 CNC mill was used, with a precision of 0.0001 in. The scale used is a Fairbanks digital scale with a precision of 0.01 g. A diagram of the flexural stiffness testing setup is shown in Fig. 2. Wings were tested approximately 24 h after extraction.

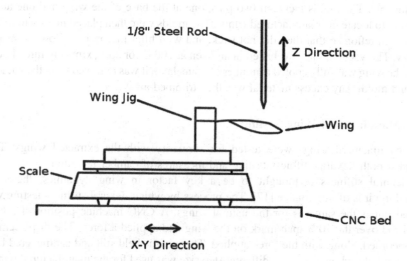

Fig. 2. Diagram of the flexural stiffness testing setup.

Additionally, in an attempt to better verify Mountcastle's conclusion that the flexural stiffness of the wings increases over time, a single pair of wings was tested repeatedly [17]. Initially, the wings were tested approximately every 30 min after their extraction from a moth. One test was run from the top and bottom for both the left and right wing every half hour. After approximately 48 h, they were tested again, this time with three tests from both directions for each wing.

3.3 Wing Manufacturing

Wing manufacturing began by printing the selected template onto a sheet of carbon fiber. A membrane material was then selected, either Icarex Ripstop Fabric, Mylar Film, or Kapton Film. The membrane material was cut into a rectangle slightly larger than the template and then taped on top of the copy paper. This was then run through the printer again, such that the ink printed directly onto the membrane material. The membrane was then removed to form the paper and attached to a hard surface, such as a wooden board, with either tape or pins. Small strips of carbon fiber were then cut to serve as the venation structure. These strips were targeted to be of similar mass as the experimentally found natural averages. Likewise, the strip for the left and right wing were taken from the same stock to further ensure their similarity. As each strip is cut, its mass was recorded. They were affixed to the membrane material with a spray adhesive. Once every vein was attached, the wing was removed from the board and attached to molds designed around the camber of the wing [19]. The natural wings were found to be represented by a third order polynomial in both the spanwise and chordwise directions, the mold's surface copies this polynomial [19]. The molds were 3D printed on a Formlabs Form 2 3D Printer using their High Temperature Resin, which was selected for its high heat deformation temperature. 3D printing allowed ease of design and the possibility of rapid adjustments. The molds included two pins, one at the base of the wing and one at the wing tip, to locate the manufactured wings. The molds were then placed in a vacuum bag covered in teflon so that they did not stick, and with filler material to allow for proper airflow. The vacuum bag was baked in an oven at 100 C for approximately three hours. Once the wing was fully cooled a number of hours later, it was removed from the vacuum bag and mold. Any excess material was then trimmed away.

3.4 Manufactured Wing Testing

The manufactured wings were tested for similarity with the extracted wings. This included both flexural stiffness testing and measures of camber retention.

Flexural stiffness is thought to be a key factor in wing dynamics, therefore, mimicking it is of importance [17]. The process by which flexural stiffness testing was carried out is the same as for the natural wings. A CNC machine positioned a long metal rod over the 70% span mark on the wing and applied a force. The displacement was recorded, along with the force applied. The wing is held still and cantilevered by a clamp and placed on a scale. A different step size was used for the manufactured wings. Both Icarex and Kapton wings were tested with a step size of 1.27 mm (0.05 in), Mylar was tested with a step size of 2.55 mm (0.1 in). As with the natural wings, three tests from both the dorsal and ventral sides were done for every wing, each of which included six data points. By using Eq. (1), the flexural stiffness was calculated.

One of the primary goals of this work was to replicate the camber of the natural wings, therefore this was evaluated in the manufactured wings. In order to test how well each wing retained its camber they were re-attached to their molds at the root tip and held in place with scotch tape. They were then placed in the CNC machine once again on top of a small sheet of silicone rubber. The CNC applied a force again at the 70% span mark using the same steel rod. The position of initial touch off was recorded. The CNC lowered the steel rod until the wings correctly deformed to the shape of the mold. This displacement was also recorded. A wing that has a smaller difference in displacement between touch off and conformation has a more similar camber, a larger displacement wing is worse camber. This test was run three times for every wing.

4   Results

The mass and stiffness of the moth wings are summarized in Table 2. Figure 3 compares the masses of the moth wings and the manufactured wings. The proportion of the mass that is due to the venation structure is also indicated. The masses of the manufactured Icarex and Kapton wings are similar to the masses of the moth wings. Figure 4 compares the flexural stiffness of the moth and manufactured wings in the dorsal and ventral directions. The manufactured wings are an order of magnitude stiffer than the moth wings.

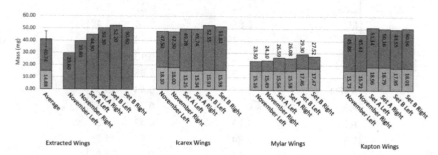

Fig. 3. Masses of Natural and Manufactured Wings. When available, the venation structure mass is the lower section of each bar. The manufactured Icarex and Kapton wings are similar to their natural counterparts.

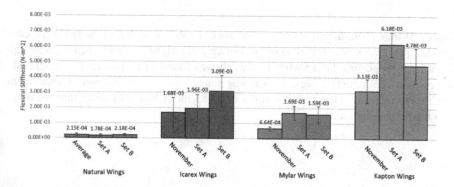

Fig. 4. Flexural stiffness from both the ventral and dorsal directions. The extracted wings are an order of magnitude less stiff than the manufactured wings.

4.1 Extracted Moth Wings

Through the extraction of wings from 23 individual moths, the average forewing mass was found to be 40.74 ± 6.56 mg. During the construction process, the venation structure was targeted to be of a similar mass to that displayed in Table 1. It was found that the average venation structure composes approximately 63% of the average wing.

When testing for the flexural stiffness over time (Fig. 5), it was difficult to see a clear trend within the first three hours. The stiffness of the left and right wings from both directions did appear to increase, however, the data did not fit any trends particularly well. That being said, all tests resulted in flexural stiffness values of the order 10^{-4} N-m^2. When tested again, at the 48 h mark, results showed a notable difference. All the wings were stiffer, in the order of 10^{-3} N-m^2.

Table 1. Wing venation mass distribution

Vein	Mass (mg)	Standard Deviation	Percent
A1	1.49	0.16	5.76
A2	0.55	0.14	2.13
Cu	2.03	0.22	7.85
Cu2	1.44	0.27	5.57
M3	0.88	0.10	3.40
M2	0.57	0.13	2.20
M1	0.69	0.13	2.67
R5	0.46	0.08	1.78
R+R4	3.97	0.44	15.35
R3	0.93	0.26	3.60
R2	1.21	0.42	4.68
R1	3.84	0.57	14.85
Re	2.57	0.57	9.94
Clump	5.23	0.80	20.22
Total Venation	25.86	1.79	100.00
Total Wing	40.74	6.56	-

Icarex Wings. Building upon previous work, new sets of Icarex wings were constructed [1]. Icarex was found to be of a marginally higher than ideal mass, although capable of replicating larger wing masses. It was found to be an order of magnitude stiffer than the natural wings. Icarex was found to have an average displacement required to return it to the correct camber of 0.683 mm which was lower than the other two membrane materials.

Table 2. Summary of natural moth wing data

	Mass (mg)		Flexural Stiffness (N-m^2)	Standard Deviation
Avarage	40.74	Dorsal	1.96E-04	5.65E-05
		Ventral	2.33E-04	7.95E-05
November Left	29.6		-	-
November Right	39.6		-	-
Set A Left	44.9	Dorsal	1.75E-04	7.17E-05
		Ventral	2.87E-04	1.15E-04
Set A Right	50.3	Dorsal	1.97E-04	6.21E-05
		Ventral	1.87E-04	2.34E-05
Set B Left	52.2	Dorsal	2.10E-04	4.45E-05
		Ventral	2.63E-04	6.46E-05
Set B Right	50.6	Dorsal	2.04E-04	4.36E-05
		Ventral	1.96E-04	3.18E-05

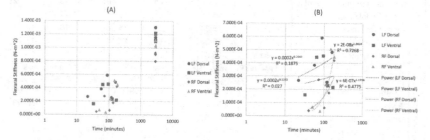

Fig. 5. Flexural stiffness versus time. (A) Flexural stiffness over 48 h. (B) Flexural stiffness of the first three hours. Flexural stiffness seems to increase over extended periods of time. The trend within the first three hours is unclear, a power function seems to be the best fit, generally producing higher R^2 values. The above figures plot the averages of test data on logarithmic axis.

Mylar Wings. Mylar wings were found to be exceptionally light. They were all below two standard deviations of the average mass. Of the three membrane materials, Mylar was the most similar in terms of flexural stiffness. Unfortunately, the most similar wing was still over 7 times stiffer than a moth wing. Mylar retains the camber of the wing less well than Icarex, with an average displacement of 1.098 mm.

Kapton Wings. Kapton wings were closest to the actual wings masses. The Kapton Set B right wing mass was only 0.04 mg greater than the extracted wing. Similarly to Icarex, Kapton was capable of replicating heavier wings. It was found to have flexural stiffness values of well over an order of magnitude higher than the natural wings. Kapton had the least camber retention of the three membrane materials, with a displacement of 1.290 mm (Fig. 6 and Table 3).

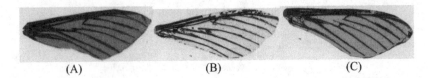

(A)   (B)   (C)

Fig. 6. Manufactured wings using different materials and templates. (A) Wing manufactured using Icarex, November Template. (B) Using Mylar, Set A Template. (C) Using Kapton, Set B Template.

Table 3. Summary of manufactured wing data

		Icarex		Mylar		Kapton	
		Overall Mass (mg)	Venation Mass (mg)	Overall Mass (mg)	Venation Mass (mg)	Overall Mass (mg)	Venation Mass (mg)
Mass	November Template Left	47.5	18.1	23.5	15.16	45.88	15.73
	November Template Right	47.3	18	24.1	15.49	45.43	15.72
	Set A Template Left	49.78	15.25	26.59	15.56	51.14	18.96
	Set A Template Right	49.74	15.34	26.08	15.58	50.16	18.79
	Set B Template Left	52.55	15.93	29.3	17.46	49.55	17.95
	Set B Template Right	51.82	15.98	27.52	17.47	50.56	18.01
		Flexural Stiffness (N-m^2)		Flexural Stiffness (N-m^2)		Flexural Stiffness (N-m^2)	
Flexural Stiffness	November Template Left	9.750E-04		6.390E-04		3.095E-03	
	November Template Right	2.387E-03		6.890E-04		3.169E-03	
	Set A Template Left	1.823E-03		1.470E-03		5.814E-03	
	Set A Template Right	2.101E-03		1.919E-03		6.547E-03	
	Set B Template Left	2.554E-03		1.210E-03		4.127E-03	
	Set B Template Right	3.627E-03		1.972E-03		5.431E-03	
		Average Displacement (mm)		Average Displacement (mm)		Average Displacement (mm)	
Camber	November Template Left	1.177		1.634		1.185	
	November Template Right	0.720		1.743		1.041	
	Set A Template Left	0.567		0.559		1.270	
	Set A Template Right	0.271		1.024		1.753	
	Set B Template Left	0.745		0.881		1.126	
	Set B Template Right	0.618		0.745		1.363	

5   Conclusions

A number of conclusions can be drawn from this work. With this manufacturing process, it is possible to fabricate wings using Icarex or Kapton that are similar in mass to extracted moth wings. Wings constructed using Mylar were found to be less massive than moth wings, and is thought to be a poor choice. Kapton is marginally the best for replicating mass.

In terms of flexural stiffness, all of the fabricated wings are too stiff. Wings made using Mylar are the least stiff. The best Mylar wing was still over seven times stiffer than the natural wing. It is plausible that changing the venation structure material may help to alleviate this problem.

Icarex retained camber the best. Kapton retained it the worst. Both Mylar and Kapton are stored on a roll. When manufactured, the wings were normally produced in a way such that the camber of the wing was in the opposite direction of the curve of the roll. This meant that the direction of roll worked negatively for camber retention. The fabrication method should be modified to take this into account.

Among these materials, Icarex is the recommended material for future work. It is capable of producing similar mass and retaining the correct camber, but the fabricated wings are an order of magnitude too stiff. In order to better mimic *M. sexta* wings, it is recommended to reevaluate the materials chosen. No doubt, better methods exist with which to manufacture wings. Future work on this project will focus on using epoxy and urethane resins to manufacture the venation structure, as well as further mapping the distribution of flexural stiffness throughout the wings. Different methods to replace the vacuum bag are also being investigated.

References

1. Moses, K.C., Michaels, S.C., Willis, M., Quinn, R.D.: Artificial Manduca sexta forewings for flapping-wing micro aerial vehicles: how wing structure affects performance. Bioinspiration Biomimetics **12**(5) (2017)
2. Michaels, S.C., et al.: Biomimicry of the *Manduca sexta* forewing using SRT protein complex for FWMAV development. In: Wilson, S.P., Verschure, P.F.M.J., Mura, A., Prescott, T.J. (eds.) LIVINGMACHINES 2015. LNCS (LNAI), vol. 9222, pp. 86–91. Springer, Cham (2015). https://doi.org/10.1007/978-3-319-22979-9_8
3. Moses, K.C., Prigg, D., Weisfeld, M., Bachmann, R.J., Willis, M., Quinn, R.D.: Simulating flapping wing mechanisms inspired by the *Manduca sexta* hawkmoth. In: Vouloutsi, V., et al. (eds.) Living Machines 2018. LNCS (LNAI), vol. 10928, pp. 326–337. Springer, Cham (2018). https://doi.org/10.1007/978-3-319-95972-6_35
4. Fearing, R.S., Chiang, K.H., Dickenson, M.H., Pick, D.L., Sitti, M., Yan, J.: Wing transmission for a micromechanical flying insect. In: Proceedings 2000 ICRA. Millennium Conference. IEEE International Conference on Robotics and Automation. Symposia Proceedings (2000)
5. Yan, J., Wood, R.J., Avadhanula, S., Sitti, M., Fearing, R.S.: Towards flapping wing control for a micromechanical flying insect. In: IEEE International Conference on Robotics and Automation (2001)
6. Wood, R.J., Avadhanula, S., Sahai, R., Steltz, E., Fearing, R.S.: Microrobot design using fiber reinforced composites. J. Mech. Des. **30**(5)
7. Wood, R.J.: The first takeoff of a biologically inspired at-scale robotic insect. IEEE Trans. Rob. **24**(2), 341–347 (2008)
8. Ramezani, A., Chung, S.-J., Hutchinson, S.: A biomimetic robotic platform to study flight specializations of bats. Sci. Robot. **2**(3) (2017)
9. Bunget, G., Seelecke, S.: BATMAV: a biologically inspired micro air vehicle for flapping flight: kinematic modeling. In: SPIE Smart Structures and Materials Nondestructive Evaluation and Health Monitoring, vol. 6928 (2008)
10. Keennon, M., Klingebiel, K., Won, H.: Development of the nano hummingbird: a tailless flapping wing micro air vehicle. In: 50th AIAA Aerospace Sciences Meeting Including the New Horizons Forum and Aerospace Exposition (2012)

11. Nguyen, Q.V., Park, H.C., Goo, N.S., Byun, D.: Characteristics of a beetle's free flight and a flapping-wing system that mimics beetle flight. J. Bionic Eng. **7**(1), 77–86 (2010)
12. Combes, S.A., Daniel, T.L.: Into thin air: contributions of aerodynamic and inertial-elastic forces to wing bending in the hawkmoth Manduca sexta. J. Exp. Biol. **206**, 2999–3006 (2003)
13. Combes, S.A., Daniel, T.L.: Flexural stiffness in insect wings I. Scaling and the influence of wing venation. J. Exp. Biol. **206**(17), 2979–2987 (2003)
14. Combes, S.A., Daniel, T.L.: Flexural stiffness in insect wings II. Spatial distribution and dynamic wing bending. J. Exp. Biol. **206**(17), 2989–2997 (2003)
15. Mountcastle, A.M., Daniel, T.L.: Aerodynamic and functional consequences of wing compliance. In: Taylor, G.K., Triantafyllou, M.S., Tropea, C. (eds.) Animal Locomotion, pp. 311–320. Springer, Heidelberg (2010). https://doi.org/10.1007/978-3-642-11633-9_25
16. Mountcastle, A.M., Combes, S.A.: Wing flexibility enhances load-lifting capabilities in bumblebees. Proc. R. Soc. B Biol. Sci.
17. Mountcastle, A.M.: Structural dynamics and aerodynamics of flexible wings in insect flight, dissertation (2010)
18. O'Hara, R.P., Palazotto, A.N.: The morphological characterization of the forewing of the Manduca sexta species for the application of biomimetic flapping wing micro air vehicles. Bioinspiration Biomimetics **7**(4) (2012)
19. O'Hara, R.P.: The characterization of material properties and structural dynamics of the Manduca sexta forewing for application to flapping wing micro air vehicle design, dissertation (2012)
20. Tobias, A.P.: Experimental methods to characterize nonlinear vibration of flapping wing micro air vehicles, thesis (2007)
21. Sims, T.W.: A structural dynamic analysis of a Manduca sexta forewing, thesis (2010)
22. Dudley, R.: The Biomechanics of Insect Flight: Form, Function, Evolution. Princeton University Press, Princeton (2000)

Robots that Imagine – Can Hippocampal Replay Be Utilized for Robotic Mnemonics?

Matthew T. Whelan[1,2(✉)], Eleni Vasilaki[1], and Tony J. Prescott[1,2]

[1] Department of Computer Science, University of Sheffield, Sheffield S10 2TN, UK
{mwhelan3,e.vasilaki,t.j.prescott}@sheffield.ac.uk
[2] Sheffield Robotics, University of Sheffield, Sheffield S1 3JD, UK

Abstract. Neurophysiological studies on hippocampal replay, which was a phenomenon first shown in rodents as the reactivation of previously active hippocampal cells, has shown it to be potentially important for mnemonic functions such as memory consolidation/recall, learning and planning. Since its discovery, a small number of neuronal models have been developed to attempt to describe the workings of this phenomenon. But it may be possible to utilize hippocampal replay to help solve some of the difficult challenges that face robotic cognition, learning and memory, and/or be used for the development of biomimetic robotics. Here we review these models in the hope of learning their workings, and see that their neural network structures may be integrated into current neural network based algorithms for robotic spatial memory, and perhaps are particularly suited for reinforcement learning paradigms.

Keywords: Hippocampal replay · Memory · Planning · Reinforcement learning

1 Introduction

Hippocampal replay, first discovered in rodents, is a phenomenon in which hippocampal cells that were previously active during awake exploratory behaviours are later replayed in the same temporal order, often during sharp-wave ripple events that compresses the time-scale of the replay event relative to the exploratory activation [10]. Hippocampal replay predominantly occurs whilst the rat is in restful states such as sleep or awake quiescence, and can occur in a 'forward' direction, such that the previously active cells are reinstated with the same temporal order [36]; or it can be in the 'reverse', such that the temporal order of the cells are reversed during a replay event [12] (see [11] for a review on hippocampal replay). But just how or why hippocampal replay occurs is still an ongoing research problem, yet current evidence suggests that it may be important for memory consolidation/recall, planning [30], and (reinforcement) learning [6].

© Springer Nature Switzerland AG 2019
U. Martinez-Hernandez et al. (Eds.): Living Machines 2019, LNAI 11556, pp. 277–286, 2019.
https://doi.org/10.1007/978-3-030-24741-6_24

The neural mechanisms of reinforcement learning can be traced back to Schultz's seminal work on dopamine as a reward-predicting error signal [35], and a recent review on the ventral basal ganglia (VBG) – a region heavily innervated with dopaminergic neurons [18] – has shown that the hippocampal region projects to and possibly receives projections from the VBG [17]. Indeed, experimentally there is strong evidence that interactions between hippocampus, VBG, and ventral tegmental area support reward-guided memory and conditioned place preference (CPP) [12,14,40]. Furthermore, recent experimental results have shown that hippocampal replays and sharp-wave ripples coordinate with bursts of activity in the ventral tegmental area [14] and ventral striatum [31], and that changes in reward modulates the rate at which hippocampal reverse replays, but not forward replays, occur [1]. It has even been shown in a recent study on humans that spatial memory is prioritized for rewarding locations "retroactively", suggesting that reward-prioritized spatial memory appears some time after an event has occurred [4]. Perhaps it is hippocampal replay in the interim that modulates the memory?

Hippocampal replay in coordination with dopaminergic activity therefore seems well suited as a potential mechanism for reinforcement learning. A number of models have looked to incorporate dopamine as a neuromodulatory third factor in three-factor learning rules for synaptic plasticity (see [13] for a review), successfully showing, for instance, behavioural changes for conditioned place preference in a simulated Morris water maze task [41]. Traditionally, reinforcement learning algorithms have only partially resembled biology, and there is certainly no mention of hippocampal replay in the main body of reinforcement learning literature (i.e. Sutton and Barto's famous text book [37]). However, some of the reinforcement learning algorithms, such as DynaQ algorithms and the deep Q-network, seem well suited as explanations for the use case of hippocampal replay with their need for offline *sequence replays* [3,6,21,24,26,37].

Memory, reinforcement learning and planning are all active challenges in the field of robotics and AI, and bioinspired models have been and are being developed to tackle these challenges [22]. Given the role hippocampal replay has in mnemonic functions, we review here a selection of the most recent studies that aim to describe the neural dynamics of hippocampal replay through computational modelling. We hope that doing so will help determine how and whether hippocampal replay could be useful for solving some of the mnemonic and learning challenges that face the robotics and AI fields.

2 Computational Models of Hippocampal Replay

Models of hippocampal replay are almost exclusively composed of neural networks with either rate-based or spiking-based neural dynamics, and most, if not all, necessitate the use of recurrent networks in order to store memory traces for later reinstatement. Furthermore, they mostly simplify the problem of place cell activation by assuming evenly distributed place fields, usually overlapping, in an environment for which specific place cells fire as a function of the agent's distance from the centre of the respective place field.

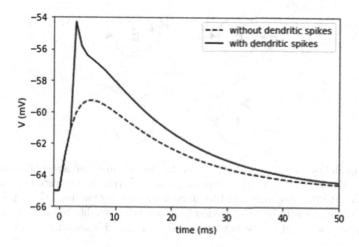

Fig. 1. Dendritic spiking causes supralinear responses to synchronous inputs (solid line) above what would be expected with a simple summation of inputs only (dashed line), important in the model by Jahnke et al. [19] for modelling forward/reverse replays and sharp-wave ripples. This plot was modelled using a standard leaky-integrate and fire neuron receiving instantaneous synchronous inputs at t = 0, with and without dendritic spiking (see main text).

We start with a spiking-based model of leaky-integrate and fire neurons by Jahnke et al. [19]. Here they exploit theta phase precession [29] to generate memory traces via spike-timing dependent plasticity. But the key inclusion in their model is to use dendritic spiking, which occurs when a high number·of synchronous inputs exceed some threshold Θ_b within a time interval of ΔT^s. This then causes a dendritic current impulse which causes an increase in membrane voltage above what would be expected without dendritic spiking (Fig. 1).

Once a dendritic spike is initiated, the dendrite enters a refractory period during which time it cannot transmit any spikes. In a linear sequence of place cells with bidirectional connections, this refractory period is important for restricting replays to only travel in a single direction, without reversing back on itself [23]. Furthermore, the supralinear nature of the dendritic impulse generates activity pulses that are reminiscent of sharp-wave ripples.

Dendritic spiking, found to occur in CA1 pyramidal cells of the hippocampus [2], offers a unique explanation for the occurrence of both sharp wave ripples and replay, and Matheus Gauy et al. [23] have extended the use of dendritic spikes, as modelled by Jahnke et al. [19], but invented a new cell type termed 'sequence cells'. The reason for this inclusion is that Jahnke et al.'s model could not account for different trajectories containing the same place cells. Having multiple trajectories emanating from the same place cell would cause replays of multiple trajectories at once. Rather, sequence cells, activated in sequential order as an agent traversed an environment, were paired with place cells via Hebbian learning. As such, one needs only save individual trajectories of sequence cells,

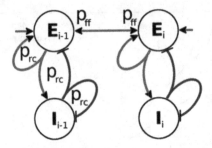

Fig. 2. A model by Chenkov et al. [7] of a synfire-like chain of cell assemblies containing excitatory (**E**) and inhibitory (**I**) cell populations, recurrently connected to each other with probability P_{rc}, and connected feedforwardly with probability P_{ff}. Replay events are characterized as activity propagation from one cell assembly to another and so on, with activity modulated by the inhibitory interneurons. Figure adapted from [7].

and reactivate them in order to reinstate the place cell sequences learned during exploration. It is worth noting that the assumption of sequence cells causes two possible issues: (1) this may necessitate an indefinite number of distinct sequences of sequence cells to account for all trajectories experienced; (2) there is no biological evidence for the existence of sequence cells (though for bioinspiration this may be irrelevant).

Matheus Gauy et al.'s model above had sequences of sequence cells arranged in a similar fashion to synfire chains, and Chenkov et al. [7] designed a similar synfire-like chain of cell assemblies. Within each cell assembly of the synfire chain was a collection of excitatory and inhibitory cells with recurrent connections (Fig. 2). By carefully designing each assembly such that there was increased inhibition for accumulating excitatory spikes, the model was able to successfully amplify activity down through the assembly sequences, mimicking replay events, but avoids explosions of activity reminiscent of synfire chain explosions and bursting. This controlled amplification allows weak memory traces, such as those that might be generated during one-shot learning episodes, to successfully re-fire. Furthermore, the increase in inhibition due to accumulating excitatory activity causes replay events to travel in a single direction only.

Refractory periods and inhibitory effects with symmetric bidirectional connections are two methods that allow reverse replays to occur, but Haga and Fukai [16] have shown that the effects of short-term plasticity could also be an explanation for reverse replay. By modelling short-term depression and facilitation at synapses, it is possible to long-term potentiate bidirectional connections in an asymmetric fashion, such that the reverse direction is potentiated more than the forward direction following a forward activation of a sequence. However, it is not clear how this model accounts for forward replay, nor how it prevents continuous reversals in the memory trace strength. For instance, reverse replays cause potentiations to favour the forward direction again, which could be useful, but a forward replay would re-potentiate the reverse direction, which is perhaps not quite clearly as useful.

It seems likely that we'd be interested in models that can support both forward and reverse replays, and perhaps the earliest model of a network incorporating both forward and reverse replay was from Molter et al. [27]. Their original model was more typical in that a traversal through a set of place cells would potentiate that trajectory more in the forward than the reverse direction, but still has non-negligible reverse connections necessary for reverse replays. They also, like in Jahnke et al.'s model [19], employed theta phase precession during memory trace formation. The model was also somewhat simpler and computationally cheaper than the above models, as it was rate-based as apposed to spiking (though both [16] and [23] include rate-based and spiking-based models). But the replays themselves in a 2D environment were similar to a wave-like propagation across the entire environment emanating from the position of replay initiation – as such it does not hold an accurate model of traversal for the environment, though it can provide replays of inexperienced paths.

Following memory trace formation it is then necessary to initiate replay events, and all models suggest that an external stimulus be input to the first (last) cell/cell assembly to initiate forward (reverse) replays. Chenkov et al. [7], however, through control of recurrent and feedforward connection probabilities, show that asynchronous-irregular spiking can spontaneously initiate replay events – whether this is of use is unknown, but a recent study with a DynaQ neural network algorithm suggests 'random' hippocampal replays are not only useful, but necessary, for converging Q-values (see Sect. 3 below).

To summarize, there have been a small number of computational models, rate-based and spiking-based, that aim to capture the dynamics of hippocampal replay. Most networks require recurrent connections, either across the whole network or within sub-assemblies that are then connected as synfire-like chains, so that memory traces can be effectively stored and, as a consequence of an external stimulus, reinstated later as a replay event. The mechanisms through which each model forms memory traces and then initiates and maintains replay events is summarized in Table 1.

It is worth noting that a small number of studies have modelled the process of sharp-wave/ripples in the hippocampus, which occurs simultaneously with a replay event [10]. Particularly they model the generation of sharp-wave/ripples via interactions of inhibitory interneurons, extra-hippocampal inputs such as septal inputs, and/or neuromodulators like acetylcholine, and the relationship between sharp-wave/ripples and replay events [8,9,34,39].

3 Hippocampal Replay for Robotics Applications

The models reviewed here are computational models with the sole intent of replicating experimental findings. But they do not prove immediately useful for practical applications, as they all require place cell representations readily available prior to replay, and offer no useful outputs post-replay. What could be missing then is a unified model of place cell, or state, representations at the input end of a hippocampal replay model, and a means for action-selection

Table 1. Summary of the hippocampal replay models. The means by which each model performs the stages required for hippocampal replay are summarized here. See main text for full details.

Model	Means for generating hippocampal replay stages			
	Memory trace formation	Replay initiation	Maintenance of replay	Forward/Reverse replay?
Jahnke et al. [19]	Spike-timing dependent plasticity with theta phase precession in recurrent network of place cells	Targeted external stimulation of place cell assemblies	Dendritic spiking with refractory periods	Forward and reverse
Matheus Gauy et al. [23]	Hebbian plasticity between pre-existing sequence cell assemblies and place cells	Targeted external stimulation of sequence cell assemblies	Dendritic spiking with refractory periods	Forward and reverse
Chenkov et al. [7]	Pre-existing synfire-like chains with probabilistic recurrent and feedforward connections	External stimulation or spontaneously through activity fluctuations	Recurrent excitatory and inhibitory cell assemblies for controlled amplification along assembly sequences	Forward and reverse
Haga and Fukai [16]	Asymmetric bidirectional recurrency via STP modified Hebbian learning	Targeted external stimulation of end place cells	Asymmetric bidirectional connection strengths provide unidirectional replay	Reverse only
Molter et al. [27]	Asymmetric bidirectional recurrency via theta phase precession Hebbian learning	Targeted external stimulation of place cells	Propagation due to strong place cell connections learned during exploration	Forward and reverse

improvement at the output end. A line a literature on each of these areas is available, but a full review of these is outside the scope of this paper.

Though a few recent studies are worth mentioning here that could integrate well with hippocampal replay. On the place cell representation end, the first is a biologically inspired SLAM algorithm, or RatSLAM, developed by Milford et al. [25], which has proven effective at capturing state representations in the form of 'pose cells.' With an accurate map represented in the form cell values, this offers itself as a candidate for replay models based upon neural networks. Alternatively, Byrne et al. model [5] hippocampal place cells, boundary vector cells and head direction cells, all neurophysiological features of the hippocampal region [28,38], which could provide a more biologically plausible model of place cell representations, whilst Jauffret et al. [20] have recently developed a model of grid cells [15] and place cells that was successfully applied for spatial navigation in a robot.

For action-selection improvement, the first is a DynaQ neural network algorithm developed by Aubin et al. [3], which is a reinforcement learning model using Q-learning and the Dyna algorithm. It too is composed of a neural network that represents states, but pairs the states with (discrete) actions. They indeed integrated a version of hippocampal replay and showed that where Q-values could not converge online due to similarities in state values, they could however converge offline via 'random' hippocampal replays. Mnih et al.'s deep Q-network (DQN) [26], in a similar fashion to the DynaQ neural network, utilized *experience replays*, which is conducted by selecting from a random uniform distribution groupings of state, action, reward and next state experiences. A list of experiences could then be denoted by $D_t = \{e_1, ..., e_t\}$ with $e_t = (s_t, a_t, r_t, s'_t)$ being an individual experience, and applying the Q-learning update for each $e_{rand} \sim U(D)$ where $U(\cdot)$ is the uniform distribution. But both these algorithms suffer from perhaps one minor issue, in that Q-values here are learned for a discrete set of actions. Though perhaps rectifiable, this could prove problematic for states that are represented continuously.

Recent work by Mattar and Daw [24] developed a Q-learning based reinforcement learning model that prioritizes Bellman backups. Such a prioritization (for which something similar is found in the model by Aubin et al. [3] and termed *prioritized sweeping*) determines whether the agent should prioritize the evaluation of upcoming decisions, or whether to perform updates in order to capture newly learned information about a reward. Prioritization of the former increases the number of forward replays, whilst for the latter reverse replays become more prominent. In this way, the model favours forward replays at the start of a trial, whilst reverse replays are favoured at the end of a trial – effects similar to that found with hippocampal replay [10].

Another challenge for robotics is the number of trials required for reinforcement learning algorithms to properly converge. This was a problem addressed by Vasilaki et al. [33,41] in a spike-based model of hippocampal place cells for a reinforcement learning Morris water maze task. They showed that whereas policy-gradient methods require either a high number of learning trials (due to small learning rates) or cause noisy eligibility traces (when learning rates are high), their model could account for effective learning within a small number of trials, as is found experimentally with rats. Interestingly, they modelled "action cells", which could possibly be found in the basal ganglia as an action selection mechanism [32], and further, unlike the models discussed above, they were able to represent actions and states as continuous, rather than discrete. Yet importantly for our discussion here, they did not employ hippocampal replay.

Hippocampal replay could offer another means to achieve the low number of learning trials required – learning is done "offline" as (perhaps noisy) repetitions of previous experience. This could therefore offer an effective and highly efficient mechanism that converges state-action values "offline", which could prove useful for robotic learning, as well as offer bioinspired learning mechanisms for biomimetic robotics. And indeed there can be a symbiotic relationship between neurophysiology and robotics, such that whilst robotics can take inspiration from biology, we may also enhance our understanding of the underlying biology by providing solutions, via behavioural robotics, of some of the functional properties that exists in biological creatures.

4   Conclusion

The discovery of hippocampal replay, via its ability to reinstate previously active place cells, along with dopaminergic activity in the basal ganglia, offers a possibly efficient "offline" mechanism that seems to be in place for post-hoc pairing of state-actions with rewards. We have therefore reviewed a number of biologically-plausible models that aim to describe the neural mechanisms of hippocampal replay in both the forward and reverse directions. Integrating biologically plausible state representations, such as place cells, with a biologically plausible action selection mechanism remains an open challenge, but incorporating hippocampal replay into the process could help understand better the underlying biology, as well perhaps aid in the development of memory and learning algorithms. Whether it can be used for robotic mnemonics and biomimetic robotics remains open for further investigation, but the groundwork seems already to be in place.

References

1. Ambrose, R.E., Pfeiffer, B.E., Foster, D.J.: Reverse replay of hippocampal place cells is uniquely modulated by changing reward. Neuron **91**(5), 1124–1136 (2016)
2. Ariav, G., Polsky, A., Schiller, J.: Submillisecond precision of the input-output transformation function mediated by fast sodium dendritic spikes in basal dendrites of CA1 pyramidal neurons. J. Neurosci. **23**(21), 7750–7758 (2003)
3. Aubin, L., Khamassi, M., Girard, B.: Prioritized sweeping neural DynaQ with multiple predecessors, and hippocampal replays. In: Vouloutsi, V., et al. (eds.) Living Machines 2018. LNCS (LNAI), vol. 10928, pp. 16–27. Springer, Cham (2018). https://doi.org/10.1007/978-3-319-95972-6_4
4. Braun, E.K., Wimmer, G.E., Shohamy, D.: Retroactive and graded prioritization of memory by reward. Nat. Commun. **9**(1), 4886 (2018)
5. Byrne, P., Becker, S., Burgess, N.: Remembering the past and imagining the future: a neural model of spatial memory and imagery. Psychol. Rev. **114**(2), 340 (2007)

6. Cazé, R., Khamassi, M., Aubin, L., Girard, B.: Hippocampal replays under the scrutiny of reinforcement learning models. J. Neurophysiol. **120**(6), 2877–2896 (2018)

7. Chenkov, N., Sprekeler, H., Kempter, R.: Memory replay in balanced recurrent networks. PLoS Comput. Biol. **13**(1), e1005359 (2017)

8. Cutsuridis, V., Hasselmo, M.: Spatial memory sequence encoding and replay during modeled theta and ripple oscillations. Cogn. Comput. **3**(4), 554–574 (2011)

9. Cutsuridis, V., Taxidis, J.: Deciphering the role of CA1 inhibitory circuits in sharp wave-ripple complexes. Front. Syst. Neurosci. **7**, 13 (2013)

10. Diba, K., Buzsáki, G.: Forward and reverse hippocampal place-cell sequences during ripples. Nat. Neurosci. **10**(10), 1241 (2007)

11. Foster, D.J.: Replay comes of age. Ann. Rev. Neurosci. **40**, 581–602 (2017)

12. Foster, D.J., Wilson, M.A.: Reverse replay of behavioural sequences in hippocampal place cells during the awake state. Nature **440**(7084), 680 (2006)

13. Gerstner, W., Lehmann, M., Liakoni, V., Corneil, D., Brea, J.: Eligibility traces and plasticity on behavioral time scales: experimental support of NeoHebbian three-factor learning rules. Front. Neural Circuits **12**, 53 (2018)

14. Gomperts, S.N., Kloosterman, F., Wilson, M.A.: VTA neurons coordinate with the hippocampal reactivation of spatial experience. Elife **4**, e05360 (2015)

15. Hafting, T., Fyhn, M., Molden, S., Moser, M.B., Moser, E.I.: Microstructure of a spatial map in the entorhinal cortex. Nature **436**(7052), 801 (2005)

16. Haga, T., Fukai, T.: Recurrent network model for learning goal-directed sequences through reverse replay. Elife **7**, e34171 (2018)

17. Humphries, M.D., Prescott, T.J.: The ventral basal ganglia, a selection mechanism at the crossroads of space, strategy, and reward. Prog. Neurobiol. **90**(4), 385–417 (2010)

18. Ikemoto, S., Yang, C., Tan, A.: Basal ganglia circuit loops, dopamine and motivation: a review and enquiry. Behav. Brain Res. **290**, 17–31 (2015)

19. Jahnke, S., Timme, M., Memmesheimer, R.M.: A unified dynamic model for learning, replay, and sharp-wave/ripples. J. Neurosci. **35**(49), 16236–16258 (2015)

20. Jauffret, A., Cuperlier, N., Gaussier, P.: From grid cells and visual place cells to multimodal place cell: a new robotic architecture. Front. Neurorobot. **9**, 1 (2015)

21. Johnson, A., Redish, A.D.: Hippocampal replay contributes to within session learning in a temporal difference reinforcement learning model. Neural Netw. **18**(9), 1163–1171 (2005)

22. Martinez-Hernandez, U., Damianou, A., Camilleri, D., Boorman, L.W., Lawrence, N., Prescott, T.J.: An integrated probabilistic framework for robot perception, learning and memory. In: 2016 IEEE International Conference on Robotics and Biomimetics (ROBIO), pp. 1796–1801. IEEE (2016)

23. Matheus Gauy, M., et al.: A hippocampal model for behavioral time acquisition and fast bidirectional replay of spatio-temporal memory sequences. Front. Neurosci. **12**, 961 (2018)

24. Mattar, M.G., Daw, N.D.: Prioritized memory access explains planning and hippocampal replay. Nat. Neurosci. **21**(11), 1609 (2018)

25. Milford, M.J., Wyeth, G.F., Prasser, D.: RatSLAM: a hippocampal model for simultaneous localization and mapping. In: Proceedings of the IEEE International Conference on Robotics and Automation, vol. 1, pp. 403–408. IEEE (2004)

26. Mnih, V., et al.: Human-level control through deep reinforcement learning. Nature **518**(7540), 529 (2015)

27. Molter, C., Sato, N., Yamaguchi, Y.: Reactivation of behavioral activity during sharp waves: a computational model for two stage hippocampal dynamics. Hippocampus **17**(3), 201–209 (2007)

28. O'Keefe, J., Dostrovsky, J.: The hippocampus as a spatial map: preliminary evidence from unit activity in the freely-moving rat. Brain Res. **34**(1), 171–175 (1971)

29. O'Keefe, J., Recce, M.L.: Phase relationship between hippocampal place units and the EEG theta rhythm. Hippocampus **3**(3), 317–330 (1993)

30. Ólafsdóttir, H.F., Bush, D., Barry, C.: The role of hippocampal replay in memory and planning. Curr. Biol. **28**(1), R37–R50 (2018)

31. Pennartz, C., Lee, E., Verheul, J., Lipa, P., Barnes, C.A., McNaughton, B.: The ventral striatum in off-line processing: ensemble reactivation during sleep and modulation by hippocampal ripples. J. Neurosci. **24**(29), 6446–6456 (2004)

32. Redgrave, P., Prescott, T.J., Gurney, K.: The basal ganglia: a vertebrate solution to the selection problem? Neuroscience **89**(4), 1009–1023 (1999)

33. Richmond, P., Buesing, L., Giugliano, M., Vasilaki, E.: Democratic population decisions result in robust policy-gradient learning: a parametric study with gpu simulations. PLoS ONE **6**(5), e18539 (2011)

34. Saravanan, V., et al.: Transition between encoding and consolidation/replay dynamics via cholinergic modulation of can current: a modeling study. Hippocampus **25**(9), 1052–1070 (2015)

35. Schultz, W.: Predictive reward signal of dopamine neurons. J. Neurophysiol. **80**(1), 1–27 (1998)

36. Skaggs, W.E., McNaughton, B.L.: Replay of neuronal firing sequences in rat hippocampus during sleep following spatial experience. Science **271**(5257), 1870–1873 (1996)

37. Sutton, R.S., Barto, A.G.: Reinforcement Learning: An Introduction. MIT press, Cambridge (2018)

38. Taube, J.S.: Head direction cells and the neurophysiological basis for a sense of direction. Prog. Neurobiol. **55**(3), 225–256 (1998)

39. Taxidis, J., Coombes, S., Mason, R., Owen, M.R.: Modeling sharp wave-ripple complexes through a CA3-CA1 network model with chemical synapses. Hippocampus **22**(5), 995–1017 (2012)

40. Trouche, S., et al.: A hippocampus-accumbens tripartite neuronal motif guides appetitive memory in space. Cell **176**(6), 1393–1406 (2019)

41. Vasilaki, E., Frémaux, N., Urbanczik, R., Senn, W., Gerstner, W.: Spike-based reinforcement learning in continuous state and action space: when policy gradient methods fail. PLoS Comput. Biol. **5**(12), e1000586 (2009)

A Robust and Efficient Cooler Design Inspired by Leaf Venation

Houpu Yao[(✉)], Rui Dai, and Hamidreza Marvi

Arizona State University, Tempe, AZ 85281, USA
hyao23@asu.edu

Abstract. After years of evolution and natural selection, leaf venation yields to a complicated pattern to achieve better transfer efficiency
together with higher structure robustness. In this paper, we use the
design of a cooler as an example to explore the benefits of using such
venation pattern. We first utilize a bio-inspired venation generation algorithm called space colonization to generate the venation patterns, which
is used as the topology of a cooler system. Numerical simulations show
that, the venation-inspired design is 10% more efficient than typical
cooler in heat conduction, while is about twice more robust under physical damage. These results demonstrate that plants arrange their venation
in a very efficient strategy, which can be a very promising source design
for both efficiency and robustness considerations.

Keywords: Bio-inspired · Leaf venation · Cooler design · Robustness

1 Introduction

The structure of leaf venation (as shown in Fig. 1a) is very complicated and has
evolved over many years [1]. Several different explanations were given by biologist
for the complexity of venation pattern: (1) for better efficiency in transporting
water and nutrients [2–4]. The core function of the veins is fluid transportation
to nourish cells, thus it is conceivable that it will tend to have high transportation efficiency. (2) supporting for the leaf weight [5–7]. It has been shown that
venation can significantly increase the mechanical strength and stiffness to serve
as mechanical reinforcement [5]. (3) providing redundancy [8,9]. Natural leaves
are subject to all kinds of damage from insects (as shown in Fig. 1b for example),
herbivore, hail and even windstorm.

Since venation has such interesting properties, researchers have started investigating the possibility to generate design configurations inspired by leaf venation patterns. For example, the branching pattern of venation has inspired people to design fuel cells [10,11], micro flow field [12], and thermal functional
materials [13]. All of these venation inspired designs have shown improved efficiency over standard designs. However, the potential of venation-like pattern in
achieving both high transport and high robustness to damage still hasn't been
explored yet.

© Springer Nature Switzerland AG 2019
U. Martinez-Hernandez et al. (Eds.): Living Machines 2019, LNAI 11556, pp. 287–294, 2019.
https://doi.org/10.1007/978-3-030-24741-6_25

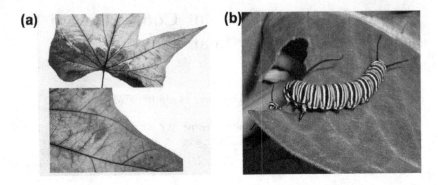

Fig. 1. Left: photograph leaf venation. Right: leaf under insect damage.

In this work, we investigate the efficiency and robustness of venation inspired design under the context of designing a cooler system based on numerical simulations. The venation structure is generated from a bio-inspired space colonization algorithm. Compared with the traditional cooler designs, the computational results corroborate that the proposed venation-inspired design can achieve a higher transportation capacity as well as processing extraordinary robustness under damage.

2   Bio-Inspired Venation Generation

In this section, we briefly review a bio-inspired algorithm called space colonization to generate the venation pattern. This generated pattern will be used to build used a cooler system in the later experiment to study both the transportation efficiency and robustness of venation based design.

The main idea of space colonization is inspired by the growth of leaves. From the biological perspective, a leaf will produce auxin (a kind of hormone) to stimulate the growth of venation, and venation will grow towards the direction with as many auxin sources as possible [14]. Once the venation is getting closer enough to an auxin source, the auxin will be depleted by the venation cells. The size of the leaf will get larger based on the span of venation, and more auxin sources will be released to further stimulate the growth of venation. This process can iterate over and over.

Space colonization is an iterative generation algorithm build on the previous described biological process. A very good illustration of this algorithm is adopted from [15] and shown in Fig. 2. The execution of the algorithm can be explained step by step as below:

- (a) Before the iteration starts, a node will be set as the beginning of venation, from where the rest of the vein (white dots) will be generated. Several auxin sources (blue dots) will be randomly initialized in the region as well.
- (b) Assign each auxin sources to different venation nodes based on the distance, as shown by the red connection.

- (c) Compute the directions for each venation node based on their associated auxin sources.
- (d) Average the directions on each venation node. Grow each venation node towards these directions.
- (e) Add newly grown venation nodes to the current venation.
- (f) Verify if the previous auxin is too close to the current venation, in other words, if it is inside the "kill distance".
- (g) Remove the auxin source if it is too close to the current venation.
- (h) Grow the size of the region of interest.
- (i) Randomly place more auxin sources in the enlarged region.
- (j) Remove the auxin sources that are close to the auxin sources in step (h).
- (k) Go back to step (b) and repeat the process.

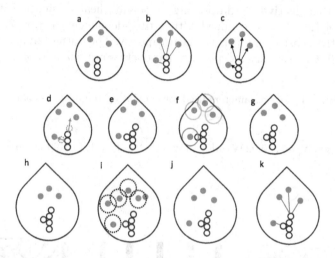

Fig. 2. Illustration of the space colonization algorithm for simulating venation growth. Figure adapted from [15]. (Color figure online)

The variables in this algorithm including the number of auxins, the kill distance, and the position of the auxin will all influence the final venation pattern. For more details on the algorithm, we encourage the readers to refer to [15].

3   Venation-Inspired Cooler Design and Analysis

In this section, a two dimensional (2D) heat conduction problem is used to demonstrate the performance of venation inspired design. The problem and configuration are defined in the first subsection, then the efficiency and robustness of venation-inspired design are investigated by the following two subsections, respectively.

3.1   Problem Setting and Design Configuration

Consider designing a cooler for the two-dimensional isotropic thermal problem in Fig. 3a. We have a uniform heat source distributed in Ω, there is zero heat conduction on Σ_N (Neumann boundary), and the temperature is fixed at zero degrees at Σ_D (Dirichlet boundary). We wish to design a cooler to cooler down the region Ω by transmitting the temperature through Σ_D.

The governing equation for the system can be written as:

$$\nabla \cdot (\kappa \nabla T) + \dot{q} = 0 \text{ on } \Omega \tag{1}$$

$$T = 0 \text{ on } \Sigma_D \tag{2}$$

$$(\kappa \nabla T) \cdot \mathbf{n} = 0 \text{ on } \Sigma_N \tag{3}$$

where T is the temperature field on region Ω, $\dot{q}$ is a heat source and κ is the material thermal conductivity. Additionally, in solving heat dissipation, the right-hand side of Eq. (1) is exchanged with a time-dependent energy term $\rho c_p \frac{\partial T}{\partial t}$, where ρ is the density and c_p is the heat capacity. The initial temperature at Ω is set at $300\,^{\circ}$C. Other related physical parameters are set in Table 1.

Table 1. The parameters used for simulating the heat dissipation

κ_1	κ_2	$\dot{q}$	c_p	ρ
$300\,\text{W/mK}$	$0.02\,\text{W/mK}$	$10\,\text{W/m}^2$	$233\,\text{J/kg.K}$	$10490\,\text{kg/m}^3$

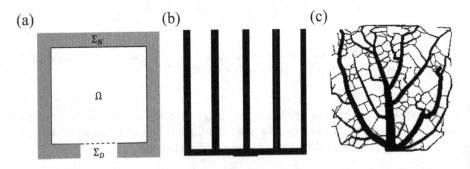

(a)   (b)   (c)

Fig. 3. (a): thermal conduction problem setting; (b): traditional conductor configuration; (c): venation-inspired conductor configuration. The coverage of conductive material for traditional and venation-inspired design is 30.7% and 30.3%, respectively.

Our objective is to reliably transfer heat from Ω through Σ_D as fast as possible. As shown in Fig. 3b and c, we tested these two different cooler configurations in the following experiments. The first configurations is a traditional design with multiple fingers, and the second one is a venation inspired design generated from the space colonization algorithm introduced in Sect. 2. We use 20 auxin sources and set kill distance to 5 to generate the venation topology. In both traditional and venation-inspired configurations, there are about 30% of the region covered by the thermal conductive material, which is marked as black. And 22.5% of one side is in contact with the external cooler, which is assumed to be at a constant temperature. The heat conductivity of the conductive material κ_1 is set to be much higher than the non-conductive base material κ_2, so that the heat conduction through venation will dominate the conduction.

3.2 Analysis of the Conductivity Efficiency

We use implicit finite difference solver to solve the heat diffusion equation Eq. 1 to obtain the temperature and heat flux distribution over the solution domain. To qualitatively compare the efficiency of different cooling configurations, we monitor the total heat flux passing through Σ_D over time. This total heat flux E can be numerically computed by summing over the heat flux over time steps:

$$E(\phi, t) = \sum_{t=0}^{t_n} q_t(\phi, x), \quad x \in \Sigma_D \tag{4}$$

where ϕ is the structure topology, and t_n is set to 800 s in the experiment. We also record the history of E over t and visualize it in Fig. 4. There is a small period at the very start (starting from initial to about 80 s) that heat conduction efficiency of traditional cooler is slightly higher resulting from more high heat conduction material around the boundary Σ_D and steady state has not reached yet. However, it can be seen that venation inspired cooler design is still able to conduct more thermal energy outside of the domain Ω for most of the time. Additionally, by the end of 800 s, the total energy conducted using venation structure is 10% higher than the traditional cooler design.

3.3 Analysis of the Structure Robustness

To investigate the robustness of the cooler design under damage, we will need to make following definitions and assumptions: We first define the robustness as how much influence an external loading will have on the performance of the cooling systems. Furthermore, following three assumptions will be made to simplify this problem:

- For a given patch of the cooler with size d, its stiffness will be proportional to the volume fraction ratio r of the venation structure.
- The patch under loading will get damaged if the deformation exceeds a certain threshold.
- If a patch is damaged, all conductive material κ_1 in this region will turn into non-conductive base material κ_2.

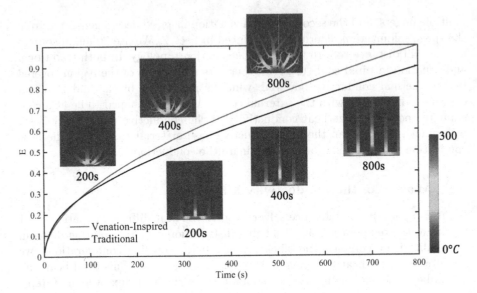

Fig. 4. Total heat conducted history. The result is normalized to be bounded in $(0, 1)$. The heatmaps above and below the curve are the temperature distribution for venation inspired cooler and traditional cooler, respectively. Captions below the heatmaps are the time stamp the heatmap is captured.

The first assumption is made reasonable because the venation structures tend to have a stronger mechanical property. Thus the more venation material exists in a patch, the harder to get this patch damaged. Based on the second assumption, we can define the "damage probability" p as the probability that a given region is likely to malfunction under a given loading magnitude. Combine these two assumptions together, we can model the relationship between p and the volume fraction ratio with a negative step function, as shown in Fig. 5a. In this experiment, we randomly pick a damaging threshold at $r = 0.4$ (we have $r \approx 0.3$ on the whole structure).

We propose to use the expectance of the drop rate of the total heat conduction E after damage as the metric to measure the robustness of a configuration ϕ. We define the expectance as ϵ, which is a function of the patch size d:

$$\epsilon(d) = \mathbb{E}_{x \in \Omega}\big(1 - E_{t_n}(\phi'(x, d))/E_{t_n}(\phi)\big) \tag{5}$$

where ϕ is the original topology, $\phi'(x, d)$ is the topology after a patch of loading with patch size d is applied at location x. As before, we still use $t_n = 800$.

We track ϵ under different damage extend d for traditional and venation-inspired cooler. The comparison is plotted in Fig. 5b with d ranging from 15% to 35% of the total region size. It can be seen that the venation-inspired design is constantly almost twice more robust than the traditional structure. This shows that plants have learned to distribute the volume of venation wisely over the leaf to achieve the maximum reliability. Firstly, it can be seen that there is a roughly linear (or piece-wise linear) relationship between d and ϵ. Furthermore, for the traditional cooler design, there exists a jump in ϵ when $d = 0.25$. This is due to the fact that the distance between the two fingers is equal to 0.25. If we reached that damage level, the transmission effect will be severely influenced. On the other hand, the venation-inspired design has constantly better performance.

In biology, it is observed that the first order veins are more influential to the conduction speed. In the meantime, first order venation will also have a stronger mechanical property that makes it unlikely to get easily damaged. Besides, there are lots of interconnections in the venation pattern and alternative heat conduction path exists if the original one is damages. This interconnection gives extra redundancy to the cooler design.

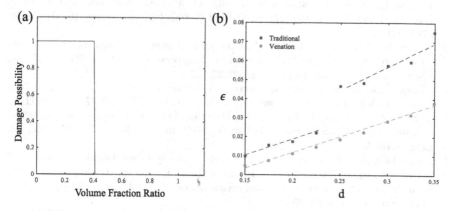

Fig. 5. (a): Illustration of the damage probability w.r.t. the volume fraction ratio. (b): Comparison of robustness under external loading.

4 Conclusions and Future Work

The thermal transportation efficiency and robustness of venation structure are explored in this paper. A bio-inspired venation generation algorithm is used to obtain the venation pattern for the conductive cooler model. An improvement of 10% in heat conduction is obtained with our venation-inspired design. What's more, the impair of the heat conduction ability due to damage in the traditional design was twice that of venation-inspired design.

Further improvements can be made in several aspects. First, a higher resolution of venation structure can be generated and fed to the numerical model. A higher level of the venation hierarchy might also improve the results. Second, different parameters in the venation generation algorithm can be optimized to obtain the most efficient network configuration. A symmetric pattern can be added to the algorithm as a constraint as well. Furthermore, designing 3D cooling systems based on venation and utilizing 3D printing techniques to fabricate these venation patterns would also be another direction worth exploring.

Acknowledgement. The authors would like to thank Kexin Jiao, Yuehui Li, Karanjodh Singh for the discussion and suggestions, and Yuexuan Yang for providing the venation photograph.

References

1. Roth-Nebelsick, A., Uhl, D., Mosbrugger, V., Kerp, H.: Evolution and function of leaf venation architecture: a review. Ann. Bot. **87**(5), 553–566 (2001). https://doi.org/10.1006/anbo.2001.1391
2. Buckley, T.N., John, G.P., Scoffoni, C., Sack, L.: How does leaf anatomy influence water transport outside the xylem? Plant Physiol. **168**(4), 1616–1635 (2015). https://doi.org/10.1104/pp.15.00731
3. Noblin, X., Mahadevan, L., Coomaraswamy, I.A., Weitz, D.A., Holbrook, N.M., Zwieniecki, M.A.: Optimal vein density in artificial and real leaves. Proc. Nat. Acad. Sci. U.S.A. **105**(27), 9140–9144 (2008). https://doi.org/10.1073/pnas.0709194105
4. Kawai, K., Okada, N.: How are leaf mechanical properties and water-use traits coordinated by vein traits? A case study in Fagaceae. Funct. Ecol. **30**(4), 527–536 (2016). https://doi.org/10.1111/1365-2435.12526
5. Niklas, K.J.: A mechanical perspective on foliage leaf form and function. New Phytol. **143**(1), 19–31 (1999). https://doi.org/10.1046/j.1469-8137.1999.00441.x
6. Laguna, M.F., Bohn, S., Jagla, E.A.: The role of elastic stresses on leaf venation morphogenesis. PLoS Comput. Biol. **4**(4) (2008). https://doi.org/10.1371/journal.pcbi.1000055
7. Jakubska-Busse, A., Janowicz, M., Ochnio, L., Jackowska-Zduniak, B.: Shapes of leaves with parallel venation. Modelling of the Epipactis sp. (Orchidaceae) leaves with the help of a system of coupled elastic beams. PeerJ **4**, e2165 (2016). https://doi.org/10.7717/peerj.2165
8. Price, C.A., Weitz, J.S.: Costs and benefits of reticulate leaf venation. BMC Plant Biol. **14**(1), 234 (2014). https://doi.org/10.1186/s12870-014-0234-2
9. Sack, L., Dietrich, E.M., Streeter, C.M., Sánchez-Gómez, D., Holbrook, N.M.: Leaf palmate venation and vascular redundancy confer tolerance of hydraulic disruption. Proc. Nat. Acad. Sci. U.S.A. **105**(5), 1567–1572 (2008). https://doi.org/10.1073/pnas.0709333105
10. Guo, N., Leu, M.C., Koylu, U.O.: Bio-inspired flow field designs for polymer electrolyte membrane fuel cells. Int. J. Hydrogen Energy **39**(36), 21185–21195 (2014). https://doi.org/10.1016/j.ijhydene.2014.10.069
11. Arvay, A., French, J., Wang, J.C., Peng, X.H., Kannan, A.M.: Nature inspired flow field designs for proton exchange membrane fuel cell. Int. J. Hydrogen Energy **38**(9), 3717–3726 (2013). https://doi.org/10.1016/j.ijhydene.2012.12.149
12. Barber, R.W., Emerson, D.R.: Optimal design of microfluidic networks using biologically inspired principles. Microfluid. Nanofluid. **4**(3), 179–191 (2008). https://doi.org/10.1007/s10404-007-0163-6
13. Alston, M.E., Barber, R.: Leaf venation, as a resistor, to optimize a switchable IR absorber. Sci. Rep. **6**, 31611 (2016). https://doi.org/10.1038/srep31611
14. Sawchuk, M.G., Edgar, A., Scarpella, E.: Patterning of leaf vein networks by convergent auxin transport pathways. PLoS Genet. **9**(2) (2013). https://doi.org/10.1371/journal.pgen.1003294
15. Runions, A., Fuhrer, M., Lane, B., Federl, P., Rolland-Lagan, A.-G., Prusinkiewicz, P.: Modeling and visualization of leaf venation patterns. ACM Trans. Graph. **24**(3), 702 (2005). https://doi.org/10.1145/1073204.1073251

Bayesian Optimization of a Quadruped Robot During 3-Dimensional Locomotion

Jiahui Zhu[1]([✉]), Shuting Li[1,2], Zhuoli Wang[1], and Andre Rosendo[1]

[1] Living Machines Lab, School of Information Science and Technology,
ShanghaiTech University, Shanghai, China
{zhujh1,wangzhl,arosendo}@shanghaitech.edu.cn
[2] College of Electronics and Information Engineering,
Sichuan University, Chengdu, Sichuan, China
lishuting.cd@gmail.com
http://lima.sist.shanghaitech.edu.cn/

Abstract. Parametric search for gait controllers is a key challenge in quadruped locomotion. Several optimization methods can be adopted to find the optimal solution by regarding it as an optimization problem. Here we adopt Bayesian optimization (BO), a global optimization method that is suitable for unknown objective functions particularly when it is hard to evaluate, which is the common case of real robot experiments. We demonstrate this process on a quadruped robot capable of 3-dimensional locomotion, and our goal is to make it move forward as far as possible. While initially probing the parametric landscape, Random Search shows that in a 10-dimensional search space of over a million combinations, only 30% of them contribute to moving forward, merely 2% results in our robot walking longer than 2 m, and none of these parameters leads to more than 3 m distance. In face of such difficult landscape BO finds near-optimal parameters after 22 iterations, and walks a range of 3 m in over 40% of its iterations. Our findings illustrate that BO can efficiently search control parameters in a 3-dimensional locomotion case, and the development of controllers for legged robots, very often plagued with manual tuning of parameters, could profit from this.

Keywords: Gait optimization · Quadruped locomotion ·
3-dimensional locomotion

1 Introduction

Legged robots overcome several limitations of traditional wheeled robots [1]. From all forms of legged robots, quadruped robots outperform one-legged and bipedal robots in stability and robustness, and possess higher mobility and versatility in walking, running, and jumping, than hexapod and octopod due to bionic reasons. Despite many advances in design and control of four-legged robots [2], the walking gait of quadruped locomotion is still fundamental yet challenging.

© Springer Nature Switzerland AG 2019
U. Martinez-Hernandez et al. (Eds.): Living Machines 2019, LNAI 11556, pp. 295–306, 2019.
https://doi.org/10.1007/978-3-030-24741-6_26

Some fitting controllers for quadruped robots have already been designed [3], but the real problem then is the parameter set-up. The performance of such controller parameters largely depends on the surrounding environment, which is unpredictable and noisy. In that case, parametric search becomes a dynamic problem and often requires artificial interactions. At the beginning, gait optimization often transfers to a trial-and-error algorithm [4], yet robots may break easily if obtained parameters perform badly. Consequently, manual tuning of parameters relies on expertise in engineering. Moreover, a variation in walking surface (e.g., angle, friction, and hardness), a change in optimization target (e.g., velocity, energy efficiency, and stability), can result in a new search of parameters. In conclusion, a quickly adaptable automatic search is in urgent need.

By considering the search for gait parameters as an optimization problem, multiple optimization techniques can be applied to find the local or global extreme. Some of the recent approaches, particularly in robotics, mainly include: gradient descent [5], genetic algorithms [6–8], and Bayesian optimization [9–13], where the first two methods each have major drawbacks. While the gradient descent method requires a known objective function as well as access to its derivatives, which are both hard to obtain in robotics experiments, genetic algorithms is time-consuming or even unfeasible when using fragile robots, requiring many generations to converge [6].

BO is a novel strategy to black-box global optimization, especially when the objective function is expensive to evaluate [14]. It uses Gaussian Processes to approximate the (true) objective function and an acquisition function to promote a balance between exploitation and exploration in the selection of the next iteration [9]. In [10,11], and [12] BO is applied in a 2-dimensional bipedal locomotion problem, where [10] is used in simulations and [11,12] being applied to a real bipedal robot. In [13] the authors show that a hexapod robot could use BO to adapt their controllers to damage.

In this article we implement BO on an open-loop quadruped robot with 3-dimensional locomotion to effectively find a near-optimal set of parameters for the controller, which is selected from a search space of 1048576 ($\approx 10^6$) combinations. We present the Methods used in this work at Sect. 2, including Gaussian Processes, Bayesian optimization, Random Search, hardware set-up, and parameter configuration. In Sect. 3, we demonstrate experimental results with several figures and further discussion, while we conclude our work in the last section.

2   Method

2.1   Gait Optimization Methods

The work of [11] suggests that the parametric search of a controller can be viewed as an optimization problem, which can be formulated as follows:

$$\max_{x \in \mathbb{R}^d} f(x) \tag{1}$$

In the realm of robotics, $f(\cdot)$ is the objective function that encodes measurement standard and in our work, it is the vertical displacement between initial and end position. Meanwhile, x are the parameters that need to be tuned.

Gaussian Processes. The fundamental work of Gaussian processes (GPs) is introduced in [15]. A Gaussian process can be defined as a probabilistic nonlinear regression and provide a method for modeling probability distributions over functions, f with mean function, m and covariance function, k:

$$f(\cdot) \sim \mathcal{GP}(m(\cdot), k(\cdot, \cdot)) \tag{2}$$

Generally speaking, any real-valued function $m(\cdot)$ can be accepted, but it is more demanding for covariance function $k(\cdot, \cdot)$, where the kernel matrix is given by (a set of elements x_1, x_2, ..., $x_m \in \chi$):

$$K = \begin{bmatrix} k(x_1, x_1) & \cdots & k(x_1, x_n) \\ \vdots & \ddots & \vdots \\ k(x_n, x_1) & \cdots & k(x_n, x_n) \end{bmatrix}$$

Kernel Functions. Here we introduce the *Matérn* kernel [15], adopted in this work and represented by:

$$k_{Matern}(d) = \sigma_p^2 \frac{2^{1-v}}{\Gamma(\nu)} \frac{\sqrt{2\nu d}^v}{l} K_\nu \frac{\sqrt{2\nu d}}{l} \tag{3}$$

where d is the Euclidean distance between two inputs, $\Gamma(\nu)$ and K_ν denotes the Gamma function and the Bessel function of order ν, and l shows the characteristic length-scale. It also takes noise into account, which is denoted by σ_p^2. *Matérn* kernel has higher flexibility for both smooth and sharp areas [16].

Gaussian Process Regression. Gaussian Processes provide us a powerful tool to parameterize probability distributions over functions [15]. Consider how GPs are used in regression. Suppose that we have drawn our data, both the training and test sets, from a zero-mean prior Gaussian distribution,

$$f(\cdot) \sim \mathcal{GP}(0, k(\cdot, \cdot)) \tag{4}$$

and decompose K as: $\begin{bmatrix} K & K_* \\ K_*^T & K_{**} \end{bmatrix}$, where star (*) marks for training sets, then the conditional distribution of the latent function $f(\cdot)$ can be written as:

$$y_* | ((x_1, y_1), ..., (x_n, y_n), x_*) \sim \mathcal{N}(K_*^T K^{-1} y, K_{**} - K_*^T K^{-1} K_*) \tag{5}$$

Particularly, if y_* is the observation of $f(x_*)$ with noise that is in zero-mean, i.i.d. Gaussian, i.e., $y_* = f(x_*) + \epsilon$, where $\epsilon \sim \mathcal{N}(0, \sigma^2)$, then we can rewrite the distribution as:

$$y_* | ((x_1, y_1), ..., (x_n, y_n), x_*)$$
$$\sim \mathcal{N}(K_*^T (K + \sigma^2 I)^{-1} y, K_{**} + \sigma^2 I - K_*^T (K + \sigma^2 I)^{-1} K^*) \tag{6}$$

Bayesian Optimization. Bayesian optimization uses Gaussian processes as the approximation of the unknown objective function. Nonetheless, GPs are gradually updated since BO samples the next selected point in each iteration.

Acquisition Functions. Bayesian optimization introduces an acquisition function to decide the next sample point. The simplest way of representing acquisition function $u(\cdot)$ is:

$$u(x) = \mu(x) + m\sigma(x) \tag{7}$$

where m is the weight to balance exploration and exploitation. When m is assigned to a high value, the acquisition function is more aggressive towards where variance is high; on the contrary, the acquisition function will prefer to choose the location where mean is high.

We choose the probability of improvement (PI) with a trade-off parameter ξ as the acquisition function in our work. PI function is defined as:

$$PI(x) = \phi(\frac{\mu(x) - y_{max} - \xi}{\sigma(x)}) \tag{8}$$

The following algorithm is the pseudo code of how we adopted Bayesian Optimization with slight modifications:

Algorithm 1. Bayesian Optimization

1: **if** $t = 1, 2$ **then**
2:     Add the upper bound and the lower bound of parameters into GPs as prior knowledge
3: **end if**
4: **for** $t = 3, 4, \cdots, 50$ **do**
5:     Optimize the acquisition function: $\mathbf{x}_t = \mathbf{x}_* = \max_{\mathbf{x}} PI(\mathbf{x})$ to find $\mathbf{x}_*$.
6:     Sample the objective function: $y_t = y_* = f(\mathbf{x}_*) + \varepsilon$.
7:     Expand the data $\mathcal{D}_{1:t} = \{\mathcal{D}_{1:t-1}, (\mathbf{x}_t, \mathbf{y}_t)\}$ and get GPs updated.
8: **end for**

Random Search. For a better understanding of the problem that we are aiming to optimize we decided to perform a Random Search (RS) with 50 iterations. A full understanding of this 10 dimensional parametric landscape is not a possibility from a real-world perspective, and RS is useful in this aspect. A comparison between RS and BO would be unfruitful, and this is not the purpose of this work. We use function $randi()$ in Matlab and the seed of the random function is set to be associated with the corresponding time, in order to prevent duplicates of generated sets of parameters.

2.2 Experimental Set-Up

The experiment was conducted at a marked arena of $4000 \times 2000\,\mathrm{mm}$ (shown in Fig. 4) and we used an oscillator as the controller for the quadruped robot. After referring to the code in the article [16], we wrote the RS and BO code in Matlab whose version was Matlab 2016b. A DELL OptiPlex 7060 series desktop was used with i7-8700 processor, 12 processor threads and 32 GB internal memory.

Experiments were carried out using RS and Bayesian optimization methods, respectively. We used the evaluation criteria for the vertical distance y (the vertical component of the initial and end positions' displacement) that the robot walked forward within 10 s, and if it went backward, the distance y was negative. A total of 50 iterations were performed for each method. In order to reduce the measurement error, four experiments were implemented for each iteration, and the average of four experiments was taken as the input of each iteration to optimize the parameters.

Oscillators. In the locomotion of animals, the oscillations of the joint angles produced by the muscular activity can have different wave forms which are usually smooth and brutal transitions are uncommon [17]. In order to facilitate practical application, it is necessary to simplify the modeling of locomotion. One way is to approximate the robot's joint angles to sinusoidal variations. According to the gait, these sine waves must have the same frequency but they can differ in phases and amplitude. In other words, a robot's motor activation can be controlled by this simple equation:

$$x(t) = x_0 + A sin(t/\tau + \varphi) \qquad (9)$$

where $x(t)$ is the current servomotor state of the robot at time t, x_o is the midpoint of the oscillations for each joint, A is the amplitude of the oscillations, τ is the time constant that determines the oscillation's frequency, and φ is the oscillation phase.

Robotic Platform. The quadruped robot *BayesAnt* mainly consists of two parts and its total size is $350 \times 350 \times 300$ mm (shown in Fig. 1). The body part, printed by onyx and carbon fiber materials, has a protective rope to prevent it from falling during walking. As for the moving parts, an Arduino nano with an Adafruit 16-Channel PWM/Servo Driver is used for controlling eight servomotors, and each leg, made of carbon fiber tubes, has two servomotors. Hip's servomotors are responsible for *BayesAnt*'s movement in the horizontal plane, and knee's servomotors are responsible for its movement in the vertical plane. Therefore, *BayesAnt* can move freely within the 3-dimensional space where its design size is limited.

Based on the real quadrupeds, *BayesAnt*'s four legs were constrained in the whole experiment, e.g., an animal's hip cannot rotate 360°. If quadruped robot *BayesAnt* walk normally, it is obvious that the knee joints should oscillate in a region below the body. On the other hand, each of the four hip joints moves in the same plane. In order to prevent *BayesAnt*'s hips from interfering with each other while walking, each hip accounts for a quarter of a circle (360°), which is 90°.

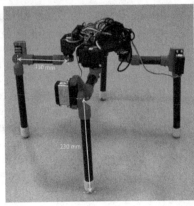

Fig. 1. The general morphology of our quadruped robot *BayesAnt* with a front view on the left and a top view on the right. The left figure shows that the hip limb's length is 130 mm and the knee limb's length is 230 mm. Due to the symmetrical design, only one of their hip limbs and knee limbs is labeled. Similarly, the right figure shows the body's size is 150 × 150 mm, so the overall size is 350 × 350 × 300 mm.

2.3   Parameter Configuration

Our quadruped robot *BayesAnt* has eight servomotors and each servomotor is controlled by an oscillator. Thus, each joint has a sinusoidal equation as shown before. A frequency of 1 Hz ($\tau = 1/(2\pi)$) is chosen as baseline for all joints. This is because it corresponds to the pace of an ordinary animal and it is slow enough for quadruped robot's servomotors to go once 180° back and forth [17]. In that case, it still has three free parameters of the oscillation and in total, there are 24-dimensional parameters.

Considering that each parameter requires a certain range, even for discrete intervals, the search space will be extremely large. For example, if there are four choices for each parameter, then the observation space is about 28 trillion (4^{24}). We decide to do a symmetrical parameter configuration which should be 12-dimensional parameters, but the parameter space is still too large. We turn the four midpoint parameters x_o of four legs' proximal and distal links into two parameters x_i, x_j (see Table 1), reducing our problem to 10-dimensional parameters. Table 1 gives a summary of the corresponding ranges or fixed values that were used. Even so, our search space is still about one million (4^{10}).

For the oscillation central angle, as discussed before, hip's servomotors are responsible for *BayesAnt*'s horizontal movement, and knee's servomotors are responsible for its vertical movement, so we took the midpoint angle of hip and knee as 2-dimensional parameters. For the oscillation amplitude, 4-dimensional parameters are set because of the symmetry of *BayesAnt*'s morphology. And as for the oscillation phase, analogous to the tetrapod's locomotion, 2-dimensional parameters are bilaterally symmetric to the hip and 2-dimensional parameters are diagonally symmetric to the knee.

Table 1. Gait parameters, left(L), right(R), forelimb(F), hindlimb(H).

Parameter		Type	Values[a]	Controls
LF/LH/RH/RF Hip_ang	$x_i(i = 1, 2, 3, 4)$	Free	[255 295 305 345]	Oscillation midpoint
LF/LH/RH/RF Knee_ang	$x_j(j = 5, 6, 7, 8)$		[215 255 295 305]	
LF/RF Hip_amp	$A_i(i = 1, 4)$	Free	[50 55 60 65]	Oscillation amplitude
LH/RH Hip_amp	$A_j(j = 2, 3)$		[60 65 70 75]	
LF/RF Knee_amp	$A_m(m = 5, 8)$		[25 30 35 40]	
LH/RH Knee_amp	$A_n(n = 6, 7)$		[20 25 30 35]	
LF/RF Hip_pha	$\varphi_i(i = 1, 4)$	Free	[−90 0 90 180]	Oscillation phase
LH/RH Hip_pha	$\varphi_j(j = 2, 3)$		[−90 0 90 180]	
LF/RH Knee_pha	$\varphi_m(m = 5, 7)$		[−90 0 90 180]	
LH/RF Knee_pha	$\varphi_n(n = 6, 8)$		[−90 0 90 180]	
Frequency	τ	Fixed	$1/(2\pi)$	Oscillation period

[a] The column described as "Values" is the range of parameters used in our code to control our quadruped robot *BayesAnt*. Since those parameters are used to change the values of Pulse-Width Modulation (PWM) which control the servomotors, they are not the exact angle at which the robot's legs move. For LF knee, LH knee, RH knee, and RF knee, when the PWM value is 300, the part below the knee of *BayesAnt* is 90° to *BayesAnt*'s body. As the PWM values increase, the parts below *BayesAnt*'s knees bend inward. For LF hip, LH hip, RH hip, RF hip, the angles between four legs and body are 45°, while the PWM values are 300. As the PWM values increase, LF hip and LH hip legs move forward. As the PWM values decrease, RH hip and RF hip legs move forward. The *Adafruit_PWMServoDriver* library sets 90 as PWM values to make servomotor turn to 0° and 540 PWM values to make servomotor turn to 270°. We cannot tell the accurate formula for the two parameters, PWM value and the degree change of servomotor, but we can tell that the degree of servomotor increase as the PWM value increase.

3 Results and Discussion

We performed two experiments, one using a RS and the second using BO to select the optimal parameters in 50 iterations. In order to show the parameter changes more clearly, the parameter values are replaced by different colors in Figs. 2 and 3, and the color bar is referred on the right.

We start by exploring the search landscape with RS as we cannot find an analytic solution for real-world 3-dimensional locomotion, so as to have a general understanding of the quality of space combinations. It is important to emphasise that a comparison between BO and RS is not the scope of this paper, as it would be an unfair comparison, and in this sense RS is solely being used to gauge how difficult this problem is. We show the results of 50 random trials in Fig. 2. In

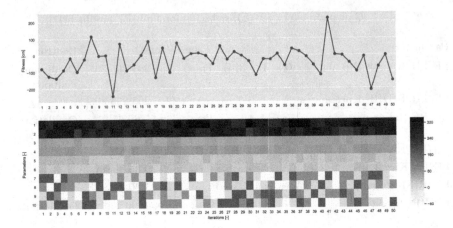

Fig. 2. The upper figure shows that the results of RS oscillate at 0, and negative values mean that our robot moves backward instead of moving forward. The lower figure illustrates how parameters change during each iteration with a heat-map. It can be seen that the color varies widely as every new trial, indicating that RS is mainly an exploratory tool.

only 30% of trials the robot could move forward, in 4% of all trials it passed the one meter mark, and in only one of those trials (trial 42) it could pass the two meter mark. In some trials the robot falls on the floor, where it is assigned zero as their distance. As expected, locomotion is a difficult problem to be optimized, specially from a model-free perspective.

The experimental results of the BO are depicted in Fig. 3, and instead of using random initial parameters we opted for trying the minimum ([255, 215, 50, 60, 25, 20, −90, −90, −90, −90]) and maximum ([345, 305, 65, 75, 40, 35, 180, 180, 180, 180]) parameter combinations, and BO only starts inferring in the third iteration. The reason for this choice is to avoid a "lucky" initial seed bootstrapping good results. Their fitness is −0.04 m and −0.15 m. The iteration 23 represents the optimal parameter combination in 50 iterations, while Bayesian optimization has a maximum distance of 3.61 m at iteration 23 (expressed by speed, it is about 0.36 m/s) with parameter combination [305, 215, 65, 70, 25, 35, −90, 90, 180, −90] and a minimum distance of −1.46 m at iteration 7 with parameter combination [305, 305, 60, 60, 30, 35, 0, 90, 90, 180].

We capture our quadruped robot *BayesAnt*'s gait under the optimal parameter combinations ([305, 215, 65, 70, 25, 35, −90, 0, 90, 180]), found with BO, with a low-speed continuous shooting, to show our experimental results clearer. The walking snapshots (shown in Fig. 4) have shown a forward maximum distance of 3.61 m in 10 s.

As the reader can see from Fig. 3, the gait parameters were initially explored until iteration 7, and then kept the oscillation phase unchanged for the exploitation. After a few trials, it returned to the exploration. Exploration and exploitation are repeatedly cross carried out, and in the end a exploitative behaviour is

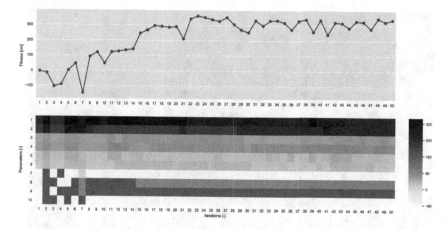

Fig. 3. The upper figure shows the result of Bayesian optimization. It suggests that only 6 trials result in moving backward, and the robot learns to walk further than 2 m after only 15 iterations. Although the method chooses a few missteps (i.e. 7th, 11th, and 21st), we can see that BO gradually improves and stabilizes the behavior. The lower figure illustrates how parameters change during each iteration with heat-map. It can be seen an alternation between exploration and exploitation through the color variation of the parameters after the 7th trial.

dominant due to the Probability of Improvement (PI) acquisition function. It uses a trade-off parameter ξ, so that it starts fairly high early in the optimization to drive exploration, and decreased toward zero as the algorithm continued (exploitation).

A few previous works also used BO on different walking robots, such as the Sony AIBO (Dimensions: $220 \times 130 \times 200$ mm) [9], the bipedal Spring Loaded Inverted Pendulum (SLIP) simulated model [10], the SLIP-based bipedal walker Fox [11], the ATRIAS bipedal robot (Dimensions: 0.9×0.9 m) [12], and the hexapod robot [13]. In [9], they use GPs with the most probable improvement and reach a maximum walking speed about 0.281 m/s. In [10], a bipedal SLIP model and BO are utilized to explore gaits with a step of 0.2 m/s. In [11], they apply GPs with Upper Confidence Bound and reach a maximum walking speed about 0.337 m/s, while ATRIAS obtains a target speed of 0.5 m/s by using BO with Determinants of Gaits (DoG) [12], and the undamaged hexapod robot's maximum speed is 0.32 m/s [13]. As for our quadruped robot *BayesAnt* (Dimensions: $350 \times 350 \times 300$ mm), it reaches a maximum speed of 0.361 m/s. As expected, robots with different dimensions will reach different optimal speeds.

3.1   2D vs 3D Locomotion

SLIP model and ATRIAS both are 2-dimensional locomotion. Especially, ATRIAS moves on a planar around a boom and calculates the Center of Mass (CoM) height at the start and end of each step which avoids the robot falling

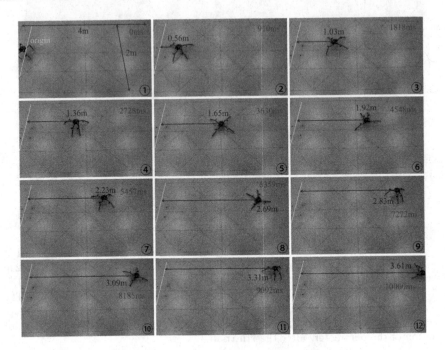

Fig. 4. Snapshots of *BayesAnt* walking on the marked arena within 10 s. We set the origin at the midpoint of the body to facilitate the measurement.

across steps. In our work, *BayesAnt* is open-loop without any sensor and CoM feedback. It is capable of 3-dimensional walking with dynamic locomotion and these properties make our robot easier to fall down than ATRIAS and SLIP. It shows our 10-dimensional parametric search problem during 3-dimensional loco-motion is a much tougher problem. Although the hexapod robot is 3-dimensional locomotion, the higher number of legs can guarantee enough foot contact with the floor to preclude the robot from rolling over.

3.2   Prior Models and Kernels

Different robots have different morphologies, and the presence of a computer simulation can accelerate the learning by creating a prior knowledge of how the gait should look like. Different kernel functions can equally affect the convergence speed: experiments with ATRIAS [12] and with the hexapod robot [13] show a faster BO convergence. Both works used simulations to search for thousands of gaits prior to the beginning of experiments, while the work from [12] used a DoG-based kernel with domain prior knowledge. In our experiments we do not use a prior knowledge, and next steps of our research will combine simulation with real-world to assess how much can be improved from this.

3.3 Iterations-Parameters Relationship

The number of iterations required usually increases with dimensions. In [12], the parameters of a 9-dimensional controller on ATRIAS are optimized and the robot successfully walks in 3 trials with 5 runs each trial, yet our quadruped robot reaches a maximum forward distance in 10-dimensional search space at iteration 23. As mentioned previously, A. 2-dimensional problems are easier than 3-dimensional locomotion and B. the presence of a prior knowledge helps the process.

4 Conclusion and Future Work

An automatic parametric search of the gait controller for real-world robot applications is a challenging task. After probing the search space with RS to see how difficult this problem is, we use Bayesian optimization on a quadruped robot which is capable of 3-dimensional locomotion. The results show that there are major advantages of BO, such as data-efficiency (requiring few iterations to reach optimum) and the consideration of noise during the optimization process. Our robot starts from zero knowledge about its morphology and after 23 iterations it reaches optimal behaviour. This methodology, if combined with controllers, can be used to quickly tune parameters after environmental/morphological changes.

Our future work will focus on the adaptation of BO during different degrees of morphological changes. For example, how BO converges after suffering damage, and how to quantify this damage to bootstrap the following learning procedure (as opposed to a new tabula rasa assumption). We are currently working on the usage of BO to investigate the effect of incremental morphological changes on the controller of a quadruped robot [18]. Our current BO model still has lots of room for improvement, such as different kernel functions, acquisition functions and ways to encode the parameter-motor relationship, and we aim to tackle these matters in the near future.

References

1. Poulakakis, I., Smith, J.A., Buehler, M.: Modeling and experiments of untethered quadrupedal running with a bounding gait: the Scout II robot. Int. J. Robot. Res. **24**(4), 239–256 (2005)
2. Seok, S., Wang, A., Chuah, M.Y., Otten, D., Lang, J., Kim, S.: Design principles for highly efficient quadrupeds and implementation on the MIT Cheetah robot. In: 2013 IEEE International Conference on Robotics and Automation, pp. 3307–3312. IEEE (2013)
3. Ijspeert, A.J.: Central pattern generators for locomotion control in animals and robots: a review. Neural Netw. **21**(4), 642–653 (2008)
4. Calandra, R., Seyfarth, A., Peters, J., Deisenroth, M.P.: Bayesian optimization for learning gaits under uncertainty. Ann. Math. Artif. Intell. **76**(1–2), 5–23 (2016)
5. Tedrake, R., Zhang, T.W., Sebastian Seung, H.: Learning to walk in 20 minutes. In: Proceedings of the Fourteenth Yale Workshop on Adaptive and Learning Systems, Beijing, vol. 95585, pp. 1939–1412 (2005)

6. Chernova, S., Veloso, M.: An evolutionary approach to gait learning for four-legged robots. In: 2004 IEEE/RSJ International Conference on Intelligent Robots and Systems (IROS) (IEEE Cat. No. 04CH37566), vol. 3, pp. 2562–2567. IEEE (2004)

7. Seo, K., Hyun, S., Goodman, E.D.: Genetic programming-based automatic gait generation in joint space for a quadruped robot. Adv. Robot. **24**(15), 2199–2214 (2010)

8. Oliveira, M., Santos, C., Costa, L., Ferreira, M.: Quadruped robot locomotion using a global optimization stochastic algorithm, vol. 1389, pp. 500–503 (2011)

9. Lizotte, D.J., Wang, T., Bowling, M.H., Schuurmans, D.: Automatic gait optimization with Gaussian process regression. In: IJCAI, vol. 7, pp. 944–949 (2007)

10. Saar, K.A., Rosendo, A., Llda, F.: Bayesian optimization of gaits on a bipedal slip model. In: 2017 IEEE International Conference on Robotics and Biomimetics (ROBIO), pp. 1812–1817. IEEE (2017)

11. Calandra, R., Seyfarth, A., Peters, J., Deisenroth, M.P.: An experimental comparison of Bayesian optimization for bipedal locomotion, pp. 1951–1958 (2014)

12. Rai, A., Antonova, R., Song, S., Martin, W., Geyer, H., Atkeson, C.: Bayesian optimization using domain knowledge on the ATRIAS biped. In: 2018 IEEE International Conference on Robotics and Automation (ICRA), pp. 1771–1778. IEEE (2018)

13. Cully, A., Clune, J., Tarapore, D., Mouret, J.-B.: Robots that can adapt like animals. Nature **521**(7553), 503 (2015)

14. Brochu, E., Cora, V.M., De Freitas, N.: A tutorial on Bayesian optimization of expensive cost functions, with application to active user modeling and hierarchical reinforcement learning. arXiv preprint arXiv:1012.2599 (2010)

15. Rasmussen, C.E.: Gaussian processes in machine learning. In: Bousquet, O., von Luxburg, U., Rätsch, G. (eds.) ML -2003. LNCS (LNAI), vol. 3176, pp. 63–71. Springer, Heidelberg (2004). https://doi.org/10.1007/978-3-540-28650-9_4

16. Rosendo, A., Von Atzigen, M., Iida, F.: The trade-off between morphology and control in the co-optimized design of robots. PLoS ONE **12**(10), e0186107 (2017)

17. Bourquin, Y., Ijspeert, A.J., Harvey, I.: Self-organization of locomotion in modular robots. Unpublished Diploma Thesis (2004). http://birg.epfl.ch/page53073.html

18. Zhu, J., Li, S., Wang, Z., Rosendo, A.: Influences of incremental mechanical damage on the Bayesian optimization of a quadruped robot. In: 2019 IEEE International Conference on Robotics and Automation (ICRA) Workshop "Towards Real-world Development of Legged Robots". IEEE (2019)

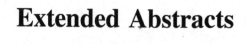

Extended Abstracts

Latent Morality in Algorithms and Machines

Xerxes D. Arsiwalla[1,2,3(✉)], Ismael T. Freire[1,3], Vasiliki Vouloutsi[1,3], and Paul Verschure[1,3,4]

[1] Institute for BioEngineering of Catalonia, Barcelona, Spain
x.d.arsiwalla@gmail.com
[2] Universitat Pompeu Fabra, Barcelona, Spain
[3] Barcelona Institue of Science and Technology, Barcelona, Spain
[4] Institució Catalana de Recerca i Estudis Avançats (ICREA), Barcelona, Spain

Abstract. Can machines be endowed with morality? We argue that morality in the descriptive or epistemic sense can be extended to artificial systems. Following arguments from evolutionary game-theory, we identify two main ingredients required to operationalize this notion of morality in machines. The first, being a group theory of mind, and the second, being an assignment of valence. We make the case for the plausibility of these operations in machines without reference to any form of intentionality or consciousness. The only systems requirements needed to support the above two operations are autonomous goal-directed action and the ability to interact and learn from the environment. Following this we have outlined a theoretical framework based on conceptual spaces and valence assignments to gauge latent morality in autonomous machines and algorithms.

Keywords: Philosophy of morality · Ethics of algorithms · Theory of mind · Qualia · Autonomous systems · Goal-directed action

1 Morality in Humans and Machines

In philosophy and social anthropology, morality has been referred to both in the descriptive and normative sense [16]. Descriptively, it refers "to certain codes of conduct put forward by a society or a group (such as a religion), or accepted by an individual for her own behavior" Normatively, it refers "to a code of conduct that, given specified conditions, would be put forward by all rational persons "[16]. This has been proposed as a definition of what morality is, rather than what constitutes the contents of a moral theory. This definition highlights two interpretations or one may even say, types of morality: a normative one and an epistemic one. The former posits an absolute sense of good and bad, whereas in the latter view, morality is a socio-cultural phenomenon. In humans, both of these require notions of free will and intentionality for behavioral manifestation. In terms of Penrose's three worlds (which is an adaptation of the Popper-Eccles interactionist trialism) [21], the Platonic, the mental and the physical world, these two senses of morality occupy different worlds. The normative one lives in the Platonic world and can be perceived

© Springer Nature Switzerland AG 2019
U. Martinez-Hernandez et al. (Eds.): Living Machines 2019, LNAI 11556, pp. 309–315, 2019.
https://doi.org/10.1007/978-3-030-24741-6_27

by conscious minds. The epistemic kind would be confined to the mental world and require physical carriers supporting mental states. Actions that are considered moral by either of the above definitions result in behaviors that reflect altruism, ethical decision-making, compassion, etc. Similar behaviors in animal groups have been studied, suggesting that morality, at least in the epistemic sense, might also manifest in animal behavior.

Can these notions of morality be extended to machines? Here we propose that epistemic morality can, in fact, be extended to machines provided we replace free will with autonomous goal-directed action, and relax the requirement of intentionality (replacing it with internal predictive models). In this sense, the ethics of machine actions, preferences and decisions is already manifest in present-day algorithms and autonomous systems executing those algorithms (see [24] and [25] for an overview on machine morality).

2   Operationalizing Machine Morality

In human and animal societies, the epistemic form of morality has its origins in socio-evolutionary arguments. Namely, that the set of behaviors that constitute morality evolved largely because they provided possible survival or reproductive benefits such as increased evolutionary success. Humans consequently evolved social emotions, such as feelings of empathy or guilt, in response to these moral behaviors [22].

From the evolutionary perspective, described above, epistemic morality can be thought of as a specific subset of social conventions, which have a categorical value system attached to them. In game-theoretic settings, conventions are typically studied as Nash equilibria of cooperative or competitive games between a group of players. Particularly, over successive trials or generations, adaptive learning mechanisms optimize behavioral policies based on cost or reward utility functions. This is generically true for many conventions, not all of which would form part of a moral code. We postulate that two additional ingredients are required to operationalize epistemic morality in a group: (i) A group theory of mind, and (ii) Encoding of valence to states of (i). The motivation for (i) comes from the role that Theory of Mind (ToM) capabilities play in cognition and consciousness. ToM refers to mental models of other agents that a given agent can acquire. This is a construct from cognitive science which seeks to explain how social agents make predictions about mental and behavioral states of other agents, including their beliefs, goals and actions. The evolutionary argument for consciousness posits that ToM became a necessary mechanism for social cooperation and competition, enabling an agent to solve the problem of inferring hidden states (mental/psychological) of other agents in complex social environments. ToM models may also include perceived intentionality. In AI and multi-agent autonomous systems, ToM is modeled using reinforcement learning for predicting actions and policies of other agents in games. While ToM itself refers to dyadic interactions, this idea has recently been extended to a group theory of mind [23]. Here, an agent forms or acquires a mental or internal model associated to a group as a whole. This may be a conspecific or heterospecific population.

When combined with the categorical value system alluded to above, one has the operational ingredients for morality. These values may refer to emotional attributions associated to mental states/representations, as well as utility assignments to internal models/states referring to a group. In cognitive science, value assignments are also referred to as valence. For simplicity, let us assume these values to be trivalent: positive, negative or neutral. Valence can be associated to objects, other agents, actions and their compositions. In biological agents, such assignments are encoded as emotional reflexes (example, the well-known fight or flight response). Here, we will specifically associate valence to all states of the group ToM that an agent has. For example, when an agent performs a specific action, valence in the agent's group ToM will be used to inform the agent whether its action will be perceived favorably or unfavorably by the group. This will prime individual behaviors towards codes of conduct that over several iterations are beneficial for the group and manifest as morality in the descriptive sense. Here, no reference to explicit intentionality or agency has been made (even though one cannot rule out implicit intentionality encoded by the developer, for example in the goals that drive the reinforcement learning). All that was needed was a level of autonomous goal-directed action sufficient to learn and generate a group ToM.

What kind of machines can have these capabilities? Most machines would be amoral or neutral by themselves. However, reward and utility based specifications in current technologies could lead to actions that from a human perspective might be perceived as moral or immoral. In particular, if an autonomous vehicle is placed in the context of the classic trolley-dilemma, it's predisposition to act one way or another, or even it's indecisiveness within that task will have real consequences. Moreover, concerning perceived morality of autonomous systems, this perception will vary from individual to individual, depending on their own ToM about the machine itself and its designer/operator. In this sense, machines implicitly have a latent morality and that makes the case for assessing the ethics of algorithms that run these systems [18,19]. In the next section, we describe a theoretical framework for making such assessments.

3   A Framework for Estimating Latent Morality in Algorithms

ToM models are typically predictive models with internal priors. In AI and cognitive systems these are often realized either as Bayesian or reinforcement learning modules [13,14] (see also [2–4,6–8]). What is important for our discussion here is not the specific representation of these ToM models but the relations and associations that these models learn and acquire about a social group as well as self relations. In other words, to assess latent morality in algorithms and autonomous systems, we first need to extract the set of concepts and associations between concepts that this system or algorithm is responsive to either by way of learning or as priors. Such a conceptual space can be represented as a network, where nodes denote objects or agents that the systems sensors recognize and edges denote similarities between objects/agents that the system has learnt to associate during social interactions. The nodes can also represent internal concepts about the system such as its internal states, drives, goals. This network of relations encodes a world model that the agent has acquired, alongside a self model.

Similar networks of concepts have been empirically constructed for human subjects in fMRI studies and are called semantic spaces [17]. In cognitive science, conceptual spaces refer to geometric spaces that encapsulate similarities between related concepts, thus representing higher-level concepts as geometric spaces [15]. In theories of consciousness such as Integrated Information Theory (IIT), the notion of a conceptual space is formulated as a Q-space (Q referring to qualia) or Q-structure [20] (see also [1,5,9–12]). In IIT, Q-spaces are computed in information space following a system's causal dynamics. Conceptual spaces are important cognitive tools that can be used for performing hierarchical inferences given new data, as in belief propagation networks. They are also useful as models of distributional semantics and higher-level concept representation. Both of these are functions that cognitive agents endowed with ToM capabilities require for social interactions.

Here, we hypothesize another cognitive feature that these spaces may help encapsulate, namely, valence. Valence can be simplified as a categorical assignment to every concept (positive, negative or neutral), that in either encoded as a prior or learnt in the course of interactions. An example of such learning is classical conditioning, where a negative valence gets associated to a concept which happens to be associated to another concept which itself carries a negative valence. More complex associations of concepts will form paths in the conceptual space. Then one needs a rule to compose individual valences to result in a valence for the complex of concepts. This will very much depend on the environment context that the agent is in and its own internal states. One way to formalize this idea is to use the construction of a measure space. A measure space is a triplet which includes a base set, an algebra over the set and a function from the algebra to denote a measure. This is how measures can be formally defined. Probabilities are one such example. In our case, the base set is the conceptual space; the algebra denotes all paths of concepts on the network; and the measure is the valence that associates the complex of concepts to a categorical value. This gives us a way to formally define valence on conceptual spaces.

How does this work in practice for algorithms? Given an algorithm that is part of an autonomous system that interacts with other agents and learns, its conceptual space will be a network of relations between all objects, agents and actions that it can identify using its sensors and act upon. This includes its internal homeostatic drives. As the system interacts and learns, this network will grow. Based on initial valences, successive concepts will acquire valences based on concept similarity. Many prediction-based algorithms, will already have valences based on utility. In simple settings, that may be enough. However, for systems as self-driving cars in complex social environments, pure utility-based judgements may be insufficient or simply not be computable within the split-second that it has to make a decision. For these purposes, a valence based on positive or negative associations (similar to fight or flight responses) would help in complex and dangerous situations. In this sense, these technologies have a latent morality and assessing or modifying valences on the conceptual space of these systems offers a way to enable ethical protocols in human-machine interactions.

4 Discussion

In this paper, we have narrowed down the concept of morality to an epistemic realization, which can be extended from humans to machines. Following arguments from evolutionary game-theory, we have identified two main ingredients required to operationalize this notion of morality in machines. The first, being a group theory of mind, and the second, being an assignment of valence. We have argued for the plausibility of these operations in machines without reference to any form of intentionality or consciousness. The only systems requirements needed to support the above two operations are autonomous goal-directed action and the ability to interact and learn from the environment. Following this we have outlined a theoretical framework based on conceptual spaces and valence assignments to gauge latent morality in autonomous machines and algorithms.

Why is this relevant for current technologies involved in human-machine interaction? Sociality and epistemic morality become relevant factors in tasks where autonomous agents will be required to cooperate with other such agents or with groups of humans. Driverless vehicles are one such example, where pre-wired reflexes are proving to be insufficient to account for all the complexities that real-world scenarios present. Another example is the use of robots by police forces and military personnel for operations involving controlling violence or rescuing hostages. Both these scenarios are a not-so-distant reality. Hence, for safe use of these technologies in society and prevention of accidents in interactions with humans, it is vital to have measures that gauge implicit ethics in algorithms. This is particularly relevant for systems involved in autonomous decision-making.

Acknowledgments. This work is supported by the EU's HR-Recycler Project. We would like to thank the two anonymous reviewers for useful suggestions.

References

1. Arsiwalla, X.D., Verschure, P.F.M.J.: Integrated information for large complex networks. In: The 2013 International Joint Conference on Neural Networks (IJCNN), pp. 1–7, August 2013
2. Arsiwalla, X.D., Herreros, I., Moulin-Frier, C., Sanchez, M., Verschure, P.F.: Is Consciousness a Control Process?, pp. 233–238. IOS Press, Amsterdam (2016)
3. Arsiwalla, X.D., Herreros, I., Moulin-Frier, C., Verschure, P.: Consciousness as an evolutionary game-theoretic strategy. In: Mangan, M., Cutkosky, M., Mura, A., Verschure, P.F.M.J., Prescott, T., Lepora, N. (eds.) Living Machines 2017. LNCS (LNAI), vol. 10384, pp. 509–514. Springer, Cham (2017). https://doi.org/10.1007/978-3-319-63537-8_43

4. Arsiwalla, X.D., Herreros, I., Verschure, P.: On three categories of conscious machines. In: Lepora, N.F.F., Mura, A., Mangan, M., Verschure, P.F.M.J.F.M.J., Desmulliez, M., Prescott, T.J.J. (eds.) Living Machines 2016. LNCS (LNAI), vol. 9793, pp. 389–392. Springer, Cham (2016). https://doi.org/10.1007/978-3-319-42417-0_35

5. Arsiwalla, X.D., Pacheco, D., Principe, A., Rocamora, R., Verschure, P.: A temporal estimate of integrated information for intracranial functional connectivity. In: Kůrková, V., Manolopoulos, Y., Hammer, B., Iliadis, L., Maglogiannis, I. (eds.) ICANN 2018. LNCS, vol. 11140, pp. 403–412. Springer, Cham (2018). https://doi.org/10.1007/978-3-030-01421-6_39

6. Arsiwalla, X.D., Signorelli, C.M., Puigbo, J.Y., Freire, I.T., Verschure, P.: What is the physics of intelligence? In: Frontiers in Artificial Intelligence and Applications: Proceedings of the 21st International Conference of the Catalan Association for Artificial Intelligence, vol. 308. IOS Press, October 2018

7. Arsiwalla, X.D., Signorelli, C.M., Puigbo, J.-Y., Freire, I.T., Verschure, P.F.M.J.: Are brains computers, emulators or simulators? In: Vouloutsi, V., Halloy, J., Mura, A., Mangan, M., Lepora, N., Prescott, T.J., Verschure, P.F.M.J. (eds.) Living Machines 2018. LNCS (LNAI), vol. 10928, pp. 11–15. Springer, Cham (2018). https://doi.org/10.1007/978-3-319-95972-6_3

8. Arsiwalla, X.D., Sole, R., Moulin-Frier, C., Herreros, I., Sanchez-Fibla, M., Verschure, P.F.: The morphospace of consciousness. arXiv preprint arXiv:1705.11190 (2017)

9. Arsiwalla, X.D., Verschure, P.: Computing information integration in brain networks. In: Wierzbicki, A., Brandes, U., Schweitzer, F., Pedreschi, D. (eds.) NetSci-X 2016. LNCS, vol. 9564, pp. 136–146. Springer, Cham (2016). https://doi.org/10.1007/978-3-319-28361-6_11

10. Arsiwalla, X.D., Verschure, P.: Measuring the complexity of consciousness. Front. Neurosci. **12**, 424 (2018)

11. Arsiwalla, X.D., Verschure, P.F.M.J.: High integrated information in complex networks near criticality. In: Villa, A.E.P., Masulli, P., Pons Rivero, A.J. (eds.) ICANN 2016. LNCS, vol. 9886, pp. 184–191. Springer, Cham (2016). https://doi.org/10.1007/978-3-319-44778-0_22

12. Arsiwalla, X.D., Verschure, P.F.: The global dynamical complexity of the human brain network. Appl. Netw. Sci. **1**(1), 16 (2016)

13. Freire, I.T., Moulin-Frier, C., Sanchez-Fibla, M., Arsiwalla, X.D., Verschure, P.: Modeling the formation of social conventions in multi-agent populations. arXiv preprint arXiv:1802.06108 (2018)

14. Freire, I.T., Puigbò, J.-Y., Arsiwalla, X.D., Verschure, P.F.M.J.: Modeling the opponent's action using control-based reinforcement learning. In: Vouloutsi, V., Halloy, J., Mura, A., Mangan, M., Lepora, N., Prescott, T.J., Verschure, P.F.M.J. (eds.) Living Machines 2018. LNCS (LNAI), vol. 10928, pp. 179–186. Springer, Cham (2018). https://doi.org/10.1007/978-3-319-95972-6_19

15. Gärdenfors, P.: Conceptual Spaces: The Geometry of Thought. MIT press, Cambridge (2004)

16. Gert, B., Gert, J.: The definition of morality (2002)

17. Huth, A.G., Nishimoto, S., Vu, A.T., Gallant, J.L.: A continuous semantic space describes the representation of thousands of object and action categories across the human brain. Neuron **76**(6), 1210–1224 (2012)

18. Kraemer, F., Van Overveld, K., Peterson, M.: Is there an ethics of algorithms? Ethics Inf. Technol. **13**(3), 251–260 (2011)

19. Mittelstadt, B.D., Allo, P., Taddeo, M., Wachter, S., Floridi, L.: The ethics of algorithms: mapping the debate. Big Data Soc. **3**(2), 2053951716679679 (2016)
20. Oizumi, M., Albantakis, L., Tononi, G.: From the phenomenology to the mechanisms of consciousness: integrated information theory 3.0. PLoS Comput. Biol. **10**(5), e1003588 (2014)
21. Penrose, R.: The road to reality: A complete guide to the laws of the universe (2004)
22. Shermer, M.: Transcendent morality? The Science of Good and Evil (2004)
23. Shum, M., Kleiman-Weiner, M., Littman, M.L., Tenenbaum, J.B.: Theory of minds: understanding behavior in groups through inverse planning. arXiv preprint arXiv:1901.06085 (2019)
24. Wallach, W., Allen, C.: Moral Machines: Teaching Robots Right from Wrong. Oxford University Press, Oxford (2008)
25. Wallach, W., Allen, C., Smit, I.: Machine morality: bottom-up and top-down approaches for modelling human moral faculties. AI Soc. **22**(4), 565–582 (2008)

A Window into the Robot 'mind': Using a Graphical Real-Time Display to Provide Transparency of Function in a Brain-Based Robot

David R. Buxton[1(✉)], Hamideh Kerdegari[2], Saeid Mokaram[3], Ben Mitchinson[1],
and Tony J. Prescott[1]

[1] Adaptive Behaviour Research Group, The University of Sheffield, Sheffield, UK
[2] Kingston University London, Kingston upon Thames, UK
[3] Speech and Hearing Research Group, The University of Sheffield, Sheffield, UK
http://abrg.group.shef.ac.uk, http://spandh.dcs.shef.ac.uk

Abstract. Biomimetic robots are often given a humanoid or animaloid form that generates useful interaction affordances through similarities to natural counterparts. This has raised concerns about the potential for deception by creating the expectation of human- or animal-like intentional states that cannot (supposedly) be generated in artefacts. Here we report on the design of a graphical user interface (GUI) to the brain-based control system of the MiRo animal-like robot that we are developing to test the value of real-time displays as a means of increasing transparency for biomimetic robots and as a tool for investigating people's understanding of the relationship between internal mental processes and behaviour.

Keywords: Biomimetic robot · Brain-based robot · Intentionality · MiRo robot · Transparency

1 Introduction

Research in robot ethics has highlighted a potential trade-off between the utility of robots in human–robot interaction settings and their functional transparency. For instance, whilst robot developers such as Breazeal and Scassellati [1] have argued that "to interact socially, a robot must convey intentionality, that is, the human mind must believe that robot has beliefs, desires and intentions", Wortham and Theodorou [2] have proposed that present-day social robots may be effective only because they instil a belief in human users about intentional states that they do not actually have. In other words, robots might serve as effective social others by deceptively concealing the reality that they are machines controlled by computer programs. This risk of deception has been highlighted by a growing number of authors; Sparrow and Sparrow [3] have described social robots as intrinsically unethical, whilst the EPSRC "Principles of Robotics" [4], developed by a panel of UK ethicists and roboticists, advocates that as manufactured artefacts, robots "should not be designed in a deceptive way to exploit vulnerable users; instead their machine nature should be transparent".

© Springer Nature Switzerland AG 2019
U. Martinez-Hernandez et al. (Eds.): Living Machines 2019, LNAI 11556, pp. 316–320, 2019.
https://doi.org/10.1007/978-3-030-24741-6_28

The notion of robot deception has proved controversial [5] and further research is needed to understand the complex relationship between utility, transparency, and deception from ethical, philosophical, and psychological standpoints. More pragmatically, it will also be helpful to understand if robots can be useful in roles where they act as social others while still remaining transparent about their internal states and processes.

Wortham and Theodorou [2] have suggested various means of increasing the functional transparency of robots to explore these issues. For instance, by generating real-time audio or textual reports of the robot's control processes [6], and/or by using graphical real-time visualisation of the robot's inner workings [7], it may be possible to help human users construct a mental model (or 'Theory of Mind') more appropriate than the erroneous one that might otherwise develop through our human tendency to anthropomorphise.

In this paper, we report on the development of a graphical user interface (GUI) for the brain-based control system of the MiRo robot that we are developing to test the value of graphical real-time displays as a means of increasing transparency. Transparency is often discussed based on the presumption that the control systems underlying robot behaviour are fundamentally different from those operating through the nervous systems of animals to generate natural behaviour. MiRo presents an interesting case study in this context, as it is controlled by a highly simplified abstraction of the control architecture of the mammalian brain [8]. In addition to demonstrating how MiRo's behaviour is controlled, this GUI could therefore also serve as an educational tool to demonstrate how brains control bodies to generate behaviour. One potential outcome is that by seeing animal-like behaviour generated by a model of the mammalian nervous system, people may develop a more mechanistic view of the internal processes underlying their own thoughts and actions.

2 GUI Overview

The MiRo graphical interface[1] (Fig. 1) is a hybrid display of dynamically updating and static information about MiRo's cognitive architecture, incoming sensory data, and internal computations that effectively represent the robot's current 'mental state'. Live data from sensory, attentional, affective, and action selection systems are presented in appropriately formatted plots and laid out in the form of an extended box–and–arrow diagram that guides understanding of how these components interact to drive behaviour. This creates a visualisation of the complete 'brainstem' level of MiRo's hierarchical cognitive architecture [8] and of information that would otherwise remain entirely hidden. Many of the dynamic plots further invite the user to click through to an enhanced view that provides access to more detailed information or explains the component in greater depth.

---

[1] Available at: https://github.com/hamidehkerdegari/graphical_interface.

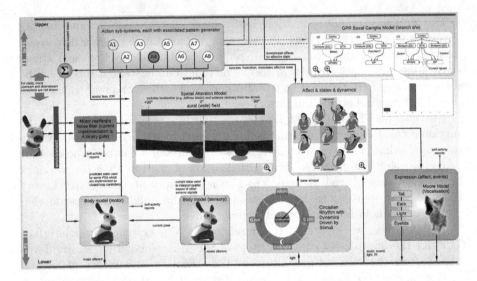

Fig. 1. Main window of the MiRo graphical interface, showing an overview of a virtual robot's cognitive state while approaching a toy ball. Component subsystems are framed in different colours; action selection is orange, spatial attention is green, circadian clock is pale blue, and affect is magenta. (Color figure online)

2.1 Component Summaries

Action selection: Displays the current input salience of each action subsystem and the corresponding level of disinhibitory output from the basal ganglia model, illustrating the important point that even when several or no high-salience inputs exist, a selection system should still select a single action strongly and unambiguously [9].

Spatial attention: Displays MiRo's visual field and aural attention indicator[2], with an enhanced view (Fig. 2) that includes MiRo's visual salience map.

Circadian clock: MiRo's internal circadian clock, which impacts affective state and drives a periodic sleep cycle.

Affect: Shows emotion, mood, and sleepiness, which are all represented by a 2D circumplex model [10] influenced by sensory and cognitive factors.

---

[2] The virtual MiRo environment does not support auditory simulation, therefore the spatial attention component shown here lacks that information.

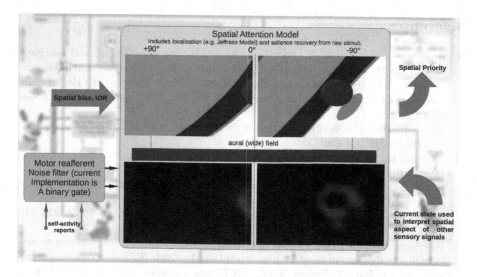

Fig. 2. Enhanced view of the spatial attention component showing MiRo's visual field *(upper)* and salience map *(lower)*. Objects attracting attention, such as MiRo's toy ball, will be highlighted in the salience map.

3   Conclusion

The graphical interface has several potential benefits. Firstly, the information presented may prove useful as a STEM teaching resource; the diagrammatic representation of a model cognitive architecture provides a visual aid that illustrates the functional connectivity of mammalian brains, and the integration of live sensory information may facilitate discussions on the problem of action selection and the role of specific brain structures. Secondly, the GUI greatly increases the transparency of MiRo's behaviour, helping to clarify the similarities and differences between MiRo's brain and human brains, to explain the functionality underlying MiRo's behaviour, and to refute beliefs that MiRo is truly conscious.

Furthermore, because the interface displays live information directly from the active 'mind' of a behaving robot, it is also interactive; not only can a user study the diagram to learn how spatial attention drives action selection and sensory stimulation modulates affect, but as they interact with MiRo they can observe the robot attending to their movements, choosing to approach them, and the increase in affect that underlies the wagging tail if they pet him.

We are interested in exploring how such operational transparency may improve human–robot relationships [2], and we are optimistic that this GUI presents a valuable opportunity to deepen the public's interest in biomimetic robots. We plan to utilise the MiRo GUI in future experimental work to explore if the benefits described here are realised in practice, and how it influences users' understanding not only of our simulated cognitive architecture, but also of their own.

References

1. Breazeal, C., Scassellati, B.: How to build robots that make friends and influence people. In: Proceedings 1999 IEEE/RSJ International Conference on Intelligent Robots and Systems. Human and Environment Friendly Robots with High Intelligence and Emotional Quotients (Cat. No. 99CH36289), vol. 2, pp. 858–863, October (1999)
2. Wortham, R.H., Theodorou, A.: Robot transparency, trust and utility. Connection Sci. **29**(3), 242–248 (2017)
3. Sparrow, R., Sparrow, L.: In the hands of machines? The future of aged care. Mind. Mach. **16**(2), 141–161 (2006)
4. Boden, M., et al.: Principles of robotics: regulating robots in the real world. Connection Sci. **29**(2), 124–129 (2017)
5. Collins, E.C.: Vulnerable users: deceptive robotics. Connection Sci. **29**(3), 223–229 (2017)
6. Wortham, R.H., Rogers, V.: The muttering robot: Improving robot transparency though vocalisation of reactive plan execution. In: 26th IEEE International Symposium on Robot and Human Interactive Communication (Ro-Man) Workshop on Agent Transparency for Human-Autonomy Teaming Effectiveness (Lisbon:) (2017)
7. Wortham, R.H., Theodorou, A., Bryson, J.J.: Improving robot transparency: real-time visualisation of robot AI substantially improves understanding in naive observers. In: 2017 26th IEEE International Symposium on Robot and Human Interactive Communication (RO-MAN), pp. 1424–1431 (2017)
8. Mitchinson, Ben, Prescott, Tony J.: MIRO: a robot "Mammal" with a biomimetic brain-based control system. In: Lepora, N., Mura, A., Mangan, M., Verschure, P., Desmulliez, M., Prescott, T. (eds.) Living Machines 2016. LNCS (LNAI), vol. 9793, pp. 179–191. Springer, Cham (2016). https://doi.org/10.1007/978-3-319-42417-0_17
9. Prescott, T.J., Redgrave, P., Gurney, K.: Layered control architectures in robots and vertebrates. Adapt. Behav. **7**(1), 99–127 (1999)
10. Posner, J., Russell, J.A., Peterson, B.S.: The circumplex model of affect: an integrative approach to affective neuroscience, cognitive development, and psychopathology. Dev. Psychopathol. **17**(3), 715–734 (2005)

Robust Postural Stabilization with a Biomimetic Hierarchical Control Architecture

Adrián Fernández Amil[1,2], Giovanni Maffei[3,5],
Jordi-Ysard Puigbò[1,2,3], Xerxes D. Arsiwalla[1,2,3],
and Paul F. M. J. Verschure[1,2,3,4(✉)]

[1] Institute for Bioengineering of Catalonia (IBEC), Barcelona, Spain
pverschure@ibecbarcelona.eu
[2] Barcelona Institute of Science and Technology (BIST), Barcelona, Spain
[3] Technology Department, University Pompeu Fabra, Barcelona, Spain
[4] Catalan Institution for Research and Advanced Studies (ICREA),
Barcelona, Spain
[5] Alpha, Telefónica, Barcelona, Spain

Abstract. Fast online corrections during anticipatory movements are a signature of robustness in biological motor control. In this regard, a previous study suggested that anticipatory postural control can be recast as a sensory-sensory predictive process, where hierarchically connected cerebellar microcircuits reflect the causal sequence of events preceding a postural disturbance. Hence, error monitoring signals from higher sensory layers inform lower layers about violations of expectations, affording fast corrections when the normal sequence is broken. Here we generalize this insight and prove that the proposed hierarchical control architecture can deal with different types of alterations in the causal structure of the environment, therefore extending the limits of performance.

Keywords: Cerebellum · Anticipatory control · Robustness · Control architecture

1 Introduction

Anticipation allows humans to maintain their bodies in desired states even when external disturbances are present [1]. That is, provided that perturbations are preceded by sensory cues, well-timed anticipatory actions are acquired to efficiently counteract them, enhancing the controllability of body posture [2]. However, after the acquisition, a person incurs in the risk of over- or under-anticipating if the perturbation or the preceding signal do not match the expectations. Therefore, theories of anticipatory motor control must account for the fast corrections needed to keep stability under variable conditions. In a previous study [3], a novel cerebellar-based control scheme called Hierarchical Sensory Predictive Control (HSPC) was compared to another architecture based on the standard theory of motor adaptation, Feedback Error Learning (FEL) [4]. Whereas HSPC casts the anticipatory control as a predictive process in the

© Springer Nature Switzerland AG 2019
U. Martinez-Hernandez et al. (Eds.): Living Machines 2019, LNAI 11556, pp. 321–324, 2019.
https://doi.org/10.1007/978-3-030-24741-6_29

sensory domain, FEL acts in the motor domain (see Fig. 1, bottom). Importantly, in HSPC, the sensory prediction error (e_d in Fig. 1) is not only used for learning, but also as an error-correction signal that informs about violations of sensory expectations. This mechanism, absent in FEL, explains the early online corrections of over-anticipations seen in "catch trials" with humans (i.e. the preceding cue is present, but the perturbation is not delivered) [3]. Here we test and validate the generality and robustness of this error-correction mechanism for a wider range of conditions, using a variation of the classical inverted pendulum problem in control theory as our reference system to compare the HSPC and FEL architectures' generalization capabilities.

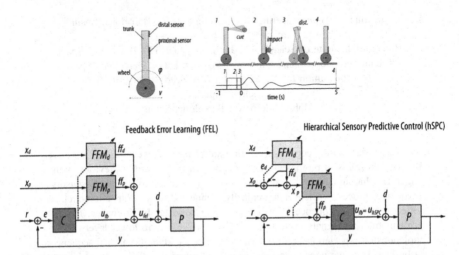

Fig. 1. **(Top)** Simulated inverted pendulum during a normal training trial. 1- distal sensing (vision). 2-proximal sensing (proprioception). 3-sensing of the angular displacement (vestibular). 4-postural stabilization. **(Bottom left)** Feedback Error Learning (FEL) architecture. Both feed-forward modules send anticipatory motor commands to the plant and learn from the output of the feedback controller. **(Bottom right)** Hierarchical Sensory Predictive Control (HSPC) architecture. The distal module sends early sensory predictions to the proximal module and learns from the sensory prediction error. The error is also added to the anticipated prediction as input to the proximal module, acting as an error correction signal. Finally, the proximal module sends *counterfactual* errors to the feedback controller and learns from the error in angle.

2 Methods

We use the same setup as in [3]. A simulated inverted pendulum was driven by a Proportional-Derivative (PD) controller by providing torque at its base. The sensory feedback corresponds to the delayed error in angle with respect to the vertical. Besides the feedback loop, two feed-forward modules (distal and proximal), acting as cerebellar adaptive filters [5], are arranged according to a sensory prediction (HSPC) or motor anticipation (FEL) hypothesis (see Fig. 1, bottom). Importantly, all the feed-forward modules have the same set of alpha-like temporal basis functions and are updated following the same learning rule: the Least Mean Squares (LMS) [6], with an eligibility trace to account for the delays between signals [7]. The experiment goes as follows (see Fig. 1, top). First, the agents (HSPC- and FEL-based) are trained for 100 trials with the same cue and perturbation. The distal cue (i.e. vision) is briefly presented before the perturbation is delivered. The perturbation itself is modeled as a brief constant force of 100 N at the center of mass of the pendulum. The proximal signal (i.e. proprioception) follows the timings of the force, with some delay. Both the distal and proprioceptive signals are modeled as rectangular functions, with magnitude 1. After training, both agents are tested without further learning for a wide range of forces and distal cues, covering an important portion of the Cue-Force space. Thus, performance surfaces are obtained, that go beyond the typical test with the catch trial.

3 Results and Discussion

As can be seen from Fig. 2 (top), both FEL and HSPC architectures acquire successful anticipatory actions that minimize the error caused by the perturbation, compared to before training (the "naive condition"). Moreover, they do so at an equal pace (shown by the acquisition curves). Furthermore, the effects of the early error-correction mechanism in HSPC can be seen during the catch trial (Fig. 2, bottom), whereas FEL incurs in a bigger self-generated peak angular error that the feedback is then forced to counteract afterward. Finally, from Fig. 3 it is shown that HSPC's robustness capabilities seen in the catch trial [3] generalize to a much wider range of conditions. The surfaces or generalization gradients show the performance landscape for both architectures, with HSPC's being flatter than FEL's. Therefore, the ("plant-agnostic") error-correction mechanism makes the hierarchical control scheme to work better under previously unseen environments, making it a more robust architecture without having

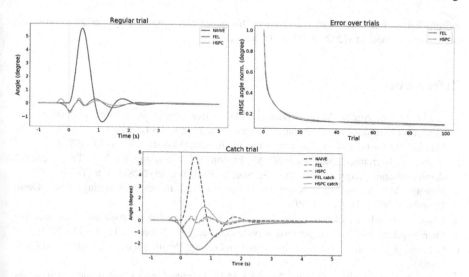

Fig. 2. (Top) Behavior (angle) of HSPC and FEL in first ("naive", feedback response) and last (trained) regular training trials (cue = 1, force = 100 N at 0 s); and the acquisition curves during training (in cumulative RMSE of angle). (Bottom) Behavior in catch trials (cue = 1, force = 0 N).

HSPC vs. FEL error in Cue-Force space

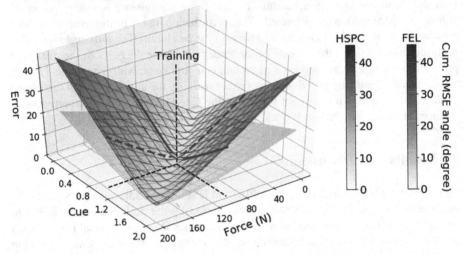

Fig. 3. Generalization gradients of FEL and HSPC for a wide range of distal cues and forces. The lines represent slices made to the surfaces at cue = 1 (dashed lines) and force = 100 N (solid lines). The errors are measured as the cumulative RMSE angle (in degrees) during the trials.

to sacrifice top performance. However, a systematic analysis of both architectures in terms of the performance-robustness trade-off is still lacking. Hence, in future work we will test both control schemes under stochastic environments, to see how uncertainty and variability affect their learning dynamics and generalization capabilities.

Acknowledgments. The work presented in this paper was supported by the European Commission under contract H2020-820742 HR-Recycler.

References

1. Shadmehr, R., Smith, M.A., Krakauer, J.W.: Error correction, sensory prediction, and adaptation in motor control. Annu. Rev. Neurosci. **33**, 89–108 (2010)
2. Massion, J.: Postural control system. Curr. Opin. Neurobiol. **4**(6), 877–887 (1994)
3. Maffei, G., Herreros, I., Sánchez-Fibla, M., Friston, K.J., Verschure, P.F.M.J.: The perceptual shaping of anticipatory actions. Proc. R. Soc. B: Biol. Sci. **2017**(284), 1–9 (1869)
4. Kawato, M.: Internal models for motor control and trajectory planning. Curr. Opin. Neurobiol. **9**(6), 718–727 (1999)
5. Dean, P., Porrill, J., Ekerot, C.-F., Jörntell, H.: The cerebellar microcircuit as an adaptive filter: experimental and computational evidence. Nat. Rev. Neurosci. **11**, 30–43 (2009)
6. Widrow, B., Stearns, S.D.: Adaptive Signal Processing. Prentice-Hall Inc., Englewood Cliffs (1985)
7. Herreros, I., Arsiwalla, XD., Verschure, P.F.M.J.: A forward model at Purkinje cell synapses facilitates cerebellar anticipatory control. In: Proceedings in Advances in Neural Information Processing Systems, pp. 3828–3836 (2016)

Auditory-Visual Virtual Reality for the Study of Multisensory Integration in Insect Navigation

Koki Makino[1]([⊠])[iD], Noriyasu Ando[1,2], Hisashi Shidara[3][iD],
Naoto Hommaru[4], Ryohei Kanzaki[1], and Hiroto Ogawa[3]

[1] Research Center for Advanced Science and Technology,
The University of Tokyo, Tokyo, Japan
makino@brain.imi.i.u-tokyo.ac.jp
[2] Department of Systems Life Engineering, Maebashi Institute of Technology,
Maebashi, Japan
[3] Department of Biological Sciences, Faculty of Science, Hokkaido University,
Sapporo, Japan
[4] Graduate School of Life Science, Hokkaido University, Sapporo, Japan

Abstract. Insects have the ability to navigate through a complex environment. It has been reported that using multisensory information improves their ability to navigate. To reveal when and how insects utilize multiple sensory information, we developed a multisensory virtual reality system for crickets (*Gryllus bimaculatus*), which enables us to manipulate auditory and visual stimuli from every direction. We investigated how visual information influenced their phonotaxis towards a conspecific male calling song. Our results showed that crickets exhibit phonotaxis under virtual reality and that a visual target with a sound source reduced the variability of the body angle towards the source. These results suggested the possibility that crickets utilize visual cues to localize sound sources. Further investigation with our system will reveal how crickets effectively utilize multiple sensory information in complex environments.

Keywords: Navigation · Visual-auditory integration · Virtual reality · Insects

1 Introduction

Insects robustly perform goal-oriented navigational tasks in complex environments despite their relatively simple nervous systems. Extensive research has been conducted on goal-oriented navigation such as visually, olfactory-, and auditory-guided behaviors [1]. These studies focused on a specific sensory input that had a dominant role in navigation. However, it is unlikely that insects rely only on a single sensory input in a real environment where such information is noisy and continuously changing. Multisensory integration improves the reliability of their internal representation of their surroundings, which in turn increases their navigational ability [2]. However, it is still unknown when and how insects utilize multisensory information because sensory inputs are constantly changing (sensory types, intensity and direction) even as a result of their own movement in a real environment.

© Springer Nature Switzerland AG 2019
U. Martinez-Hernandez et al. (Eds.): Living Machines 2019, LNAI 11556, pp. 325–328, 2019.
https://doi.org/10.1007/978-3-030-24741-6_30

Auditory navigation (phonotaxis) of female crickets is a well-studied navigational ability in insects [3] and is an ideal model to investigate multisensory integration for navigation, because crickets have various behavioral repertories associated with multiple sensory stimuli [4, 5]. Virtual reality (VR) is a useful technique for investigating multisensory information handling during navigation. The most established VR system in neuroethology involves a trackball combined with visual stimulation, in which a tethered animal explores a virtual space through the rotation of a ball triggered by its own walking [6]. This framework is also advantageous for further analysis of the neural activity associated with navigational tasks. However, most of the VR systems have been limited to vision, and there have been few studies on VR systems that can manipulate both auditory and visual information [7, 8] as well as auditory alone [9].

In this study, we developed a multisensory VR system that allowed us to control both auditory and visual stimuli to a tethered walking cricket and investigated the effect of a visual cue on phonotaxis.

2 Materials and Methods

2.1 Auditory-Visual Virtual Reality

We designed a VR system consisting of an array of 16 speakers and four LCD displays (frame rate, 60 Hz) surrounding a cricket tethered to a trackball (illuminance 96.9 lx; Fig. 1). A 7–21-day-old adult female cricket (*Gryllus bimaculatus*) was tethered to the trackball and its walking behavior was determined using two optical mice. The position and heading of the cricket relative to a sound source (male calling song) or a visual target (black circle, Michelson contrast 0.99) on a virtual space were calculated to set the parameters of both auditory (intensity and direction) and visual stimuli (size and direction). Our system allows us to present both stimuli from all directions, which is a requirement for the study of virtual navigation in a fully two-dimensional space. Moreover, this is advantageous compared to previous auditory-visual VRs [7, 8] wherein the range of the direction of the stimulus was limited to the frontal region.

2.2 Behavioral Experiment

A sound source and a visual target were placed 500 mm from a cricket in a virtual arena. Although our system can modulate both sound intensity and image size in relation to the distance from the cricket, we set these parameters at constant values to facilitate behavioral responses in this study. The sound intensity was set at 75 dB, which was high enough to elicit phonotaxis, and the image size was set at a visual angle of 30°, which was large enough to elicit visually-guided antennal tracking when moved. The experiments were conducted under four conditions: no stimuli (spontaneous walking, $N = 15$), visual target only ($N = 15$), sound only ($N = 17$), and sound with a visual target ($N = 18$); each trial lasted for five minutes. The position and heading of the cricket in the virtual arena were recorded at 100 Hz. We quantified the rate of localization as an index of navigational performance, calculated as the number of trials in which the cricket reached within 20 mm from the sound source or the visual target divided by all the number of trials. The stability of heading was quantified as its variability, calculated as the interquartile range (IQR) of the angle between the body axis and the source direction during the first trip to the source.

Fig. 1. Presentation of a visual target and trackball system with a speaker array

3 Results

When the calling song was presented, 82.4% of crickets localized the sound source (Fig. 2A, B), whereas none of the 15 crickets localized the same position without any stimuli. This indicated that our VR system effectively elicited phonotaxis of crickets in the virtual arena. Four out of 15 crickets localized the visual target without the song; however, the localization rate was significantly lower than that with the song ($P < 0.05$, Fisher's exact test with the Bonferroni-Holm correction). The visual target with the song scored the highest localization rate of 83.3%; however, the rate was not significantly different from that with the song alone. On the other hand, the IQR of the body angle relative to the source was smaller when both stimuli were presented compared to when only the song was presented ($P < 0.001$, Wilcoxon rank sum test, Fig. 2C). These results indicated that crickets utilized the visual information to better orient themselves towards the sound source.

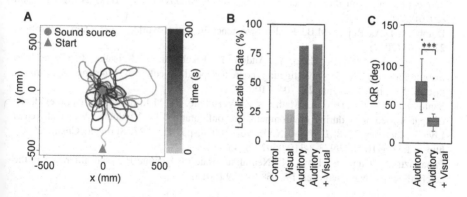

Fig. 2. Locomotion in the virtual arena. (A) Trajectory of a cricket in response to a sound source, (B) Localization rate, (C) Comparison of the variability of the heading

4   Discussion

Our auditory VR adequately elicited cricket phonotaxis and the additional presentation of the visual target affected body orientation. The capability to present both stimuli from every direction in our system allows crickets to receive multiple sensory inputs throughout the two-dimensional virtual space. Therefore, our system fulfills the requirements to reveal the utilization of multiple sensory inputs for navigation in cricket phonotaxis. Further investigation with our VR system will reveal how crickets effectively utilize multiple sensory information in more complex environments.

VR systems allow experimental animals to behave more freely in a virtual space. However, it should be noted that the results may differ from the actual behavior in a natural environment. Although increasing the number of sensory inputs in VR is one of the ways to improve the experimental design, the accumulation of errors derived from the trackball system or the inertia of the ball itself must be considered. Comparison of the behavior exhibited by animals in a virtual and real environment is necessary to fill this knowledge gap.

Acknowledgement. This work was supported by JSPS KAKENHI on Innovative Areas 'Systems Science of Bio-Navigation' (16H06544).

References

1. Namiki, S., Kanzaki, R.: The neurobiological basis of orientation in insects: insights from the silkmoth mating dance. Curr. Opin. Insect Sci. **15**, 16–26 (2016)
2. Frye, M.A.: Multisensory systems integration for high-performance motor control in flies. Curr. Opin. Neurobiol. **20**, 347–352 (2010)
3. Hedwig, B.: Pulses, patterns and paths: neurobiology of acoustic behaviour in crickets. J. Comp. Physiol. A **192**, 677–689 (2006)
4. Bohm, H., Schildberger, K., Huber, F.: Visual and acoustic course control in the cricket *Gryllus bimaculatus*. J. Exp. Biol. **159**, 235–248 (1991)
5. Haberkern, H., Hedwig, B.: Behavioural integration of auditory and antennal stimulation during phonotaxis in the field cricket *Gryllus bimaculatus*. J. Exp. Biol. **219**, 3575–3586 (2016)
6. Dombeck, D.A., Reiser, M.B.: Real neuroscience in virtual worlds. Curr. Opin. Neurobiol. **22**, 3–10 (2012)
7. Yamashita, A., Ando, N., Sano, Y., Andoh, T., Takahashi, H., Kanzaki, R.: Closed-loop locomotion analyzer for investigating context-dependent collision avoidance systems in insects. J. Robot. Soc. Jpn. **27**, 704–710 (2011)
8. Santos-Pata, D., Escuredo, A., Mathews, Z., Verschure, P.F.M.J.: Insect behavioral evidence of spatial memories during environmental reconfiguration. In: Vouloutsi, V., et al. (eds.) Living Machines 2018. LNCS (LNAI), vol. 10928, pp. 415–427. Springer, Cham (2018). https://doi.org/10.1007/978-3-319-95972-6_45
9. Funamizu, A., Kuhn, B., Doya, K.: Neural substrate of dynamic Bayesian inference in the cerebral cortex. Nat. Neurosci. **19**, 1682–1689 (2016)

Brainless Quasi-quadruped Robot Resembling Spinal Reflex and Force-Velocity Relationship of Muscles

Yoichi Masuda[1]([⊠]), Masato Ishikawa[1], and Akio Ishiguro[2]

[1] Osaka University, 2-1, Yamadaoka, Suita, Osaka 565–0871, Japan
{masuda,ishikawa}@mech.eng.osaka-u.ac.jp
[2] Tohoku University, 2-1-1 Katahira, Aoba-ku, Sendai 980–8577, Japan
ishiguro@riec.tohoku.ac.jp

Abstract. The aim of this study was to determine the conditions that allow for the generation of gait in quadruped animals using a brainless simple quasi-quadruped robot having two functions of quadruped animals. We included a reflex circuit and an actuator characteristics in the robot that were inspired by two animal functions, i.e., the spinal reflex (through the group I extensor afferent) and the force-velocity relationship of muscles. The robot, however, did not include a microprocessor or a gait generator. Our robot was able to reciprocate gait autonomously by adjusting phase differences between the limbs using only an analog reflex circuit and an actuator characteristics. Embedding two abovementioned functions in the robot allowed it to propel its body by adjusting the phase differences between the limbs.

Keywords: Quadruped robot · Reflex · Actuator dynamics · Decentralized autonomous control · Brainless control

1   Introduction

Gait is the pattern of periodic movement of the limbs of legged animals during locomotion. Various gait generation models and robotic models have been proposed [1,2]. However, the source of gait generation in legged animals has not been clearly identified as locomotion in animals is a result of complex interactions between the brain, central nervous system, body and uncertainties in the environment. The aim of the research was to determine the conditions for generating gait in quadruped animals. In achieving our aim, we used a simple quasi-quadruped robot with two functions of quadruped animals.

We developed a quasi-quadruped robot having fore-wheels and hind-limbs to investigate the generation of gait in quadruped locomotion. The first function we

This work is supported by JST CREST and JSPS grant-in-aid for Scientific Research (S) JP17H06150.

U. Martinez-Hernandez et al. (Eds.): Living Machines 2019, LNAI 11556, pp. 329–333, 2019.
https://doi.org/10.1007/978-3-030-24741-6_31

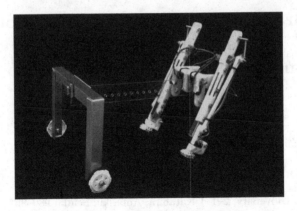

Fig. 1. Brainless quasi-quadruped robot having no microprocessor or gait generator.

integrated in our robot was spinal reflex through an analog reflex circuit. The analog reflex circuit resembled the spinal reflex of the group I extensor afferent in quadruped animals. It was integrated as an experiment on cat hindlimb during walking by [3] in which stimulation of the group I extensor afferents were simulated showed a prolonged stance phase and delays in the beginning of swing phase. The analog circuit we used comprised of a push switch and two DC motors. The second function integrated was an actuator which had characteristics comparable to the force-velocity relationship of animal muscles [4]. Experiments and simulations conducted using robotic models have shown that the dynamics of DC motors can function as a sensory feedback [5], contributing to coordinating the gait of a walking robot [6]. DC motors were also integrated in our robot to serve as sensory feedback mechanisms. The dynamics of DC motors that were embedded in each joint of hindlimbs adjusted the phase differences between the limbs.

2   Quasi-quadruped Robot

The simple quasi-quadruped robot we developed had two limbs, and each limb had a push switch and two low-torque DC motors (Pololu 75:1). Figure 1 shows an overview of the simple quasi-quadruped robot we developed. The design of our robot was based on two functions of quadruped animals, i.e., reflex through the group I pathways [3] and the force-velocity relationship of muscles [4].

2.1   Sensory Feedback Using Simple Reflex Circuit

The robot had a sensory feedback circuit in each limb independently to allow it to propel its body and adjust the timing of the stance-to-swing phase transition. The reflex circuit in each robot limb was inspired by the sensory feedback of group I extensor afferents in quadruped animals. A simple sensory feedback mechanism as illustrated in Fig. 2 was designed to mimic the stimulation of

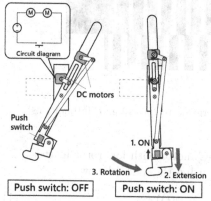

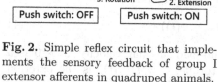

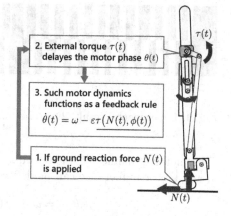

Fig. 2. Simple reflex circuit that implements the sensory feedback of group I extensor afferents in quadruped animals.

Fig. 3. Mechanism that implements the force-velocity characteristics of animal muscles. The torque-velocity characteristics of the motors coordinate gait.

the group I extensor afferent comparable to the cat hindlimb locomotion of [3]. The switch turned on when the robot walked at the beginning of stance phase and switched off when the foot made contact with the ground. The switch was connected to the DC motors in series and thus the motors ran until the limb was unloaded. The DC motors were also connected to the hip and knee joints through the slider-crank mechanisms. This allowed for the hip joint to propel the body forward when the hip motor rotated and the knee slider extended to kick the ground mimicking animal extensors. Two springs attached to the DC motors mimicked flexor muscles and pulled back the DC motors when the switch was turned off allowing for stance-to-swing transition. This resulted in a delay in the initiation of the swing phase as the limb loaded, and consequently, the stance phase was prolonged, as was observed in the experiment by [3].

2.2 Force-Velocity Relationship

Animal muscles have a force-velocity relationship. The force generated by a muscle is a function of its velocity. Animal muscles decrease their contraction speed as the tensile force increases. An experiment [6] showed that the torque-velocity characteristics of DC motors in a walking robot aided in adjusting the phase differences between the limbs, and such motor dynamics function as a kind of sensory feedback [5]. We also integrated a similar sensory feedback mechanism into our robot to aid in coordinating gait. The force-velocity relationship of muscles was mimicked in the brainless simple quasi-quadruped robot by exploiting the dynamics of the electric motors, as illustrated in Fig. 3.

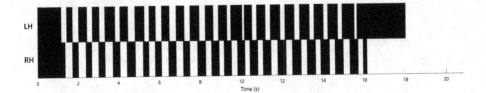

Fig. 4. Experimental result. The robot emerges a reciprocal gait autonomously.

The motor dynamics of a low-torque DC motor with low rotor inertia, friction, and motor inductance can be defined using the model below.

$$\dot{\theta}(t) = \omega - \varepsilon\tau(N(t), \phi(t)) \tag{1}$$

where $\theta(t)$ is the motor angle, ω is the no-load angular velocity, $\varepsilon > 0$ is a sensitivity of the motor to the external torque, $\tau(N(t), \phi(t))$ is the external torque that is a function of ground reaction force $N(t)$ and the joint angle $\phi(t)$. When a ground reaction force $N(t)$ (in the direction opposing the limb motion) is applied to the robot's foot, an external torque $\tau > 0$ is applied to the motor shaft, thereby causing the angular velocity $\dot{\theta}$ to decrease. The torque-velocity relationship of low-torque DC motors allows for robots to slow-down the limb motion and support their body mass.

3   Results and Conclusion

Figure 4 illustrates the gait diagram of the robot. Although the robot we developed had no microprocessor or gait generator, it was able to autonomously conduct reciprocal gait. The results suggest that the spinal reflex through the group I extensor afferents and the force-velocity relationship of muscles are the source of gait generation in quadruped animals. In support of our results, we recommend that future work be conducted through the development of a quadruped robot that reproduces the characteristics of reflex pathway and muscle dynamics more accurately. More extensive studies need to be conducted to allow for a better understanding of gait transitions of quadruped robot.

References

1. Ijspeert, A.J.: Central pattern generators for locomotion control in animals and robots: a review. Neural Netw. **21**(4), 642–653 (2008)
2. Aoi, S., et al.: Adaptive control strategies for interlimb coordination in legged robots: a review. Front. Neurorobotics **11**, 39 (2017)
3. Whelan, P.J., Hiebert, G.W., Pearson, K.G.: Stimulation of the group I extensor afferents prolongs the stance phase in walking cats. Exp. Brain Res. **103**(1), 20–30 (1995)
4. Scott, S.H., Brown, I.E., Gerald, E.L.: Mechanics of feline soleus: I. Effect of fascicle length and velocity on force output. J. Muscle Res. Cell Motil. **17**(2), 207–219 (1996)

5. Masuda, Y., Minami, Y., Ishikawa, M.: Actuator synchronization for adaptive motion generation without any sensor or microprocessor. In: Asian Control Conference (ASCC 2017), Australia, Goald Coast (2017)
6. Masuda, Y., Naniwa, K., Ishikawa, M., Osuka, K.: Weak actuators generate adaptive animal gaits without a brain. In: IEEE International Conference on Robotics and Biomimetics (ROBIO 2017), China, Macau SAR (2017)

Cellular Level Analysis of the Locomotor Neural Circuits in *Drosophila melanogaster*

Ryo Minegishi[1(⊠)], Kai Feng[2], and Barry Dickson[1,2]

[1] Janelia Research Campus, HHMI,
19700 Helix Drive, Ashburn, VA 20147, USA
minegishir@janelia.hhmi.org
[2] Queensland Brain Institute, University of Queensland,
QBI Building 79, University of Queensland, St Lucia, QLD 4072, Australia

Abstract. To investigate the neural mechanisms of insect locomotion, we aimed to generate genetic reagents to manipulate the specific cell types in the thoracic ganglion of *Drosophila melanogaster*. By using the split-Gal4 technique, we have generated ~1000 lines which can drive reporters or modulators in the specific cell types. We used these split-GAL4 lines to analyze the anatomy of individual cell types. Furthermore, we have screened their functions in locomotion by optogenetic activation. We observed a wide range of activation phenotypes, including the initiation and stopping of locomotion. These genetic resources will enable us to analyze the anatomy and function of insect locomotor circuits at the cellular level.

Keywords: Locomotion · Insect · Central nervous system · Split-Gal4 · Optogenetics

1 Introduction

Insects perform sophisticated legged locomotion. They execute gait pattern change and speed control in response to the environmental conditions by their comparatively small number of neurons. Command signals from the brain, rhythmic neural activities in the central pattern generator and sensory feedback are thought to control locomotion jointly. A few neurons supporting this concept have been identified, and models which explain leg coordination have been suggested [1, 2]. However, because of technical limitations, most of the neurons in the central nervous system (CNS) have not yet been well characterized, and it is difficult to manipulate individual neurons for testing the models. On the other hand, the recent progress of microscopic technology and data science is trying to make a whole central nervous system connectivity map [3]. To ascertain the specific functions of individual neurons, and how they are integrated into motor control circuits, we need methods to monitor and perturb their activity at cellular resolution.

Insects have a distributed CNS, with locomotor actuation centers located in the thoracic ganglion. We aim to analyze the locomotor circuits in the ventral nerve cord (VNC) of *Drosophila melanogaster*, which is a combined structure of the thoracic ganglion and the abdominal ganglion and analogous to the spinal cord in vertebrates. We seek to acquire genetic reagents to express activity reporters and modulators in specific cell types in the VNC.

© Springer Nature Switzerland AG 2019
U. Martinez-Hernandez et al. (Eds.): Living Machines 2019, LNAI 11556, pp. 334–337, 2019.
https://doi.org/10.1007/978-3-030-24741-6_32

2 Split-Gal4 System

We use the split-Gal4 system to target the intersection of two enhancer elements, each of which drives expression of one of the two split halves of the GAL4 transcription factors. Two hemi-drivers of GAL4 are DBD (GAL4's DNA-binding domain) and AD (activation domain) [4, 5] (Fig. 1(A)). In cells that express both enhancers, a functional GAL4 is reconstituted, thereby activating any transgene under GAL4/UAS control. Candidate AD and DBD pairs were selected by examining the expression patterns of several thousand GMR and VT (Vienna Tile) GAL4 lines [6, 7] which are generated by Gerry Rubin Lab and Barry Dickson Lab. Each contains an enhancer element that labels a subset of neurons in the CNS, and the AND operation between two of those elements creates even sparser labeling of neurons. We have screened over 6000 intersections of the split-Gal4 pairs and have generated ~ 1000 stable lines which have specific expression in a single or very few cell types (Fig. 1(B)).

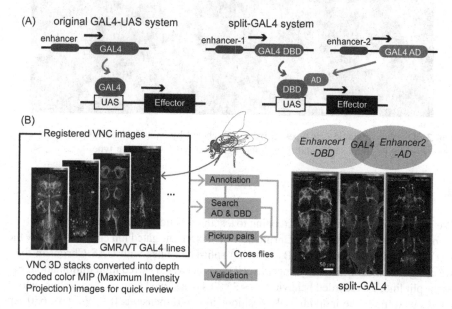

Fig. 1. Strategy to generate split-Gal4 line

3 Anatomical Analysis

For the anatomical analysis, we registered neuron images to compare them in the same 3D coordinate space, which is defined by a template VNC created from averaged VNC images. For each sample, we imaged the expression pattern of neurons by genetically encoded fluorescent markers and the whole VNC neuropil by immunohistochemistry staining of a synaptic marker. We aligned the images using the parameters that non-rigidly transform the VNC neuropil image into that of template.

The VNC can be subdivided into 3 segments of thoracic ganglion, and abdominal ganglion. Each thoracic ganglion consists of left and right hemispheric structure, which corresponds to the 6 legs. We categorized VNC cell types into 4 groups based on their segmental and hemispheric projection patterns in the thoracic ganglion (Fig. 2). (1) Local type: Neurons arborizing in a single hemisphere of a single segment, (2) Intra-segmental type: Neurons projecting between left and right hemisphere, but confined to a single segment, (3) Inter-segmental type: Neurons projecting among 2 or 3 segments, (4) Ascending type: Neurons projecting from VNC to brain. So far, 800 distinct cell types are represented by sparse split-Gal4 lines.

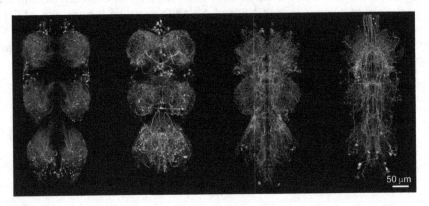

Fig. 2. Overlay of single cell types in the VNC labeled by split-Gal4 technique. From left to right: Local type, Intra-segmental type, Inter-segmental type, Ascending type.

4   Behavioral Screening

We also performed behavioral screening to test the functional role of each VNC cell type by optogenetic activation using Chrimson which is a light-gated ion channel to allow the fast depolarization of neurons. By crossing split-Gal4 lines with UAS-Chrimson flies, we can get the flies which have specific cell types activated by red light illumination. For each split line, we recorded behavior of ~25 flies in a sloped arena with a ceiling, which allows us to track the individual fly positions in two dimensions [8]. We gave 630 nm red lights in a sequential manner (5 s duration, 9 times with 30 s intervals) and acquired the changes of locomotor parameters (forward, backward, left, right and turn) in response to the stimuli. Characteristic locomotion phenotypes including initiation and stopping of locomotion as well as speed increasing or decreasing were observed in flies with cell-type-specific activation. In this screening, we also tested multiple lines which have expression in the same cell type with different levels. We could observe the behavior repeatedly in the different split-Gal4 lines which have the expression in the same cell types.

5 Conclusion and Future Works

We have generated the split Gal4 lines which can drive reporters and modulators in specific cell types. By using these genetic reagents, we could label and manipulate the neurons in the single cell resolution.

Segmentation of single neuron shapes enables us to analyze detailed comparison and generate the compatible data with electron microscope data to analyze their connectivity with their functions by identifying the neurotransmitters. We also started analyzing their leg movement, leg joint angle kinematics and stepping patterns in both activation and silencing experiments.

The genetic reagents, and the initial anatomical and behavioral analysis, provide the foundation for a detailed investigation of the circuit mechanisms underlying insect locomotion.

References

1. Burrows, M.: The Neurobiology of an Insect Brain. Oxford University Press on Demand (1996)
2. Bidaye, S.S., Bockemühl, T., Büschges, A.: Six-legged walking in insects: how CPGs, peripheral feedback, and descending signals generate coordinated and adaptive motor rhythms. J. Neurophysiol. **119**, 459–475 (2017). https://doi.org/10.1152/jn.00658.2017
3. Zheng, Z., et al.: A complete electron microscopy volume of the brain of adult Drosophila melanogaster. Cell **174**, 730–743.e22 (2018). https://doi.org/10.1016/j.cell.2018.06.019
4. Pfeiffer, B.D., et al.: Tools for neuroanatomy and neurogenetics in Drosophila. Proc. Natl. Acad. Sci. **105**, 9715–9720 (2008). https://doi.org/10.1073/pnas.0803697105
5. Luan, H., Peabody, N.C., Vinson, C.R., White, B.H.: Refined spatial manipulation of neuronal function by combinatorial restriction of transgene expression. Neuron **52**, 425–436 (2006). https://doi.org/10.1016/j.neuron.2006.08.028
6. Tirian, L., Dickson, B.: The VT GAL4, LexA, and split-GAL4 driver line collections for targeted expression in the Drosophila nervous system. bioRxiv. 198648 (2017). https://doi.org/10.1101/198648
7. Dionne, H., Hibbard, K.L., Cavallaro, A., Kao, J.C., Rubin, G.M.: Genetic reagents for making split-GAL4 lines in Drosophila. Genetics **209**, 31–35 (2018). https://doi.org/10.1534/genetics.118.300682
8. Branson, K., Robie, A.A., Bender, J., Perona, P., Dickinson, M.H.: High-throughput ethomics in large groups of Drosophila. Nat. Methods **6**, 451–457 (2009). https://doi.org/10.1038/nmeth.1328

Using Two IMU Sensors to Simulate Lower Body Stance

Connor Morrow[✉], Remigius Stecher, and Alexander Hunt

Department of Mechanical and Materials Engineering,
Portland State University, Portland, OR 97207, USA
comorrow@pdx.edu

Abstract. This paper presents initial findings that are a stepping stone to creating a sensor suite that monitors human posture with limited inertial measurement units. The focus is on using two inertial measurement units, one on each lower leg, to try to recreate the posture of the lower body. We compare a complementary filter and a biologically inspired filter for defining leg angle. Our results show that lower leg stance and hip position can be calculated through the use of both filters, with the complementary filter offering a less computationally intensive result while also being more accurate at tracking.

Keywords: IMU sensor · AHRS · Vestibular emulation

1 Introduction

Understanding human posture, stance, and balance is important for the health of an aging populace, where falling becomes a primary concern. In the United States, falls are the leading cause of fatal and non-fatal injuries among individuals 65 and older [1]. Developing an easy solution to monitor center of mass and posture to prevent falls would dramatically improve the quality of life for individuals aged 65 and older. By knowing the position of their legs and torso, the center of mass can be calculated [2], which allows for early detection of when a fall is imminent.

A way of detecting limb position and posture is through the use of inertial measurement units (IMU sensors). IMU sensors collect rotational velocity and linear acceleration data. Combining this data provides an attitude and heading reference system (AHRS) that can describe the motion and orientation of the sensor, which, when attached to a body segment, can track the limbs as well. IMU sensors are desirable for recording human posture due to their small size, portability, and low cost. This paper compares two methods for filtering IMU sensor data in the context of tracking lower leg position and hip displacement. The first is the complementary filter [3] and the other is a bio-inspired filter which emulates the human vestibular system [5]. The vestibular emulating filter

Supported by Portland State University.

U. Martinez-Hernandez et al. (Eds.): Living Machines 2019, LNAI 11556, pp. 338–341, 2019.
https://doi.org/10.1007/978-3-030-24741-6_33

was chosen to evaluate how well a biologically inspired filter would compare with a traditional filter. The main contribution of this work is it provides a unique investigation of determining hip height with a reduced number of IMU sensors when compared to previous methods [6].

2   Methods

2.1   Experimental Setup

The goal of the experiment was to identify if the complementary filter or vestibular emulating filter would be better at monitoring lower leg position and angle. The experiment was conducted with one participant, with an IMU sensor attached to the outside of their shank, 8 cm below the knee of each leg.

The participant entered a squat and stood back up several times, while being recorded by video next to a measuring stick. Hip height was calculated manually through video analysis and used to validate the two sensor fusion algorithms.

2.2   Complementary Filter

The complementary filter is used to help eliminate gyro drift in the IMU sensors. The method first multiplies the angular velocity signal by the sampling time and adds it to the previous calculated angle. This intermediate angle is then multiplied by a gain between 0 and 1. Another angle is formed by the tangents of the acceleration vector's components, which is also multiplied by a gain, equal to 1 minus the gyro gain. For this experiment, the gyroscope gain was set to 0.9, and the accelerometer gain was set to 0.1. The gyroscope angle and the angle formed by the acceleration vector data are then summed together to find the overall angle of rotation. The resulting angles provided an absolute rotation matrix, describing the rotated orientation of the lower leg.

$$\theta_t = Gain_{gyroscope} \times (\theta_{t-1} + \omega_t \times t_s) + Gain_{accelerometer} \times tan(\frac{a_1}{a_2}) \quad (1)$$

2.3   Vestibular Emulating Filter

The other filter investigated is a bio-inspired filter developed by Mergner et al. [5]. The vestibular system uses biological analogs to IMU sensors for balance control, and transfer functions have been developed to emulate the system. Figure 1 shows the block diagram of the algorithm, including the biologically inspired transfer functions used to filter the data coming from the sensors. Rotation matrices are calculated from the resulting estimated gravity vector, $\hat{g}$, and the IMU sensor's originally detected gravity vector, found during the start up of the experiment.

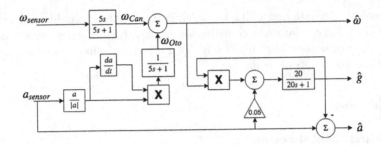

Fig. 1. Block diagram which represents the vestibular emulating algorithm, based on Mergner's et al. paper [5].

3   Results

The results of the experiment show that the position of the hip height calculated from the complementary filter closely matches the· height retrieved from the camera validation method (Fig. 2). The vestibular emulated filter, however, has a significant phase lag between the hip height found from the camera. To quantify the accuracy of both results, the root mean squared error was calculated between the normalized heights calculated by both algorithms and the normalized heights from the validation techniques.

$$RMS = \sqrt{\frac{1}{N}\sum_N(h_{algorithm} - h_{validation})^2} \qquad (2)$$

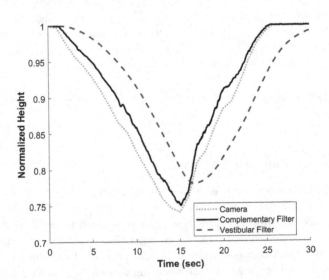

Fig. 2. Normalised experimental hip heights compared to the validation methods. The complementary filter determined hip height follows the camera height closely, while the vestibular filter has significant phase lag.

The complementary filter has an RMS of 0.020 compared to the camera validation. The vestibular filter performs worse than the complementary filter. Compared to the camera system, the vestibular filter has an RMS of 0.061.

4 Conclusion

The results demonstrate how a limited number of IMU sensors can be used to determine hip height during motion. The complementary filter does a better job than the vestibular algorithm of tracking the IMU sensor orientation for a very low computational cost. The low RMS of 0.020 means a fair amount of confidence can be put into the use of the complementary filter when tracking leg orientation.

4.1 Future Work

The insights found here are one step to further experiments. The complementary filter should be next tested to see how well it performs in a more dynamic environment, specifically during gait. Another comparison to look into is the accuracy of a quarternion based AHRS algorithm for tracking limbs, namely the gradient descent method detailed by Madgwick et al. [4].

References

1. Burns, E.R., Stevens, J.A., Lee, R.: The direct costs of fatal and non-fatal falls among older adults — United States. J. Saf. Res. **58**, 99–103 (2016). https://linkinghub.elsevier.com/retrieve/pii/S0022437516300172
2. Dumas, R., Chàze, L., Verriest, J.P.: Adjustments to McConville et al. and Young et al. body segment inertial parameters. J. Biomech. **40**(3), 543–553 (2007). https://linkinghub.elsevier.com/retrieve/pii/S0021929006000728
3. Islam, T., Islam, M.S., Shajid-Ul-Mahmud, M., Hossam-E-Haider, M.: Comparison of complementary and Kalman filter based data fusion for attitude heading reference system, Dhaka, Bangladesh, p. 020002 (2017). http://aip.scitation.org/doi/abs/10.1063/1.5018520
4. Madgwick, S.O.H., Harrison, A.J.L., Vaidyanathan, R.: Estimation of IMU and MARG orientation using a gradient descent algorithm. In: 2011 IEEE International Conference on Rehabilitation Robotics, Zurich, pp. 1–7. IEEE, June 2011. http://ieeexplore.ieee.org/document/5975346/
5. Mergner, T., Schweigart, G., Fennell, L.: Vestibular humanoid postural control. J. Physiol. Paris **103**(3–5), 178–194 (2009). https://linkinghub.elsevier.com/retrieve/pii/S0928425709000436
6. Yi, C., Ma, J., Guo, H., Han, J., Gao, H., Jiang, F., Yang, C.: Estimating three-dimensional body orientation based on an improved complementary filter for human motion tracking. Sensors **18**(11), 3765 (2018). http://www.mdpi.com/1424-8220/18/11/3765

Analyzing the Interplay Between Local CPG Activity and Sensory Signals for Inter-leg Coordination in *Drosophila*

William Nourse[1]([⊠]) [iD], Nicholas Szczecinski[1,2], Moritz Haustein[2], Till Bockemühl[2], Ansgar Büschges[2], and Roger Quinn[1]

[1] Case Western Reserve Universtiy, Cleveland, OH 44106, USA
nourse@case.edu
[2] Zoological Institute, University of Cologne, Cologne 50674, Germany

Abstract. Leg coordination is important for walking robots. Insects are able to effectively walk despite having small metabolisms and size, and understanding the neural mechanisms which govern their walking could prove useful for improving legged robots. In order to explore the possible neural systems responsible for inter-leg coordination, leg positional data for walking fruit flies of the species Drosophila melanogaster was recorded, where one individual leg was amputated at the base of the tibia. These experiments have shown that when amputated, the remaining stump oscillates in a speed-dependent manner. At low walking speeds there is a wide range of possible stump periods, and this variance collapses down to a minimum as walking speed increases. We believe this behavior can be explained by noisy pattern generation networks (CPGs) within the legs, with intra-leg load feedback and inter-leg global signals stabilizing the network. In this paper, this biological data will be analyzed so that a simplified neuromechanical model can be designed in order to explain this behavior.

Keywords: Drosophila · Sensory feedback · Inter-leg coordination

1 Introduction

A robot with the neuromechanical design of an insect could be successful in walking, and accordingly many robots have been designed to mimic the behavior seen in insects and arthropods, including the praying mantis [4] and lobster [1]. One area of active study within insect locomotion is inter-leg coordination, where behavioral studies on stick insects [3] and fruit flies [5] have been performed. Previous work has studied the behavior of walking flies where various legs were amputated [2]. We aim to further analyze this behavior observed in *Drosophila* so that we may design better walking controllers for legged robots.

This work was funded by National Science Foundation (NSF) Award #1704436.

© Springer Nature Switzerland AG 2019
U. Martinez-Hernandez et al. (Eds.): Living Machines 2019, LNAI 11556, pp. 342–345, 2019.
https://doi.org/10.1007/978-3-030-24741-6_34

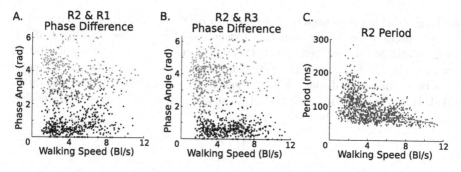

Fig. 1. R2 phase and period with respect to walking speed in body-lengths per second. Each data point corresponds to a single DEP event of R2. Shown in (A) and (B) are the phase locations of the specific DEP between the previous and next AEP in R1 or R3, respectively. Color refers to the DEP timing, with black corresponding to the first DEP after the reference AEP, green to the second, and purple to the third and beyond (color figure available online). Shown in (C) are the periods between R2 DEPs, and their corresponding walking speeds. An exponential regression curve for (C) is shown in red.

2   Methods

All analysis was performed on data collected following the methods presented in [2]. 12 males of *Drosophila melanogaster* had their right middle leg (R2) amputated distal to the femur, were tethered and placed on an air-supported polypropylene sphere, and were recorded by a high-speed video camera as they walked. Eighty-three trials of data were collected, with the data consisting of recorded timestamps corresponding to the anterior and posterior extreme positions (AEP and PEP) of the intact right front and hind legs (R1 and R3), as well as dorsal and ventral extreme positions (DEP and VEP) of R2.

The behavior of R2 was characterized through analysis of the oscillation period and the phase relationships between R2 and the intact legs (R1 and R3). Phase differences between the legs were computed using

$$\Phi_{R2} = \frac{t^{DEP} - t_{-}^{AEP}}{t_{+}^{AEP} - t_{-}^{AEP}} \tag{1}$$

where Φ_{R2} is the phase offset of R2, t^{DEP} is the timestamp where R2 reaches a DEP, t_{-}^{AEP} is the timestamp of the reference leg AEP immediately preceding t^{DEP}, and t_{+}^{AEP} is the following reference leg AEP. This calculates where the given R2 DEP falls within the AEP period of a reference leg, with the resulting data shown in Fig. 1. The data presented here appears different than shown in [2], as more data is present at slower walking speeds. At these slow walking speeds, it is possible for R2 to exhibit several consecutive DEPs between each reference AEP. Due to this and the varied scattering of the phase and period information across a range of walking speeds, it was necessary to characterize this variable behavior. The data was sorted into bins based on the fly's average walking speed between each pair of reference AEPs, then each bin was described using a probability density function to compare the relative likelihood of different states within a given speed. Polar histograms of the phase information are presented in Fig. 2, and the period information in Fig. 3. The experimental data rarely had long durations at one speed, so phase drift could not be quantified. However, the data analyzed in [2] showed preferential inter-leg latencies, suggesting that phase drift is not present.

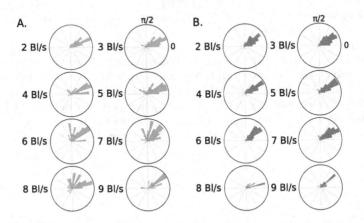

Fig. 2. Probability density functions of R2 phase information. (A) and (B) are the density functions of the first DEP points seen in Fig. 1 (A) and (B) with respect to R1 and R3. Data was sorted into bins by average walking speed (body-lengths/second) between reference AEPs, with each bin represented by a different polar histogram.

3 Results and Discussion

In order to construct a model of the behavior exhibited by *Drosophila* in [2], we needed to further quantify the relationship between the intact legs and stump. As shown in Fig. 2, it appears that the phase relationship between the amputated R2 and the intact R3 is nearly identical across all walking speeds. This suggests that there is some mechanism of direct phase influence between the intact R3 and the stump, which induces a DEP in the R2 stump at a constant point within the period of R3. The phase relationship between the amputated R2 and the intact R1 also appears to be similar across all walking speeds, although the range of possible phase offsets is more varied. This suggests that the phase coupling between R2 and R3 is stronger than between R2 and R1.

Figure 3 suggests that there is a speed-dependent factor affecting the stump's oscillation period. At low walking speeds there appears to be a wide range of possible oscillation periods centered at a slow period, then as walking speed increases the range of possible periods narrows and the average period decreases. This also suggests that the stump's period is not affected by the phase resetting shown in Fig. 2, and could be induced by a separate neural mechanism.

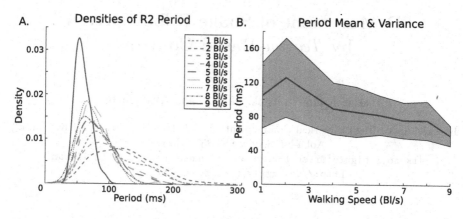

Fig. 3. Probability density functions of R2 period. Shown in (A) are the density functions of the R2 DEP periods, as seen in Fig. 1(C). Points were sorted into bins based on average walking speed, where each bin has a separate density function. Average periods and variances per walking speed are given in (B).

We believe that these results provide particular insights into a potential source for the behavior observed in [2]. Based on our results, we argue that the period of the central pattern generator (CPG) for the R2 stump is naturally noisy, but would be stabilized and regulated by proprioceptive and load feedback if the leg were intact. Without load feedback the stump's period fluctuates until the walking speed increases, increasing the amplitude of velocity feedback and stabilizing the CPG's period. We intend to modify our previously described neuromechanical insect leg model [4] by incorporating these noisy CPG networks and load feedback pathways hypothesized in this work, as well as incorporating multiple legs.

References

1. Ayers, J., Witting, J.: Biomimetic approaches to the control of underwater walking machines. Philos. Trans. Roy. Soc. A Math. Phys. Eng. Sci. **365**(1850), 273–295 (2007)
2. Berendes, V., Zill, S.N., Büschges, A., Bockemühl, T.: Speed-dependent interplay between local pattern-generating activity and sensory signals during walking in Drosophila. J. Exp. Biol. **219**(23), 3781–3793 (2016)
3. Cruse, H.: What mechanisms coordinate leg movement in walking arthropods? Trends Neurosci. **13**(1), 15–21 (1990)
4. Szczecinski, N.S., Quinn, R.D.: MantisBot changes stepping speed by entraining CPGs to positive velocity feedback. In: Mangan, M., Cutkosky, M., Mura, A., Verschure, P.F.M.J., Prescott, T., Lepora, N. (eds.) Living Machines 2017. LNCS (LNAI), vol. 10384, pp. 440–452. Springer, Cham (2017). https://doi.org/10.1007/978-3-319-63537-8_37
5. Wosnitza, A., Bockemühl, T., Dübbert, M., Scholz, H., Büschges, A.: Inter-leg coordination in the control of walking speed in Drosophila. J. Exp. Biol. **216**(3), 480–491 (2013)

3D Movement of Snake Robot Driven by *Tegotae*-Based Control

Takeshi Kano[✉], Naoki Matsui, and Akio Ishiguro

Research Institute of Electrical Communication, Tohoku University, 2-1-1 Katahira,
Aoba-ku, Sendai 980-8577, Japan
{tkano,ishiguro}@riec.tohoku.ac.jp, naoki.matsui.31@gmail.com
http://www.cmplx.riec.tohoku.ac.jp/

Abstract. Snakes possess versatile gait patterns and use them appropriately to adapt to various environments. To reproduce this ability, we have previously proposed a decentralized control scheme for snake robots based on *Tegotae*, a Japanese concept describing how well a perceived reaction matches an expectation. Here we extend our previous control scheme. Both pitch and yaw joints are embedded in a snake robot, and contact points with the ground as well as lateral bending of the body are controlled by the extended control scheme. We validate the proposed control scheme via real-world experiments with the robot developed.

Keywords: Snake robot · *Tegotae*-based control

1 Introduction

Snakes have various gait patterns such as lateral undulation, concertina locomotion, sinus-lifting, and sidewinding (Fig. 1) [1–4]. They use them appropriately according to the current circumstances encountered. It is likely that there exists an ingenious mechanism underlying this behavior, and its clarification will benefit the development of robots that function well in harsh environments such as disaster areas. However, snake-like robots previously developed [3,4] could only exhibit specific types of gait patterns, and the essential mechanism for the emergence of situation-dependent gait patterns is still unclear.

To address this issue, we have previously proposed an autonomous decentralized control scheme based on *Tegotae*, a Japanese concept describing how well a perceived reaction matches an expectation [5,6]. We demonstrated via simulations and real-world experiments that some of the gait patterns can be well reproduced. However, because our previous work focused on 2D movement, we could not reproduce the locomotion patterns in which contact points with the ground change spatiotemporally, such as sidewinding. In this study, we extend the previous control scheme to 3D and demonstrate with a snake-like robot implementing both pitch and yaw joints that sidewinding can be well reproduced by using the extended control scheme.

© Springer Nature Switzerland AG 2019
U. Martinez-Hernandez et al. (Eds.): Living Machines 2019, LNAI 11556, pp. 346–350, 2019.
https://doi.org/10.1007/978-3-030-24741-6_35

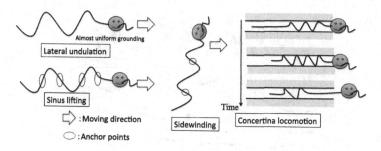

Fig. 1. Gait patterns of snakes.

2 Model

A schematic of the body is shown in Fig. 2(a). Several segments are concatenated one-dimensionally wherein the pitch and yaw joints are implemented alternatively. Force sensors are embedded at each body part between the yaw and pitch joints on both sides of the body. The target angles of the ith yaw and pitch joints at time step t are denoted by $\bar{\theta}_i^y(t)$ and $\bar{\theta}_i^p(t)$, respectively. The joint torques are generated so that the real joint angles approach the target joint angles.

Except for the most anterior joints which are controlled by a motor command from a higher level controller, the target joint angles are updated each time step as follows:

$$\bar{\theta}_i^y(t+1) = \theta_{i-1}^y(t) + \sigma_y \tanh \left(\kappa_y \sum_{j=i-n_h}^{i+n_f} |S_i(t)| \tau_j^y(t) \right), \tag{1}$$

$$\bar{\theta}_i^p(t+1) = \theta_{i-1}^p(t) + \sigma_p \tanh \left(\kappa_p \sum_{j=i-n_h}^{i+n_f} S_i(t) \tau_j^y(t) \right), \tag{2}$$

where σ_y, σ_p κ_y, and κ_p are positive constants, and $\tau_j^y(t)$ is a torque generated at the jth yaw joint. The first terms on the right-hand sides of Eqs. (1) and (2) denote the curvature derivative control [7] wherein torques proportional to the curvature derivative of the body curve are generated so that bodily waves propagate from the head to the tail.

The second terms on the right-hand sides of Eqs. (1) and (2) denote a sensory feedback based on *Tegotae*, which is described as the product of the torque, *i.e.*, intended action, and the contact forces, *i.e.*, reaction [5,6]. This feedback works as shown in Fig. 2(b). When a torque generated to bend the body rightward (red arrows in Fig. 2(b)(i)) resulted in receiving a contact force from the left (blue arrow in Fig. 2(b)(i)), the contact force assists propulsion (*i.e.*, good *Tegotae*), and the feedback works to generate further torques along the yaw axis so that the contact force increases. Moreover, torques along the pitch axis are generated so that the body is pushed against the ground. Meanwhile, when a torque

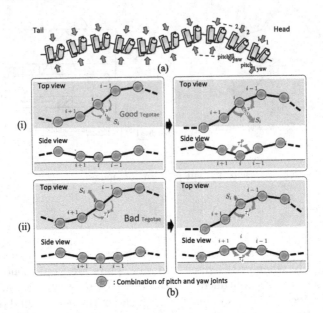

Fig. 2. Schematic of the model. (a) body structure. The pitch and yaw joints are implemented alternatively. Arrows denote the locations of the force sensors. (b) Schematic of the *Tegotae*-based control: (i) and (ii) show the cases of good and bad *Tegotae*, respectively (detailed explanations are provided in the main text). (Color figure online)

generated to bend the body rightward (red arrows in Fig. 2(b)(ii)) resulted in receiving a contact force from the right (blue arrow in Fig. 2(b)(ii)), the contact force impedes propulsion (*i.e.*, bad *Tegotae*), and the feedback works to generate further torques along the yaw axis so that the contact force decreases. Moreover, torques along the pitch axis are generated so that the body lifts off the ground.

Note that the proposed control scheme is equivalent to our previous control scheme when $\bar{\theta}_i^p(t)$ is set to zero.

3   Robot Experiment

The overview of the developed robot HAUBOT VIII is shown in Fig. 3(a). The robot consists of 24 segments concatenated one-dimensionally. Yaw and pitch joints are embedded alternatively between the adjacent segments, and they are driven by servo motors (ROBOTIS, Dynamixel AX-12). The motors generate torques proportional to the difference between the target and real joint angles. Seals (colltex, climbing skins) are attached at the bottom of the segments so that friction coefficient along the forward direction is smaller than that along the backward direction.

Sensors are embedded at each body part between yaw and pitch joints on both sides of the body. Detailed structure of a sensor is shown in Fig. 3(b). Springs are embedded on both sides of the body, and the inner structure can move along

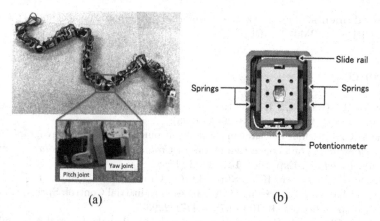

(a)   (b)

Fig. 3. Snake-like robot HAUBOT VIII: (a) overview and (b) detailed structure of each segment.

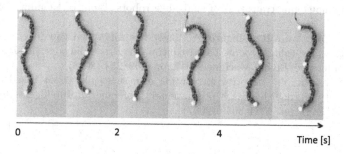

Fig. 4. Experimental result. The robot exhibits sidewinding.

a slide rail. The displacements of the springs are detected by potentiometers (ALPS, RDC1014A09). In this way, reaction forces from the environment can be estimated.

Figure 4 shows an experimental result when the motor command from the higher center is given by an asymmetric periodic function. The robot exhibited sidewinding; thus, the proposed control scheme qualitatively reproduced the gait pattern of real snakes.

4   Conclusion

We extended the *Tegotae*-based control scheme for snake-like robots from 2D to 3D, and demonstrated that sidewinding, which was not reproduced in the 2D model, can be reproduced. Unlike the previous works [3,4], the proposed control scheme enables to reproduce the locomotion patterns of snakes in a self-organized manner. We believe that further improvement of the hardware and the control scheme will lead to achieve more adaptive locomotion.

Acknowledgments. This work was supported by Japan Science and Technology Agency, CREST (JPMJCR14D5).

References

1. Moon, B.R., Gans, C.: Kinematics, muscular activity and propulsion in gopher snakes. J. Exp. Biol. **201**, 2669–2684 (1998)
2. Jayne, B.C.: Muscular mechanisms of snake locomotion: an electromyographic study of the sidewinding and concertina modes of *Crotalus Cerastes Nerodia Fasciata and Elaphe Obsoleta*. J. Exp. Biol. **140**, 1–33 (1988)
3. Liljebäck, P., Pettersen, K.Y., Stavdahl, Ø., Gravdahl, J.T.: Snake Robots. Modelling, Mechatronics, and Control: Advances in Industrial Control. Springer, London (2012). https://doi.org/10.1007/978-1-4471-2996-7
4. Hirose, S.: Biologically Inspired Robots (Snake-like Locomotor and Manipulator). Oxford University Press, Oxford (1993)
5. Kano, T., Yoshizawa, R., Ishiguro, A.: Tegotae-based decentralised control scheme for autonomous gait transition of snake-like robots. Bioinsp. Biomim. **12**, 046009 (2017)
6. Kano, T., Yoshizawa, R., Ishiguro, A.: Snake-like robot that can generate versatile gait patterns by using *Tegotae*-based control. In: Proceedings of the 7th International Conference, Living Machines 2017, pp. 249–254 (2018)
7. Date, H., Takita, Y.: Adaptive locomotion of a snake like robot based on curvature derivatives. In: IEEE/RSJ International Conference on Intelligent Robots and Systems (IROS), pp. 3554–3559 (2007)

Exploring the Potential of the Animal-Like Robot MiRo as a Therapeutic Tool for Children Diagnosed with Autism

Maria Panagiotidi[1]($\boxtimes$), Simon Wilson[3], and Tony Prescott[2]

[1] Department of Psychology, School of Health and Society,
University of Salford, Salford, UK
m.panagiotidi@salford.ac.uk

[2] Sheffield Robotics and Department of Computer Science,
The University of Sheffield, Sheffield, UK
t.j.prescott@sheffield.ac.uk

[3] Ysgol Y Deri, Sully Road, Penarth, Vale of Glamorgan CF64 2TP, UK
SWilson@yyd.org.uk

Abstract. Autism spectrum disorder (ASD) is a neurodevelopmental condition characterized by social interaction and communication deficits and the presence of restricted, repetitive patterns of behaviour. One potential intervention for ASD is animal-assisted therapy, which can improve physiological and psychological health. Animal-assisted therapy, however, is not widely accepted or possible due to potential negative effects of animals on vulnerable populations, health and safety concerns, and cost. Robot-assisted therapy could be offered as an alternative and result in similar health benefits. The MiRo robot, a companion biomimetic robot, has the potential to be used as a social healthcare robot. The aim of the proposed study is to investigate the effects of an interaction with MiRo on a group of children with ASD. In particular, the effect of MiRo on children's mood, well-being, and involvement will be examined. The results of this study would allow us to examine the potential companion robots have to be used in robot therapy and social healthcare.

Keywords: Social robotics · Robot-assisted therapy · MiRo robot · Biomimetics

1 Introduction

Autism spectrum disorder (ASD) is a neurodevelopmental condition characterized by social interaction and communication deficits and the presence of restricted, repetitive patterns of behaviour [1]. A number of potential interventions have been proposed for this condition but they all typically require time, resources, and labour and can put substantial strain on both families and caregivers [2]. One potential intervention is animal-assisted therapy (AAT). Research on human-animal interactions has shown that interactions with animals make a positive difference to the physiological and psychological health of people (e.g. by lowering blood pressure and heart-rate, by reducing loneliness) [3]. AAT can have a strong impact on the behaviour of children with

U. Martinez-Hernandez et al. (Eds.): Living Machines 2019, LNAI 11556, pp. 351–354, 2019.
https://doi.org/10.1007/978-3-030-24741-6_36

autism. In particular, existing evidence suggests that after a session with an animal children show increased social interaction and communication as well as decreased problem behaviours, autistic severity, and stress [4]. AAT, however, is not widely accepted or possible in a number of cases due to possible negative effects of animals on vulnerable populations, like infections, bites, allergy, and rashes. This concern can be of particular importance in the case of individuals with autism, who report higher levels of allergies [5].

A number of robots mimicking characteristics of pets (biomimetic) have been developed that could be used instead of animals (e.g. Aibo, Paro, MIRO). Robot-assisted therapy (RAT) could be offered as an alternative to individuals who do not have access to an animal and result in similar health benefits [6]. The MiRo robot [7, 8] a companion biomimetic robot, created by Consequential Robotics, a spin-out from the University of Sheffield, has the potential to be used as a social healthcare robot. MiRo is capable of emulating familiar mammalian body language using a control system based on a simplified model of the mammalian brain [7]. This allows it to effectively communicate emotional state and intent in a similar manner to that of an animal [6, 7].

Preliminary evidence from studies in neurotypical children suggests that they are more involved in a motor task when they interact with a robot rather than with a virtual agent [9]. This suggests that robots have the potential to motivate students in learning [10]. There is growing evidence suggesting that some individuals with ASD prefer robots to non-robotic toys or humans and that they show an intrinsic interest in technology [11, 12]. Additionally, individuals with autism have difficulty interpreting facial expressions and other social cues in social interaction [13]. As a result, they often avoid social interactions since people appear to be unpredictable and confusing. Furthermore, children with ASD prefer predictable and structure environments and interactions [14]. Animal-like robots have a potential advantage in that they are not replacing human interaction with a child with autism rather they have the potential to augment it. A study by Stanton et al. [15] showed that children with ASD benefit in terms of increased verbal and reciprocal exchanges from interacting with Sony's robot dog *Aibo* compared to a mechanical dog without sensory or AI capabilities. An animal-like robot such as MiRo, therefore, appears to be a suitable starting point for therapeutic interventions. In particular, MiRo displays the emotion it "experiences" by changing its colour [6], and acts in a predictable manner, making it particularly appealing to individuals with autism.

Even though MiRO has the potential to be used as an intervention with autistic populations, no study so far has examined its effectiveness. The aim of the proposed study is to investigate the effects of a brief interaction with MiRo on a group of children with ASD. In particular, the effects on mood, well-being, and involvement will be examined. The results of this study would allow us to examine the potential companion robots have to be used in robot therapy and social healthcare and could have a direct impact on the lives of individuals with autism. We here provide an outline of the planned study and expect to report preliminary findings in an extended version of this paper.

2 Methodology

2.1 Participants

Forty children aged 11–16 diagnosed with autism will be recruited from the *YsGol Y Deri* Special Educational Needs (SEN) school in Wales. Information about the students' IQ scores will be collected in collaboration with the school's educational psychologist.

2.2 Procedure

Participants and their legal guardians will be asked to sign the consent form and complete The Self-Assessment Manikin (SAM) [16], a non-verbal pictorial assessment, which measures emotional responses to stimuli. The teacher will complete the Leuven Well-being and Involvement Scales [17]. The Leuven scale is widely used in education and is a way to measure children's 'well-being' and 'involvement'.

Participants will be then be introduced to MiRo and be asked to interact with it (visual or tactile interaction). The maximum length of interaction will be 15 min but participants will be able to stop at any point after the start of the session. The duration as well as the type of interaction will be analysed. The next step will involve removing MiRO from the room and asking participants to complete SAM for the second time. The participants will then return to class and the researcher will complete the Leuven. To assess whether the effect of the session is long lasting, the Leuven scale will also be recorded at the end of the school day.

3 Data Analysis

Differences in scores in the two scales before MiRO is introduced and after the brief interaction will be examined. We hypothesise that a brief session with a biomimetic robot will improve the mood of the children and will result in higher levels of involvement and well-being. In addition to this, the time spent interacting with the robot will also be analysed as well as the type of interaction, that will be coded for a number of characteristics (e.g. visual, tactile).

4 Discussion

The results of this study will allow us to assess whether robot therapy is a potential effective intervention for children with ASD. In addition to this, long-lasting effects of the short interaction will be examined by comparing Leuven scores before the interaction and at the end of the school day. This will be the basis for a number of future studies further investigating the effectiveness of RAT. Similar interventions could be used for disorders often co-diagnosed with autism, such as Attention Deficit Hyperactivity Disorder (ADHD) [18].

References

1. American Psychiatric Association: Diagnostic and Statistical Manual of Mental Disorders, 5th edn. Arlington (2013)
2. Mackintosh, V.H., Goin-Kochel, R.P., Myers, B.J.: "What do you like/dislike about the treatments you're currently using?" a qualitative study of parents of children with autism spectrum disorders. Focus Autism Dev. Disabil. 27(1), 51–60 (2012)
3. Nimer, J., Lundahl, B.: Animal-assisted therapy: a meta-analysis. Anthrozoös 20(3), 225–238 (2007)
4. O'Haire, M.E.: Animal-assisted intervention for autism spectrum disorder: a systematic literature review. J. Autism Dev. Disord. 43(7), 1606–1622 (2013)
5. Miyazaki, C., et al.: Allergies in children with autism spectrum disorder: a systematic review and meta-analysis. Rev. J. Autism Dev. Disord. 2(4), 374–401 (2015)
6. Collins, E.C., Prescott, T.J., Mitchinson, B.: Saying It with light: a pilot study of affective communication using the MiRo robot. In: Wilson, S.P., Verschure, P.F.M.J., Mura, A., Prescott, T.J. (eds.) Living Machines 2015. LNCS (LNAI), vol. 9222, pp. 243–255. Springer, Cham (2015). https://doi.org/10.1007/978-3-319-22979-9_25
7. Mitchinson, B., Prescott, T.J.: MiRo: A robot "mammal" with a biomimetic brain-based control system. In: Lepora, N.F.F., Mura, A., Mangan, M., Verschure, P.F.M.J., Desmulliez, M., Prescott, T.J.J. (eds.) Living Machines 2016. LNCS (LNAI), vol. 9793, pp. 179–191. Springer, Cham (2016). https://doi.org/10.1007/978-3-319-42417-0_17
8. Prescott, T.J., Mitchinson, B., Conran, S.: MiRo: an animal-like companion robot with a biomimetic brain-based control system. In: Proceedings of the Companion of the 2017 ACM/IEEE International Conference on Human-Robot Interaction, pp. 50–51. ACM (2017)
9. Fridin, M., Belokopytov, M.: Embodied robot versus virtual agent: involvement of preschool children in motor task performance. Int. J. Hum. Comput. Interact. 30(6), 459–469 (2014)
10. Conti, D., Di Nuovo, S., Buono, S., Di Nuovo, A.: Robots in education and care of children with developmental disabilities: a study on acceptance by experienced and future professionals. Int. J. Soc. Robot. 9(1), 51–62 (2017)
11. Dautenhahn, K., Werry, I.: Towards interactive robots in autism therapy: background, motivation and challenges. Pragmatics Cogn. 12(1), 1–35 (2004)
12. Diehl, J.J., Schmitt, L.M., Villano, M., Crowell, C.R.: The clinical use of robots for individuals with autism spectrum disorders: a critical review. Res. Autism Spectr. Disord. 6(1), 249–262 (2012)
13. Uljarevic, M., Hamilton, A.: Recognition of emotions in autism: a formal meta-analysis. J. Autism Dev. Disord. 43(7), 1517–1526 (2013)
14. Wong, C., Kasari, C.: Play and joint attention of children with autism in the preschool special education classroom. J. Autism Dev. Disord. 42(10), 2152–2161 (2012)
15. Stanton, C.M., Kahn, P.H., Severson, R.L., Ruckert, J.H., Gill, B.T.: Robotic animals might aid in the social development of children with autism. In: Paper Presented at the 3rd ACM/IEEE International Conference on Human-Robot Interaction (HRI), Amsterdam (2008)
16. Bradley, M.M., Lang, P.J.: Measuring emotion: the self-assessment manikin and the semantic differential. J. Behav. Ther. Exp. Psychiatry 25(1), 49–59 (1994)
17. Laevers, F., Vandenbussche, E., Kog, M., Depondt, L.: A Process-Oriented Child Monitoring System for Young Children. Centre for Experimental Education, Leuven, Belgium (1994)
18. Panagiotidi, M., Overton, P.G., Stafford, T.: Co-occurrence of ASD and ADHD traits in an adult population. J. Attention Disord. 1087054717720720 (2017)

Hierarchical Behaviour for Object Shape Recognition Using a Swarm of Robots

Adrian Rubio-Solis[1(✉)] and Uriel Martinez-Hernandez[2(✉)]

[1] ACSE Department, University of Sheffield, Sheffield, UK
a.rubiosolis@sheffield.ac.uk
[2] EEE Department, University of Bath, Bath, UK
u.martinez@bath.ac.uk

Abstract. A hierarchical cognitive architecture for robot exploration and recognition of object shape is presented. This cognitive architecture proposes the combination of multiple robot behaviours based on (1) Evolutionary, (2) Fuzzy Logic and (3) Bayesian approaches. First, the Evolutionary approach allows a swarm of robots to locate and reach an object for exploration. Second, Fuzzy Logic is used to control the exploration of the object shape. Third, the Bayesian approach allows the robot to detect the orientation of the walls of the object being explored. Once the exploration process finishes, the swarm of robots determine whether the object has a rectangular or circular shape. This work is validated in a simulated environment and MATLAB using a swarm of E-puck robots. Overall, the experiments demonstrate that simple robots are capable of performing complex tasks through the combination of simple collective behaviours while learning from the interaction with the environment.

Keywords: Swarm robotics · Hierarchical control · Bayesian perception

1 Introduction

It has been demonstrated that in social organisms, collective decisions arise from a democratic consensus by pooling individual interactions and estimates about the environment [1]. Particularly in ant foraging, information retrieval about food sources is a collective process that involves individual activities as well as behaviourally integrated groups [2]. Based on the principles of self-organisation, ant foraging is a societal activity that has inspired a number of researchers in the area of robotics to create algorithms for different purposes. Examples of applications include search and rescue in hostile environments, demining and removal of toxic material. Some of the benefits from the foraging approach in swarm robotics are the robustness, collective intelligence and emerging behaviours to unexpected events. In this paper, a hierarchical cognitive architecture, composed of evolutionary aggregation, fuzzy logic, and Bayesian perception, is proposed for the control of the collective behaviour of a group of robots with basic computation capabilities [3], for exploration and identification of geometric shapes.

© Springer Nature Switzerland AG 2019
U. Martinez-Hernandez et al. (Eds.): Living Machines 2019, LNAI 11556, pp. 355–359, 2019.
https://doi.org/10.1007/978-3-030-24741-6_37

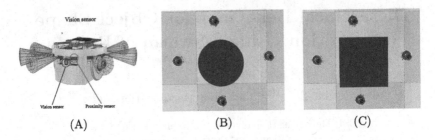

Fig. 1. (A) E-puck robot and (B,C) Examples of objects for shape recognition.

2   Methods

2.1   Robot Platform and Sensory System

This work employs the E-puck robot platform, which is a differential wheel miniature robot [4]. The E-puck is equipped with eight infrared sensors to evaluate
either the proximity of obstacles or the intensity of the surrounding environment
and a colour CMOS camera with a resolution of 640 × 480 pixels. The E-puck
robot and its sensors are shown in Fig. 1. The implementation of the hierarchical
cognitive architecture in the E-puck, is performed using two development tools
for robotics; V-REP and ENKI simulators.

2.2   Hierarchical Architecture for Control of Robot Behaviour

The proposed hierarchical cognitive architecture implements three robot
behaviours (a) evolutionary aggregation, (b) fuzzy logic theory and (c) Bayesian
perception for exploration and recognition of object shapes using a swarm of
robots. Examples of the object shapes used for exploration and the hierarchical
cognitive architecture are shown in Figs. 1B,C. The initial task for all robots
in the arena is to aggregate around the object and find the closest clear edge.

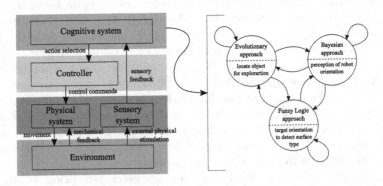

Fig. 2. Hierarchical architecture for robot control for the exploration of object shape.

For this process of aggregation, each robot employs a recurrent neural controller (Fig. 3A) that evolves a stochastic and deramdomised self-adaptation evolutionary strategy CMA-ES. The sensor data used for the aggregation process is collected from the camera as a binary input. Once the robots are aggregated around the object, the E-puck robots determine the orientation of the object shape. For this process, the robots employ proximity sensor data with a Bayesian formulation (Fig. 3B). This approach allows the robots to naturally accumulate evidence for accurate and robust decision-making processes [5]. Thus, using the data from the 8 proximity sensors, the robot is capable to estimate its orientation or angle with respect to the object edge being explored. This information is used by the robot for object exploration. This process is controlled with a Fuzzy Logic method which is implemented using an Interval Type-2 Fuzzy Logic Controller (IT2 FLC) [6], which receives as input the orientation estimation (Fig. 4). Thus, the robot makes decisions to move forward, backward, to the left or right according to the orientation estimated. These processes are repeated to perform the exploration of the whole object, and determine if it has a polygonal or circular shape. Finally, the E-puck robots emit a red or blue colour light to indicate that the object explored has circular or polygonal shape, respectively (Fig. 2).

3   Results

This preliminary study analysed the hierarchical behaviour of a swarm of E-puck robots for exploration of an object in a simulated environment. This architecture was implemented in MATLAB and the robots and objects were simulated in V-REP. MATLAB received signals from the camera, proximity sensors, and motor values from all robots. These data were processed and the output control signals were sent to V-REP to control the speed and movement of each robot during the exploration of the object shape. Figure 5 shows the processes performed by the robot for exploration of the object shape. First, the robots search for an object using data from the camera, and then, they start moving towards the object.

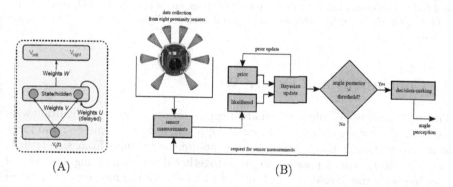

(A)   (B)

Fig. 3. (A) RNN for robot aggregation behaviour. (B) Bayesian method for estimation of the robot orientation or angle with respect to the object edge begin explored.

Second, the robots start the angle detection using proximity sensors to place the robot in position for exploration of the object shape. Third, the robots start moving forward and backward to collect data from the object edges using the proximity sensors. Then, each robot estimates if the corresponding edge belongs to a polygonal or circular object. Finally, the robots make a consensus, using majority vote, to determine if the complete shape of the object is polygonal or circular, displaying a blue or red colour light. The hierarchical architecture was tested using objects with different shapes such as triangles, squares, rectangles and circles. These experiments were repeated 10 times for each object, achieving a mean error of 10% for the recognition of object shape with a swarm of robots.

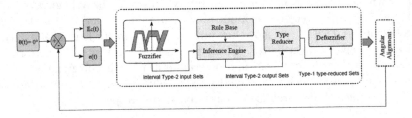

Fig. 4. Fuzzy Logic Controller for object exploration by the E-puck robot.

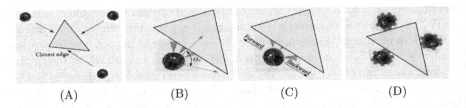

Fig. 5. Robots performing (A) aggregation to reach the object, (B) angle estimation and (C) forward and backward movements for edge angle perception. (D) Robots emit a blue light if the object shape is polygonal and red light otherwise. (Color figure online)

4   Conclusions and Future Work

This work presented a hierarchical architecture for object shape recognition with a swarm of robots using an evolutionary approach, a Bayesian method and fuzzy logic. Even though this work presented preliminary results from simulations, they showed that it is possible to bring together different learning and control paradigms for the development of intelligent robots. In the future work, we plan to implement this cognitive architecture using real E-puck robots for autonomous exploration and recognition of shapes from object in the real world.

References

1. Berdahl, A., Torney, C.J., Ioannou, C.C., Faria, J.J., Couzin, I.D.: Emergent sensing of complex environments by mobile animal groups. Science **339**(6119), 574–576 (2013)
2. Traniello, J.F.: Foraging strategies of ants. Ann. Rev. Entomol. **34**(1), 191–210 (1989)
3. Johnson, M., Brown, D.S.: Evolving and controlling perimeter, rendezvous, and foraging behaviors in a computation-free robot swarm (No. AFRL-RI-RS-TP-2016-005). Air Force Research Laboratory/RISC Rome United States (2016)
4. Mondada, F., et al.: The e-puck, a robot designed for education in engineering. In: Proceedings of the 9th Conference on Autonomous Robot Systems and Competitions, vol. 1, no. CONF, pp. 59–65 (2009)
5. Martinez-Hernandez, U., Dodd, T.J., Evans, M.H., Prescott, T.J., Lepora, N.F.: Active sensorimotor control for tactile exploration. Robot. Auton. Syst. **87**, 15–27 (2017)
6. Wagner, C., Hagras, H.: Toward general type-2 fuzzy logic systems based on zSlices. IEEE Trans. Fuzzy Syst. **18**(4), 637–660 (2010)

Development of Omnidirectional Mobile Treadmill for Neuroethology

Shunsuke Shigaki[1]($\boxtimes$) (iD), Kazushi Sanada[2] (iD), and Daisuke Kurabayashi[3] (iD)

[1] Osaka University, Osaka, Japan
shigaki@arl.sys.es.osaka-u.ac.jp
[2] Yokohama National University, Kanagawa, Japan
sanada-kazushi-sn@ynu.ac.jp
[3] Tokyo Institute of Technology, Tokyo, Japan
dkura@irs.sc.e.titech.ac.jp

Abstract. We developed an omnidirectional mobile treadmill for measuring the adaptive behavior of an insect. We focused on the odor source search problem to construct it. We employed a male silkworm moth *Bombyx mori*, which searches a female by walking, as an experimental insect. We evaluated the performance of the omnidirectional mobile treadmill by performing an odor source search experiment. As a result of the search experiment, the silkworm moth on the mobile treadmill was able to reach the odor source with 100% success rate. Therefore, we succeeded in developing the insect behavior measurement system and the drive system of the omnidirectional mobile treadmill.

Keywords: Omnidirectional mobile treadmill · Silkworm moth · Odor source search

1 Introduction

In recent years, there were many kinds of research which focused on the specific abilities possessed by living organisms, and many studies have been conducted to apply them to artificial systems. Animals have unique abilities depending on the species, and it is important to first understand the behavior of the animal in order to apply such abilities to an artificial system. It is thought that the adaptability of animals is caused from the interaction of environmental and physical characteristics and neural information processing [1]. Therefore, if it is possible to simultaneously measure the behavior of the moving animal in the real environment and the brain neural activity that controls that behavior, we might elucidate the selection process of situation-adaptive behaviors. However, the previous biological experiments have been carried out under controlled environmental conditions. In other words, experiments have been conducted in a special environment for the animal, and it may be difficult to measure the adaptability that occurs in a natural environment.

This work was partially supported by JSPS KAKENHI Grant Number JP18H05889, JP19K14943.

U. Martinez-Hernandez et al. (Eds.): Living Machines 2019, LNAI 11556, pp. 360–364, 2019.
https://doi.org/10.1007/978-3-030-24741-6_38

Therefore, in this research, we developed an omnidirectional mobile tread-mill. The omnidirectional mobile treadmill itself moves according to the amount of movement of the animal; therefore, the measurement target executes a task in a real environment while being on the measurement device. In previous research, a system was proposed in which an insect controls a differential wheeled robot to investigate sensory-motor integration of the insect [2]. However, this system might have difficulties to correctly reflect the behavior of the insect which is a multi-legged animal because it employs a differential wheeled type that has a constraint condition in the moving direction. For that reason, we add one degree of freedom to the drive system and construct the omnidirectional mobile tread-mill. We use an adult male silkworm moth (*Bombyx mori*) as in the previous research [2] as model organisms in this research and focus on its female searcha-bility [3][4]. In addition, we evaluate by performing an odor source search exper-iment whether the constructed omnidirectional mobile treadmill has the same movement performance as the behavior output of the silkworm moth.

In order to verify the system, the odor source search experiment of this research is conducted not under the natural environment such as outdoor but under a controlled environment (indoor).

2 Problem Statement

We mainly construct and evaluate an insect behavior measurement system which consists of the treadmill system and a drive system for movement. Specifically, we construct the system to satisfy the following two points; (i) construction of a treadmill capable of measuring the moving speed and direction of the silkworm moth in real time, (ii) construction of a drive system that can move in a one-on-one relationship with insect behavior. In order to evaluate the performance of the omnidirectional mobile treadmill, we actually mount the silkworm moth on the mobile treadmill and carry out odor source search experiments.

If the system moves according to the amount of movement of the silkworm moth and it can be localized to the odor source (pheromone) with a success rate of over 90%, we succeed in constructing the insect behavior measurement system and the drive system for movement [2].

3 Construction of Omnidirectional Mobile Treadmill

Figure 1(a)(b) illustrates an omnidirectional mobile treadmill for a silkworm moth. Moreover, Fig. 1(c) shows the system configuration of the insect behavior measurement system and the drive system. By installing optical mouse sensors (MA-MA6W, Sanwa Supply, Japan) on the x and y axes of the sphere for mea-suring moth behavior, it is possible to measure the behavior output of the moth with three degrees of freedom (v_x, v_y, ω) as shown in Fig. 1(b). We read the out-put of the optical mouse sensor using the Arduino Pro Mini (SparkFun, USA) via the Mini USB Shield (Circuits@Home). The read optical mouse sensor value

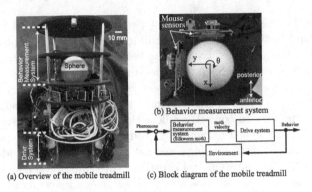

(a) Overview of the mobile treadmill   (c) Block diagram of the mobile treadmill

Fig. 1. Outline of the mobile treadmill

was sent to the main board (Arduino Mega, Arduino Holding, USA) via serial communication, and we calculated the moving speed of the silkworm moth. By adopting an omni-wheel as the drive system, it responded to the behavior output of the three-degree-of-freedom silkworm moth. By controlling the three omni-wheels independently according to the movement of the silkworm moth, it became possible to track its movement. The control cycle of the measurement system and the drive system was 100 Hz.

4   Odor Source Search Experiment

4.1   Experimental Conditions

We set up the odor source search experiment in the same way as the conditions for similar study as shown in Fig. 2(a) [2][5]. As the odor source, sex pheromones (Bombykol, 1000 ng) were soaked in filter paper and placed in a glass tube. We fed an air of 1.0 L/min into the glass tube and diffused the pheromone into the search field by a fan placed behind the odor source. Before and after the experiment, we ventilated the room in order to avoid accumulation of pheromone. The omnidirectional mobile treadmill was placed 1.0 m away from the odor source. At this time, we set the initial heading angle to two conditions: (1) facing the odor source direction (0°), and (2) 30° inclined to the odor source. We used two individual silkworm moth in each of the initial heading angle conditions and repeated five times experiments with the same individual. The search succeeded if the omnidirectional mobile treadmill reached within 0.2 m radius of the odor source.

4.2   Results

Figure 2(b) shows the results of the search success rate and the search time. As shown in Fig. 2(b), the omnidirectional mobile treadmill steered by the silkworm moth could reach the odor source with a success rate of 100% regardless of the initial heading angle. In addition, search time was about 10 s longer when

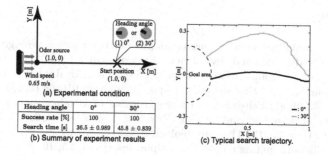

Fig. 2. Odor source search experiment environment and result.

the initial heading angle had 30° inclined to the odor source. Figure 2(c) shows typical behavior trajectories for each initial heading angle. The black and gray solid line in Fig. 2(c) is the trajectory at the initial heading angle 0° and 30°, respectively. Although the trajectory deviated in the y-axis direction by giving the initial heading angle, the odor source search is realized by selecting the behavior appropriately according to the acquired amount of odor information. Therefore, we succeeded in developing the insect behavior measurement system and the drive system of the omnidirectional mobile treadmill.

5   Conclusion and Future Work

In this paper, we developed an insect behavior measurement system and the drive system of an omnidirectional mobile treadmill, which is an apparatus for measuring neural activity of insects moving in a real environment. We carried out the odor source search experiment using the omnidirectional mobile treadmill on which a silkworm moth was mounted, and it could reach the odor source with a success rate of 100 % under any conditions. This means that we succeeded in developing the insect behavior measurement system and the drive system of the mobile treadmill correctly measuring the movement speed of the silkworm and moving accordingly.

In this paper, we plan to perform additional experiments to strengthen the system evaluation because the number of trials and the experimental conditions (initial attitude angle) are a few.

In the future, we will install an amplifier to the mobile treadmill to measure neural signals, and measure the behavior and neural activity of the silkworm moth simultaneously during the female search.

Furthermore, we will verify how common this system is by mounting other insects.

References

1. Asama, H.: Mobiligence: emergence of adaptive motor function through interaction among the body, brain and environment. Environment **1** (2007)
2. Ando, N., et al.: Odour-tracking capability of a silkmoth driving a mobile robot with turning bias and time delay. Bioinspir. Biomim. **8**, 016008 (2013)
3. Kanzaki, R., et al.: Self-generated zigzag turning of Bombyx mori males during pheromone-mediated upwind walking (Physology). Zoolog. Sci. **9**, 515–527 (1992)
4. Namiki, S., Kanzaki, R.: The neurobiological basis of orientation in insects: insights from the silkmoth mating dance. Curr. Opin. Insect Sci. **15**, 16–26 (2016)
5. Shigaki, S., et al.: Time-varying moth-inspired algorithm for chemical plume tracing in turbulent environment. IEEE Robot. Autom. Lett. **3**, 76–83 (2017)

Evaluation of the Facial Expressions of a Humanoid Robot

Vasiliki Vouloutsi[1,2(✉)], Klaudia Grechuta[1,2], and Paul F. M. J. Verschure[1,2,3]

[1] The Synthetic Perceptive, Emotive and Cognitive Systems group SPECS,
Institute for Bioengineering of Catalunya (IBEC), Barcelona, Spain
{vvouloutsi,pverschure}@ibecbarcelona.eu
[2] Barcelona Institute of Science and Technology (BIST), Barcelona, Spain
[3] Catalan Institute of Advanced Studies (ICREA), Barcelona, Spain
https://www.specs-lab.com

Abstract. Facial expressions are salient social features that crucial in communication, and humans are capable of reading the messages faces convey and the emotions they display. Robots that interact with humans will need to employ similar communication channels for successful interactions. Here, we focus on the readability of the facial expressions of a humanoid robot. We conducted an online survey where participants evaluated emotional stimuli and assessed the robot's expressions. Results suggest that the robot's facial expressions are correctly recognised and the appraisal of the robots expressive elements are consistent with the literature.

Keywords: Facial expressions · Human-robot interaction · Emotion recognition

1 Introduction

The face and more specifically facial cues play an important role in social perception [1], as they allow to infer the emotional and mental states of others. It seems that social features (such as human faces or bodies) are more salient compared to neutral scenes (like plants or scenery) [2]. Such findings led to a plethora of studies concerning to how we perceive and process faces. More specifically, facial expressions are crucial in communication, and humans are very apt in reading the messages facial expressions convey and the emotions they display [3].

As robots gain popularity, it is important to design them in way that allows humans to understand and intuitively interpret communication channels (such as facial expressions) in a transparent way [4]. Here, we concentrate on the expression and readability of the facial expressions of the humanoid robot iCub. Key regions of the face, such as the eyes or mouth have been identified as salient cues for emotion recognition [5] and different combinations produce a variety of expressions. Usually, a robot's capability for expression is limited, and the purpose of this study is to establish a valid scale of facial expressions that are correctly recognised by humans.

© Springer Nature Switzerland AG 2019
U. Martinez-Hernandez et al. (Eds.): Living Machines 2019, LNAI 11556, pp. 365–368, 2019.
https://doi.org/10.1007/978-3-030-24741-6_39

2 Methods

For this study, we used the iCub humanoid robot. Its face consists of eyes, ears, eyebrows and mouth. The eyebrows and mouth are displayed via strips of LEDs while the eyes include eyelids whose openness or closeness can be controlled by a motor. In total, their combination provides us with approximately 480 different facial expressions.

To evaluate the readability of the iCub's facial expressions, we conducted an online survey in which users evaluated a stimulus using the Self Assessment Manikin (SAM) [6] and the Affective Slider (AS) [7]. The SAM is a non-verbal pictorial assessment technique to measure self-reported valence and arousal associated with a person's affective state. Each scale consists of nine items. We also used the Affective Slider for higher precision. The Affective Slider is a digital self-reporting tool composed of two slider controls for the quick assessment of a stimulus in terms of valence (positive or negative) and arousal (intensity). A depiction of the SAM scale and the AS can be seen in Fig. 1A.

The presented stimuli consisted of pictures of the iCub with various configurations of its mouth, eyebrows and eye-opening. We assessed the affective response of the robot's expression as opposed to an avatar and created three alternative versions of the head (tin, random shape and no head) to examine whether the anthropomorphic shape of the head would play a role in appraisal (Fig. 1B). Additionally, we showed images of the KDEF [8] and the IAPS (International Affective Picture System) database [9] (Fig. 1C). The last two categories served to ensure that participants could correctly recognise a facial expression and appraise an affective stimulus.

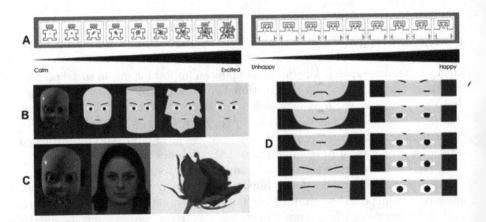

Fig. 1. Examples of the experimental setup. (A) the SAM (top) and AS (bottom) scale for arousal (left) and valence (right) (B) images of the variation of the iCub's face stimuli with the same facial expression (C) images of affective stimuli: the iCub, a photo of the KDEF database and an illustration of the IAPS database (the real image is not represented here to ensure the validity of the database) (D) variations of the expressive elements of the iCub.

To avoid any biases, we randomised the position of the stimuli (right/left) and the position of the SAM and AS. Additionally, to avoid any possible effects of the previous image, upon the evaluation of each stimulus, a black screen appeared for 3 s. All images were aligned to the same eye position. Before the survey, participants signed a consent form, were introduced to the scope of the study and provided us with demographic data (like gender and age).

As the test space was quite large and to eliminate certain stimuli, we performed a pilot (pretest) study with only the cartoon versions of the iCub to determine if the shape of the head affected the recognition of emotion and if the scale of the eye-opening was essential or not. The level of the eye-opening ranged from 0.0 to 1 with intervals of 0.1. The results of the pretest suggested no perceptual differences in several of the ranges of eye-opening and hence, we chose the following values of eye aperture: 0, 0.4, 0.6, 0.8 and 1 where 0 is shut and 1 completely open. The selected combinations of facial features can be found in Fig. 1D.

In total, 33 participants (19 females, between 19 and 52 years old) took part in the study and each stimulus was evaluated on average eight times.

3   Results

First, we examined the correlation between the two affective scales (SAM and AS). We found a strong significant positive correlation (Spearman's rank order) between the two affective scales for both arousal ($r_s = 0.874$, $p < 0.001$) and valence ($r_s = 0.961$, $p < 0.001$). Thus, we used the Affective Slider's results for the evaluation of the proposed stimuli. Then we assessed the participants' evaluation of the affective images. Our results suggest that the participants were able to recognise a facial expression correctly and found no significant differences between their evaluation of the affective images and the IAPS scores. We, therefore, did not exclude any participant.

Due to the small sample on our data, we could not evaluate whether the recognition of the facial expression between the robot image and avatar was different. We then examined the correlation between the mouth configurations and valence or arousal of the data acquired from the Affective Slider. We found a significant positive correlation between the mouth and valence ($r_s = 0.926$, $p < 0.001$), but not arousal ($r_s = 0.074$, $p = 0.424$). Results suggested that the happier the mouth, the more positive it is perceived. Results were consistent with the literature on how the mouth contributes to the facial expression in terms of valence.

We found a medium significant positive correlation between the eye opening and arousal ($r_s = 0.458$, $p < 0.001$) but not valence ($r_s = 0.074$, $p > 0.5$). Results suggested that the wider the eyes open, the more "intense" the expression was perceived. Our results were consistent with the literature regarding the eye-opening and the perceived arousal of the emotion. Finally, we examined the correlation between the position of the eyebrow and valence or arousal. We found a significant positive correlation between the position of the eyebrows and arousal ($r_s = 0.657$, $p < 0.001$) but not valence ($r_s = 0.08$, $p > 0.05$). Consequently, the more close the eyebrows were to the eyes, the more "intense" the facial expression was perceived. Results were consistent with the literature regarding the intensity of expression and the position of the eyebrow (for example in the case of anger).

4   Conclusion

This study aimed to evaluate the readability of the facial expressions of the iCub. Our results suggested that the robot's facial expressions were correctly recognised. Additionally, the results were consistent with the literature, as we found a positive correlation between the robot's mouth configuration (ranging from happy, to neutral to sad in a variety of intensities) and valence and eye aperture and arousal. The contribution of this work is twofold. On the one hand, we evaluated the readability of the iCub's facial expressions, and on the other, the results of this study will inform the expression system of the robot for future interactions.

References

1. Little, A.C., Jones, B.C., DeBruine, L.M.: The many faces of research on face perception. Philos. Trans. Roy. Soc. B Biol. Sci. **366**, 1634–1637 (2011)
2. Wagner, D.D., Kelley, W.M., Heatherton, T.F.: Individual differences in the spontaneous recruitment of brain regions supporting mental state understanding when viewing natural social scenes. Cereb. Cortex **21**(12), 2788–2796 (2011)
3. Knapp, M., Hall, J., Horgan, T.: Nonverbal Communication in Human Interaction. Cengage Learning, Boston (2013)
4. Duffy, B.R.: Anthropomorphism and the social robot. Robot. Auton. Syst. **42**(3), 177–190 (2003)
5. Calvo, M.G., Fernández-Martín, A., Nummenmaa, L.: Facial expression recognition in peripheral versus central vision: Role of the eyes and the mouth. Psychol. Res. **78**(2), 180–195 (2014)
6. Bradley, M.M., Lang, P.J.: Measuring emotion: the self-assessment manikin and the semantic differential. J. Behav. Ther. Exp. Psychiatry **25**(1), 49–59 (1994)
7. Betella, A., Verschure, P.F.: The affective slider: a digital self-assessment scale for the measurement of human emotions. PloS one **11**(2), 1–11 (2016)
8. Lundqvist, D., Flykt, A., Öhman, A.: The karolinska directed emotional faces (KDEF), CD ROM from Department of Clinical Neuroscience, Psychology section, Karolinska Institutet, vol. 91, p. 630 (1998)
9. Lang, P.J., Bradley, M.M., Cuthbert, B.N.: International affective picture system (IAPS): Technical manual and affective ratings, The Center for Research in Psychophysiology, University of Florida, Gainesville, FL, vol. 2 (1999)

Towards a Temperature-Responsive Pinecone-Inspired Actuator Using Silicone Encapsulated Hydrogels

Nickolas P. Walling$^{(\boxtimes)}$ ⓘ, Hemma Philamore,
Kira B. Landenberger ⓘ, and Fumitoshi Matsuno ⓘ

Kyoto University, Kyoto-shi, Kyoto-fu 615-8510, Japan
walling.paul.55s@st.kyoto-u.ac.jp

Abstract. Many plants exhibit actuation in response to environmental stimuli; osmotic influx and efflux of water due to environmental changes in temperature and humidity causes cells to swell and contract. Hydrogels are superabsorbent networked polymers containing hydrophilic units. The large strains produced by hydrogels on the absorption of water resembles the behavior of plant cells that drive actuation through the exchange of water with the surrounding environment. Here we present a soft, silicone actuator, driven by hydrogel expansion and contraction. The blocking force produced by the actuator was investigated. Sodium polyacrylate (2.91 N) and PMOVE (0.56 N), imitate the actuation of plants in response to environmental stimuli. The novel encapsulation of hydrogel within a passive silicone body increased the complexity of motion achievable and blocking force. However, the actuator demonstrated a slower response due to reduced contact surface between the hydrogel and the surrounding water. By utilizing hydrogels, we present an environmentally responsive actuator, driven by hydrogel expansion, which mimics the bimorph actuation of plants, including pinecones, in response to hydration and dehydration.

Keywords: Biomimetic actuation · Soft actuation and robotics · Hydrogels

1 Introduction

Plants have diversified to inhabit the entire planet thanks to numerous mechanisms for survival in challenging environments. Conifers have cones that release seeds in warm, dry conditions and close when wet [1]. This behavior is due to environmentally responsive structures within the plant tissue which expand upon the absorption of water. This mechanism is passively driven due to the fiber orientation in the pinecone scales, a structural feature rather than an active one, meaning that even dead tissue can actuate in this manner.

Hydrogels are polymer networks which absorb water to produce large strains. They have been used in the design of systems which imitate the osmotic actuation of plant cells. Some hydrogels exhibit a thermally responsive transition from hydrophilic to

© Springer Nature Switzerland AG 2019
U. Martinez-Hernandez et al. (Eds.): Living Machines 2019, LNAI 11556, pp. 369–373, 2019.
https://doi.org/10.1007/978-3-030-24741-6_40

hydrophobic states enabling the design of structures that respond to changes in ambient temperature just as the pinecone responds to moisture [2].

In our previous research, we demonstrate the use of sodium polyacrylate hydrogel swelling to drive a Pneunet-inspired [3], silicone-bodied, bimorph actuator (Fig. 1) [4]. However, reverse deswelling behavior is impractically slow due to the lack of a stimulus-based phase transition in sodium polyacrylate. In this study we investigate the blocking force response of poly(2-methoxyethyl vinyl ether) (PMOVE), a hydrogel which exhibits a temperature responsive hydrophilic to hydrophobic phase transition, and compare its performance to sodium polyacrylate. By combining passive silicone structures with actuation driven by thermo-responsive hydrogels, we demonstrate a highly novel, totally self-contained actuator capable of complex motion and suitable force output for practical, macro-scale applications.

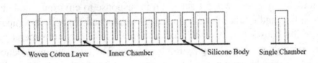

Woven Cotton Layer   Inner Chamber   Silicone Body   Single Chamber

Fig. 1. Schematic of bimorph actuator tested in [4] consisting of repeating silicone chambers

2 Methodology

2.1 Hydrogel Fabrication and Selection

Cross-linked sodium polyacrylate powder was purchased from Nacalai Tesque, Inc. PMOVE gels were synthesized via living cationic polymerization using the following method: 2-methoxyethyl vinyl ether (MOVE; Maruzen Petrochemical; monomer, 1,4-cyclohexanedimethanol divinyl ether (DVE; 98% mixture of isomers, Sigma-Aldrich; crosslinker (10%), ethyl acetate (1st Grade, Wako) added base, the bifunctional initiator ((cyclohexane-1,4-diylbis(methylene))bis(oxy))bis(ethane-1,1-diyl) diacetate (synthesized according to the method for 1-(isobutyoxy)ethyl acetate, [5]) and dichloromethane (Super Dehydrated, Wako) were added to baked glassware under nitrogen, cooled to 0 °C and cool ethyl aluminum chloride (1.0 M in hexane, TCI) was added to initiate the polymerization; after gel formation, additional polymerization was quenched using an ammonium methanol solution; gels were washed thoroughly with methanol and then water prior to use.

2.2 Force Testing Experimental Setup

Swelling. The blocking force of a single silicone chamber filled with 0.11 g of air-dried granular hydrogel was measured using an RS Pro Force Gauge (FG-6005SD) (Fig. 2). The chamber was immersed in approximately 50 mL of deionized water at 25 °C for 2,434 min and 4,430 min for sodium polyacrylate and PMOVE respectively. The chamber containing sodium polyacrylate ruptured after 2,434 min, so the test was terminated. An ABS planar surface was placed on top of the chamber to allow for an even contact area with the force gauge. The blocking force of a continuous piece of PMOVE (0.235 g) not housed in silicone while transitioning from a hydrophobic to hydrophilic phase was measured for approximately 1,400 min.

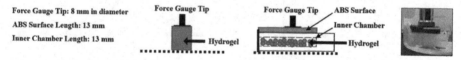

Fig. 2. Setup of blocking force experiments for continuous (left) and granular (right) samples

Deswelling. Approximately 350 mL of 80 °C water was added to the beaker containing the PMOVE-filled. The PMOVE was allowed to deswell until the exerted force below the minimum reading of the force gauge. The chamber was placed in deionized water at 80 °C and transferred to deionized water at 25 °C where the blocking force was again measured with the procedure mentioned above. Two trials using PMOVE were conducted. The chamber used in PMOVE Trial 1 was exposed to air for two days prior to submersion in water while the chamber used in PMOVE Trial 2 was directly transferred from water at 25 °C to water at 80 °C. After 30 min the blocking force of the chamber was measured using the procedure mentioned above.

3 Results and Discussion

3.1 Swelling

The blocking force produced by both materials increased temporally, with the rate of increase decreasing with time. The maximum magnitude of the blocking force recorded during the experiment was approximately 6 times greater for sodium polyacrylate than for PMOVE, but the steep slope of the graph indicates that the blocking force of the sodium polyacrylate has not peaked (Fig. 3a). After exhibiting a hydrophobic to hydrophilic phase transition, the blocking force of continuous and granular PMOVE reached 0.3 N between 20 and 77 times faster than air-dried granular PMOVE but resulted in a smaller overall force output (Fig. 3a, b). Granular PMOVE inside a silicone chamber may produce a larger blocking force than an unhoused, continuous piece (Fig. 3b). The sharp drop in force for the continuous sample (Fig. 3b) may be due to the sample breaking as cracks were observed after it was removed from the testing setup. While measuring the blocking force of a second continuous piece of PMOVE, a slight perturbation to the testing setup within the first minute of measurement caused the hydrogel to break and cease exerting a blocking force. These results demonstrates that unhoused, continuous PMOVE is unsuitable for use in actuators due to its fragility.

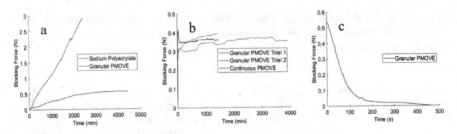

Fig. 3. Blocking force when after: (a) being air-dried, (b) a hydrophobic to hydrophilic phase transition, and (c) a hydrophilic to hydrophobic phase change. Figure 3b was filtered using a moving average at 450 points

3.2   Deswelling

The blocking force of the PMOVE chamber decreased to 0.03 N, the minimum unit resolution of the force gauge, within 4 min (Fig. 3c) demonstrating significantly faster actuation than during swelling.

4   Conclusions

We build on our previous work demonstrating the first use of a soft actuator, driven by hydrogel expansion within a passive silicone body comprised of multiple repeating units, by comparing the blocking force of a single unit when actuated using thermally responsive (PMOVE) and non-thermally responsive (sodium polyacrylate) hydrogel. We justified the use of encapsulating granular hydrogels in silicone rather than using a continuous piece by demonstrating that unencapsulated continuous PMOVE is too fragile for use in practical applications and that granular PMOVE produces a similar maximum force output. The rapid thermal response of PMOVE, during de-swelling in particular, shows its suitability for inclusion in the actuator to produce a reversible, thermally driven, self-contained bimorph. The trade-off is a significantly lower blocking force compared to sodium polyacrylate. In future work we will investigate the use of PMOVE in place of sodium polyacrylate as the driving material in a Pneunet-inspired actuator with the aim of producing more complex, temperature-driven actuation than previously achieved using thermo-responsive hydrogels.

Acknowledgements. This work would not have been possible without the support of the Wagoner Foreign Study Scholarship and the Center for Civic Leadership at Rice University. This research was supported by Sekisui Chemical Co. 2-Methoxyethyl vinyl ether was generously provided by Maruzen Petrochemical Co., Ltd.

References

1. Harlow, W.M.C., et al.: J. Forest. **62**(8), 538–540 (1964)
2. Tan, Y., et al.: Macromol. Rapid Commun. **39**(8), 1700863 (2018)
3. Ilievski, F., et al.: Angew. Chem. **123**, 1930–1935 (2011)
4. Walling, N., et al.: A soft bimorph actuator using silicone-encapsulated hydrogels. In: Robosoft 2019, Late Breaking Results, Seoul, South Korea (2019)
5. Aoshima, S., Higashimura, T.: Macromolecules **22**, 1009–1013 (1989)

Evaluation of 3D-Bioprinted Materials and Culture Methods Toward Actuator Driven by Skeletal Muscle Cells

Naoki Yamada[1]([✉]), Masahiro Shimizu[1], Takuya Umedachi[2], Toshihiro Ogura[3], and Koh Hosoda[1]

[1] Graduate School of Engineering Science, Osaka University,
1-3, Machikaneyama, Toyonaka, Osaka 560-8531, Japan
{yamada.naoki,shimizu,hosoda}@arl.sys.es.osaka-u.ac.jp
[2] Graduate School of Information Science and Technology, The University of Tokyo,
2-11-16, Yayoi, Bunkyo, Tokyo 113-0032, Japan
[3] Institute of Development, Aging and Cancer, Tohoku University,
4-1, Seryo, Aoba, Sendai, Miyagi 980-8575, Japan

Abstract. Soft actuators powered by skeletal muscle cells provide robots flexibility and adaptability. In developing actuators, reproducibility must be ensured. For this, We used a 3D-Bioprinter. The 3D bioprinter can set print parameters according to a program. Opposed to the conventional methods, the skeletal muscle cell-driven actuator can be produced automatically, while ensuring reproducibility. 3D-Bioprinter has huge merits, however, there are many problems in order to develop cell-driven actuators. In this work, we used BIO X (3D bio-printer, CELLINK) and examined materials and culture methods. We successfully printed GelMA and Collagen 1 A and cultured cells in both Attached Gel culture and gel embedded culture.

Keywords: 3D-Bioprinter · Skeletal muscle cells · Soft robotics

1 Introduction

Biohybrid system, in which some components are replaced with bio-based materials, provide an engineering system with flexibility and adaptability. In a biohybrid system, we focused on cell-driven actuator powered by skeletal muscle cells. Cell-driven actuators are composed of skeletal muscle cells and extracellular matrix, similar to living muscle. The cell-driven actuator used for mimicking living things or movement of controllable soft robots [5]. So far, swimming [4], arm joint rotation [3], locomotion [1] have been recreated in robots actuated by cell-driven actuators. These actuators that have a simple 2D arrangement

Supported partially by grant in aid for scientific research on JP18H05467, and JP17K19978 from the Ministry of Education, Culture, Sports, Science and Technology of Japan.

U. Martinez-Hernandez et al. (Eds.): Living Machines 2019, LNAI 11556, pp. 374–377, 2019.
https://doi.org/10.1007/978-3-030-24741-6_41

of cells or are fabricated manually are a success to actuate robots. However, for further development, we have to ensure reproducibility and to fabricate 3D structure cell-driven actuators. To solve this problem, we used a 3D-Bioprinter(Biox, CELLINK). 3D-Bioprinter can print 3D objects using soft materials like gelatin or collagen andprint them programmatically. Therefore, 3D-Bioprinter provide the development of cell-driven actuator with reproducibility and ability to fabricate 3D complex designed. There are some researches about 3D-Bioprinted tissues with muscle cells [2,5], however we have many problems to print soft materials for cell-driven actuators and to culture cells that make driving force. One of the problems is about materials that 3D-Bioprinter use and about the suitable method of distributing cells to tissues for 3D-Bioprinter. In order to solve these problems, we tried to print the GelMA and the Collagen 1 A and culture skeletal muscle cells on and in the printed gel. As a result, we could successfully print both materials and culture cells.

2   Result

2.1   Printability of GelMA and Collagen 1 A and Cultivation of Skeletal Muscle Cells

First, we examined the printability of Collagen 1(Nitta Gelatin). We printed collagen 1 with these parameters: (pressure) 10 kPa, (printhead temperature) 10 °C, (printhead speed) 5 mm/s, (density of cell) 2.0×10^6 cells/ml, (density of collagen) 3.0 mg/ml. Collagen 1 A has low printability to print using BIO X. Although the viscosity of Collagen varies with temperature, once gelation begins, it cannot be returned to sol. We could print collagen in the shape of a square, however, it was hard to maintain its shape, so we printed water-solution surrounding the printed collagen as a frame. As a result, we could print Collagen using a frame, and succeeded in culturing cells(Myoblast Culture kit(containing medium) F-6, COSMO BIO). After 5 days from seeding cells, cells on and in collagen started self-contraction, which lasted for 12 days.

Next, we successfully used GelMA(CELLINK) to culture the skeletal muscle cells using Attached Gel Culture method and Gel Embedded Culture method. We printed GelMA with these parameters: (pressure) 50 kPa, (printhead temperature) 26 °C, (printhead speed) 20 mm/s, (density of cell) 5.0×10^5 cells/ml, (density of GelMA) <Attached Gel Culture> 8.0 mg/ml, <Gel Embedded Gel Culture> 3.0 mg/ml. The viscosity of GelMA was adjusted by controlling its temperature, and a temperature range allowing for high printability was identified. The viscosity of GelMA reversibly changes with temperature. We confirmed that the cells were alive in and on the GelMA, however, GelMA proved too brittle to withstand long-term culture. GelMA containing LAP is cross-linked by UV to maintain the three-dimensional structure. In this experiment, GelMA could maintain the structure for 2, 3 days, however, after 8 days some or all of GelMA had dissolved in the culture solution. It takes about 8 days to mature skeletal muscle cells for use as an actuator, so GelMA maybe not suitable as a material for cell-based bio-actuator considering strength.

2.2   Culture Methods

We succeeded in culturing cells in two methods, particularly in Attached Gel
Culture, many skeletal muscle cells seeded are fallen through the surface of
the printed gel. When we spread the collagen manually on the bottom of the
culture dish, cells maturation progressed and a high density of cells could be
observed. So, if we can attach cells to any place, a high contractile force can be
obtained. However, attaching cells to an arbitrary surface is often very difficult.
On the other hand, Gel Embedded culture was mixed with GelMA or Collagen in
advance, so cells were in the whole printed gel, removing the necessity for attachment. Although cells matured well in Attached Gel culture, cells maturation was
inhibited and cells maturation in the gel did not progress enough.

As a result, we succeeded in culturing cells using both methods. Each method
has its advantages and disadvantages. Further research is necessary to learn more
about culture methods to produce 3D-designed bio-actuator (Fig. 1).

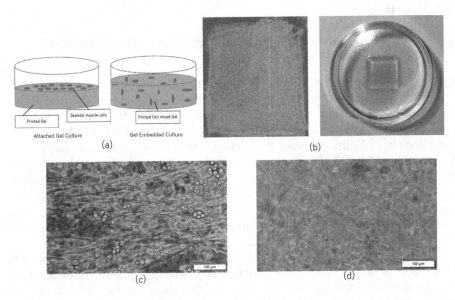

Fig. 1. (a)Attached Gel culture and Gel Embedded culture. (b)Printed collagen 1 A
mixed skeletal muscle cells. Square 10 mm on a side and height is about 0.5 mm.
(c)Skeletal muscle cells cultured 8 days in Attached Gel Culture method. (d)Skeletal
muscle cells cultured 8 days in Gel Embedded Culture method.

3   Conclusion

In conclusion, GelMA and Collagen can be printed using BioX. Also, skeletal
muscle cells can be cultured in and on both materials. However, GelMA cannot maintain shapes because of its brittle nature. Collagen has low printability,
however, Collagen is suitable for bio-actuator materials because of strength and

capacity for cell maturation within it. In this work, we observed that cells could grow both in and on gel printed with BIO X. Collagen was found to be more suitable than GelMA for production of bio-actuators. Comparing two the culturing methods, Attached Gel Culture method was found to be better as we could obtain contractile force from a small number of cells. However, a disadvantage of this method was the difficulty involved with attaching the cells to the surface of the printed gel. In Gel Embedded Culture method, cells are mixed before printing, so it is possible to design three-dimensional shapes.

4   Future Works

We will improve the printability of Collagen in future works. We will try ColMA that is Collagen-based bio-ink (CELLINK) and culture skeletal muscle cells with ColMA printed.

Secondly, we will attempt to create 3D actuators using the Attached Gel Culture method, which currently produces only 2D actuators. For this, we try a method of alternating cell and gel layers to create a 3D actuator. Before this, we will devise a method of seeding cells on Gel to ensure that cells adhere to it for this method.

Lastly, we will examine the contraction force of three-dimensional shape bio-actuator cultured by the two methods, Attached Gel Culture and Gel Embedded Culture. We will examine the relative suitability of either culturing method for 3D bio-actuator fabrication.

References

1. Cvetkovic, C., et al.: Three-dimensionally printed biological machines powered by skeletal muscle. Proc. Nat. Acad. Sci. **111**(28), 10125–10130 (2014)
2. Mestre, R., Patiño, T., Barceló, X., Anand, S., Pérez-Jiménez, A., Sánchez, S.: Force modulation and adaptability of 3D-bioprinted biological actuators based on skeletal muscle tissue. Adv. Mater. Technol. **4**(2), 1800631 (2019)
3. Morimoto, Y., Onoe, H., Takeuchi, S.: Biohybrid robot powered by an antagonistic pair of skeletal muscle tissues. Sci. Robot. **3**(18) (2018). https://doi.org/10.1126/scirobotics.aat4440, http://robotics.sciencemag.org/content/3/18/eaat4440
4. Park, S.J., et al.: Phototactic guidance of a tissue-engineered soft-robotic ray. Science **353**(6295), 158–162 (2016)
5. Ricotti, L., et al.: Biohybrid actuators for robotics: A review of devices actuated by living cells. Sci. Robot. **2**(12) (2017). https://doi.org/10.1126/scirobotics.aaq0495, https://robotics.sciencemag.org/content/2/12/eaaq0495

Learning in Growing Robots: Knowledge Transfer from Tadpole to Frog Robot

Yiheng Zhu[1,2]([✉]), Jonathan Rossiter[1,2], and Helmut Hauser[1,2]

[1] Department of Engineering Mathematics, University of Bristol, Bristol, UK
{yiheng.zhu,jonathan.rossiter,helmut.hauser}@bristol.ac.uk
[2] Bristol Robotics Laboratory, Bristol, UK

Abstract. Inspired by natural growing processes, we investigate how morphological changes can potentially help to lead and facilitate the task of learning to control a robot. We use the model of a tadpole that grows in four discrete stages into a frog. The control task to learn is to locomote to food positions that occur at random positions. We employ reinforcement learning, which is able to find a tail-driven swimming strategy for the tadpole stage that transitions into a leg-driven strategy for the frog. Furthermore, by using knowledge transferred from one growing stage to the next one, we were able to show that growing can benefit from guiding the controller optimization through morphological changes. The results suggest that learning time can be reduced compared to the cases when learning each stage individually from scratch.

Keywords: Biomimetic robotics · Knowledge transfer · Reinforcement learning · Morphological computation

1 Introduction

Biological systems are remarkably robust and adaptive, and they are able to control their highly complex bodies seemingly with ease. One of the reasons is that some biological systems grow. Their morphological structures are simple in the early stages and can therefore be easily controlled. Consequently, it is almost trivial to find a good and simple control policy. During growth, the complexity of the body increases and the corresponding control structure adapts by exploiting previous experience, which means it does not have to learn from scratch. A potential interpretation is that the morphological changes introduced by the growing process serve as guidances for the controller optimization. Work by Bongard [1] shows that such controllers are more robust and can be learnt faster. However, in that work a genetic algorithm was used, which is a population-based method, to obtain these controllers. To improve the learning efficiency, we propose to adopt reinforcement learning and show how this could be advantageous in the case of a robot model that grows stepwise from a tadpole to a frog structure. This concept of reusing and transferring knowledge has been explored previously by shaping [2], lifelong learning [3], curriculum learning [4], and transfer learning [5].

© Springer Nature Switzerland AG 2019
U. Martinez-Hernandez et al. (Eds.): Living Machines 2019, LNAI 11556, pp. 378–382, 2019.
https://doi.org/10.1007/978-3-030-24741-6_42

We form a sequence of four structurally ordered robot models inspired by the meta-morphosis of the frog (Xenopus Laevis). These range from the tadpole form (actu-ated tail), through the froglet form (actuated tail and legs), and finally to the frog form (actuated legs only). The task is to repeatedly reach an item of food spawned at random positions. The reinforcement learning algorithm applied in the robots is proximal policy optimization (PPO) [6]. The policy and value networks trained from the previous stage are transferred directly to bias the learning process for later stages, which is compared to learning from scratch at each stage. We experimen-tally show that knowledge transfer in growing robots serves as desirable parame-ter initialization for later stages, which accelerates learning, compared to learning from scratch.

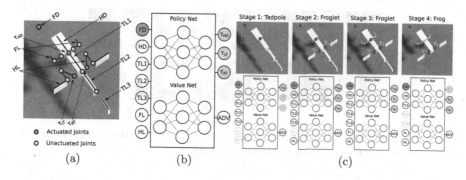

Fig. 1. Model robot growth and network change. (a) Model notations: HD (head), TL1 (tail 1), TL2 (tail 2), TL3 (tail 3), FL (forelimb), HL (hindlimb), FD (food), τ_{HD} (head torque), τ_{LT} (left thigh torque), τ_{RT} (right thigh torque), and ADV (action value advantage). (b) Sensor inputs on the left, neural networks in the middle, actuator outputs on the right. Policy network for decision making (upper) and value network for stabilizing cumulative reward estimation (lower). (c) Models and networks of 4 stages for tadpole to frog metamorphosis: tail-driven tadpole (stage 1), tail-leg-driven froglet without forelimbs (stage 2), tail-leg-driven froglet with forelimbs (stage 3), and leg-driven frog (stage 4). (Color figure online)

2   Method

Model Structure. The Unity ML-Agents toolkit [7] is used for physical simu-lation and learning. The body of the tadpole/frog robot consists of four cuboids in sequence, which are head, tail 1, tail 2, and tail 3 (Fig. 1(a)). Two three-link hindlimbs are connected to tail 1 where the feet have large areas for providing thrust while thighs and calves are relatively slim. Two two-link forelimbs are connected to the head, which have limited contribution to swimming [8]. Pas-sive springs in all hinge joints between adjacent cuboids bring the robot back to its default position when no external force is applied. The learnt controller needs to exploit the unactuated degrees of freedom. We approximate the inter-action between robot and water by applying linear and angular drag to all body parts. In this way, realistic underwater locomotion for the tadpole/frog robot is simulated with relatively low computational complexity.

Model Inputs and Outputs. We define the sensor inputs (states) and actuator outputs (actions) as follows. For sensing, the robot's state consists of the positions, velocities, angles, and angular velocities of all body parts, which is close to a complete description of its configuration, and we can therefore say the Markov property is approximately satisfied. In terms of actuation, the tadpole/frog robot can apply continuous torques, $\tau \in [-2, 2]$ Nm, to three hinge joints: (i) the joint between head and tail 1, (ii) the joint between tail 1 and left thigh, and (iii) the joint between tail 1 and right thigh (blue nodes in Fig. 1).

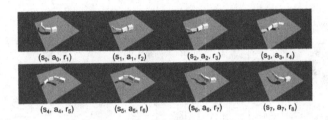

Fig. 2. A sample trajectory with 8 frames: s for state, a for action, and r for reward. Subscripts denote frame counts in the current trajectory.

Sampling. Reinforcement learning algorithms repeat between sampling and optimization to iteratively improve a policy, in which the policy maps sensor inputs (state) to actuator outputs (action). Figure 2 is a sample trajectory of the tadpole robot swimming from the frame when the food is spawned (s_0) to the frame when it reaches the food (s_7). There are 8 frames in this sample trajectory, but the lengths of trajectories can vary depending on when the tadpole robot reaches the food or hits the arena's boundary. The robot's 2D position is defined by $x \in (-5, 5)$ m and $y \in (-5, 5)$ m. Each frame is treated as a sample tuple, (s_t, a_t, r_{t+1}), where the tadpole robot at state s_t takes action a_t based on its policy and gets a scalar reward r_{t+1}. The reward value is 1.0 for the frame when the tadpole robot reaches the food (s_7 in Fig. 2), otherwise the reward value is always 0.0. Each time the food is reached, it is respawned at a random position in $x \in (-4, 4)$ m and $y \in (-4, 4)$ m with equal probability.

Optimization. TensorFlow [9] is used as the neural network library for policy optimization. We follow the policy gradient framework where the policy parameters are iteratively updated following the ascent direction of reward value. The policy gradient algorithm adopted is proximal policy optimization (PPO) [6], which is a first-order optimization method that strikes a balance among simplicity, data efficiency, scalability, and robustness. We use a feedforward policy network with 2 hidden layers, 128 hidden neurons per layer, and a value network of the same structure for caching and averaging rewards.

3   Results

To investigate the effect of knowledge transfer from the tadpole to the frog robot, we perform two experiments: (i) learning from scratch for all 4 stages separately and (ii) learning with policy and value networks transferred from previous stages.

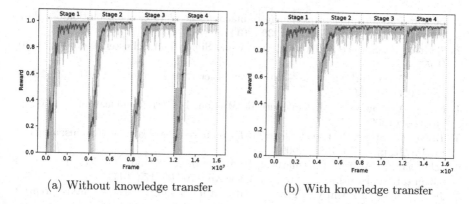

(a) Without knowledge transfer   (b) With knowledge transfer

Fig. 3. Cumulative reward versus frame. (a) Without knowledge transfer: each stage is trained from scratch. (b) With knowledge transfer: policy and value networks are transferred from the previous stage.

Figure 3 summarizes the results. On the left (Fig. 3(a)), all stages are learnt from scratch, while on the right (Fig. 3(b)), knowledge (policy and value networks) are reused from previous stages. It can be observed that knowledge transfer serves as a good strategy to accelerate convergence. Especially, from stage 2 to stage 3 we can see that reusing previous knowledge is beneficial. On the other hand, moving from stage 1 to stage 2 the advantage of knowledge transfer, although clearly seen, is not that prominent. The difference is that from stage 1 to stage 2 we add additional actuators and legs, which is a significant morphological change, while between stage 2 and stage 3 we only add small passive forelimbs, which do not change the dynamics significantly. This might point to the fact that we have to consider further, smaller steps between stage 1 and stage 2 to achieve smoother transfer of knowledge. Finally, interestingly, the morphological change between stage 3 and stage 4 is significant as well, as we remove almost a third of the body by removing the tail, however, this part only contributes to passive dynamics and, therefore, allows smooth knowledge transfer. We plan to investigate these questions further in future work.

4   Conclusion

In this paper, we study knowledge transfer in a growing tadpole/frog robot which learns an underwater food-seeking task. By directly transferring converged policy and value networks from one stage to the next, we show that learning is accelerated when knowledge is transferred between different physical morphologies, for example as a robot grows. This is expected to have advantage in future morphologically adapting robots.

References

1. Bongard, J.: Morphological change in machines accelerates the evolution of robust behavior. PNAS **108**(4), 1234–1239 (2011)
2. Skinner, B.: Science and Human Behavior. Simon and Schuster, New York City (1953)
3. Thrun, S.: Is learning the nth thing any easier than learning the first?. In: NIPS, pp. 640–664 (1996)
4. Bengio, Y., Louradour, J., Collobert, R., Weston, J.: Curriculum learning. In: ICML, pp. 41–48 (2009)
5. Taylor, M., Stone, P.: Transfer learning for reinforcement learning domains: a survey. In: JMLR, pp. 1633–1685 (2009)
6. Schulman, J., Wolski, F., Dhariwal, P., Radford, A., Klimov, O.: Proximal policy optimization algorithms. arXiv preprint arXiv:1707.06347 (2017)
7. Juliani, A., et al.: Unity: a general platform for intelligent agents. arXiv preprint arXiv:1809.02627 (2018)
8. Tassava, R.A.: Forelimb spike regeneration in Xenopus laevis: testing for adaptiveness. JEZ-A **301**(2), 150–159 (2004)
9. Abadi, M., et al.: A system for large-scale machine learning. In: USENIX, pp. 265–283 (2016)

Author Index

Printed in the United States
By Bookmasters